DISCOVERING SQL

Discovering SQL

Discovering SQL

A HANDS-ON GUIDE FOR BEGINNERS

Alex Kriegel

Wiley Publishing, Inc.

Discovering SQL

Published by
Wiley Publishing, Inc.
10475 Crosspoint Boulevard
Indianapolis, IN 46256
www.wiley.com

Published simultaneously in Canada

ISBN: 978-1-118-00267-4

ISBN: 978-1-118-09279-8 (ebk)
ISBN: 978-1-118-09277-4 (ebk)
ISBN: 978-1-118-09278-1 (ebk)

Manufactured in the United States of America

10 9 8 7 6 5 4 3 2 1

For general information on our other products and services please contact our Customer Care Department within the United States at (877) 762-2974, outside the United States at (317) 572-3993 or fax (317) 572-4002.

Wiley also publishes its books in a variety of electronic formats. Some content that appears in print may not be available in electronic books.

Library of Congress Control Number: 2011922790

To Liana

ABOUT THE AUTHOR

ALEX KRIEGEL is an Enterprise Systems Architect for the Oregon Health Authority. He has over 20 years of professional experience designing and developing software, implementing and administering enterprise RDBMS, as well managing software development processes. Alex graduated from National Technical University of Belarus with a Master's of Science in Physics of Metals. He also holds several industry certifications, including PMP from Project Management Institute, TOGAF 8 Certified Practitioner from the Open Architecture Group, Certified Scrum Master from Scrum Alliance, and Microsoft Certified Technology Specialist (MCTS) from Microsoft.

Alex provides online training and consulting services through the `www.agilitator.com` website.

Alex is author of *Microsoft SQL Server 2000 Weekend Crash Course* (Wiley, 2001) and a co-author on several other tiles: *SQL Bible* (Wiley, 2003), *SQL Functions* (Wrox, 2005), Introduction to *Database Management* (Wiley, 2007) and *SQL Bible, 2nd Edition* (Wiley, 2008). His books have been translated into Chinese, Portuguese and Russian.

ABOUT THE TECHNICAL EDITOR

BORIS TRUKHNOV is a Principal Oracle Engineer for NexGen Data Systems, Inc. He has been working with relational databases (primarily Oracle) since 1994. Boris is an author of several technical books published in US and translated into Portuguese, Chinese, and Russian, including *SQL Bible* (1st and 2nd editions) and *Introduction to Database Management.*

Boris's areas of expertise include RAC, ASM, RMAN, performance tuning, database and system architecture, platform migrations, and system upgrades.

Boris is an Oracle 11g Database Administrator Certified Professional (OCP) and Oracle Real Application Clusters Administrator (OCE).

CREDITS

EXECUTIVE EDITOR
Robert Elliott

PROJECT EDITOR
Christopher J. Rivera

TECHNICAL EDITOR
Boris Trukhnov

PRODUCTION EDITOR
Rebecca Anderson

COPY EDITOR
Nancy Sixsmith

EDITORIAL DIRECTOR
Robyn B. Siesky

EDITORIAL MANAGER
Mary Beth Wakefield

FREELANCER EDITORIAL MANAGER
Rosemarie Graham

ASSOCIATE DIRECTOR OF MARKETING
David Mayhew

PRODUCTION MANAGER
Tim Tate

VICE PRESIDENT AND EXECUTIVE GROUP PUBLISHER
Richard Swadley

VICE PRESIDENT AND EXECUTIVE PUBLISHER
Barry Pruett

ASSOCIATE PUBLISHER
Jim Minatel

PROJECT COORDINATOR, COVER
Katie Crocker

PROOFREADER
Carrie Hunter, Word One New York

INDEXER
Johnna VanHoose Dinse

COVER DESIGNER
Ryan Sneed

COVER IMAGE
© Henry Chaplin / iStockPhoto

ACKNOWLEDGMENTS

I would like to thank Robert Elliott, executive editor at Wiley Publishing for the wonderful opportunity to work on this book, and for the patience with which he helped me to navigate the editorial process. His friendly managerial style and valuable insights helped to keep the project on track and on time.

Many thanks to the Wiley Editorial team, especially to my project editor, Christopher Rivera, for the patience and meticulousness in preparing the text for publication. His suggestions and guidance helped to make this book better.

I would like to thank my technical editor and my friend, Boris M. Trukhnov, for the thorough technical editing of the book and his illuminating insights into the subject.

I would like to thank Robert M. Manning for helping with SQuirreL Universal SQL Client introduction (Appendix D) and to the entire SQuirreL development project team for the work that went into delivering this great free open source application.

My thanks go to Dzmitry Aliaksandrau, CCNA, for preparing screenshots for the database products used in the book and help in putting together the presentations. I'd like to thank Andrey Pfliger for help with testing SQL scripts in the book and suggestions on how to make the content more accessible for the readers.

CONTENTS

INTRODUCTION

THE INFORMATIONAL DELUGE shows no signs of abating. We are inundated with data from the TV, from the Internet, and from advertisements stuffed in our mail boxes, virtual and otherwise. Unfortunately, as the quantity of information increased, its quality declined dramatically: Books were replaced by journals; then magazines; then newspapers; then web pages, blogs, and finally, tweets. The information becomes ever-more voluminous and ever-less trustworthy. Even worse, in the age of the Internet data never really disappears; it keeps accumulating, tucked away in files, logs, and databases. According to Google's former CEO Eric Schmidt, we create as much data in two days as we did from the first written record until 2003 (a date as good as any); this is about five *exabytes* (that is five billion gigabytes!) of data in just two days, and the pace keeps accelerating.

When electronic data storage became a reality, it brought about its own set of rules: To make sense out of the data, one had to learn the language. Relational database theory was so far the most successful attempt to bring electronic data under control, and it brought Structured Query Language (SQL) to go along with it.

The relational databases and SQL have evolved quite a bit since the 1970s when they made their first appearance, and the concepts embedded into the database SQL might appear counterintuitive to the uninitiated. By unraveling the SQL story, the reader will understand the rationale behind it and will learn to appreciate both the power and the limitations of SQL.

WHO THIS BOOK IS FOR

This books starts at the beginning, and no prior knowledge of SQL or relational databases is assumed. Along the way, on a voyage of discovery, you will participate in the creation of the sample database, which not only incorporates all SQL concepts taught in the book but also undergoes several refactoring iterations to introduce data modeling, query tuning and optimization, and set of best practices for everything SQL.

This book is for computer programmers ready to add relational database programming to their skill sets, for the business users who want more power over the data locked away in their databases, and everybody else who might be interested in learning the powerful language, the lingua franca of the relational databases.

Readers with previous database experience might want to skim through the first couple of chapters and delve into more advanced topics, or they might decide to revisit the first principles introduced in these chapters; the choice is yours.

WHAT THIS BOOK COVERS

The book covers the current release of the SQL Standard, SQL:2008, but it mostly focuses on the practical side of the language, highlighting the differences between particular implementations. It provides examples using SQL implementations in the latest versions of the following modern database systems either available for download as free express editions, or as free open source software. The most popular desktop database packages, Microsoft Access and OpenOffice, are also covered:

- IBM UDB2 9.7
- Oracle 10g
- Microsoft SQL Server 2008/2005/2000
- MySQL 5.1/5.5
- PostgreSQL 9.0
- Microsoft Access 2007/2010
- OpenOffice 3.2 BASE (with embedded HSQLDB)

HOW THIS BOOK IS STRUCTURED

The book takes a holistic approach, introducing the reader to the concepts of the relational databases in general, and SQL in particular, by gradually building an understanding of the subject through the iterative process of refactoring the ideas, where each concept introduced at the beginning will be revisited in greater detail later on, illuminating the interconnectedness of the underlying principles.

Chapter 1 introduces the story behind SQL and the relational theory behind it. It is a whirlwind tour in which the basic concepts are introduced; all further chapters build upon it. The distinction between data and information is illuminated, and foundations are laid for further exploration. The chapter gives an overview of the relational database management systems (RDBMSs) used in this book.

We revisit these concepts again in Chapter 2 and add some more. The amorphous data becomes structured as it is being analyzed and conformed to the relational model. The "fridge magnets" paradigm becomes the "chest drawer" one, and then morphs into a bona fide relational database table.

The relational model is further explored in Chapter 3, as we step through the basics of the database design and normalization process. The SQL tools for working with normalized data are introduced. Dynamic SQL makes it appearance in this chapter.

To highlight both the power and limitations of SQL as a set-based language, some of the most popular procedural extensions (such as Oracle's PL/SQL and Microsoft's Transact-SQL) are discussed in Chapter 4. This chapter will also introduce SQL functions as a means of alleviating innate deficiencies of the language when dealing with a record-based logic.

Aggregate data are explored in Chapter 5, summarizing the power and limitations of the approach. The aggregate SQL functions introduced in the previous chapter are taken to the next level to show how SQL works with data stripped of its individuality.

Chapter 6 deals with subqueries when data sets are being staggered, and data discovery is based upon multilevel data filtering, one query providing selection criteria to another. The subqueries are precursors to the more SQL attuned JOIN(s), a recurring theme throughout the book.

The power of SQL comes from its ability to deal with data locked in relational tables. Chapter 7 explores the ways SQL can combine this data into a single data set.

This book introduces basic SQL concepts, opening the door for further exploration, and Chapter 8 lays out the next steps of this voyage, with concepts you might consider to explore further later on.

Chapter 9 deals with performance optimization, describing general approach and best practices in optimizing your queries and database environment.

Chapter 10 discusses how relational databases work in multiuser environments, and what mechanisms were implemented in SQL to deal with concurrent data access.

SQL is all about structure and order — it is Structured Query Language, after all! But the real data comes in every shape and size, and Chapter 11 shows how SQL accommodates semistructured (XML documents), unstructured (text files), and binary (such as pictures and sounds) data.

Chapter 12 briefly discusses the latest developments, such as columnar databases, NoSQL databases, object databases, and service oriented architecture (SOA), and how they relate to SQL.

Appendix A describes, step by step, the procedure for installing the sample Library database and populating it with an initial set of data with specific instructions for each of the seven databases discussed in this book. The SQL scripts for this are available for download from the book's supporting websites.

Appendix B provides step-by-step instructions for installing relational database software packages used in this book.

Appendix C describes facilities provided with each of the respective databases to access, create database objects, and manipulate data stored in the tables.

Appendix D introduces the open source project SQuirreL Universal SQL client that can be used to access every database used in this book via Java Database Connectivity (JDBC) interface. It describes, step by step, the process of setting up and configuring the software.

WHAT YOU NEED TO USE THIS BOOK

To make the most out of this book, we recommend downloading and installing the relational database software used throughout the book. Most of the software is free or available on a free trial basis. You'll find step-by-step instructions in Appendix B.

CONVENTIONS

To help you get the most from the text and keep track of what's happening, we used a number of conventions throughout the book.

TRY IT OUT

Try It Out is an exercise you should work through, following the text in the book.

1. It usually consists of a set of steps.
2. Each step has a number.
3. Follow the steps through with your copy of the database.

How It Works

After each *Try It Out*, the code you typed will be explained in detail.

Boxes with a warning icon like this one hold important, not-to-be-forgotten information that is directly relevant to the surrounding text.

The pencil icon indicates notes, tips, hints, tricks, or asides to the current discussion.

As for styles in the text:

- We *highlight* new terms and important words when we introduce them.
- We show keyboard strokes like this: Ctrl+A.
- We show file names, URLs, and code within the text like so: `INSERT INTO...SELECT FROM`.

We present code in two different ways:

```
We use a monofont type with no highlighting for most code examples.
We use bold to emphasize code that is particularly important in the present context
or to show changes from a previous code snippet.
```

SUPPORTING WEBSITES AND CODE

As you work through each chapter, we recommend that you download the SQL scripts to create and populate the database. The code is available at `www.wrox.com or at www.agilitator.com`. You can use the search box on the website to locate this title. After you have located this book, click the Download Code link to access the files that can be downloaded. You can download the files via HTTP or FTP. All the files are stored as ZIP files.

The ISBN for this book is 978-1-118-00267-4. You may find it easier to search by the ISBN than by the title of the book.

You can also download the code from the main WROX download page: `www.wrox.com/dynamic/books/download.aspx`. Click the link to the Discovering SQL: A Hands-On Guide for Beginners to access the files that can be downloaded.

ERRATA

We make every effort to ensure that there are no errors in the text or in the code. However, no one is perfect, and mistakes do occur. If you find an error in one of our books, like a spelling mistake or a faulty piece of code, we would be very grateful for your feedback. By sending in errata, you may save another reader hours of frustration, and at the same time, you will be helping us provide even higher quality information.

To find the errata page for this book, go to `www.wrox.com` and locate the title using the Search box or one of the title lists. Then, on the book details page, click the Book Errata link. On this page, you can view all errata that have been submitted for this book and posted by Wrox editors. You may also contact the author via e-mail at discovery@agilitator.com. A complete book list, including links to each book's errata, is also available at `www.wrox.com/misc-pages/booklist.shtml`.

If you don't spot "your" error on the Book Errata page, go to `www.wrox.com/contact/techsupport.shtml` and complete the form there to send us the error you have found. We'll check the information and, if appropriate, post a message to the book's errata page and fix the problem in subsequent editions of the book.

P2P.WROX.COM

For author and peer discussions, join the P2P forums at `p2p.wrox.com`. The forums are a Web-based system for you to post messages relating to Wrox books and related technologies, and interact with other readers and technology users. The forums offer a subscription feature to e-mail you topics of interest of your choosing when new posts are made to the forums. Wrox authors, editors, other industry experts, and your fellow readers are present on these forums.

At `p2p.wrox.com`, you will find a number of different forums that will help you, not only as you read this book but also as you develop your own applications. To join the forums, just follow these steps:

1. Go to `p2p.wrox.com` and click the Register link.
2. Read the terms of use and click Agree.
3. Complete the required information to join, as well as any optional information you want to provide, and click Submit.
4. You will receive an e-mail with information describing how to verify your account and complete the joining process.

You can read messages in the forums without joining P2P, but in order to post your own messages, you must join.

Once you join, you can post new messages and respond to messages that other users post. You can read messages at any time on the Web. If you want to have new messages from a particular forum e-mailed to you, click the Subscribe to this Forum icon by the forum name in the forum listing.

For more information about how to use the Wrox P2P, be sure to read the P2P FAQs for answers to questions about how the forum software works, as well as many common questions specific to P2P and Wrox books. To read the FAQs, click the FAQ link on any P2P page.

Discovering SQL

1

Drowning in Data, Dying of Thirst for Knowledge

Information may be the most valuable commodity in the modern world. It can take many different forms: accounting and payroll information, information about customers and orders, scientific and statistical data, graphics, and multimedia, to mention just a few. We are virtually swamped with data, and we cannot (or at least we'd like to think about it this way) afford to lose it. As a society, we produce and consume ever increasing amounts of information, and database management systems were created to help us cope with informational deluge. These days we simply have too much data to keep storing it in file cabinets or cardboard boxes, and the data might come in all shapes and colors (figuratively speaking). The need to store large collections of persistent data safely, and "slice and dice" it efficiently, from different angles, by multiple users, and update it easily when necessary, is critical for every enterprise.

Besides storing the information, which is what electronic files are for, we need to be able to find it when needed and to filter out what is unnecessary and redundant. With the informational deluge brought about by Internet *findability*, the data formats have exploded, and most data comes unstructured: pictures, sounds, text, and so on. The approach that served us for decades — shredding data according to some predefined taxonomy — gave in to the greater flexibility of unstructured and semistructured data, and all this can still fit under the umbrella of a database (a broader concept than the "data banks" of the 1970s).

The databases evolved to accommodate all this, and their language, which was designed to work with characters and numbers, evolved along with it. The concept of gathering and organizing data in a database replaced with the concept of a data hub ("I might not have it, but I know where to find it") with your data at the core, surrounded with ever less related (and less reliable) data at the rim.

When does data transform into information? When it is organized and is given a context. Raw data collection does not give you much. For example, the number 110110 could be a decimal number 54 in binary representation; November 1, 2010, the date of D. Hamilton Jackson Memorial Day commemorating establishment of the first press in the U.S. Virgin Islands; House Committee Report #110 for the 110th U.S. Congress (2007–2008), you get the idea.

To transform data into information, you can aggregate the data, add context, cross-reference with other data, and so on. This is as far as databases can take you. The next step, transforming information into knowledge, normally requires human involvement.

DATA DELUGE AND INFORMATIONAL OVERLOAD

One of the reasons behind building a database of your information is to filter the information specific to your needs, to separate the wheat from the chaff. Anybody who uses Internet search engines such as Google or Bing can attest that results brought back are far from being unambiguous because the search engine tries to find the best matches in the sea of relevant, tangentially relevant, and absolutely irrelevant information. Your database is created to serve your unique needs: to track your sales, your employees, and your book collection. In doing so, it might reach out and get some additional information (for example, getting a book's information from Amazon.com), but it will be information specific to your particular needs.

Another important aspect of the database is security. How secure do you need your data? Can anybody see it and modify? Does it need to be protected from unauthorized access due to compliance requirements and simply common sense?

Database management systems, otherwise known as DBMSs, answer all these questions, and more.

Database Management Systems (DBMSs)

What makes a database management system a system? It's a package deal: You get managed storage for your data, security, scalability, and facilities to get data in and out, and more. These are things to keep in mind when selecting a DBMS. The following sections describe a few of the factors that you should consider.

Storage Capacity

Will the selected DBMS be sufficient for current and future needs? If you intend to store your favorite recipes or manage your home library, you might decide to use a desktop database such as Microsoft Access. When you need to store terabytes of information (for example, New York Stock Exchange financial transactions for the last 50 years), you should shop for an enterprise class DBMS such as Oracle, Microsoft SQL Server, or IBM DB2.

Number of Users

If you are the only user of your database, you might not need some of the features designed to accommodate concurrent data use in your database. The current version of Microsoft Access, for instance, supports up to 255 concurrent users (in practice, actual numbers will depend on many factors, including network, bandwidths, and processing power). And with advanced clustering technologies, there is theoretically no limit on the number of users in an enterprise DBMS such as Oracle.

Security

How secure do you want your data to be? You might not be overly concerned if your favorite recipes are stolen, but you'd want your banking or health information to be as secure as possible (and there are regulations to mandate certain levels of protection for various kinds of data collected). One of the major differentiators between enterprise class DBMSs and their desktop counterparts is a robust, finely grained security implementation. A simple file that is a Microsoft Access database is more insecure than a server-based IBM DB2 installation with multiple levels of protection.

Performance

How fast does your database need to be? Can you wait minutes for the information to come back, or must you have a subsecond response, as in a stock trading platform? The answers tie into the question about concurrent users and also scalability. Some DBMSs are inherently slower than the others, and should not be deployed in environments they cannot handle.

Scalability

As Yogi Berra used to say, "Predictions are hard, especially about the future." Databases must be able to accommodate changing business needs. While one cannot anticipate all the changes down the road, one could make an educated guess based upon likely scenarios and industry trends. Your business will change (growths, acquisitions), and your database needs will change with it. You can bet that your data will live longer than the database it lives in. The operating system might change (mainframe, UNIX/Linux, Windows); the programming environments might change (COBOL, C/C++, Java, .Net); regulations might change, but your data must endure, and not entirely for sentimental reasons.

Any of the modern enterprise DBMSs will get a decent score on any of these factors; ultimately, your business needs will dictate the technology choice. Expert advice will be needed for large production deployment, and qualified database administrators to keep your database in the best shape possible. Once you master the language, your data could be transformed into information; it will be up to you to take it to the next level: knowledge.

Costs

Of course, it is important to consider costs associated with installing and operating a database. Vendors might charge hundreds of thousands of dollars for an enterprise class DBMS or it could be had for free as an open source DBMS. Remember: "There ain't no such thing as a free lunch." An open source DBMS might save you money in upfront costs, but would quickly catch up in expertise, time, tools availability, and maintenance costs later on. The total cost of ownership (TCO) must be considered for every DBMS installation.

Recording Data

As far as recorded history goes, humans kept, well, records. Some philosophers even argue that one of the major differences between humans and animals is the ability to record (and recall) past events.

Oral Records

In all probability, oral records were the first kind of persistent storage that humans mastered. The information was transmitted from generation to generation through painstaking memorization; mnemonic techniques such as melody and rhyming were developed along the way. Information transmitted orally was highly storage-dependent, and could deteriorate (as in a game of Chinese whispers) or disappear altogether after an unfortunate encounter by the bearer with a lion, a shark, or a grizzly bear.

Pictures

Pictures such as petroglyphs or cave paintings were much sturdier and somewhat less dependent on vagaries in an individual's fate. They were recorded on a variety of media: clay, stone, bark, skin; and some have survived to the modern age. Unfortunately, much of the context for these pictures was lost, and their interpretation became a guessing game for the archeologists.

Written Records

The beginning of written records, first pictographs and then hieroglyphs, dates back to around 3000 BC, when the Sumerians invented wedge-shaped writing on clay tablets, or cuneiform. This activity gradually evolved into a number of alphabets, each with its own writing system, some related, some autochthonous. This opened the door to storing textual information in pretty much the same form that we use even now. The medium for the writing records also improved over time: clay, papyrus, calf skin, silk, and paper.

Printed Word

Recording and disseminating the information was a painstakingly manual process. Each record had to be copied by hand, which severely limited access to information. The next step was to automate the process with printing. First came woodblock printing, with the earliest surviving example in China dating back to 220 AD. This sped up the process dramatically; a single woodblock could produce hundreds of copies with relatively little effort. The invention of movable type, first by the Chinese and Koreans (1040 and 1230, respectively) and then by Johannes Gutenberg in 15th century Europe, led to dramatically increased access to information through automated duplication. Still, single storage (book) could only be used by a single user (reader) at a time, and searching was a painstaking manual process, even with invention of indexing systems (a list of keywords linked to the pages where these keywords were used).

All of the Above

Technological advances made it possible to accumulate information in a variety of media (text, pictures, and sounds). Not until electronic data storage was developed did it become possible to store them all together and cross-reference them for later automated retrieval. The data had to be digitized first.

Analog versus Digital Data

Up until the invention of the first computers, most information was created and stored in human-readable format. Various mechanical systems were invented to facilitate storage and retrieval of the information, but the information itself remained analogous: print, painting, and recorded sound. Sounds recorded on LP disks are analog, and sounds recorded on CD are digital. The most dedicated audiophiles claim that a CD is but an approximation of the real sound (and they are correct), but most people do not notice the difference. One cannot deny the convenience afforded by a digital CD (or, better yet, an audio file stored on one's computer).

The idea to represent data in binary format came independently to several people around the world, with MIT engineer Claude Shannon formulating principles of binary computation in 1938, and German scientist Konrad Zuse creating a fully functional binary computer in 1941. It turns out that a binary system is uniquely suited for the electrical signal processing; it was humans' turn to adapt to a machine.

The familiar letters and punctuation were translated into combinations of ones and zeroes, starting with the Extended Binary Coded Decimal Interchange Code (EBCDIC), developed by IBM in the early 1950s; through the American Standard Code for Information Interchange (ASCII) character-encoding scheme introduced in the early 1960s; to the advent of Unicode, which made its debut in 1991. The latter system was designed to accommodate every writing system on Earth, and can currently represent 109,000 characters covering 93 distinct scripts.

While initial efforts were focused on representing characters and numbers, the other types of data were not far behind. Pictures and then sounds became digitized and eventually made their way into databases.

To Store or Not to Store?

In 1956, IBM was selling five megabyte persistent storage drives for a whopping $10,000 per megabyte (no wonder it had to make this agonizing decision to store dates as two digits instead of four; also known as the Y2K problem); this came down to just under $200 per megabyte in 1981 (Morrow Designs). In August 2010, a Western Digital 1 terabyte hard drive was selling for $70, which translates into 122 megabytes per one cent!

When storage was dear, people had to be very selective about what data they wanted to keep; with costs plummeting, we've set our sights on capturing and storing *everything*.

The Holy Grail of the DBMS for years was to structure and organize data in a format that computers could manipulate; the preferred way was to collect the data and sort it, and then store it in bits and pieces into some sort of a database (it was called a *data bank* in those days, with policies to match). You had to own all your data. With the proliferation of the Internet, this is no longer the case. Distributed data is now the norm; instead of bringing the data in, you might choose to store information about where the data could be found and leave it at that.

Of course, you may need to keep some of your data closer to the vest (financial data and personal data, for example). Storing the actual data will give you full control of how this data is accessed and modified; this is what databases do best.

With all this dizzying variety of data formats, one needs to make a decision on how this data is to be stored. Despite advances in processing unstructured data, organizing it into taxonomies (a process called *data modeling*; see Chapters 2 and 3 for more information) has distinct benefits both in speed and flexibility. Breaking your data down into the smallest bits and pieces requires a lot of upfront effort, but it gives you an ability to use it in many more ways than when stored as monolithic blocks. Compare a Lego bricks castle with a premolded plastic castle. The latter stays a castle forever, while the former could be used to build a racing car model, if needed. The tradeoffs between structured and unstructured data (and everything in-between) will be discussed in Chapter 11.

Relational Database Management Systems

This book is about SQL, the language of relational databases, or relational database management systems (RDBMSs). Since the theoretical foundations was laid down in the 1970s by Dr. Codd, quite a few implementations have come into existence, and many more are yet to come.

Many people consider DB2 to be the granddaddy of all databases, given that the very term *relational* was introduced by IBM researcher Dr. Edgar Frank Codd in 1969, when he published his paper, "Derivability, Redundancy, and Consistency of Relations Stored in Large Data Banks" in an IBM research report. This assertion is contested by others who point to Oracle's version 2 commercial release in 1979; Multics Relational Data Store sold by Honeywell Information Systems in 1976; or the Micro DBMS experimental designs (pioneering some of the principles formulated by Dr. Codd two years later) of the University of Michigan from 1968 (the last instance of Micro DBMS in production was decommissioned in 1998). The RDBMS road is marked by a multitude of milestones (and an occasional gravestone) of other RDBMS products, including IBM PRTV (1976); IBM SQL/DS (1980); QBE(1976); Informix (1986); Sybase (1986); Teradata (1979); and Ingres, an open source project that gave inspiration to many other successful systems such as PostgreSQL (1996), Nonstop SQL (1987), and Microsoft SQL Server (1988) — to mention but a few. These systems used different dialects of primordial SQL: SEQUEL, QUEL, Informix-SQL, and so on. It was not until 1987 when the first attempt was made to standardize the language; arguably, the battle is still going on.

The current RDBMS market is split among heavyweight proprietary relational databases Oracle (48 percent), IBM (25 percent), and Microsoft (18 percent); smaller proprietary systems Teradata and Sybase, each with a distant 2 percent; and the other vendors, as well as open source databases, comprising about 10 percent of the total market.

For a sizeable enterprise, selecting a database foundation for their applications is a decision not to be taken lightly. Not only does it cost tens of thousands of dollars in upfront licensing fees for the software, and hundreds of thousands of dollars in maintenance and support fees, but it is also an important factor in determining the overall enterprise architecture that aligns all other investments in software, hardware, and human resources. Although migrating from one RDBMS to another became easier in recent years, still the mere thought of it might give your CFO nightmares.

IBM DB2 LUW

IBM is a long-term front-runner in the RDBMS arena, from the mainframe world with the MVS family of operating systems, to z/OS, and later to UNIX and Windows. The current version is IBM DB2 9.7 LUW (Linux, UNIX, and Windows).

The IBM DB2 9.7 keeps the absolute record in transaction processing speed (see Chapter 9 for more information) and comes in a variety of editions, from Advanced Server Enterprise to a free (albeit limited) DB2 Express-C edition used to run samples provided with this book.

DB2 in its version 9.7 is still only compliant with the ANSI/ISO SQL 92 Entry standard (see later in this chapter) and supports some of the more advanced features from other standards organizations such as the Open Geospatial Consortium, JDBC, X/Open XA, as well as bits and pieces of the latest SQL:2008 Standard. In addition to its own built-in procedural extension language, SQL PL, it also provides support for Oracle's PL/SQL, Java, and even Microsoft's .NET family languages for creating stored procedures (see Chapter 4 for more information).

Oracle

Oracle traces its roots back to the first release of Oracle version 2 in 1979, initially for older VAX/VMS systems, with UNIX support following in 1983. Over the years, it added support for most of the features specified in SQL Standard, culminating in the latest release of Oracle 11g, which claims compliance with the "many features" of the latest release of SQL:2008 Standard.

Oracle holds second place in the high-performance transaction processing benchmarking and is at the center of the company's ecosystem. It is a secure, robust, scalable, high-performance database that has dominated the UNIX market for decades. In addition to SQL support, it comes with a built-in procedural language, PL/SQL (see Chapter 4 for more information on procedural extensions), as well as support for general programming languages such as Java.

At of the time of this writing, the latest version is Oracle 11g; the free express edition is available only for Oracle 10g, which has some limits on the data storage size and number of processors (CPUs) the RDBMS is capable of utilizing. The express edition has full support for all SQL features discussed in this book.

Microsoft SQL Server

SQL Server began as partnership between Sybase, Microsoft, and Ashton-Tate, with the initial idea to adapt existing UNIX-only Sybase SQL Server to then-new IBM operating system OS/2. Ashton-Tate later dropped out of the partnership, and the IBM OS/2 operating system faded into oblivion. Microsoft and Sybase were to share the world, being careful not to step on each other's toes. Microsoft was to develop and support SQL Server on Windows and OS/2, and Sybase was to take over UNIX platforms. The partnership formally ended in 1994, although at its core, Microsoft SQL Server still used fair chunks of Sybase technology. In 1998, beginning with the release of Microsoft SQL Server 7.0, the last traces of Sybase legacy were eliminated, and a brand spanking new RDBMS set out to conquer the world (the Windows world, that is). As of today, Microsoft holds about 20 percent of the RDBMS market, though on Windows it reigns supreme.

The latest version as of this writing is Microsoft SQL Server 2008 Release 2; a limited Express edition available for free that supports all features of SQL covered here.

Microsoft Access

Microsoft Access, known lately as Microsoft Office Access, is a desktop relational database (relatively relational, as some might quip). It purports to be an integrated solution combining elements of a relational database engine, application development infrastructure (complete with built-in programming language and programming model), and reporting platform. Unlike other RDBMSs discussed in the book, this is a file-based database and as such has inherent limitations in performance and scalability. For example, while the latest version theoretically allows for up to 255 concurrent users, in practice anything more than a dozen users slows the performance to a crawl. It also supports only a subset of SQL Standard, as well as a number of features available in its own environment only.

One of the features is linking in tables from remote databases that allow it to be used as an application front end to any ODBC/OLEDB-compliant database.

PostgreSQL

PostgreSQL evolved from a project at the University of California at Berkeley lead by Michael Stonebraker, one of the pioneers of the relational databases theory. The principles that went into the original Ingres project, and its successor PostgreSQL, also found their way into many other RDBMs products such as Sybase, Informix, EnterpriseDB, and Greenplum.

The first version of PostgreSQL (with this exact name) came in 1996; it was released in version 6.0 the next year, and remained an open source project maintained by group of dedicated developers. There are numerous commercial versions of PostgreSQL; most notable is EnterpriseDB, a private company that offers enterprise support (along with variety of proprietary management tools) for the product and has convinced many high-profile customers such as Sony and Vonage to rely on an open source RDBMS for some critical enterprise class applications.

PostgreSQL is arguably the closest in terms of support for the SQL standards in addition to a number of features found nowhere else. Unlike its peers (such as MySQL), it provided referential integrity and transactional support from the beginning. It also comes with built-in support for the PL/pgSQL procedural extension language, as well as the capability to adapt virtually any other language to the same purpose.

MySQL

MySQL was first developed by Michael Widenius and David Axmark back in 1994, with its first release in 1995. It was initially positioned as a lightweight, fast database to serve as the back end for data-driven websites. Even though it was lacking many features of the more mature RDBMS products, it was fast in serving information and "good enough" for many scenarios. (To be really fast, MySQL can bypass referential integrity constraints and ditch transactional support; see Chapters 3 and 10 for additional information.) Plus you could not beat the price; it was free. No wonder it grew up to be the most popular relational database among small- and medium-sized users. There were a number of other free database products on the market that lacked features, near-commercial polish, or both. Not one of the big guys — Oracle, IBM, Microsoft, and Sybase — offered free express versions of their respective RDBMSs back then. MySQL was acquired by Sun Microsystems in 2008, which was subsequently swallowed by Oracle.

Currently, Oracle offers a commercially supported version of MySQL as well as a Community Edition. Following this acquisition, a number of fork versions sprang up, such as MariaDB and Percona Server, committed to maintain free status under the General Public License (GPL), one of the least restrictive open source licenses.

The latest released version of MySQL is 5.5, with version 6 on the horizon. It is multiplatform (Linux/UNIX/Windows), and supports most of the features of SQL:1999; some of the features depend on the selected options (for example, a storage engine).

The storage engine option is a feature unique to MySQL, which allows handling of different table types differently. Each engine comes with unique capabilities and limitations (transactional support, index clustering, storage limits, and so on). A database table could be created with different storage engine options, with the default being MyISAM engine.

HSQLDB and OpenOffice BASE

Hyper Structured Query Language Database (HSQLDB), a relational database management system implemented in the Java programming language, is available as open source under the Berkley Software Distribution (BSD) license (meaning pretty much free for all).

This is a default RDBMS engine shipped with the OpenOffice.org BASE, a desktop database positioned to compete in the same market as Microsoft Access. It is a relational database, robust, versatile, and reasonably fast, and is supported on multiple platforms including Linux, various flavors of UNIX, and Microsoft Windows. It claims to be almost fully compliant with SQL:1992 Standard, which covers most of the SQL subset discussed in this book.

An adaptation of HSQLDB serves as an embedded back end to the OpenOffice.org suite component BASE and became part of the suite starting with version 2.0. Like Microsoft Access, the OpenOffice BASE can connect to a variety of RDBMSs, provided that there is a suitable driver; a number of Java Database Connectivity (JDBC) and ODBC (Open Database Connectivity) drivers are available and ship with the product.

Following Oracle's acquisition of OpenOffice and its uncertain status as an open source project under Oracle's patronage, the OpenOffice.org community decided to start a new project called LibreOffice, *with the intent of implementing all the functionality of OpenOffice as free software under the original BSD license.*

Relational databases are not the only game in town. Some of the older technologies, seemingly forever defeated by relational database theory, came back, helped by ever faster/cheaper hardware and software innovations. The quest for better performance and ease of creating applications spawned research into columnar and object-oriented databases, frameworks that make the "all data in one bucket" approach workable, domain-specific extensions (such as geodetic data management or multimedia), and various data access mechanisms. We discuss this topic in Chapter 12.

WHAT IS SQL?

Before the advent of commercially available databases, every system in need of persistent storage had no choice but to implement its own, usually in some proprietary file format (binary or text) that only this application could read from and write to. This required every application that used these files to be intimately familiar with the structure of the file, which made switching to a different storage all but impossible. Additionally, you had to learn a vendor-specific access mechanism to be able to use it. Relational model dealt with complexities of data structures, organizing data on logical level, but it had nothing to say about the specifics of storage and retrieval except that it had to be set-based and follow relational algebra rules. Left to their own devices, the early RDBMSs implemented a number of languages, including SEQUEL, developed by Donald D. Chamberlin and Raymond F. Boyce in the early 1970s while working at IBM; and QUEL, the original language of Ingres. Eventually these efforts converged into a workable SQL, the Structured Query Language.

SQL is a RDBMS programming language designed to define relational constructs (such as schemas and tables) and provide data manipulation capabilities. Unlike many programming languages in general use, it does not exist outside the relational model. It cannot create stand-alone programs; it can only be used inside RDBMSs. This is a declarative type of language. It instructs the database about what you want to do, and leaves details of implementation (*how* to do it) to the RDBMS itself. In Chapter 2, we will go over the elements of the language in detail.

From the very beginning there were different dialects bearing the same SQL name, some of them quite different from each other. This worked for the vendors, as it assured lock-in to specific technology, but it also defied the purpose of creating SQL in the first place.

The SQL Standard

To bring greater conformity among vendors, the American National Standards Institute (ANSI) published its first SQL Standard in 1986 and a second widely adopted standard in 1989. ANSI released updates in 1992, known as SQL92 and SQL2, and again in 1999: SQL99 and SQL3. Each time, ANSI added new features and incorporated new commands and capabilities into the language.

The ANSI standards formalized many SQL behaviors and syntax structures across a variety of products. These standards become even more important as open source database products (such as MySQL, mSQL, and PostgreSQL) grow in popularity and are developed by virtual teams rather than large corporations.

The SQL Standard is now maintained by both ANSI and the International Standards Organization (ISO) as ISO/IEC 9075 standard. The latest released standard is SQL:2008, and work is underway to release the next version of the standard to accommodate new developments in the way RDBMSs collect and disseminate data.

Dialects of SQL

Even with a standard in place, the constantly evolving nature of the SQL Standard has given rise to a number of SQL dialects among the various vendors and products. These dialects most commonly evolved because the user community of a given database vendor required capabilities in the database before the ANSI committee created a standard. Occasionally, though, a new feature is introduced by the academic or research communities due to competitive pressures from competing technologies. For example, many database vendors are augmenting their current programmatic offerings with Java (as is the case with Oracle and Sybase) or .Net (Microsoft's SQL Server Integration Services, embedded common language runtime [CLR]).

Nonetheless, each of these procedural dialects includes conditional processing (such as that controlled through IF … THEN statements), control-of-flow functions (such as WHILE loops), variables, and error handling. Because ANSI had not yet developed a standard for these important features at the time, RDBMS developers and vendors were free to create their own commands and syntax. In fact, some of the earliest vendors from the 1980s have variances in the most fundamental language elements, such as SELECT, because their implementations predate the standards. Some popular dialects of SQL include the following:

- PL/SQL — Found in Oracle. PL/SQL, which stands for Procedural Language/SQL and contains many similarities to the general programming language Ada; IBM DB2 added (limited) support for Oracle's PL/SQL in version 9.5.

- **Transact-SQL** — Used by both Microsoft SQL Server and Sybase Adaptive Server. As Microsoft and Sybase have moved away from the common platform they shared early in the 1990s, their implementations of Transact-SQL have also diverged, producing two distinct dialects of Transact-SQL.
- **SQL PL** — IBM DB2's procedural extension for SQL, introduced in version 7.0, provides constructs necessary for implementing control flow logic around traditional SQL queries and operations.
- **PL/pgSQL** — The name of the SQL dialect and extensions implemented in PostgreSQL. The acronym stands for Procedural Language/postgreSQL.
- **MySQL** — MySQL has introduced a procedural language into its database in version 5, but there is no official name for it. It is conceivable that with Oracle's acquiring the RDBMS it might introduce PL/SQL as part of the MySQL.

Not the Only Game in Town

Over the years there were many efforts to improve upon SQL and extend it beyond original purpose. With the advent of object-oriented programming, there came demand to store objects in the database; proliferation of Internet and multimedia increased demand for storage, indexing and retrieval of the binary information and XML data, and so on. While SQL standards were keeping pace with these and other demands, some decided to create a better mousetrap and came up with some ingenious ideas. For instance, HTSQL is a language that allows you to query data over Internet HTPP protocol; Datalog was envisioned as a data equivalent of Prolog, an artificial intelligence language; and MUMPS (going back to the 1960s!) mixes and matches procedural and data access elements.

The latest entry came from the NoSQL family of databases that depart from conventional relational database theory and eerily reminds us of a data bucket with key/value indexed storage. We will have a brief discussion about evolution of SQL in the last chapter of this book.

LET THERE BE DATABASE!

There is a bit of groundwork to be performed before we could submit our SQL statements to RDBMSs. If you have followed the instructions in Appendix B, complemented by the presentation slides on the accompanying book sites (both at `www.wrox.com` and at `www.agilitator.com`), you should have an up-and-running one (or all) of the RDBMSs used in this book; alternatively, you should have Microsoft Access or OpenOffice BASE installed. Please refer to Appendix B for step by step installation procedures for the RDBMS, and to Appendix A for instructions on how to install the Library sample database.

The following, with minor modifications, will work in server RDBMSs: Oracle, IBM DB2, Microsoft SQL Server, PostgreSQL, and MySQL. In Microsoft Access and OpenOffice BASE/HSQLDB, you'd need to create a project.

The concept of a database, a logically confined data storage (exemplified by the now rarely used term *data bank*), managed by a program is rather intuitive. When using a desktop database such as Microsoft Access, your database is a file that Access creates for every new project you start; the server-based RDBMSs use a similar concept, though the details of implementation are much more complex. Fortunately, the declarative nature of SQL hides this complexity. It tells what needs to be done, not how to do it.

In the beginning, there was a database. The database we will use throughout the book will contain all the books we have on the shelves; a book tracking database that stores titles, ISBN numbers, authors, price, and so on — quite helpful in figuring out what you have.

The following statement creates a database named LIBRARY in your RDBMS (as long as it is Microsoft SQL Server, IBM DB2, PostgreSQL and MySQL; things are a bit different with Oracle, which subscribes to a different notion of what is considered a database; see Appendix A for more details).

```
CREATE DATABASE library;
```

If you have sufficient privileges in the RDBMS instance, the preceding statement will create a database, a logical structure to hold your data, along with all supporting structures, files, and multitudes of other objects necessary for its operations. You need to know nothing about these; all the blanks are filled with default values. Behold the power of a declarative language!

Oracle's syntax would be similar to this:

```
CREATE USER library IDENTIFIED BY discover;
```

With USER being roughly an equivalent of the DATABASE in other RDBMS. A discussion of the similarities and differences between the two are outside scope of this book.

Of course, there is much more to creating a database that would adequately perform in a production environment; there are a myriad of options and tradeoffs to be considered, but the basic data storage will be created and made available to you with these three words.

Once created, a database can be destroyed just as easily, using SQL's DROP statement; you cannot destroy objects that do not exist (and the RDBMS will warn you about it should you attempt to):

```
DROP DATABASE library;
```

In Oracle, of course, you'd be dropping a USER.

Now the database is gone from your server; in Microsoft Access and OpenOffice BASE, this is equivalent to deleting corresponding files.

Due to certain differences in terms of usage across RDBMSs, the concept of database *is different among various proprietary databases. For example, what SQL Server defines as a database is in a way similar to both the SCHEMA and USER in Oracle, but in the context of this book, these differences are not particularly important.*

Creating a Table

Now that we have a database, we can use it to create objects *in* the database, such as a table. A *table* is place where all your data will be stored, and this is where common sense logic and that of RDBMS begin to diverge.

If your refrigerator is anything like ours, you will have all kind of things held to its surface by magnets, some goofy keepsakes from a trip to a zoo, a calendar sent to you by your friendly insurance agent, your kid's school menu (and school attendance phone line), a shopping list, photos of your dog, photos of your children, the pizza hotline... Think of it as your personal database. You could just stick anything to it: text, pictures, calendars, and what not. In contrast, the RDBMS is much more particular. It will ask you to sort your data according to data types. A detailed discussion of data types will take place later, in Chapter 2. Here, we just stick to the data type most intuitively understood and best dealt with by the RDBMS: the text.

Creating a table is just as easy as creating the database in the previous example, with a minor difference of specifying a name for the table column and its data type:

```
CREATE TABLE myLibrary (all_my_books VARCHAR(4000));
```

The column ALL_MY_BOOKS is defined as a character data type (see Chapter 2 for more information of data types), and it can hold as many as 4,000 characters.

As you might have guessed, there is much more to the CREATE TABLE syntax than the preceding example implies. A full syntax listing all options in any given RDBMS would span more than one page, and mastering these options requires advanced understanding of SQL, for which this book is but a first step.

As you'll see in Chapter 2, a table, once created, can be modified (altered), or dropped from the database altogether. The SQL provides you with full control over the database objects, with power to create, change, and destroy.

TRY IT OUT Creating a Database in Microsoft SQL Server 2008

Creating a database is normally a database administrator's task, especially in a production environment; there are too many options and tradeoffs to consider to leave everything set to the default. For our purposes, we can use the basic syntax, however. There are several ways to create a database in Microsoft SQL Server, and using SQL Server Management Studio Express is arguably the easiest one. Follow these steps:

1. Make sure that you have your SQL Server instance up and running (refer to Appendix B for installation instructions).
2. Start SQL Server Management Studio Express by going to the Microsoft SQL Server 2008 menu option (this exercise assumes that SQL Server is installed on your local computer so you can connect automatically with Windows Authentication).

3. The first screen you see is a prompt to connect to your server. If not already filled by default, select the server type Database Engine, the server name .\SQLEXPRESS (if you followed the instructions in Appendix B; otherwise, select another name from the drop-down box; it only displays instances of SQL Server visible from your computer), and authentication set to Windows Authentication.
4. Click the Connect button.
5. SQL Server Management Studio Express will display a window with several panes; for the purposes of this tutorial, we are only interested in the New Query button located in the upper-left corner of the window, right under the File menu (shown in Figure 1-1). Click the New Query button.

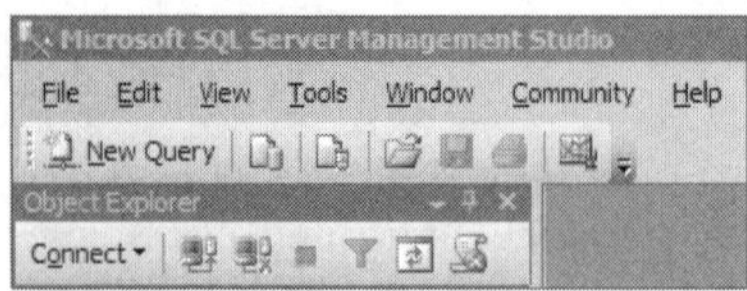

FIGURE 1-1

6. A new query window would appear in the middle of the window; this is where you will enter your SQL commands.
7. Type in the SQL statement for creating a database:

```
CREATE DATABASE library;
```

8. Click the Execute button located on the upper toolbar, as shown in Figure 1-2.

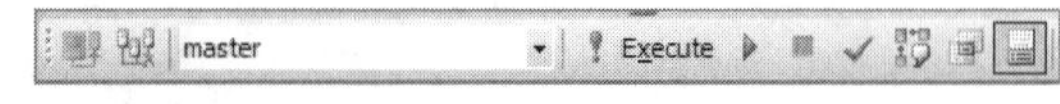

FIGURE 1-2

9. Observe the message "Command(s) completed successfully" in the lower pane, Messages tab.
10. Your newly created database will appear on the Databases list in the pane on the left, with the title Object Explorer (see Figure 1-3). Click the plus sign next to the node Databases node.

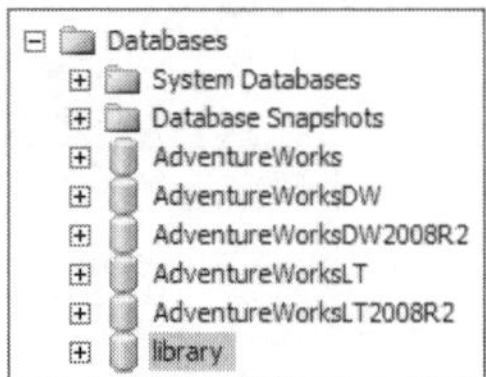

FIGURE 1-3

How It Works

Microsoft SQL Server takes out much of the complexity from creating the database process. Behind the scenes, the SQL Server created several files on the hard drive of your computer (or on an external storage device), created dozens of entries in the Windows registry and the SQL Server–specific configuration files, and created additional supporting objects for the database operations (you can take a look at these by expanding the node LIBRARY in your newly created database).

By omitting all optional configuration options, your database was created using all the default values: storage file names, locations, and initial sizes; collation orders; and so on. While this is not a recipe for creating an optimally performing database (see Chapter 9 for optimization considerations), it will be adequate for the purposes of this book.

Getting the Data In: INSERT Statement

The myLibrary table in our LIBRARY database is now ready to be populated with data, which is a task for the INSERT statement. Since the stated purpose of our database is to keep track of the books, let's insert some data using one of the books we do have on our shelf, *SQL Bible*. Here is some data.

```
SQL Bible by Alex Kriegel Boris M. Trukhnov Paperback: 888 pages
Publisher: Wiley; 2 edition (April 7, 2008)  Language: English
ISBN-13: 978-0470229064
```

This is a lot of information and all in one long string of characters. The INSERT statement would look like follows:

```
INSERT INTO myLibrary VALUES ('SQL Bible by Alex Kriegel Boris M. Trukhnov
Paperback: 888 pages Publisher: Wiley; 2 edition (April 7,2008)
Language:English ISBN-13: 978-0470229064');
```

The keywords INSERT, INTO, and VALUES are the elements of the SQL language and together instruct the RDBMS to place the character data (in the parentheses, surrounded by single quotation marks) into the myLibrary table. Note that we did not indicate the column name; first because we have but a single column in which to insert, and second because RDBMS is smart enough to figure out what data goes where by matching a list of values to the implied list of columns. Both parentheses and quotation marks are absolutely necessary: the former signifies a list of data to be inserted, and the latter tells the RDBMS that it is dealing with text (character data type).

In database parlance, we have created a record in the table. There are many more books on the shelf, so how do we enter them? One way would be to add all of them on the same line, creating a huge single record. Although that is possible, within limits, it would be impractical, creating a pile of data not unlike the refrigerator model we discussed earlier: easy to add and difficult to find. Do I hear "multiple records"? Absolutely!

The previous statement could be repeated multiple times with different data until all books are entered into the table; creating a new record every time. Instead of a refrigerator model with all data all in one place, we moved onto "chest drawer model" with every book having a record of its own.

TRY IT OUT Inserting Data into a Column

Make sure you are at the step where you can enter and execute SQL commands. Repeat Steps 1 through 6 of the first Try It Out exercise and then run these statements to insert four records in your single table, single column database:

1. Type in (or download from a website) the following queries:

```
USE library;
INSERT INTO myLibrary VALUES ('SQL Bible by Alex Kriegel Boris M. Trukhnov
Paperback: 888 pages Publisher: Wiley; 2 edition (April 7,2008) Language:English
ISBN-13:     978-0470229064');

INSERT INTO myLibrary VALUES ('Microsoft SQL Server 2000 Weekend Crash Course by
Alex Kriegel Paperback: 408 pages Publisher: Wiley (October 15, 2001)
Language:English ISBN-13: 978-0764548406');

INSERT INTO myLibrary (all_my_books ) VALUES ('Letters From The Earth by Mark Twain
Paperback: 52 pages Publisher: Greenbook Publications, LLC (June 7, 2010)
Language:English ISBN-13: 978-1617430060');

INSERT INTO myLibrary (all_my_books ) VALUES ('Mindswap by Robert Sheckley
Paperback: 224 pages Publisher: Orb Books (May 30, 2006)
Language:English ISBN-13: 978-0765315601');
```

2. Click the Execute button located on the upper toolbar, as shown on Figure 1-2.
3. Observe four confirmations "(1 row(s) affected)" in the Messages tab in the lower window.

How It Works

The INSERT statement populates columns in the table by creating a record, a single row of data. The list of columns could be omitted as the list of values corresponds exactly to the list of columns (see later in this chapter for more information). If a column is specified, it has to appear in parentheses without any quotation marks; and the corresponding data goes into the list after the VALUES keyword, in parentheses, with quotation marks around the data to indicate the character nature of the value.

Give Me the World: SELECT Statement

Now that we have our data, we could query it to find out exactly what we have. The SELECT statement will help us to get the data out of the table; all we need is to tell it what table and what column.

```
SELECT all_my_books FROM myLibrary;
```

While it did produce a list of the books' information, it is far cry from being useful. Let's face it; it is a mess of a data, and the only advantage from being stored in a relational database is that it can be easily recalled, and possibly printed. What about search? To find out whether you have a specific book, you'd have to pull all the records and *manually* go over each and every one of them! Hardly a result you would expect from a sophisticated piece of software, which is RDBMS.

We need a way to address specific keywords in the records that we store in the table, such as the book title or ISBN number. A standard programming answer to this problem is to parse the record: chop it into pieces and scroll them in a loop looking for a specific one, repeating this process for each record in the table. The SQL cannot do any of this without vendor-specific procedural extensions. This would defy declarative nature of the language and would require intimate understanding of the data structure. Let's take another look at the first record of data we entered:

```
SQL Bible by Alex Kriegel Boris M. Trukhnov Paperback: 888 pages
Publisher: Wiley; 2 edition (April 7, 2008)  Language: English
ISBN-13: 978-0470229064
```

How would you go about chopping the record into chunks? What would be the markers for each, and how do you distinguish a book title from an author? Using a blank space for this purpose would put "SQL" and "Bible" into different buckets while they logically belong together. How do we know that "by" is a preposition, and not part of the author's name? The answer comes from the structured nature of SQL, which is, after all, a *structured* query language; we need more columns. Splitting the one unwieldy string into semantically coherent data chunks would allow us to address each of them separately as each chunk becomes a column unto its own. Back to the CREATE TABLE (but let's first drop the existing one):

```
DROP TABLE myLibrary;
```

Create a new one according to the epiphany we just had:

```
CREATE TABLE myLibrary
(
     title         VARCHAR(100)
   , author        VARCHAR(100)
   , author2       VARCHAR(100)
   , publisher     VARCHAR(100)
   , pages         INTEGER
   , publish_date  VARCHAR(100)
   , isbn          VARCHAR(100)
   , book_language VARCHAR(100)
)
```

A single column became eight columns with an opportunity to add a ninth by splitting the authors' first and last names into separate columns (this is part of the data modeling process to be discussed in Chapter 3). For now, we've used the same data type, albeit shortened the number of characters, with a single exception: We made the PAGES column a number for reasons to be explained later in this chapter. You might also consider changing the data type of the column PUBLISH_DATE. Normally, a date behaves differently from a character, and the DBMS offers a date– and time–specific data type.

Now that we don't have to dump all data into the same bucket, we can be much more selective about data types, and use different types for different columns. It is not recommended that you mix up the data types when inserting or updating (see later in this chapter) the columns.

We will revisit data types again later in this chapter, and in more detail in Chapter 2.

You might have noticed that we have two "author" columns in our table now, to accommodate the fact that there are two authors. This raises the question of what to do when there is only one author, or when there are six of them. These questions will be explored in depth in a data modeling session in Chapters 2 and 3; here we just note that unused columns are populated automatically with default values, and if you find yourself needing to add columns to your table often, it might be the time to read about database normalization (see Chapter 3).

Now we need to populate our new table. The process is identical to the one described before, only the VALUES list will be longer as it will contain eight members instead of one. All supplied data must be in single quotes with the exception of the one going to PAGES column; quotes signify character data, absence thereof means numbers:

```
INSERT INTO myLibrary VALUES (
    'SQL Bible'
   ,'Alex Kriegel'
   ,'Boris M. Trukhnov'
   ,'Wiley'
   ,888
   ,'April 7,2008'
   ,'978-0470229064'
   ,'English');
```

As long as we keep the order of the values matching the structure of the table exactly, we do not need to spell out the columns, which are the placeholder labels for the data, but if the order is different or if you insert less than a full record (say, three out of eight columns), you must list the matching columns as well:

```
INSERT INTO myLibrary (
     title
   , author
   , book_language
   , publisher
   , pages
   , author2
   , publish_date
   , isbn
)VALUES (
    'SQL Bible'
   ,'Alex Kriegel'
   ,'English'
   ,'Wiley'
   ,888
   ,'Boris M. Trukhnov'
   ,'April 7,2008'
   ,'978-0470229064');
```

Repeat the previous statement with different sets of data for each of the books on the shelf. (Yes, some data entry clerks hate their jobs, too.) Alternatively, you can just download a ready-to-go script from the book's accompanying website, and install it following the instructions in Appendix A. You'll get all you information you need in a structured format, ready to be queried with SQL:

```
INSERT INTO myLibrary(title, author, book_language, publisher, pages, publish_date,
 isbn) VALUES ('Microsoft SQL Server 2000 Weekend Crash Course','Alex Kriegel'
,'English','Wiley',408, 'October 15, 2001','978-0764548406');

INSERT INTO myLibrary(title, author, book_language, publisher, pages, publish_date,
 isbn) VALUES ('Mindswap','Robert Sheckley' ,'English','Orb Books',224,'May 30,
2006','978-0765315601');

INSERT INTO myLibrary(title, author, book_language, publisher, pages, publish_date,
 isbn) VALUES ('Jonathan Livingston Seagull','Richard Bach' ,'English','MacMillan',
100, '1972','978-0075119616');

INSERT INTO myLibrary(title, author, book_language, publisher, pages, publish_date,
 isbn) VALUES ('A Short History of Nearly Everything','Bill Bryson'
,'English','Broadway',624, 'October 5, 2010','978-0307885159');
```

What happens if you omit both the column name and the value? The columns listed in the statement will get populated, but the omitted column would stay empty. To signify this emptiness, the SQL marks it as having NULL value.

In the preceding examples, the values for the AUTHOR2 column will be populated with NULL(s). As you will see in Chapter 2, a NULL has a special meaning in the database, and behaves according to rather specific rules.

To save yourself some typing, you might want download scripts for this chapter from www.wrox.com, *or from* www.agilitator.com. *The installation procedures are described in Appendix A.*

Here is a SELECT query that returns all the records you've entered into the myLibrary table:

```
SELECT  title
      , author
      , author2
      , publisher
      , pages
      , publish_date
      , isbn
      , book_language
) FROM myLibrary;
```

Instead of listing all columns, we could have used a handy shortcut provided by SQL, an asterisk symbol (*) that instructs the RDBMS to fetch back all columns.

```
SELECT * FROM myLibrary;
```

The results of this query eerily resemble what we've just discarded for being unstructured, with a minor distinction: The data is displayed in separate columns. It makes all the difference!

First, we can now combine data in any order by just shuffling the columns around or asking for specific columns instead. For example, to produce a list of authors and titles only, we could just execute this query:

```
SELECT  title
      , author
      , author2
) FROM myLibrary;
```

Second, and much more important, is the ability to address these columns by name in a WHERE clause. This clause serves as a filter, allowing you to select records that match some specified condition, such as all books written by Alex Kriegel or only these published by Wiley. The syntax of the query is very intuitive, and resembles English:

```
SELECT * FROM myLibrary WHERE publisher = 'Wiley';
```

The results of the query list only records where the value stored in the PUBLISHER column equals 'Wiley' (note that the value is also enclosed in single quotes to notify the database that this is a character data type we are comparing).

The WHERE clause allows you to narrow down your search to a specific record or a set of records matching your criteria, as there might be millions of records in your database. This is where power of SQL as a set-based declarative language comes forward. With a simple statement that is not unlike a simple English sentence, you can comb through the records returning only a subset of the result, without worrying how this data is stored, or even where it resides. The previous SELECT statements will return identical results when run in Microsoft Access, Oracle, PostgreSQL, MySQL, SQL Server or IBM DB2.

Another important component of the WHERE clause is the use of operators. The previous query used an equivalence operator, filtering only the records in which the publisher's name equals 'Wiley'. You could just as easily ask for books that were *not* published by Wiley using the non-equal operator:

```
SELECT * FROM myLibrary WHERE publisher <>'Wiley';
```

Several operators could be strung together to provide ever more stringent selection criteria using AND and OR logical operators. For instance, to find a book published by Wiley and written by Alex Kriegel, you might use the following query:

```
SELECT * FROM myLibrary
    WHERE publisher = 'Wiley' AND author= 'Alex Kriegel';
```

The query returned only records satisfying *both* criteria; using the OR operator would bring back results satisfying *either* criterion, and not necessarily together. You need to be careful when using operators as they apply *Boolean* logic to the search conditions, and results might be quite unexpected unless you understand the rules.

The logic of operators will be further explored in Chapter 2, along with syntactical differences among the vendors and precedence rules.

TRY IT OUT Exploring the SELECT Statement

Here, we are going to take SELECT statement for a spin using the Microsoft SQL Server 2008 environment. Repeat Steps 1 through 6 of the first Try It Out exercise to get to the stage where you can enter and execute SQL commands.

1. Type in the following statements to insert data into the table:

```
USE library;
INSERT INTO myLibrary (title, author , book_language , publisher , pages ,
author2 , publish_date , isbn)VALUES ('SQL Bible','Alex Kriegel','English',
'Wiley',888,'Boris M. Trukhnov','April 7,2008' ,'978-0470229064');

INSERT INTO myLibrary(title, author, book_language, publisher, pages, publish_date,
isbn) VALUES ('Microsoft SQL Server 2000 Weekend Crash Course','Alex Kriegel'
,'English','Wiley',408, 'October 15, 2001','978-0764548406');

INSERT INTO myLibrary(title, author, book_language, publisher, pages, publish_date,
isbn) VALUES ('Mindswap','Robert Sheckley' ,'English','Orb Books',224,'May 30,
2006','978-0765315601');

INSERT INTO myLibrary(title, author, book_language, publisher, pages, publish_date,
isbn) VALUES ('Jonathan Livingston Seagull','Richard Bach' ,'English','MacMillan',
100, '1972','978-0075119616');
```

```
INSERT INTO myLibrary(title, author, book_language, publisher, pages, publish_date,
isbn) VALUES ('A Short History of Nearly Everything','Bill Bryson'
,'English','Broadway',624, 'October 5, 2010','978-0307885159');
```

2. Click the Execute button located on the upper toolbar, as shown earlier in Figure 1-2.
3. Observe five confirmations "(1 row(s) affected)" in the Messages tab in the lower pane window.
4. The following statement will select all rows and all columns from the table (the display of the actual records in these examples are omitted because of space limitations):

```
SELECT * FROM myLibrary;

(5 row(s) affected)
```

5. To narrow the search, add a WHERE clause:

```
SELECT * FROM myLibrary
    WHERE publisher = 'Wiley';

(2 row(s) affected)
```

6. To narrow it even further, specify two filtering criteria in the WHERE clause: only books published by Wiley and only those that have more than 800 pages:

```
SELECT * FROM myLibrary
    WHERE publisher = 'Wiley' and pages > 800;
```

(1 row(s) affected)7. To select only specific columns, execute the following statement:

```
SELECT title , author  FROM myLibrary
title                                            author
---------------------------------------------- ----------------------
SQL Bible                                        Alex Kriegel
Microsoft SQL Server 2000 Weekend Crash Course   Alex Kriegel
Mindswap                                         Robert Sheckley
Jonathan Livingston Seagull                      Richard Bach
A Short History of Nearly Everything             Bill Bryson

(5 row(s) affected)
```

How It Works

The inserted data is stored in the table, each chunk in a column of its own, together constituting a record; this allows for addressing specific columns by name when selecting the data.

Step 4 instructs the database engine to return all available records from the myLibrary table; instead of listing all columns in the SELECT list, the query uses the asterisk symbol shortcut.

Steps 5 and 6 progressively narrow the returned result set by adding filtering criteria to the query as part of the WHERE clause; they use SQL operators to specify the equality and "greater than" conditions.

The last step demonstrates the ability to select only specific columns for the records returned and addressing them by name. They appear in the order specified in the query regardless of how they were entered or stored in the table.

Good Riddance: the DELETE Statement

Getting rid of unwanted information is just as important as getting it into the database in the first place. In the case of the Library database, a book might be lost or sold, and there is no need to keep the data any longer. The SQL provides a DELETE statement to deal with the situation. To delete all records from a table, you would use the following statement:

```
DELETE FROM myLibrary;
```

There is no need to use FROM keyword in many RDBMS, just a table name would suffice, but some will insist. Now the records are gone, and you have an empty table in the database that you could populate again using the same INSERT scripts found on `www.wrox.com` or `www.agilitator.com`.

Can these records be restored? It depends. In order to be able to undo changes made to the data in the RDBMS, you need to perform all operations in the context of a transaction that, at the end, would either commit all the changes (making them permanent) or roll them back (restoring the data to the original state). We will discuss transactional support in Chapter 10.

The DELETE statement could be much more selective in its approach if used together with WHERE clause you encountered earlier. To delete a specific set of records, you need to specify criteria. The following query will indiscriminately delete all records satisfying the WHERE clause condition:

```
DELETE FROM myLibrary
    WHERE publisher = 'Wiley';
```

All Wiley titles will be gone from your table, which might not be quite what you wanted. How do you pinpoint a single record to be removed from possible thousands sitting in your table? You need to specify a set of criteria that *uniquely* identify this record. Here's an example:

```
DELETE FROM myLibrary
    WHERE publisher = 'Wiley' AND pages = 888;
```

You can't get any more unique than this, right? Actually, you can: Although improbable, it is not impossible for a large database to have more than one record satisfying the previous criteria. The better way is to go by ISBN code that is unique:

```
DELETE FROM myLibrary
    WHERE isbn='978-0470229064';
```

What do you do when a record does not contain an easily identifiable unique marker? There are several ways to ensure the uniqueness of a record in the table (see Chapters 3 and 8), but here we'll introduce a concept of a special column which purpose, among the others, will be to uniquely identify records in the table (also called PRIMARY KEY by the initiated). Had you numbered the records as you entered them into the table, there would be an easy way to refer to a specific record; and assuming that your special column does not allow duplicate numbers, there would be no ambiguity in your deleting a single record. Unfortunately, this would require changing the table structure again.

TRY IT OUT Deleting Records from a Table

Let's delete some records from a table created in Microsoft SQL Server 2008. Repeat Steps 1 through 6 of the first Try It Out exercise to get to the stage where you can enter and execute SQL commands.

1. The following query blows all records from the myLibrary table:

```
USE library;
DELETE myLibrary

(5 row(s) affected)
```

2. Click the Execute button located on the upper toolbar, as shown earlier in Figure 1-2.
3. Insert the records anew:

```
USE library;
INSERT INTO myLibrary (title, author , book_language , publisher , pages , author2
, publish_date , isbn)VALUES ('SQL Bible','Alex Kriegel','English','Wiley',888,
'Boris M. Trukhnov','April 7,2008' ,'978-0470229064');

INSERT INTO myLibrary(title, author, book_language, publisher, pages, publish_date,
isbn) VALUES ('Microsoft SQL Server 2000 Weekend Crash Course','Alex Kriegel'
,'English','Wiley',408, 'October 15, 2001','978-0764548406');

INSERT INTO myLibrary(title, author, book_language, publisher, pages, publish_date,
isbn) VALUES ('Mindswap','Robert Sheckley' ,'English','Orb Books',224,'May 30,
2006','978-0765315601');

INSERT INTO myLibrary(title, author, book_language, publisher, pages, publish_date,
isbn) VALUES ('Jonathan Livingston Seagull','Richard Bach' ,'English','MacMillan',
100, '1972','978-0075119616');

INSERT INTO myLibrary(title, author, book_language, publisher, pages, publish_date,
isbn) VALUES ('A Short History of Nearly Everything','Bill Bryson'
,'English','Broadway',624, 'October 5, 2010','978-0307885159');
```

4. Click the Execute button located on the upper toolbar, as shown earlier in Figure 1-2.
5. Delete a more selective group of records: all books with the exception of those published by Wiley. Type in the following SQL statement, and click the Execute button:

```
DELETE myLibrary
    WHERE publisher <> 'Wiley';

(3 row(s) affected)
```

How It Works

The SQL command submitted to the database engine instructs it to delete all records from the myLibrary table. Five records disappear from the database. In order to continue, you must reinsert the records so you have some data with which to work.

Step 5 demonstrates that the records could be deleted, selectively based upon conditions specified in the WHERE clause of the query. Only three of the five satisfied the criterion *WHERE publisher <> 'Wiley'* and were deleted.

One way to add a new column to a table would be to drop the entire table and re-create it from scratch with a new column; in fact, this was the only way for many RDBMSs for a long time. Now, we just alter the table to sneak a column in (or remove it, for that matter). While the complete syntax is rather complex and differs significantly from RDBMS to RDBMS, the basic syntax is deceptively simple:

```
ALTER TABLE myLibrary
ADD COLUMN book_id INTEGER;
```

This will add an empty column to the myLibrary table of the numeric data type INTEGER. (When it comes to computers, numbers are what they understand best; in fact, the numbers are all they understand.) All human-readable characters, sounds, and pictures are internally represented as long chains of binary numbers: ones and zeroes. To add data to this new column we would have to use the UPDATE statement, the subject of the next section in this chapter.

Some of the DBMSs might have a slightly different syntax for adding columns. For instance, Microsoft SQL Server does not need the keyword COLUMN, inferring what needs to be added from the statement itself, so that the query for SQL Server would look like this:

```
ALTER TABLE myLibrary
ADD book_id INTEGER;
```

Deleting unwanted columns from the table is just as easy except you have to use DROP statement:

```
ALTER TABLE myLibrary
DROP COLUMN book_id;
```

Removing a column requires you to know only its name and that of the table of which it is a part. No data type or any other qualifiers are needed. There are ramifications to be considered when modifying table structure, especially when the table is not empty or columns are being used by some other table in the database. Please see Chapters 2, 7, and 8 for more information.

Notice the distinction between the DELETE and DROP statements: You use DELETE to get rid of the data and you use DROP to destroy database objects such as tables, views, procedures, or the database itself. As you'll learn in Chapter 2, these statements belong to different branches of SQL, data manipulation and data definition languages, respectively.

I Can Fix That: the UPDATE Statement

One of the main benefits of electronic data storage is its flexibility, nothing is written in stone, parchment, or even paper. The data can be created, deleted, or modified at will. So far, you've learned how to get the data in and out, and how to get rid of the data. The UPDATE statement allows you to modify data by changing the existing values for the columns. If you have suddenly discovered that the page number you've entered is wrong, you could fix it by running the following statement:

```
UPDATE myLibrary SET pages = 500;
```

Because the column data type is number (INTEGER), there is no need to enclose 500 in brackets (this is the rule for all numeric data types in all RDBMSs).

The problem with the preceding statement is that the value of 500 will be entered into *every record* in the table, hardly a result we've intended. Just as with DELETE, we have to be much more selective when modifying the data, updating only the records we want to update, and leaving the rest alone. This is the job for the WHERE clause, and again we need some marker that would uniquely identify a record:

```
UPDATE myLibrary SET pages = 500
    WHERE isbn='978-0470229064';
```

If you've discovered that you have more than one column to update for the record, you could add all these to the UPDATE comma-separated list:

```
UPDATE myLibrary SET
    pages = 500
  , title = 'SQL Bible, 2nd Edition'
         WHERE isbn='978-0470229064';
```

The UPDATE operation is implemented in such a way as to allow for using the existing data to be used as a filtering criterion. For instance, you could find the book by its title and change the title in the same query:

```
UPDATE myLibrary SET title = 'SQL Bible, 2nd Edition'
         WHERE title = 'SQL Bible';
```

Of course, after the data is changed, the preceding query won't be able to find the same record again using the same WHERE clause criterion. The same principle could be applied when the new data you're supplying includes the exiting data as a component. To add the '2nd Edition' qualifier to 'SQL Bible' we do not have to supply the whole string, just the second part of it, and use the concatenation operator:

```
UPDATE myLibrary SET title = title + ', 2nd Edition'
         WHERE title = 'SQL Bible';
```

The preceding syntax with the plus sign ('+') as concatenation operator is valid in Microsoft SQL Server only. Oracle and PostgreSQL use the || operator; Microsoft Access uses the ampersand (&); and IBM DB2, MySQL, and HSQLDB prefer to use the SQL function CONCAT. See Chapter 2 for information on SQL operators and SQL functions, respectively.

So far it was implied that columns are being updated with the same data type: characters to characters and numbers to numbers. What happens when you mix the data type and try to insert or update? For example, what would happen if you tried to update a character column with a number? The answer is the same dreaded "it depends." Some RDBMSs will choke on the incompatible data, and spit out an error message; others will try their best within compatibility limits to convert the data into the data type of the column. The latter *modus operandi* is known as implicit data type conversion, whose uses and misuses will be discussed in Chapter 2.

TRY IT OUT Modifying Table Structure with the ALTER Statement, and Table Data with the UPDATE Statement

To explore the scenario mentioned earlier, let's add a numeric column to our table and populate it with data in Microsoft SQL Server 2008.

First, we need to make sure we are at the step where we can enter and execute SQL commands. Repeat Steps 1 through 6 of the first Try It Out exercise, repeat the steps to create and populate the myLibrary table as shown in exercises 2 and 3, and then follow these instructions:

1. To add a column to a table, type in the following:

```
USE library;
ALTER TABLE myLibrary
ADD book_id INTEGER;
```

2. Click the Execute button located on the upper toolbar, as shown on Figure 1-2.
3. Observe the message "Command(s) completed successfully" in the lower pane of the Messages tab.
4. Query your table to make sure that the column appears at the end of the data set, and is empty (NULL), as shown in Figure 1-4.

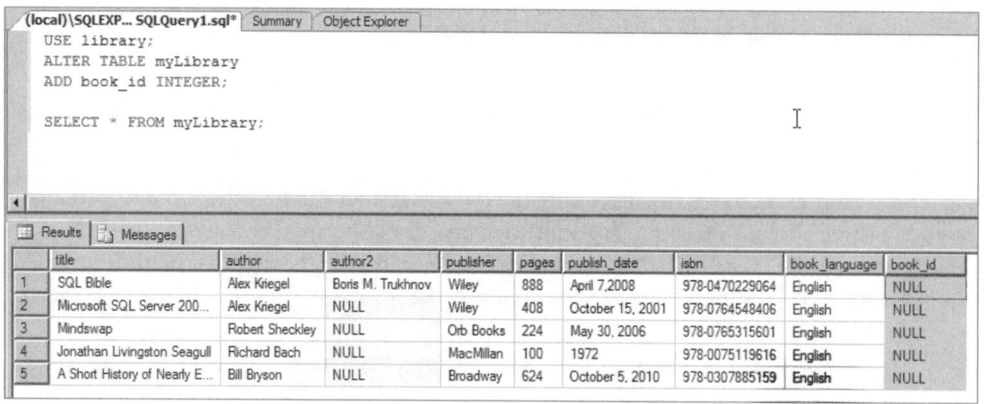

	title	author	author2	publisher	pages	publish_date	isbn	book_language	book_id
1	SQL Bible	Alex Kriegel	Boris M. Trukhnov	Wiley	888	April 7,2008	978-0470229064	English	NULL
2	Microsoft SQL Server 200...	Alex Kriegel	NULL	Wiley	408	October 15, 2001	978-0764548406	English	NULL
3	Mindswap	Robert Sheckley	NULL	Orb Books	224	May 30, 2006	978-0765315601	English	NULL
4	Jonathan Livingston Seagull	Richard Bach	NULL	MacMillan	100	1972	978-0075119616	English	NULL
5	A Short History of Nearly E...	Bill Bryson	NULL	Broadway	624	October 5, 2010	978-0307885159	English	NULL

FIGURE 1-4

5. Now we need to update the new column because all it contains currently is NULL(s). Delete every statement from the query window and type in the following commands:

```
USE library;
UPDATE myLibrary SET bk_id = 1 WHERE isbn='978-0470229064';
UPDATE myLibrary SET bk_id = 2 WHERE isbn='978-0764548406';
UPDATE myLibrary SET bk_id = 3 WHERE isbn='978-0765315601';
UPDATE myLibrary SET bk_id = 4 WHERE isbn='978-0075119616';
```

6. Click the Execute button located on the upper toolbar, as shown on Figure 1-2.
7. Observe four confirmations "(1 row(s) affected)" in the Messages tab in the lower pane window.
8. Verify that the data indeed was inserted by executing a SELECT query against the myLibrary table:

```
USE library;
SELECT bk_id, isbn FROM myLibrary;

bk_id          isbn
-----------    ---------------
1              978-0470229064
2              978-0764548406
3              978-0765315601
4              978-0075119616
NULL           978-0307885159
```

9. The following statement updates all columns in a single query, effectively replacing record #1:

```
USE library;
UPDATE myLibrary SET
    isbn = '978-1617430060'
  , pages = 52
  , title = 'Letters From The Earth'
  , author = 'Mark Twain'
  , author2 = NULL
  , publisher = 'Greenbook Publications, LLC'
  , publish_date = 'June 7, 2010
WHERE bk_id = 1;
```

10. Run the SELECT statement from Step 8 to verify the changes:

```
USE library;
SELECT bk_id, isbn FROM myLibrary;

bk_id          isbn
-----------    ---------------
1              978-1617430060
2              978-0470101865
. . .
NULL           978-0307885159
```

How It Works

The first statement in the batch indicates that the commands are to be executed in the context of the Library database; it only needs to be executed once at the beginning of the session (see Chapter 10 for more information). The ALTER TABLE command adds a column of INTEGER numeric data type to the myLibrary table created in previous exercises; the newly created columns contain only NULL(s) at this point, indicating the absence of any data. The UPDATE statements populate this column for specific records uniquely identified by setting the WHERE clause to filter for the ISBN column in the same table. Without it, the BK_ID column will be updated with the same value for all records.

As you can see from the output produced by the SELECT statement in Step 8, only four records have data in the BK_ID column now; for the rest of the records it is empty.

In Step 9 we are using the UPDATE statement to replace the contents of the entire record, column by column, ending up with a different book in our database. Because the book does not have a co-author, the value is plugged with NULL to indicate absence of any data. Had it been omitted, the column would retain the previous value.

In a multiuser environment, the problems with modifying the data are that somebody else might be reading or modifying it at the same time. This gives rise to a number of potential data integrity problems. The RDBMSs solve this problem with various locking mechanisms discussed in Chapter 10. The trick here is not to overdo it, as locking could potentially slow the database down. A popular open source database (MySQL, for instance) has different storage mechanisms for the databases used mostly to serve the information (SELECT) and those in need of data integrity protection.

SUMMARY

We produce and consume ever-increasing amounts of information, and database management systems were created to help us cope with the informational deluge.

Database management systems (DBMSs) accumulate and manage data in various forms, text, images, and sounds, both structured and unstructured. The underlying format for all electronically stored data is digital. DBMSs built upon the relational model are called RDBMS (Relational Database Management Systems).

The RDBMSs manage both data and access to it, applying security policies, and auditing activity. There is a multitude of databases on the market, from desktop to enterprise class servers, from proprietary to open source. A variety of factors must be considered for each RDBMS package deployment: storage capacity, scalability, security, and costs, to name a few. The most popular enterprise class RDBMS packages include Oracle, IBM DB2, and Microsoft SQL Server; the popular open source contenders are PostgreSQL and MySQL; desktop databases are represented by Microsoft Access and OpenOffice embedded HSQLDB.

The Structured Query Language (SQL) is lingua franca of the relational database management systems (RDBMSs) and has roots in IBM research conducted in the late 1960s. The first attempt to standardize SQL was by the American National Standards Institute (ANSI) in 1986, and the current standard is SQL:2008, endorsed by the International Standards Organization (ISO). Despite the published standard, virtually every RDBMS supports its own dialect of SQL, each being somewhat different in syntax and implementation details. In addition, many RDBMSs support procedural extensions introducing procedural logic in an otherwise set-based declarative language.

For each RDBMS system discussed in the book, the basic element is the table residing in a database. The table organizes data into rows and columns of specific data types; and SQL provides language constructs to insert and manipulate the data trough statements such as INSERT, SELECT, DELETE, and UPDATE.

RDBMSs provide an inherently multiuser environment and facilities to ensure data integrity as different users work with the same data at the same time.

Breaking and Entering: Structured Information

Let's take a closer look at the whirlwind of concepts introduced in the first chapter: database, database object, table, schema, and instance. Despite being around for a long time, there is still a fair amount of confusion regarding what a relational database management system (RDBMS) is because each one has somewhat different ideas on the subject. Yet you have to have a clear understanding of the concepts behind the terminology. Your data will live inside these objects, tucked into tables, and bound by the rules.

In the broadest terms, a *database* is a logical abstraction that describes a collection of interrelated objects managed as a unit. This would accommodate Microsoft Access, which for all intents and purposes is a file; and OpenOffice BASE, which is a pass-through to another relational database with an embedded Hyper Structured Query Language Database (HSQLDB) engine as a default. In Microsoft SQL Server, PostgreSQL, and MySQL contexts, a database is a collection of objects under common ownership managed by the software instance; whereas for Oracle, DB2, and DB2 UDB a database is a bunch of files managed by the software. What Microsoft calls *database*, Oracle refers to as *schema*; both are almost identical to a user in Oracle's context.

This is the bad news, but there is good news, too. On a fundamental level, we are dealing with physical files and the processes that manage them, and the particulars of them are primarily of concern to the database administrators, not Structured Query Language (SQL) users. When you get to the point when you can submit a SQL statement to the RDBMS, most of these concepts are already implemented, and you are ready to model your data.

A REALLY BRIEF INTRODUCTION TO DATA MODELING

According to Wikipedia, *data modeling* in software engineering is the process of creating a data model by applying formal data model descriptions using data modeling techniques. Well, this is all honky dory, but what does it actually mean? Data modeling is the first step where software abstraction touches the real world. The time has come to translate your idea into the relational system: rows, columns, and relations.

Relations, which make your database relational, *will be discussed in the next chapter.*

There are three main levels of data modeling: conceptual, logical, and physical. Each layer refers to a degree of elaboration culminating with a model that can be translated into SQL statements and implemented in RDBMS of your choice. Each of the levels deals with certain steps to be taken when defining your database objects. Table 2-1 presents a matrix of the steps for each modeling level.

TABLE 2-1: Developing Data Model Stages

STEPS	CONCEPTUAL	LOGICAL	PHYSICAL
Entities	YES		
Relationships	YES	YES	
Attributes		YES	
Primary Keys		YES	YES
Foreign Keys		YES	YES
Tables/Views			YES
Columns			YES
Data Types			YES

Conceptual Modeling

Conceptual modeling deals with the highest level of abstractions: entities and relationships. *Entities* refer to the actual physical objects or abstract concepts in your requirements. If you are modeling data for a library, you might think of books, authors, borrowers, and librarians; if you are creating a data model for a bank, your entities would be accounts, clients, money, and so on.

Relationships model the way these entities interact. In the preceding example, a book can have several authors, and a client can have several accounts. While a librarian could potentially relate to an author, it won't be something that you need to track in your database by establishing a relationship between authors and librarians. The relationships are defined through *primary* and *foreign* keys, which we'll introduce in the next chapter.

Logical Modeling

Logical modeling is the next step in data modeling. Here you begin by thinking of attributes. Does an author have a name? A date of birth? Does a book have an identification number? A number of pages? The trick is to distinguish between *attributes* (properties) that you want to track as opposed to those that are irrelevant. What would be the value of recording information about an author's eye color or dieting habits? If information seems to be superfluous to the purpose of your design, ditch it.

Physical Modeling

Physical modeling is the final modeling stage. This is where your abstract ideas gain concreteness. You are getting ready to translate ideas into scripts and implement them in an actual RDBMS of your choice. This is the stage when you define the names for your tables (which might be different from the entities' names), names for your columns, and most importantly, *data types*. What is a data type? Glad you asked; it is the subject of the next section.

WHY CAN'T EVERYTHING BE TEXT?

RDBMSs were created to store information, and human *readable* information comes in letters and numbers. You might have heard that computers use nothing but ones and zeroes to represent information. These are the numbers, and they are used to represent letters. So far, so good. What about dates? The date 10112010 would be October 11, 2010 in the United States. For most of Europe it would be November 10, 2010; in China the first four digits might be interpreted as 1011. What about pictures? There are massive amounts of ones and zeroes packed according to specific file formats: JPEG, PNG, BMP, and TIFF, to name a few. How about sounds? I am sure you've heard about WAV and MP3 files. Video? AVI, MPEG, and so on.

To computers, they are all ones and zeroes, but humans need more than that. Humans are programmed (no pun intended!) to deal with different types of information. We "intuitively" can tell an image from a time, a date from text, and sound from a number, so we created computers in our own image and programmed them to treat data types differently.

There is an historical reason for introducing data types to SQL: a dearth of storage space. Some of you might remember the millennium scare, where havoc was to occur because the year was represented by two digits instead of four. By the same token, if the numbers were presented as numbers in binary system, only 2 bytes (16 bits) would be required. If we were to use characters for the same purpose, we would need 6 bytes (3 times as many) to accommodate numbers greater than 9999 (including 1 byte for the plus/minus signs). It does not sound like much these days, but back in the 1970s when the foundations were being laid, it was a huge deal.

Data types also help to tune up database performance. For instance, ubiquitous XML data (see Chapter 11 for more information) can be represented as text. After all, it *is* text, but text processing is not optimized for the structured nature of the XML documents. With the exception of desktop RDBMSs, every single RDBMS decided to implement a very specific XML data type to address the issue.

Another reason for data types' existence is their role in enforcing *domain integrity* (discussed in detail in the next chapter). This refers to the ability of a specific data type to enforce constraints. For instance, without a DATE data type, it might be possible to enter a date such as October 48. Trying to insert invalid data into a data type–constrained field would result in an error, such as Microsoft SQL Server's "out-of-range *datetime* value" error, for example.

Before we can enter the data into our relational database, we have to break the data into pieces of specific data types, such as characters, numbers, and pictures. This information is reconstituted by a client application later on.

Character Data

It is only logical to start with character data; after all, this is what we normally deal with when collecting, transforming, and distributing information.

Fixed Length and Variable Strings

All character strings in SQL can be of fixed length or varying length. The difference is rather simple, but the devil is in the details.

A character string can be defined as a sequence of characters that belong to a predefined *character set*. A character set is the language your database stores; you might remember specifying *collation order* or *locale* during the RDBMS setup process (not Oracle 10g Express, which makes decisions based on your computer settings or when standard installation option was selected). The length of the string is the number of characters in the sequence. So far, so good. As long as everybody uses English, there is no problem, but this is not the case in the modern world. This is where internal representation enters the scene: bits and bytes. A character can be represented by one or more bytes; most of the Latin-based languages fall into the former category, and everybody else is in the latter. Therein lies the problem.

Byte is a computer term for a unit of information storage that consists of 8 bits. Each bit can either be 1 or 0, and the combination of 8 bits allows us to store 256 distinct values (or 256 different characters represented by numbers from 0 to 255), which form the foundation of the American Standard Code for Information Interchange (ASCII) character set. Considering that English contains only 26 characters, 256 looks like a lot, but it's not. We'd need separate holders for uppercase and lowercase letters, punctuation marks, digits, math symbols, unprintable characters for line feed/carriage return, and so on. This barely leaves space for the characters used in other languages based on the Latin alphabet (French with its *accent grave*, and German with *umlauts*, for instance), let alone those that aren't. There are about 3,000 different languages in the world, both dead and living; in addition to constructed languages such as J. R. R. Tolkien's Quenya, Sindarin, and Khuzdul with its *tengwar* and *cirth* scripts; or Klingon's *plqaD* script from the fictional Star Trek universe!

While there were attempts to remedy the situation with extended code pages, ultimately the solution came with the introduction of Unicode. It is a standard double-byte character set that assigns a unique number to every single character, so it can represent many more characters than ASCII (the latest count is 109,449 characters that cover 93 scripts). The Unicode standard is the result of development coordinated by a nonprofit organization named the Unicode Consortium. The first version of Unicode, Unicode 1.0, was introduced in 1991, and since then it has been adopted by such industry leaders as Apple, HP, IBM, Microsoft, Oracle, SAP, Sun, Sybase, Unisys, and many others. (The current version, Unicode 6.0, was released in October, 2010.)

Unicode is required by modern standards such as XML, Java, JavaScript, CORBA, WML, and HTML, and is governed by the ISO/IEC10646 standard. It is supported in most operating systems, all modern browsers, major RDBMS vendors, and many other products. The emergence of the Unicode standard and the availability of tools supporting it are among the most significant recent global software technology trends.

SQL "thinks" in characters, but computers count bits and bytes. If you define a string to be of a fixed length, say 10 characters long, the system allocates a certain number of bytes in memory or on a computer hard disk. If your character set is Latin-based, a total of 10 bytes will be allocated for the string, but if you use a double-byte character set, as in Simplified Chinese, 20 bytes will be allocated. It does not matter whether the actual value to be stored in that string is exactly that many bytes, half as many, or just one character long; it will occupy the whole allocated space (unused bytes will be padded with blank characters), so all strings will have exactly the same length.

If you define a string variable as a varying length string with a maximum of 10 characters to store, the behavior will be different. The actual memory or disk space required to hold the value will be allocated dynamically, as needed. Only strings that are 10 characters long will have all 10 characters allocated to them, but if you have a string that is only 2 characters, only 2 bytes of storage will be allocated.

As you can imagine, this flexibility comes with a performance price tag because the RDBMS must perform the additional task of dynamic allocation. A standard piece of advice when you need to squeeze the last drop of performance out of the database is to profile your data and allocate fixed-length strings for values that always come in predefined lengths (for example, Social Security numbers or state codes). Just don't forget to have checks in place for your inserts; an attempt to insert 11 characters into a field defined as CHAR(10) would result in an error. Also, when comparing two character strings, variable-length strings wouldn't care much about trailing blanks but fixed-length strings would.

You might have noticed that in the Library database all string fields in the tables are defined as variable character strings big enough to accommodate most common scenarios. This was a conscious choice in the case of a database that does not have to perform at its peak, queried by thousands of concurrent users. For example:

```
CREATE TABLE authors(
  au_id             bigint        NOT NULL
  au_first_name     varchar(50)   NULL
  au_middle_name    varchar](50)  NULL
  au_last_name      varchar](50)  NULL
  au_notes          xml           NULL
)
```

Here you see one numeric data type (BIGINT), three variable length strings (VARCHARs), and one XML data type. All data types were chosen based on specific business requirements and assumptions about their respective properties. For instance, it was assumed that the author's name would never exceed 50 characters.

The MySQL and PostgreSQL have support for the SQL Standard data types, while OpenOffice BASE/HSQLDB and Microsoft Access dump everything into TEXT, an equivalent of VARCHAR.

Tables 2-2 and 2-3 list the implementation of character data types in selected RDBMSs, including some implementation-specific varieties. You'd be well advised to stick with the standard whenever possible: CHAR and VARCHAR. This will give you some modicum of assurance that your SQL code might be portable across different databases.

TABLE 2-2: Selected Character String Data Types: Oracle, DB2, and SQL Server

SQL STANDARD	ORACLE 11G	DB2 9.7	MS SQL SERVER 2008
CHARACTER	CHARACTER	CHARACTER	CHARACTER
VARYINGVARCHAR	VARYING VARCHAR VARCHAR2 LONG VARCHAR	VARYING VARCHAR LONG VARCHAR	VARYING VARCHAR TEXT
CLOB or CHARACTER LARGE OBJECT	CLOB	CLOB	VARCHAR(MAX)
NCHAR	NCHAR	GRAPHIC	NCHAR
NCHAR VARYING(n)	NCHAR VARYING NVARCHAR2	VARGRAPHIC LONG VARGRAPHIC	NVARCHAR
NATIONALCHARACTER LARGE OBJECT	NCLOB	DBCLOB	NVARCHAR(MAX)

Unlike every other RDBMS that has implemented the VARCHAR data type, Oracle has VARCHAR and VARCHAR2. While currently they are synonymous, this behavior will change in the future. Oracle's documentation recommends always *using VARCHAR2 for variable length strings, noting that VARCHAR "is scheduled to be redefined as a separate data type used for variable-length character strings compared with different comparison semantics." It is usually wise taking the vendor at its word.*

Binary Strings

A *binary string* is a sequence of bytes in the same way that a character string is a sequence of characters, but unlike character strings that usually contain information in the form of text, a binary string is used to hold nontraditional data such as images, audio and video files, program executables, and so on. Binary strings can be used for purposes similar to those of character strings (to store documents in Microsoft Word or Adobe PDF format), but the two data types are not compatible. The difference is like text and a photo of the same text. To keep things separate, in this book we deal only with "real" binary data types, covered later in this chapter. The binary string data types are listed in Table 2-3 as CLOB, NCLOB, DBCLOB, and so on.

TABLE 2-3: Selected Character String Data Types: PostgreSQL, MySQL, MS Access, and HSQLDB

SQL STANDARD	POSTGRESQL	MYSQL	MS ACCESS	HSQLDB (OPENOFFICE BASE)
CHARACTER	CHARACTER	CHAR	TEXT	CHARACTER
VARYINGVARCHAR	VARCHAR		TEXT	VARCHAR
CLOB or CHARACTER LARGE OBJECT	TEXT	LONGTEXT MEDIUMTEXT TINYTEXT	MEMO	LONGVARCHAR OBJECT
NCHAR	VARCHAR TEXT	VARCHAR LONGTEXT MEDIUMTEXT TINYTEXT	TEXT MEMO	CHARACTER
NCHAR VARYING	VARCHAR	VARCHAR LONGTEXT MEDIUMTEXT TINYTEXT	TEXT MEMO	VARCHAR LONGVARCHAR
NATIONALCHARACTER LARGE OBJECT	VARCHAR TEXT	VARCHAR LONGTEXT	TEXT MEMO	LONGVARCHAR OBJECT

Character versus Special Files

It might be a little bit confusing to learn that plain text documents can be stored as character strings and a Word document has to be treated as a binary string. A Word or Adobe PDF file is a text document from a user's point of view, but from a computer storage perspective, it is not. In addition to plain text characters, it contains many special markers and instructions that only MS Word or Adobe Acrobat software can interpret. The same is true for any other special files: bitmaps, spreadsheets, audio and video files, and so forth. You can think of it in this way: a special file (for example, .doc, .xls, .bmp, or .avi) is like a Blu-ray disc for a DVD player, whereas a program (MS Word, Excel, Paint, or Adobe Acrobat) is like a DVD player. You have to have a DVD player to play a disc, and it has to be the right disc. If you try to play a Blu-ray disc in a standard DVD player, it won't work. Just try to open a Word or PDF documents with Notepad, and you will see what we are talking about.

TRY IT OUT Text or Binary?

Let's try to open Microsoft Word or Adobe Acrobat documents with the ubiquitous Notepad program on a Windows machine. The Word files would have a file extension (the last three or four characters in the name of the file, following the dot) of .doc or .docx, depending on the version of software used to create it; Adobe Acrobat files have an extension of .pdf. The basic text editor, Notepad, which has shipped with every Windows computer since time immemorial (Windows 3.1, that is) understands text only, and will interpret anything as a character.

Here are the steps to open a binary file in Notepad on a Windows-based computer.

1. Locate a .doc, .docx, or .pdf file on your computer.
2. Highlight the file by clicking it (single click!).
3. Without moving your mouse, right-click to get the pop-up menu.
4. Navigate to the Open With menu and click Choose Program.
5. Scroll the list of programs to find Notepad and select it with a single click.
6. Make sure that the check box at the bottom of the pop-up window with the caption "Always use the selected program to open this kind of file" is *not* checked (otherwise, all files with this extension will be opened by Notepad).
7. Click OK.

This is how the first several lines look when a PDF file is opened with Notepad on my computer:

```
%PDF-1.4%
âãÏÓ
2767 0 obj<</Linearized 1/L 448187/O 2770/E 50012/N 58/T 392798/H [ 693 1011]>>
Endobj
xref
2767 19
0000000016 00000 n
```

How it Works

Because the Adobe Acrobat PDF is a binary file, it contains, in addition to the text, information about fonts, positioning, coloring, and all other formatting. This information is a set of instructions that Adobe Acrobat understands and can interpret to display human readable text and any other objects that might be embedded into the document, such as pictures, diagrams, and so on.

Numeric Data

After the characters come numbers. A number is a number is a number, right? Ugh, no. They come in all shapes and colors, figuratively speaking, split into two broad categories: exact numbers and approximate ones.

Exact Numbers

Exact numbers can either be whole integers (counting pencils, people, or planets) or have decimal points (prices, weights, or percentages). Numbers can be positive and negative; they can have precision and scale. And RDBMSs accommodate them all.

Precision determines the maximum total number of decimal digits that can be stored (both to the left and to the right of the decimal point). *Scale* specifies the maximum number of decimals allowed. Exact numeric data types are summarized in Tables 2-4 and 2-5.

The scale and precision for NUMERIC and DECIMAL values often cause confusion. Just remember that precision specifies the maximum number of all *digits allowed for a value. For example, suppose that a table has these columns:*

field1 — NUMERIC(10,4); can hold up to 999,999.9999

field2 — NUMERIC(10,2); can hold up to 99,999,999.99

field3 — NUMERIC(10,0); can hold up to 9,999,999,999

To determine the maximum number of figures before the decimal point, subtract scale from precision. If you try to insert a value with more figures before the decimal point than the column allows, you will get an error, but values with more decimal points than specified will simply be rounded (the exact behavior depends on implementation).

TABLE 2-4: Exact Numeric Data Types: Oracle, DB2, and SQL Server

SQL STANDARD	ORACLE 11G	DB2 9.5	MS SQL SERVER 2008
INTEGER	NUMBER(38) INT	INTEGER BIGINT	INTEGER BIGINT
SMALLINT	SMALLINT NUMBER(38)	SMALLINT	SMALLINT TINYINT
NUMERIC	NUMERIC DECIMAL NUMBER	NUMERIC DECIMAL	NUMERIC DECIMAL MONEY SMALLMONEY

TABLE 2-5: Exact Numeric Data Types: PostgreSQL, MySQL, MS Access, and HSQLDB

SQL STANDARD	POSTGRESQL	MYSQL	MS ACCESS	HSQLDB (OPENOFFICE BASE)
INTEGER	INTEGER BIGINT	INTEGER BIGINT	NUMBER (INTEGER, LONG INTEGER	INTEGER BIGINT
SMALLINT	SMALLINT	SMALLINT TINYINT	NUMBER (INTEGER)	SMALLINT TINYINT
NUMERIC	NUMERIC	NUMERIC	NUMBER	NUMERIC

Approximate Numbers

Approximate numbers are numbers that can't be represented with absolute precision (or don't have a precise value). Approximate numeric data types are summarized in Tables 2-6 and 2-7.

TABLE 2-6: Approximate Numeric Data Types: Oracle, DB2, and SQL Server

SQL STANDARD	ORACLE 11G	DB2 9.5	MS SQL SERVER 2008
FLOAT	FLOAT NUMBER	FLOAT	FLOAT
REAL	REAL NUMBER	REAL	REAL
DOUBLE PRECISION	DOUBLE PRECISION NUMBER	DOUBLE PRECISION	DOUBLE PRECISION

To stand out in the crowd, Oracle offers only one data type, NUMBER, to represent all numeric data for its RDBMS. To comply with SQL Standard, it also has numerous synonyms for it. Behind the scenes, INTEGER and SMALLINT will translate into NUMBER(38); NUMERIC and DECIMAL will be substituted with NUMBER. The NUMBER data type stores zero, positive, and negative fixed and floating-point numbers with magnitudes between 1.0×10^{-130} *and* $9.9...9 \times 10^{125}$ *with 38 digits of precision. Oracle insists that having one numeric data type for all numeric data does not hurt performance, given the fact that "the space is allocated dynamically."*

TABLE 2-7: Approximate Numeric Data Types: PostgreSQL, MySQL, MS Access, and HSQLDB

SQL STANDARD	POSTGRESQL	MYSQL	MS ACCESS	HSQLDB (OPENOFFICE BASE)
FLOAT	FLOAT	FLOAT	NUMBER (DECIMAL)	FLOAT
REAL	REAL	REAL	NUMBER (DECIMAL)	REAL
DOUBLE PRECISION	DOUBLE	DOUBLE	NUMBER (DOUBLE)	DOUBLE

Each numeric data type has limits, a range of values that it can represent which is pretty consistent across the RDBMS. The value ranges for some common numeric types are presented in Table 2-8.

TABLE 2-8: Value Ranges for the Numeric Data Types

DATA TYPE	STORAGE SIZE (BYTES)	RANGE	NOTES
INTEGER	4	-2,147,483,648 to +2,147,483,647	Implemented in all RDBMSs
TINYINT	1	0 through 255	MS SQL Server only
SMALLINT	2	–32,768 to + 32,768	Implemented in all RDBMSs
BIGINT	8	-9,223,372,036,854,775,808 to +9,223,372,036,854,775,808	Implemented in all RDBMSs
MONEY	8	– 922,337,203,685,477.5808 to + 922,337,203,685,477.5807	MS SQL Server only
SMALLMONEY	4	– 214,748.3648 to + 214,748.3647	MS SQL Server only
REAL	*4*	The range is from negative 3.402E + 38 to negative 1.175E – 37, or from positive 1.175E – 37 to 3.402E + 38. It also includes 0.	Implemented in all RDBMSs
FLOAT	*4 to 8*	The number can be zero or can range from –1.79769E + 308 to –2.225E – 307, or from 2.225E – 307 to 1.79769E + 308.	Implemented in all RDBMSs (if only as synonyms)
DOUBLE	*8*	The number can be zero or can range from –1.79769E + 308 to –2.225E – 307, or from 2.225E – 307 to 1.79769E + 308.	Implemented in all RDBMSs

Literals for the Number

Most of the time, the numbers are hidden in the database, neatly tucked away in the bits and bytes the RDBMS allocates for them. Once in awhile, you might need to use numbers as a value inserted in your query, and databases can be very particular in what format you supply them.

Literals for numbers are represented as strings, optionally preceded by plus or minus signs, with an optional decimal part for NUMERIC and DECIMAL data types separated by a dot (.):

```
123
-34.58
+89.1018
UPDATE books SET bk_price = 16.99 WHERE bk_id = 8;
```

Oracle allows the option of enclosing literals in single quotes:

```
'123'
'-888.34'
```

MS SQL Server has literal formats for MONEY and SMALLMONEY data types represented as strings of numbers with an optional decimal point and prefixed with a currency symbol:

```
$16
$123456.14
```

For instance, this syntax will be valid in MS SQL Server and nowhere else:

```
UPDATE books SET bk_price = $16.99 WHERE bk_id = 8;
```

Approximate numbers add scientific notation to represent the numbers in two parts separated by the letter *E* (either lower- or uppercase). Both parts can include plus or minus; the part number can also include a decimal point:

```
+1.23E2
-8.745e2
-8.44488E+002
```

The value of the constant is the product of the first number and the power of 10 specified by the second number.

Once Upon a Time: Date and Time Data Types

Handling dates and times is probably one of the most confusing and inconsistent topics in SQL. Partly this stems from the inconsistency of the human-devised system of tracking day and time. Try to explain this to a Martian: 365 days in a year (except when it's 366) comprising 12 months made of alternating 30 or 31 days, and one month of 28 (except when it is 29), each day consisting of 24 hours, and so on. It's a daunting task, to be sure! The relational databases model the real world, so they had to accommodate this complexity. Accommodate they did, with DATE, TIME and DATETIME data types:

- `DATE` is a structure that consists of three elements: year, month, and day. The year is a 4-digit number that allows values from 0000 through 9999 (that's right, the year 10,000 problem is looming), the month is a 2-digit element with values from 01 through 12, and the day is another 2-digit figure with a range from 01 through 31. SQL Standard defines the semantics of dates and times using the structure described previously, but implementers are not required to use that approach, provided the implementation produces the same results. One vendor can choose something similar to the preceding structures; others can implement characters, numbers with different scale, and so on.
- `TIME` consists of hour, minute, and second components. The hour is a number from 00 to 23, the minute is a two-digit number from 00 to 59, and the second is either another integer from

00 to 61 or a decimal number with a minimum scale of 5 and minimum precision of 3 that can hold values from 00.000 to 61.999.

- DATETIME combines both DATE and TIME into a single type with date range from January 1, 1753, through December 31, 9999, and time range of 00:00:00 through 23:59:59:997; the allocated storage is 8 bytes. This data type found in Microsoft SQL Server beginning from version 2005.

The DATE data type behaves differently from implementation to implementation. IBM DB2, for instance, has DATE and TIME data types separately, whereas Oracle and Microsoft SQL Server bundle time into the date field; the OpenOffice BASE built-in HSQLDB database follows the IBM approach, and so on.

Much of the complexity of the date and time handling is hidden by the RDBMS's internal representation; what appears as a familiar string, "October 29, 2010" is stored as a complex data type in which each of the components — months, days, and years — is represented by a DECIMAL, and the entire structure is rolled up into a DATE data type, leaving the RDBMS to handle the details.

The dates and times get into the database as literals (using explicit or implicit conversion) as a return result from a function, or as a conversion. The RDBMSs have implemented a number of SQL functions to help handle this peculiar data type, please refer to Chapter 4 for more information. For instance, to insert today's date into a field defined a DATE data type, the Microsoft SQL Server might use the GetDate() built-in function (there are equivalents across all RDBMSs. Please refer to the Wrox book *SQL Functions: Programmers Reference* for more information.

```
INSERT INTO books(
                 bk_id
                ,bk_title
                ,bk_ISBN
                ,bk_publisher
                ,bk_published_year
                ,bk_price
                ,bk_page_count
                ,bk_bought_on
                ,bk_hard_cover
                ,bk_cover_pic
                ,bk_notes)
      VALUES
                (1
                ,'SQL Bible'
                ,'978-0470229064'
                ,'Wiley'
                ,2008
                ,39.99
                ,888
                ,GetDate()
                ,0
                ,NULL
                ,NULL);
```

This statement will insert today's date into the BK_BOUGHT_ON field. Substituting the explicit conversion expression CAST('10-10-2009' as SMALLDATETIME) or the implicit conversion expression '10-10-2009' would also enter a date into the field. The implicit conversion SQL functions are briefly touched in this chapter and are discussed in greater detail in Chapter 4.

As if there were not enough complexity, there is also an issue with time zones. If both your client and the RDBMS server are located within the same time zone, the date and time will be (in theory, at least) the same, and when your application inserts new records and uses one of the built-in SQL functions to stamp it with today's date, the results are as expected: Today is today for both you and your server. Now, imagine that your RDBMS server is located halfway around the globe. What date will go with your record: yours (8 o'clock in the morning) or your server's (8 o'clock in the afternoon)? The difference might not be only hours but also days and even months. To help with this situation, your RDBMS might provide TIME ZONE, as Oracle does, which would allow your application to use either your SESSION (local time) or the server's own time, as well as specify offsets for both. For information on SESSION, see Chapter 10.

While it might be apparent to humans that some literal strings are veritable dates, computers have no such insight and try to treat anything as a date if so instructed, which, of course, would result in an error. How do you do date data type validation? Microsoft has implemented the ISDate(<literal string>) function that returns either 1 (TRUE) or 0 (FALSE), indicating whether a particular string can be converted into a date data type; none of the other RDBMSs has similar functions (though custom functions can be created).

Once dates are in the database, you need to take extra care manipulating them. For instance, if you compare two dates that have the same day, month, and year component but differ in time they will be evaluated as "not equal." Be sure to compare apples to apples. There are many date- and time-related functions to help you compare dates, extract date parts, and even do date arithmetic. All this and more is discussed in Chapter 4.

Binary Data

Binary data are for computers to understand and interpret so that humans can understand. Prime examples of binary data are pictures, only your image editor knows how to arrange these ones and zeroes into a picture of your aunt Sally, Adobe Acrobat documents, the contents of a PDF file that were pried open earlier in this chapter, and so on.

There is not much you can do with binary data in SQL besides storing it and retrieving it on demand. To store binary data, the RDBMSs have introduced a number of binary data types that are listed in Chapter 11 (in Table 11-6). Chapter 11 also explains how to get the binary data in and out of an RDBMS, which is not a trivial task at all.

Table 2-9 presents selected SQL data types from several RDBMSs.

TABLE 2-9: Most Frequently Used SQL Data Types Combined

SQL SERVER 2008	ORACLE 10G	IBM DB2 9.7	POSTGRESQL 9.0	MYSQL 5.5	MS ACCESS	OPENOFFICE BASE HSQLDB
char	char	char	char	char	char	char
varchar	varchar	varchar	varchar	varchar	varchar	varchar

SQL SERVER 2008	ORACLE 10G	IBM DB2 9.7	POSTGRESQL 9.0	MYSQL 5.5	MS ACCESS	OPENOFFICE BASE HSQLDB
integer	integer	integer	integer	integer	number	integer
smallint	smallint	smallint	smallint	smallint	number	smallint
real float double	real float double	r real float double	real float double	real float double	number	real float double
decimal	decimal	decimal	decimal	decimal	number	decimal
datetime	date	date	date	date	date	date
datetime	date	time	time	time	time	time
varbinary binary image sql_variant	blob clob long	graphic vargraphic clob blob	bytea	blob binary varbinary	OLE Object	binary varbinary longvarbinary
XML	XMLType	XML	XML	n/a	n/a	n/a

IT'S A BIRD, IT'S A PLANE, IT'S ... A NULL!

True to its nature, computers need to be told not only when there is data, but also when there isn't. Humans can readily understand that "zero books" and "no books" refer to the same thing; computers will treat the two as different values. A special marker, NULL, was introduced to address the issue.

Much Ado About Nothing

NULL is a special database concept introduced to represent the absence of value, a void. Despite what some RDBMSs might have implemented, a NULL is neither a zero nor an empty string; it is a special value that can be substituted for an actual value for any data type allowed in the column. NULLs are usually used when the value is unknown or meaningless. A NULL value can later be updated with some real data; it can even become a zero or an empty string, but by itself it is neither.

For example, when you buy a new book, you might not have a few particulars such as cover picture or ISBN number. In such situations, the NULL values are appropriate for these fields.

SQL standards explicitly state that each data type should include a NULL value that is neither equal to any other value nor is a data type unto its own, but instead stands for an unknown value. NULL has been implemented by all RDBMSs.

Most of the time, NULL behaves according to its nature, hiding away and pretending to be invisible. Once in awhile, it surfaces to alter the way you are doing your queries forever.

For instance, comparing NULLs is far from obvious. A NULL is never equal to a NULL!

TRY IT OUT Discovering NULLs

NULLS are curious animals, and should be approached cautiously. In this exercise, you will see how NULLs behave in the wild.

1. Open an SQL client of your choice and connect to an RDBMS (we will use the Microsoft SQL Server 2008 Query Analyzer window).
2. To make sure you have NULL values in your table, insert one:

```
USE library;
INSERT INTO books (bk_id) VALUES (100);
```

3. Issue a SELECT statement to verify the presence of NULLs:

```
SELECT bk_id, bk_title, bk_ISBN from books WHERE bk_id = 100;
bk_id     bk_title  bk_ISBN
------    --------  -----------
100       NULL      NULL
```

4. Now, try to find records that contain NULL in the bk_ISBN field:

```
SELECT bk_id, bk_title, bk_ISBN from books WHERE bk_ISBN = NULL;
(0 row(s) affected)
```

5. Well, maybe this is the literal; how about records where one NULL field equals another NULL field? Admittedly, this is an improbable query, but still...

```
SELECT bk_id, bk_title, bk_ISBN from books WHERE bk_ISBN = bk_Title;
(0 row(s) affected)
```

6. A NULL needs a very particular approach; it is not equal, it *IS*. The following query will do the trick:

```
SELECT bk_id, bk_title, bk_ISBN from books WHERE bk_ISBN IS NULL;
bk_id     bk_title  bk_ISBN
------    --------  -----------
100       NULL      NULL
```

How It Works

A NULL value in the database represents an absence of any value and can't be compared using standard comparison operators (see more on operators later in this chapter). A special keyword IS was introduced to address the issue (as well as some workarounds, such as MySQL's NULL-safe comparison operator <=>; it is the only reliable way to find NULL values. This behavior is consistent across all RDBMSs.

NULLs can cause you serious troubles if not understood in context of your data. They will play tricks with your aggregate functions queries when you get down to counting and grouping your records (see Chapter 5 for more details).

NULLs can wreak havoc with your arithmetic. For example, suppose you want to calculate the difference between two numeric columns, and one of the columns has a NULL value. The results might surprise you: 19.99 + 0 = 19.99 (as expected), but 19.99+ NULL = NULL. The very same is true for any other mathematical operator (multiplication, division, or subtraction). Whereas division by zero will throw an error, division by NULL will serenely return NULL.

You need to pay attention to NULLs when you manipulate strings. For instance, a simple string concatenation (using a concatenation operator; see the next section for more information) will suddenly return NULL if any of the components is a NULL:

```
SELECT 'aaa' || 'BBB' AS result from dual; -- Oracle, DB2, PosgreSQL syntax
SELECT 'aaa' + 'BBB' AS result; -- MS SQL Server/Access syntax

result
--------
aaaBBB
```

The query predictably returns the "aaaBBB" string as the result, but the simple substitution of NULL for any of the component strings will bring back NULL:

```
SELECT 'aaa' + NULL AS result; -- MS SQL Server/Access syntax

result
--------
NULL
```

This behavior is identical across all RDBMSs, regardless of whether concatenation operators or concatenation functions are used (see Chapter 4 for more information on SQL Functions). To check whether the value is NULL, some RDBMSs supply functions (for example, ISNULL, introduced by SQL Server, or NVL, supplied by Oracle) or the expressions IS NULL and IS NOT NULL.

The NULL swallows anything it contacts, and a special built-in SQL function COALESCE was introduced; it returns the first non-NULL expression from the list of arguments passed in. See Chapter 4 for more information on this (and other functions).

The inability to compare NULLs using the Equals (=) and Not Equal to (<>) comparison operators was not always the default behavior of the SQL. There were times when NULL could be compared this way - in fact, it was the only allowable behavior.

The SQL-92 standard (yes, the 92 stands for the year when it was introduced) required you to use these operators when comparing NULL values. This atavistic behavior still lurks under the polished veneer of a respectable RDBMS. Microsoft SQL Server allows you to specify the SQL-92–compliant behavior of your environment by setting ANSI_NULL parameter ON and return to modern times by switching it OFF. (The ANSI prefix stands for the American National Standards Institute.)

```
SET ANSI_NULLS ON
SET ANSI_NULLS OFF
```

None of the Above: More Data Types

There are quite a few data types that we haven't mentioned yet; there are a several dozen different types out there, and vendors come up with new data types all the time. Some of these data types are so RDBMS-specific that they have no meaning outside the context, and some require knowledge of advanced SQL concepts. Yet there are a few which you ought to be aware of: BOOLEAN, BIT, and XML.

BOOLEAN

The staples of binary logic are TRUE and FALSE values. Even though this data type was introduced in SQL standard almost since the beginning, very few RDBMSs implemented it as such. The exceptions are the user-friendly desktop databases, such as Microsoft Access and OpenOffice BASE, which offer intuitive (Yes/No) data types.

MySQL has introduced a BOOLEAN data type that is but a synonym for TINYINT(1), where the value of zero is interpreted as FALSE, and any non-zero value evaluates to TRUE. PostgreSQL implements this data type natively and allows the literal values to be entered as TRUE/FALSE, YES/NO, Y/N, and 1/0 to represent TRUE and FALSE, respectively; it also allows for NULL to be used as a third state value (as discussed later in this chapter).

Oracle, IBM DB2, and Microsoft SQL Server do not have the BOOLEAN data type (even though IBM supports BOOLEAN as the data type for *variables* declared in custom functions and stored procedures).

BIT

The BIT data type can be either 0 or 1, and as the name suggests, it occupies exactly 1 bit of storage. This can be the underlying data type for the BOOLEAN data type in Microsoft SQL Server, Oracle, and IBM DB2. Using BIT as BOOLEAN requires the interpreting logic to be implemented in the client application.

Here are some examples of RDBMS specific data types: Microsoft SQL Server's SQL_VARIANT and Oracle's ROWID.

The former is supposed to be able to accommodate different data types supported by the SQL Server. Despite this claim to universal data type storage, it has quite a few exceptions, including XML, TEXT, IMAGE, and user-defined data types. The latter, ROWID, is used to store addresses for a physical location on the disk where the record lives. These data types have no direct equivalents anywhere else.

XML Data Type

XML stands for eXtensible Markup Language and is used to construct structured documents that combine both human-readable and machine-readable characteristics. The XML specification is maintained and developed by W3C, the main international standards organization for the World

Wide Web. The idea is to present information along with instructions on how this data (or data and metadata, in computer lingo) are to be interpreted. Here's an example of an XML document:

```
<books>
<book>
<title> Discovering SQL</title>
</book>
</books>
```

Despite its similarity to the more familiar HTML, a markup language used to create web pages, it has a different role. The HTML focuses on presenting the data in some layout; XML is dealing with the data.

The XML data type and its implementations in the RDBMS are discussed in greater detail in Chapter 11.

DDL, DML, AND DQL: COMPONENTS OF SQL

While SQL purports to be a single language, it is not. There are subtle distinctions, both within and outside of the language.

By now, it has become abundantly clear that there are several SQL in existence, similar in many ways, but distinct enough to pose problems when moving SQL statements between RDBMSs. In fact, there are distinct areas within the language itself.

When SQL is used to create, modify, or destroy objects within an RDBMS, it puts on its Data Definition Language (DDL) hat. Here you have the CREATE, ALTER, and DROP statements, plus a couple of others.

The Data Manipulation Language (DML) is the domain of INSERT, UPDATE, and DELETE, which you use to manipulate data.

Some bundle the Data Query Language (DQL) into DML, arguing that it also manipulates data. There are merits to this argument, not least that there is but a single member in this category: the SELECT statement.

Additionally, you might hear about the Transaction Control Language (TCL), which includes transaction statements such as COMMIT, ROLLBACK, or SAVEPOINT (see Chapter 10 for more information on transactions); and the Data Control Language (DCL), which deals with GRANT(ing) and REVOKE(ing) privileges to RDBMS objects.

The formal classification does not affect the way you use the language, but it will help you to be better prepared for a discussion with software developers and when taking your SQL mastery to the next level. As a Chinese saying has it, wisdom begins with calling things by their true names.

REFACTORING DATABASE TABLE

Now that you know about data types, you need to bring your tables up to standard by identifying which columns can be served better with which data type. The refactoring table does not equal refactoring database design (this will be the subject of the next chapter), but it will prepare you to take this step. All the statements used in this section are DDL statements.

How do you alter the past? One way is to drop everything and start anew. The DML statement DROP will serve the purpose.

DROP TABLE

Once dropped, the table can't be restored unless you were careful enough to drop it as part of the transaction (see Chapter 10 for details on transactional support). Not every RDBMS has transactional support for DDL statements. Microsoft SQL Server, Oracle, and IBM DB2 have it; MySQL and PostgreSQL don't. Neither Microsoft Access nor HSQLDB embedded into OpenOffice BASE has it.

Because a table occupies physical space, it is prudent to remove it. The DROP TABLE statement removes logical objects associated with it, such as INDEX (see Chapter 9 for more details on indices), constraints, and triggers (see Chapter 4). The syntax is virtually identical across all RDBMSs:

```
DROP TABLE <table_name>;
```

Sometimes you need to use a fully qualified name, including the table's schema, and you need to have the privileges assigned to you as a user to do so (see Chapter 10 for more information on database privileges).

If a table has referential constraints (explained in detail in Chapter 3), you can't drop such a table without either disabling or dropping the constraints first.

As fragmented as SQL is — and the situation has improved dramatically with SQL Standard's committee work — there are occasional sparks of consistency. CREATE and DROP are two of them; the syntax for creating and destroying all database objects is virtually identical across all RDBMSs — a glimpse of things to come.

CREATE TABLE

Once the table is successfully dropped, you can re-create it with all the changes that you did not put in the first time; you can't create a table with the same name that already exists in the database schema. No overloading here! The basic syntax for creating a table where you supply the table name and list of fields of particular types can quickly grow hairy, stretching across pages with numerous optional clauses.

Most of the time, you just use CREATE TABLE, list the fields (columns), and add constraints (DEFAULTS, CHECK, referential constraints, and so on; see Chapters 3 and 8 for more details). This is how we will continue doing it throughout this book and we'll leave the rest to the DBA to worry about. Here is an example of how a basic table can be created with minimum effort (it uses Microsoft SQL Server data types; you can use other data types suitable for your RDBMS):

```
CREATE TABLE books(
 bk_id bigint] NOT NULL,
 bk_title varchar(100) NULL,
 bk_ISBN varchar(50) NULL,
```

```
bk_publisher varchar(100) NULL,
bk_published_year int NULL,
bk_price smallmoney NULL,
bk_page_count int NULL,
bk_bought_on smalldatetime] NULL,
bk_hard_cover bit NULL,
bk_cover_pic varbinary(max) NULL,
bk_notes xml NULL)
```

Note that we have not specified where this table is created, how it will be managed, or what additional constraints for the table might be. These details can seriously affect performance of your database (and will be discussed in Chapter 9).

Important distinctions are the scope and type of table. In many RDBMSs, one is allowed to create permanent as well as temporary tables. The permanent tables are those we've been using so far, while temporary tables, as the name implies, have limited lifespans — usually (but not always) limited to that of the client session (see Chapter 10 for information on sessions). The following statement creates a temporary table in Oracle's syntax (which is representative of most other RDBMSs):

```
CREATE GLOBAL TEMPORARY TABLE tmp_Intermediate
( field1 INTEGER
, field2 VARCHAR2(20)
);
```

Microsoft syntax is slightly different:

```
CREATE #tmp_Intermediate
( field1 INTEGER
, field2 VARCHAR2(20)
);
```

The hash sign indicates the fleeting nature of the created table. The table automatically disappears once the user disconnects from the database. A double hash (##) gives the temporary table global scope, meaning that this table is visible to different users, and will disappear once all users disconnect — a subtle but important difference.

Once a temporary table is created, you can use it just as any other table for INSERT, UPDATE, and DELETE. Temporary tables can be used as intermediate storage or a workbench for your results, and are mostly used in stored procedures (see Chapter 4).

Temporary tables have a number of restrictions that do not apply to permanent tables. Full discussion of these nuances is beyond the scope of this book. Temporary tables are defined in SQL Standard, and all RDBMSs offer an ability to create temporary tables, though there are a lot of implementation differences.

ALTER TABLE

Is there a better way to rewrite the past? Indeed, there is: Enter the ALTER statement. Say you've created a table only to discover that you've added a superfluous field, specified a field (column) of the wrong type, or missed the column you need and need to add one. The ALTER statement can take on these jobs, and then some.

SQL Standard does not allow you to use the ALTER statement to change a data type, but it allows you to drop and re-create a field, which amounts to the same thing.

With ALTER, you can change the object by renaming it or changing its RDBMS–specific advanced characteristics (for example, move it to a different TABLESPACE in Oracle):

```
ALTER TABLE books RENAME to new_books;
```

Before renaming a table, you have to understand all the ramifications of the action because other objects might depend on the table (we'll discuss these in subsequent chapters). Once you rename it, all these dependencies will be broken. Not all RDBMSs approach the table-renaming task in the same fashion. While ALTER...RENAME will work with Oracle, PostgreSQL, and MySQL, it will not work in Microsoft products or in BD2 or OpenOffice BASE/HSQLDB.

Microsoft SQL Server uses system stored procedures (see Chapter 4) to rename objects (including tables and columns). This command will do the trick of renaming the BOOKS table into the NEW_BOOKS table:

```
EXEC sp_rename 'books','new_books'
```

IBM DB2 employs a separate RENAME statement:

```
RENAME books TO SYSTEM NAME new_books
```

All warnings regarding renaming database objects fully apply here; proceed with extreme caution!

Adding a new column to a table is rather straightforward. The following statement alters the table by adding a column NEW_COLUMN1 of CHAR data type of exactly one character length:

```
ALTER TABLE books ADD new_column1 CHAR(1);
```

This basic syntax is virtually identical across all RDBMSs, including the default COLUMN keyword being optional (with the exception of Microsoft Access and HSQLDB/OpenOffice BASE, which require the COLUMN keyword to be there).

Adding more than one column at a time is also supported:

```
ALTER TABLE books ADD
  new_column1 CHAR(1)
, new_column2 INT
, new_column3 DATETIME;
```

If the column you are trying to add already exists, the RDBMS will warn you about it by throwing an error.

Some databases, notably IBM DB2, place additional restrictions on altered tables before you can have access to them. Only specific commands can be issued against the altered table; for example, you can drop or rename it, or alter it some more. To bring the table back online, to be accessible, you must execute the REORG TABLE command to notify the RDBMS that the modifications are all done.

Modifying an existing column is more convoluted, especially if data are already there. With the ALTER statement, you can rename the column, change its data type, or add constraints. For instance, the following syntax is used by different RDBMSs to modify columns:

```
-- Oracle syntax
-- multiple changes are allowed
ALTER TABLE books
  MODIFY new_column1 CHAR(2) NOT NULL
 ,MODIFY new_column2 BIGINT

-- IBM DB2 syntax
-- multiiple changes are allowed
ALTER TABLE books
   ALTER COLUMN new_column1 SET DATA TYPE CHAR(2)
  ,ALTER COLUMN new_column1 SET NOT NULL
  ,ALTER COLUMN new_column2 SET DATA TYPE BIGINT

-- Microsoft SQl Server 2008 and MS Access
-- only one column at the time can be altered
-- cannot be renamed using ALTER statement
ALTER TABLE books
   ALTER COLUMN new_column1 CHAR(2)
ALTER TABLE books
   ALTER COLUMN new_column2 BIGINT

-- PostgreSQL
ALTER TABLE distributors
    ALTER COLUMN new_column1 TYPE CHAR(2)
   ,ALTER COLUMN new_column2 TYPE BIGINT;
ALTER TABLE books RENAME COLUMN new_colum1 TO old_column1;
-- MySQL
-- only one column at the time can be altered
-- changing data type requires column name to appear twice
-- same syntax used to rename columns, CHANGE could be substituted for MODIFY
ALTER TABLE books CHANGE new_column2new_column2BIGINT;
ALTER TABLE books CHANGE new_column2old_column2INTEGER;
```

Some RDBMSs such as Microsoft SQL Server 2008 will not allow you to alter columns of TEXT, NTEXT, and IMAGE data types. Oracle will prevent you from decreasing the size of a character data type (or lower precision, total number of digits, for numeric types) non-empty column, HSQLDB does not support renaming columns at all, and so on.

Getting rid of the objects requires the same universal DROP working in conjunction with ALTER statements; the syntax is surprisingly consistent across all RDBMSs, with minor differences as shown in the following. Some RDBMSs allow you to drop several columns in a single statement; some don't.

```
-- Oracle syntax
ALTER TABLE books
 DROP (new_column2, new_column1);

-- Microsoft SQL Server 2008 and MS Access
-- IBM DB2, PostgreSQL and MySQL
ALTER TABLE books
 DROP COLUMN new_column2;
```

An RDBMS worth its salt would prevent you from dropping all the columns. An attempt to drop the last column would result in a stern warning: "A table must have at least one data column," or something similar.

POPULATING A TABLE WITH DIFFERENT DATA TYPES

Populating a table with different data types is a snap as long as you match the type and supply the expected format: Strings need to be enclosed in single quotes (though some RDBMSs allow you to mix and match), number literals are provided as-is, and so on.

Literal in programming context means "hard-coded value," and you might have heard that this is a bad word in software development circles. Yet when SQL statements are constructed, prior to being submitted for execution, all the values (with the exception of these supplied by DEFAULT constraints) must be properly formatted literals.

Let's construct an INSERT statement for the BOOKS table:

```
INSERT INTO books(
             bk_id
            ,bk_title
            ,bk_ISBN
            ,bk_publisher
            ,bk_published_year
            ,bk_price
            ,bk_page_count
            ,bk_bought_on
            ,bk_hard_cover
            ,bk_cover_pic
            ,bk_notes)
     VALUES
            (1
            ,'SQL Bible'
            ,'978-0470229064'
            ,'Wiley'
            ,2008
            ,39.99
            ,888
            ,GETDate()
            ,0
            ,NULL
            ,NULL)
```

A brief examination of the structure should tell you that the only required value you need to supply is BK_ID because it has a NOT NULL constraint on it; everything else can be populated with default NULLs:

```
INSERT INTO books (bk_id) VALUES (8)
```

The preceding statement will insert a new row into the table and leave all fields but one empty, filled with default NULLs signifying absence of any data. Any attempt to insert a new record without involving BK_ID will fail with an error message informing you that the RDBMS can't insert the value NULL into column 'bk_id', table 'books' because the column does not allow NULLs. INSERT fails. The actual wording will vary from RDBMS to RDBMS, but the message is unmistakable: If a field is defined with the NOT NULL constraint, it has to be filled with some value upon INSERT (it can't be updated with NULL value later on, either). We will discuss the statement in greater length later in this chapter.

Character data, numbers, and even dates can be added to your INSERT statements relatively easily as part of your standard SQL. Even XML data, being essentially a string, follows the same rules. Getting binary data into your database is much trickier: You can painstakingly resort to typing in long sequences of binary or hexadecimal codes representing your binary content. Or you can rely on some RDBMS-specific mechanism such as the Microsoft SQL Server OPENROWSET keyword (that allows importing binary files residing on your computer) or FILESTREAM (that allows streaming remote content to populate your binary fields). So far, these efforts remain proprietary and differ greatly among the RDBMSs, even among those supporting this functionality.

The most common way is to use an external client written using some database access mechanism (JDBC, ODBC, or OLEDB) that supports binary data inserts, and, of course, requires custom programming. It essentially does the "painstaking binary typing," but being done by a machine makes it fast and efficient.

One of the optimization techniques for handling binary data is to leave it outside the RDBMS altogether and only store information on how to find it when requested: a path to a file, a URL to a remote image, and so on.

The methods are described in greater detail in Chapter 11, which deals with unstructured and semistructured data.

Implicit and Explicit Data Conversion

With so many data types flying around, how do we ever get reports out of this thing in normal human readable text? Why, by using conversion, of course!

Conversion is not for humans only; RDBMSs routinely use it when asked to perform tasks where intent is either implied or explicitly stated; thus the conversions are either implicit or explicit, respectively.

An *implicit conversion* occurs when the RDBMS tries to guess what the purpose of the command was. Suppose that you have decided to concatenate several strings following some of the examples we introduced earlier in this chapter, and the final result is an address, complete with the zip/postal codes and the house number. The following query would get you the desired result:

```
SELECT  '123' + '-' + '152' + ' Avenue, ' + '09071'
---------------------
123-152 Avenue, 09071
```

So far, so good; a decent although non-existent address. Now, what would happen if we accidentally dropped the hyphen and "Avenue," the non-numeric values?

```
SELECT  '123' + '152' + '09071'
-----------
12315209071
```

Our intent is still clear. By enclosing every component in single quotes, we convey to the RDBMS our intent to get a character string back, even if it would represent numbers. To give the computer a hint that we want these strings to be treated as numbers, we need to get rid of quotes, at least for one of the components. By making '123' a number by stripping the single quotes around it, the result is quite different:

```
SELECT  123 + '152' + '09071'
-----------
9346
```

Now the SQL engine realizes that we want to add the numbers, even though some of them are supplied as literal strings, by virtue of having one noncharacter added in the expression: 123. It implicitly converted all the strings into numbers, and added the numbers together.

It gets even more interesting as the RDBMS tries to be even smarter. If we decide to strip it of its character identifiers, the quotes, not from the first or second of the members in the expression but from the last one, '09071', the result will be different yet again:

```
SELECT  '123' + '152' + 09071
-----------
132223
```

Huh? What happened is the RDBMS engine concatenated the first two members, '123' and '152', into a string '123152', and then implicitly converted it into a number and added as a bona fide number to the last member.

There are limits to the RDBMS' guessing power. In order to be implicitly converted, the data types must be of compatible types. The RDBMS can't convert letters into numbers (the word 'one' will not be converted to 1); it can't convert dates into numbers and numbers into binary images, and so on. Some RDBMSs are stricter than others in enforcing conversion rules, and some disallow implicit conversions altogether.

The point of the story is that you will be well advised never to rely on implicit conversions, even if your RDBMS allows you to. Always use explicit conversions.

In case you need more convincing not to use implicit conversion in your code, consider the following reasons:

- Negative performance impact: It takes additional processing cycles to second-guess your intentions.
- Implicit conversions rely on additional configuration parameters (for example, a national character set) and might return inconsistent values as a result.
- Being proprietary by definition, implicit conversion algorithms are not guaranteed to work across different versions of the RDBMS or across different RDBMSs at all.
- It is much easier to understand (and maintain) your code when your intentions are stated upfront, without the need to guess them.

Explicit conversion happens when you do not allow the RDBMS to guess your intentions and tell it upfront how you want your data types to be treated. Explicit conversion is accomplished with the help of generic conversion functions such as CAST and CONVERT, introduced in Chapter 4. Both are used to convert one data type to another explicitly, within the bounds of compatibility, of course. Many RDBMSs have additional data type–specific functions that convert everything to characters, numbers, or dates. They are handy shortcuts to a more convoluted (and more powerful) syntax provided by the two conversion functions mentioned previously.

SELECT STATEMENT REVISITED

The SELECT statement — along with INSERT, UPDATE, and DELETE — are the four pillars of SQL, and you need to master them to be considered a fluent, if not a native speaker. We discussed this statement briefly in Chapter 1; now let's take a closer look.

Selecting Literals, Functions, and Calculated Columns

There are many things to select from in a database, and tables are not the only game in town. In the examples on implicit data conversion, you've already seen how we can perform arithmetic and strings concatenation using SELECT and literal values (Microsoft SQL Server syntax):

```
SELECT 1+2 AS SumOfTwo, 'one' + 'two' AS TwoStrings;

SumOfTwo     TwoStrings
----------- ------------
3            onetwo
```

Note that because we do not refer to a table (well, Oracle would ask for selecting `FROM dual`, and IBM insists that such expressions were selected `FROM sysibm.sysdummy1`); no `FROM` statement is required.

This also can be expanded to include calculated columns and functions (SQL functions are covered in Chapter 4). If, for instance, you'd need to see how much your books would cost in Japanese Yen, all you have to do is to multiply its price value by the exchange rate:

```
SELECT bk_price * 80.6829 AS PriceInYen
FROM books;

PriceInYen
-----------
3226.50917100
```

Adding SQL functions to the mix is just as easy, and you get to alias the resulting columns! Using Microsoft SQL Server's built-in `GetDate()` function (more about functions in Chapter 4), we can get the today's date as result of our SELECT query:

```
SELECT GetDate() as Today;
Today
-----------------------
2010-10-31 18:27:34.450
```

Setting Vertical Limits

In order to extract data from one or more tables, we use the SELECT statement. We have already seen it in its simplest form:

```
SELECT * FROM <table>
```

The preceding statement retrieves all the data from a table. What if we don't want all the data? What if you are only interested in the title and the publisher of all the books in our library?

SELECT allows us to specify what data we want retrieved. Setting vertical limits is easy; just specify the columns from which you want to see data and ignore the rest:

```
SELECT bk_title, bk_publisher FROM dbo.books;

bk_title        bk_publisher
-----------      ---------------
SQL Bible         Wiley
SQL Bible         Wiley
. . .
SQL Functions     Wrox
```

The preceding statement will produce a result set with only two columns for all records we have added to the table.

Alias: What's in a Name?

Two different types of folks use databases: those who put them together and those who use them, and they have vastly different objectives. The former strives to create a database that not only satisfies business requirements but is also easy to program and easy to maintain. They will name objects in the database from a developer's point of view: cryptic notations that make programming easier, but might leave the users guessing.

Naming conventions in database programming is a hot topic: Everybody and their cousin seem to have some ideas on how it "should be." Not long ago, it was customary to code data types into the column names; the rationale was that it would be easy for the programmers to use them if they knew what data type the column was just by looking at it. Modern developer tools made this a somewhat less pressing issue, and readability became more important. Whatever naming convention you've decided to adopt, the important thing is to stick with it for consistency's sake.

The SQL alias feature allows you to put user friendly names to otherwise cryptic programmer argot:

```
SELECT bk_title as Book, bk_publisher as Publisher FROM dbo.books

Book           Publisher
-----------      ---------------
SQL Bible         Wiley
. . .
SQL Functions  Wiley
```

Now, this looks just a little more civilized. It is called *aliasing* a column name.

A column is not the only database object that can be aliased in a SELECT statement; we can also alias table names. This would not make much sense if we are selecting from a single table, but we'll give it a try all the same:

```
SELECT bk_title as Book, bk_publisher as Publisher FROM dbo.books b
```

The benefits of this aliasing will become more obvious when we start SELECTing data from a bunch of different tables in one fell swoop (in a single SELECT statement).

We will discuss various ways to join tables in Chapter 7, but for now let's just see how we can add the authors to the books and publishers to a single result set.

In our database, there are three tables we will need to interrogate at once in order to achieve that:

```
books
authors
books_authors
```

We need these separate tables because one book may have several authors, and the same author may have written several books. The relational theory behind this will be explained in Chapter 3, but for now, just accept that in RDBMS lingo this is called a many-to-many relationship between the books and the authors. A separate table is needed to tie together every book to each of its authors and every author to each book.

Our query may now look like this, and don't worry about all the INNER JOINing. Note that we need to repeat the names of the tables over and over again (just to make the point, we have even added them as qualifiers to the field names, which is not necessary here, but may be necessary if several tables happen to have columns with the same name):

```
SELECT
 books.bk_title AS Book
,books.bk_publisher AS Publisher
,authors.au_last_name AS Author
FROM  authors INNER JOIN
books_authors ON authors.au_id = books_authors.au_id INNER JOIN
      books ON books_authors.bk_id = books.bk_id;
```

To translate the preceding query into plain English: "For each pair of [book, author] as found in the BOOKS_AUTHORS table, go fetch the corresponding book and publisher from the BOOKS table and the corresponding author from the AUTHORS table."

Let's see how a bit of aliasing will help us to make it more manageable:

```
SELECT
 b.bk_title AS Book
,b.bk_publisher AS Publisher
,a.au_last_name AS Author
FROM  authors a INNER JOIN
      books_authors ba ON a.au_id = ba.au_id INNER JOIN
      books b ON ba.bk_id = b.bk_id;
```

It looks a lot more compact, not to mention that it saved you a fair amount of typing. Both the column alias and the table alias can (but do not have to) be preceded by *AS*. In our examples, we used AS with the field name aliases, but not with the table name aliases.

Setting Horizontal Limits

So far, with only a few exceptions, we selected everything the table can furnish. It might be okay for our little library, but as you can imagine, things grow hairy pretty quickly, and issuing indiscriminate `SELECT`s on a table with a million rows might not be quite as feasible. You must narrow down your search to what you are looking for (or make your best guess).

The WHERE clause provides the needed selectivity. Suppose that we want to retrieve all the books published by a particular publisher. For this purpose, we can use the WHERE keyword. It works like this:

```
SELECT bk_title as Book, bk_publisher as Publisher FROM dbo.books
WHERE bk_publisher='Wiley';
```

Only books published by Wiley will be retrieved. In fact, you don't even need the Publisher column in our result; it will just be Wiley, Wiley, Wiley all the way down. You've successfully filtered out all other records that you don't want at the moment.

In case you don't quite remember the name of the publisher you are interested in, you can use the LIKE operator (discussed later in this chapter):

```
SELECT bk_title as Book, bk_publisher as Publisher FROM dbo.books
WHERE bk_publisher LIKE 'W%';
```

This query concerns itself with the publisher, whose name starts with a *W*.

The usefulness of the WHERE clause goes much further than limiting results horizontally; it also is being used to establish relationships when combining data from two or more tables. It is used to JOIN the tables on a set of criteria (as seen a few pages ago, and the full discussion awaits you in Chapter 7).

DISTINCT

Here is another way to whittle down the number of records to a meaningful few. Suppose that we only want to get the list of all the publishers, without their respective books. We can do this as follows:

```
SELECT bk_publisher as Publisher FROM books;
```

Unfortunately, we are liable to get more than we have bargained for; if a publisher has published 20 different books, the name will be repeated in our result 20 times! Ugh. Let's narrow things down a bit, make things more distinct:

```
SELECT DISTINCT bk_publisher as Publisher FROM books;
```

Ah, that's better. Now we get a single row for each publisher, no matter how many times it appears in the table books. Note that this time we've asked for the BK_PUBLISHER field only because the

DISTINCT keyword applies to a combination of the columns; that is, the entire set must be distinct in the set, and the combination BK_TITLE, BK_PUBLISHER is unique throughout our database:

```
bk_title        bk_publisher
--------------  --------
SQL Bible       Wiley
```

Selecting a distinct book title alone will bring us the entire collection (unless you happen to keep multiple records for multiple copies you may have); selecting only publishers will ensure that each publisher appears only once.

What about NULLs? After all, we've just been told that a NULL is never equal to another NULL; surely they must be distinct! Well, for the DISTINCT filter, a NULL is a NULL is a NULL. If you have 20 records and half of them are NULLs, the query asking for distinct values from this column will return but a single NULL. So in the preceding examples with 20 records and 10 of them being NULL, the SELECT DISTINCT will bring 11 distinct records, including one NULL.

Get Organized: Marching Orders

The order in which data is returned to you would most likely reflect the order in which it is stored in the table, and not necessarily the one in which it was entered. Things could get dicey when there was a lot of INSERT and DELETE operations on the table, and some RDBMS impose additional rules. Fortunately, SQL provides the means by which you can organize the data as it's being returned to you by a query.

ORDER BY

This keyword is used to sort the result of a query. In general, the order of rows in the data set produced by a query is undetermined. `ORDER BY` defines the desired order. The following query lists all the books and their prices, from least to most expensive:

```
SELECT bk_title as Book, bk_price as Price FROM dbo.books
ORDER BY bk_price
```

The column that is used to determine the order need not be a part of the result, either. We can rewrite the preceding query to show the books only, without the prices, but still in the least-to-most-expensive order:

```
SELECT bk_title as Book FROM dbo.books
ORDER BY bk_price
```

One or more fields may be specified for the ordering.

```
SELECT bk_title as Book FROM dbo.books
ORDER BY bk_published_year, bk_price
```

The preceding query will produce a list of books in which the oldest-published editions will come first, followed by the newer books. Within each year, the least expensive books will precede the more expensive ones.

ASC and DESC

By default, the order of the returned records is ascending (from A to Z), but modifiers ASC and DESC may be used to define the sorting explicitly. Let's reverse the sorting order of the published year:

```
SELECT bk_title as Book FROM dbo.books
ORDER BY bk_published_year DESC, bk_price
```

This is identical to...

```
SELECT bk_title as Book FROM dbo.books
ORDER BY bk_published_year DESC, bk_price ASC
```

In both cases, the new editions will now precede the old, while the expensive books within each year will still appear after the cheaper ones.

TOP and LIMIT

Being able to extract a predefined number of records comes in handy. The TOP keyword is used to limit the number of rows in the data set that results from a query in Microsoft SQL Server and Microsoft Access. Suppose that we are interested only in some recent editions. We can design a query thus:

```
SELECT TOP 5 bk_title as Book FROM dbo.books
ORDER BY bk_published_year DESC;
```

This query will give us the first 5 rows of the result. Keep in mind that behind the scenes the rows are first selected and sorted in descending order, and only then will the first five be returned. Ordering the rows in ASC order will bring the first five rows from the top, after they have been sorted in ascending order.

This approach is frequently used to find the row with the ultimate value of some sort (the latest date, the greatest price, the earliest year...). For example, to find the most expensive book ever published by Wiley, we may query as follows:

```
SELECT TOP 1 bk_title as Book FROM dbo.books
WHERE bk_publisher='Wiley'
ORDER BY bk_price DESC;
```

Unfortunately, the syntax across the RDBMSs varies significantly. Every other RDBMS had its own ideas about how this functionality needed to be implemented before the SQL Standards committee chimed in on the issue in 2008. Here's how the query would look in different RDBMSs:

- Oracle:

```
SELECT bk_title as Book FROM dbo.books
WHERE ROWNUM <=5
ORDER BY bk_published_year DESC;
```

- DB2, PostgreSQL (with some additional keywords):

```
SELECT bk_title as Book FROM dbo.books
ORDER BY bk_published_year DESC FETCH FIRST 5 ROWS ONLY;
```

- PostgreSQL, MySQL, HSQLDB:

```
SELECT bk_title as Book FROM dbo.books
ORDER BY bk_published_year DESC LIMIT 5;
```

Used in conjunction with ORDER BY, these statements can return either top or bottom records. Other RDBMSs such as PostgreSQL and MySQL offer the ability to offset counts (for example, start with the tenth record from the top):

```
SELECT bk_title as Book FROM dbo.books
ORDER BY bk_published_year DESC OFFSET 10 FETCH 5 FIRST ROWS ONLY
```

Incidentally, this corresponds to SQL Standard, introduced in 2008.

INSERT, UPDATE, AND DELETE REVISITED

While the SELECT statement seems to draw all the attention of the end user, developers responsible for implementing business logic for the applications hold INSERT, UPDATE, and DELETE statements in equal respect. After all, they are concerned with getting the data in, managing it there as long as needed, and retiring it when the need is gone. Proper use of the statements is the hallmarks of a well-behaved database.

INSERT

We used INSERT in Chapter 1 and throughout Chapter 2, but as you have probably guessed, there is more to it.

The classic INSERT requires you to list all columns in the table and supply corresponding values for each column. For instance, the full insert into the BOOKS table might look like this:

```
INSERT INTO books
          (bk_id
           ,bk_title
           ,bk_ISBN
           ,bk_publisher
           ,bk_published_year
           ,bk_price
           ,bk_page_count
           ,bk_bought_on
           ,bk_hard_cover
           ,bk_cover_pic
           ,bk_notes)
     VALUES
           ( 1
           ,'SQL Bible'
           ,'978-0470229064'
           ,'Wiley'
           ,2008
           ,39.99
           ,888
           ,CAST('10-10-2009' as smalldatetime)
           ,0
           ,NULL
           ,NULL)
```

This is fairly intuitive: a list of columns (in any order), and a matching list of values (in matching order), formatted for appropriate data types (string, numbers, dates), and off we go. The shortened version of the same statement would get rid of the columns list:

```
INSERT INTO books
     VALUES
            ( 1
            ,'SQL Bible'
            ,'978-0470229064'
            ,'Wiley'
            ,2008
            ,39.99
            ,888
            ,CAST('10-10-2009' as smalldatetime)
            ,0
            ,NULL
            ,NULL)
```

While handy, this syntax imposes two major restrictions: You must list values for all columns in the table and you must supply them in the exact order in which they are listed in the table. Therefore, even though there is but a single column in the entire table that is a required value, you must supply all values for the statement to execute it successfully. When column names are listed, you can decide for yourself which fields you want to populate and which can be left to be filled with DEFAULT values specified in the DDL definition of your table:

```
INSERT INTO books
           (bk_id
            ,bk_title
            ,bk_ISBN)
     VALUES
            ( 1
            ,'SQL Bible'
            ,'978-0470229064');
```

DEFAULT values are constraints placed upon columns instructing RDBMSs to fill in a predefined value if none was supplied in the INSERT statement. The DEFAULT value might be a literal (hard-coded) value or be defined by a function, and is defined as part of CREATE TABLE statement or added with an ALTER TABLE statement. One of the examples of the DEFAULT value is auto-increment, wherein the value inserted is generated as an increased sequence of numbers (more on auto-increment fields in Chapter 8).

You can decide whether reduced readability, reduced flexibility, and imposed restrictions are worth saving keystrokes typing the full list of columns, but with few exceptions it is the best practice to state your intentions upfront. We recommend using verbose syntax to avoid potential troubles.

The INSERT statement has no use for the WHERE clause. The inserted row just gets appended to the last one in the table, which continues to grow with each insert; you have no control where the new record gets inserted. The workaround for the situation when you need to know the exact logical location in the sequence might be to update with a subsequent insert performed as single transaction (see Chapter 10 for more information).

SELECT INTO

The SELECT statement has a couple more tricks up its sleeve. For instance, it can be used to clone tables. The Microsoft SQL Server SELECT INTO statement allows you to create an exact replica of an existing table, complete with data:

```
SELECT * INTO old_books FROM books;
```

The preceding syntax is also supported by PostgreSQL, while Oracle and MySQL offer similar functionality with somewhat different syntax:

```
INSERT INTO old_books SELECT * FROM BOOKS;
```

If the OLD_BOOKS table does not exist, it will be created (and you'll need sufficient privileges to do so; see Chapter 10 for more on privileges). If it does exist, an error will be generated.

These statements, whatever the syntax, can be used with all clauses afforded by SQL. You can limit them both vertically and horizontally by deploying the arsenal of SQL tools described in this chapter and throughout the book (WHERE clause, LIMIT, operators, and so on), or you can specify an impossible condition in the WHERE clause, in which case only the table structure will be copied and no data transferred.

An important distinction between the original and the cloned table is that none of the constraints (with a few exceptions, such as IDENTITY and NOT NULL) will be transferred to the new table. This behavior is RDBMS-dependent and will differ widely among the respective RDBMSs.

There are a few scenarios in which using INSERT is impossible because of constraints placed upon the table. The primary example is tables with referential integrity constraints. A record in the child table can't be inserted unless there is a corresponding record in the parent table already (see Chapter 3 for an explanation of terms and underlying concepts). Another example is an IDENTITY column (a concept in which the RDBMS is instructed to insert sequentially increasing numbers automatically) and the variants of similar constructs across other database systems.

UPDATE

Once the record is in the tables, it can be modified — within reason. The UPDATE statement can change values in the record's columns, but it can't do anything else. The updated values have to be replaced with the same (or compatible) data type; refer to the section on implicit conversion earlier in this chapter.

The basic syntax is identical across the RDBMSs:

```
UPDATE books SET bk_publisher = 'Wiley';
```

Here we are updating the BOOKS table, and setting the value of the BK_PUBLISHER column, whatever it might be, to a literal value. There is only one problem with the statement: All records will be set to "Wiley," even those published by other guys. Not quite what we wanted, right?

To add more selectivity to the query, you need to use the WHERE clause:

```
UPDATE books SET bk_publisher = 'Wiley'
WHERE bk_id = 1
```

Of course, you need to know which BOOK_ID to update. Alternatively, you can use comparison operators (covered later in this chapter) to pinpoint the record. Because we know that *SQL Bible* was published by Wiley, the following statement will hit the target:

```
UPDATE books SET bk_publisher = 'Wiley'
WHERE bk_title= 'SQL Bible';
```

The UPDATE statement enables modifying more than one column at a time; the changes are made to the same record (or respective records). Use the previous query as an example with Microsoft SQL Server syntax and the SQL GetDate()function to update the field with the current date (for more information on SQL functions and their uses, see Chapter 4):

```
UPDATE books
       SET bk_publisher = 'Wiley', bk_bought_on = GetDate()
WHERE bk_title = 'SQL Bible';
```

To modify the preceding query for the RDBMS of your choice, just replace the GetDate() function with the function valid for your particular database: Now() for PostgreSQL, MySQL, HSQLDB, and MS Access; SYSDATE for Oracle; and the CURRENT DATE special register for IBM DB2.

The values in the table can be updated based upon values from some other table (which would require a subquery in the WHERE clause) or it can be calculated on the fly based upon values from the very same one. For instance, if you move from the United States to Canada and want to see the prices of the books you've collected in Canadian dollars instead of American, you can use the SELECT statement to convert them. Multiply each value by the exchange rate (this is the recommended approach because exchange rates fluctuate over time) as follows (note that this assumes that prices are in U.S. dollars to begin with and affects all books in the table):

```
SELECT bk_title AS Title
    , bk_price * 1.01827 AS CanadianDollarsPrice
FROM books
```

If you decide to persist this data into the database, you can issue an UPDATE statement:

```
UPDATE books SET bk_price = bk_price * 1.01827;
```

Now all your books are priced in Canadian dollars (with the exchange rate valid on October 10, 2010). Note that we are using the very *existing* value from the field to calculate the new one — no need to supply the literal value.

Just as some columns can't be INSERTed into, some can't be UPDATEd. These are the usual suspects: constrained columns (identity, primary key, and so on); updating these columns would generate an error.

DELETE

Getting rid of data is easy, just DELETE it. The only question is what to delete. The following statement wipes out the entire table:

```
DELETE FROM <table name>;
```

If you are in a hurry, FROM can also be omitted in some RDBMSs:

```
DELETE <table name>;
```

It looks scary, but keep in mind that DELETE is a DML statement and it can't destroy an object. This is what DROP, a DML counterpart, does best. Not every RDBMS supports this shortcut, so you'll be well advised to use a more readable DELETE FROM syntax.

Deleting the records does not have to be an all-or-nothing process. The approach can be more nuanced when a WHERE clause is deployed, but you need to know what criteria to specify. To delete a specific record, you need to know what identifies it as unique in the entire table (such as PRIMARY KEY; see the next chapter for the definitions). The following statement inserts and deletes a dummy record with ID 1000 and leaves the rest of the values to their defaults:

```
INSERT INTO books (bk_id) VALUES (1000)
DELETE FROM books WHERE  bk_id = 1000;
```

But trying to remove a record that has references in other tables (for example, BK_I = 1) results in an error. Here is an example of how it might look in Microsoft SQL Server 2008:

```
DELETE FROM books WHERE  bk_id = 1;

Msg 547, Level 16, State 0, Line 1
The DELETE statement conflicted with the REFERENCE constraint "FK_bk_au_books".
The conflict occurred in database "library", table "dbo.books_authors"
, column 'bk_id'.
The statement has been terminated.
```

Had the table been self contained, this statement would have removed the record from the table, but in the relational world, it's a rare table that is an island. Referential constraints make it necessary either to drop the constraint before the deletion or start from "child-most" tables (BOOKS_AUTHORS, SEARCH_BOOKS, and LOCATION), removing the records referring to the BK_ID 1 in the BOOKS table. This behavior is consistent throughout every RDBMS that supports referential integrity constraints (see the next chapter), including all relational databases discussed in this book.

Tracking down all references can be a lengthy and tedious procedure, requiring an intimate knowledge of the data model. To help with the job, some RDBMSs began to offer the ON DELETE CASCADE option as part of their DDL definitions for the FOREIGN KEY constraints (there is also a corresponding ON UPDATE CASCADE option). This functionality is RDBMS-dependent, and using it has lots of conditions attached to it. Please check the vendor's documentation.

When pinpointing a single record, you specify a range and you need to use operators (discussed later in this chapter). For instance, to remove all records in which the bought-on date is earlier than October 29, 2000, you might use the following statement, which also converts a literal string into a DATETIME type of Microsoft SQL Server:

```
DELETE FROM books
WHERE  bk_bought_on < CAST('October 29, 2000' AS DATETIME);
```

All operators are fair game and can be used in any combinations; they will be applied according to the rules of precedence (see later in this chapter for more details).

DELETE can be used on only a single table at a time; you cannot delete from two or more tables in one statement. However, if you ever need to do so, you can use batch grouping to group the statements into a transaction to be executed as a single unit (please see Chapter 10 for more information).

A record in one table can be deleted based upon a value from another table or tables. This requires a subquery to be used in the WHERE clause of the DELETE command (discussed in Chapter 6).

TRUNCATE That Table!

Deleting all data from a table is easy and the TRUNCATE statement makes it even easier! The difference is subtle but crucial. The DELETE statement is monitored (logged) by the RDBMS, and, with a bit of effort, is reversible; the TRUNCATE statement is swift and merciless: The data are blown out without chance of redemption (unless you wrapped the statement in a transaction; see Chapter 10 for more details). Unlike the DELETE statement, if a table has triggers defined for it — special programming modules triggered by events in the table (see Chapter 4 for more details) — they will not be activated.

The basic syntax valid across all RDBMSs in this book is simple. Here's how you truncate a table in one fell swoop:

```
TRUNCATE TABLE <table name>;
```

Depending on a particular RDBMS implementation, it can have many optional RDBMS-specific qualifiers that you might have to take into consideration.

Neither OpenOffice BASE's HSQLDB nor Microsoft Access supports the TRUNCATE statement. The trick of using their respective embedded programming languages can accomplish a similar functionality, however.

The statement comes with some strings attached, and the options and restrictions vary across RDBMS implementations. First, TRUNCATE is a solitary affair. Only a single table can be truncated at a time. Because of its totality, you can't use the WHERE clause; it won't do you any good when all rows are removed. Furthermore, a table that has FOREIGN KEY constraints (see the next chapter) can't be truncated in Microsoft SQL Server or Oracle; you have to drop the constraint first. The same action is perfectly valid in PostgreSQL, however, when you add the CASCADE clause to the statement.

SQL OPERATORS: AGENTS OF CHANGE

Operators are fulfilling an important go-between function, connecting data, comparing data, and changing behavior of SQL statements. *Operators* in SQL are defined as symbols and keywords that are used to specify an action to be performed on one or more expressions called *operands* (the parts on which the operator operates).

All operators can be split into two broad categories:

- **Unary operators** — Applied to only one operand at a time; a typical format is `<operator><operand>`.
- **Binary operators** — Applied to two operands at a time; they usually appear in the format `<operand><operator><operand>`.

Arithmetic and String Concatenation Operators

Arithmetic operators, as the name implies, are used for arithmetic computations. The use of the arithmetic operators is very intuitive (elementary school stuff), and they can be used in virtually every clause of the SQL statement. Table 2-10 provides a selected list of arithmetic operators.

TABLE 2-10: Selected Arithmetic Operators

OPERATOR	DESCRIPTION
+	Addition: Adds two numbers or (in the case of Microsoft SQL Server) concatenates strings. With this exception, the usage is identical across all three databases. Valid for all RDBMSs.
-	Subtraction: Subtracts one numeric value from another. The usage is identical across all RDBMSs. It is also used as a sign identity or unary negation operator.

continues

TABLE 2-10 *(continued)*

OPERATOR	DESCRIPTION
*	Multiplication: Multiplies one number by another. The usage is identical across all RDBMSs.
/	Division: Divides one number by another. The usage is identical across all RDBMSs.

The string concatenation operator is a binary operator that glues two character strings together (as we've already seen with NULL examples in the preceding section) and is similar to the addition operator that adds two numbers. String concatenation operators are listed in Table 2-11.

TABLE 2-11: String Concatenation Operators

<table>
<tr><th>OPERATOR</th><th>DESCRIPTION</th></tr>
<tr><td>||</td><td>Concatenation operator: Concatenates character strings; valid for Oracle, DB2, PostgreSQL, and HSQLDB (OpenOffice BASE).</td></tr>
<tr><td>+</td><td>String concatenation operator in Microsoft SQL Server.</td></tr>
<tr><td>CONCAT</td><td>String concatenation operator (DB2 only): Used as an SQL function in other RDBMSs such as MySQL.</td></tr>
</table>

While doing arithmetic in SQL is relatively easy, you must pay attention to the data type used in the operations; for numeric values, that would mean the precision and scale of the result; for datetime, the range of the resulting values; and so on.

Some databases (such as Oracle) will perform implicit conversion (whenever possible) if data types are not compatible with the operator (for example, a string value used with the addition operator); the others will require explicit conversion into a compatible data type to perform an operation.

Comparison Operators

Comparison operators are used to compare two or more values. They are usually found in the `WHERE` clause of a `SELECT` statement, although they can be used in any valid SQL expression.

The usage is identical across all three databases except for the nonstandard operators `!<` and `!>`.They are recognized by DB2 9.7 and Microsoft SQL Server 2008, but are excluded from every other RDBMS. The nonstandard *not equal to* operator, `!=`, can be used in all three dialects; another *not equal to* operator, `^=`, is recognized only by Oracle and DB2.

Table 2-12 lists the comparison operators.

TABLE 2-12: Comparison Operators

OPERATOR	DESCRIPTION
=	Equals: implemented across all RDBMSs
>	Greater than: implemented across all RDBMSs

OPERATOR	DESCRIPTION
<	Less than: implemented across all RDBMSs
>=	Greater than or equal to: implemented across all RDBMSs
<=	Less than or equal to: implemented across all RDBMSs
<>	Not equal to: implemented across all RDBMSs
!=	Not equal to: implemented across all RDBMSs
^=	Not equal to: Oracle and DB2 only
!<	Not less than: DB2 9.7 and Microsoft SQL Server only
!>	Not greater than: DB2 9.7 and Microsoft SQL Server only

Logical Operators

These operators are used to evaluate some set of conditions, and the returned result is always a value of TRUE, FALSE, or "unknown." Table 2-13 presents full list of SQL logical operators.

Oracle lists logical operators as SQL conditions. *It was referred in previous versions as comparison operators or logical operators. DB2 uses the term* predicates *instead of* operators, *and so on. Pick your flavor.*

TABLE 2-13: SQL Logical Operators

OPERATOR	ACTION
ALL	Evaluates to TRUE if all of a set of comparisons are TRUE.
AND	Evaluates to TRUE if both Boolean expressions are TRUE. Some RDBMSs use && instead of the keyword.
ANY	Evaluates to TRUE if any one of a set of comparisons is TRUE.
BETWEEN	Evaluates to TRUE if the operand is within a range.
EXISTS	Evaluates to TRUE if a subquery contains any rows.
IN	Evaluates to TRUE if the operand is equal to one of a list of expressions.
LIKE	Evaluates to TRUE if the operand matches a pattern.

continues

TABLE 2-13 *(continued)*

OPERATOR	ACTION
NOT	Reverses the value of any other Boolean operator.
OR	Evaluates to TRUE if either Boolean expression is TRUE.
SOME	Evaluates to TRUE if some of a set of comparisons are TRUE; is not supported by HSQLDB (OpenOffice BASE).

ALL

ALL compares a scalar value with a single-column set of values. It is used in conjunction with comparison operators and is sometimes classified as a comparison operator. It returns TRUE when a specified condition is TRUE for all pairs; otherwise, it returns FALSE. An example of its usage is given in Chapter 6.

ANY | SOME

The ANY | SOME operator compares a scalar value with a single-column set of values. The keywords ANY and SOME are completely interchangeable. The operator returns TRUE if a specified condition is valid for any pair; otherwise, it returns FALSE. An example of its usage is given in Chapter 6, dealing with *subqueries*.

In Microsoft SQL Server and DB2, operators ANY | SOME *can be used with a subquery only. Oracle allows them to be used with a list of scalar values. Other RDBMSs do not recognize the SOME keyword.*

BETWEEN <expression> AND <expression>

The BETWEEN operator allows for "approximate" matching of the selection criteria. It returns TRUE if the expression evaluates to be greater or equal to the value of the start expression, and is less than or equal to the value of the end expression. Used with negation operator NOT, the expression evaluates to TRUE only when its value is *less* than that of the start expression or *greater than* the value of the end expression.

The AND *keyword used in conjunction with the* BETWEEN *operator is not the same as the* AND *operator explained later in this chapter.*

The following query retrieves data about books, specifically book price and book title, from the BOOKS table, where the book price is in the range between $35 and $65:

```
SELECT bk_id,
       bk_title AS Title,
```

```
       bk_price AS Price
FROM   books
WHERE  bk_price BETWEEN 35 AND 65

bk_id Title                                             Price
----- ------------------------------------------------- -------------
1     SQL Bible                                         39.99
2     Wiley Pathways: Introduction to Database Management 55.26
10    Jonathan Livingston Seagull                       38.88
```

Note that the border values are included into the final result set. This operator works identically across all RDBMSs and can be used with a number of different data types: dates, numbers, and strings.

Although the rules for evaluating strings are the same, the produced results might not be as straightforward as those with the numbers because of alphabetical order of evaluation.

Another way to accomplish this task is to extract and compare appropriate substrings from the product description field using a string function, as explained in Chapter 4.

IN

This operator matches any given value to that on the list, either represented by literals, or returned in a subquery. The following query illustrates the usage of the `IN` operator:

```
SELECT bk_id,
       bk_title AS Title,
       bk_price AS Price
FROM   books
WHERE  bk_price IN (26.39, 39.99, 50, 40)
bk_id     Title                    Price
--------- ------------------------ -----
        6 SQL Bible                39.99
        9 SQL Functions            26.39
```

Because we do not have products priced exactly at $40 or $50, only two matching records were returned.

The values on the `IN` list can be generated dynamically from a subquery (see Chapter 6 for more information).

The data type of the expression evaluated against the list must correspond to the data type of the list values. Some RDBMSs would implicitly convert between compatible data types. For example, Microsoft SQL Server 2008 and Oracle 11g both accept a list similar to `10,15,'18.24', 16.03`*, mixing numbers with strings; whereas DB2 generates an error* `SQL0415N, SQLSTATE 42825`*. Check your RDBMS on how it handles this situation.*

The operator IN behavior can be emulated (to a certain extent) by using the OR operator. The following query makes the result set identical to that returned by the query using a list of literals:

```
SELECT bk_id,
       bk_title AS Title,
       bk_price AS Price
FROM   books
WHERE  bk_price = 39.99 OR bk_price = 26.39;
bk_id     Title                     Price
--------- ------------------------  -----
        6 SQL Bible                 39.99
        9 SQL Functions             26.39
```

Using the NOT operator in conjunction with IN returns all records that are *not* within the specified list of values, either predefined or generated from a subquery.

EXISTS

The EXISTS operator checks for the existence of any rows with matched values in the subquery. The subquery can query the same table, different table(s), or a combination of both (see Chapter 6). The operator acts identically in all three RDBMS implementations.

The EXISTS usage resembles that of the IN operator (normally used with a correlated query; see Chapter 6 for details).

The EXISTS *operator will evaluate to* TRUE *with any non-empty list of values. For example, the following query returns all records from the table* PRODUCT *because the subquery always evaluates to* TRUE.

Using the operator NOT in conjunction with EXISTS brings in records corresponding to the empty result set of the subquery.

LIKE

The LIKE operator belongs to the "fuzzy logic" domain. It is used any time criteria in the WHERE clause of the SELECT query are only partially known. It utilizes a variety of wildcard characters to specify the missing parts of the value (see Table 2.14). The pattern must follow the LIKE keyword.

TABLE 2-14: Wildcard Characters Used with the LIKE Operator

CHARACTER	DESCRIPTION	IMPLEMENTATION
%	Matches any string of zero or more characters	All RDBMSs
_ (underscore)	Matches any single character within a string	All RDBMSs

CHARACTER	DESCRIPTION	IMPLEMENTATION
[]	Matches any single character within the specified range or set of characters	Microsoft SQL only
[^]	Matches any single character *not* within specified range or set of characters	Microsoft SQL only

The following query requests information from the BOOKS table of the LIBRARY database, in which the book title (field BK_TITLE) starts with SQL:

```
SELECT bk_id,
       bk_title
FROM   books
WHERE  bk_title LIKE 'SQL%'
cust_id_n   cust_name_s
--------- --------------------------------
        1 SQL Bible
        4 SQL Functions
```

Note that blank spaces are considered to be characters for the purpose of the search.

If, for example, we need to refine a search to find a book whose title starts with SQL and has a second part sounding like LE ("Puzzle"? "Bible"?), the following query would help:

```
SELECT bk_id,
       bk_title
FROM   books
WHERE  bk_title LIKE 'SQL% _ibl%'
bk_id       bk_title
---------   ------------------------------
        1   SQL Bible
```

In plain English, this query translates as "All records from the BOOKS table where field BK_TITLE contains the following sequence of characters: The value starts with SQL, followed by an unspecified number of characters and then a blank space. The second part of the value starts with some letter or number followed by the combination *IBL*; the rest of the characters are unspecified."

In Microsoft SQL Server (and Sybase), you also can use a matching pattern that specifies a range of characters. Additionally, some RDBMSs have implemented regular expressions for pattern matching, either through custom built-in routines or by allowing creating custom functions with external programming languages such as C# or Java.

The ESCAPE clause in conjunction with the LIKE operator allows wildcard characters to be included in the search string. It allows you to specify an escape character to be used to identify special characters within the search string that should be treated as "regular." Virtually any character can be designated as an escape character in a query, although caution must be exercised to not use characters that might be encountered in the values themselves (for example, the use of the percent or L as an escape character produces erroneous results). The clause is supported by all three major databases and is part of SQL Standard.

The following example uses an underscore sign (_) as one of the search characters; it queries the INFORMATION_SCHEMA view (see Chapter 10 for more details) in Microsoft SQL Server 2008:

```
USE master
SELECT table_name,
       table_type
FROM   INFORMATION_SCHEMA.TABLES
WHERE  table_name LIKE 'SPT%/_F%' ESCAPE '/'
table_name       table_type
---------------  ----------
spt_fallback_db  BASE TABLE
spt_fallback_dev BASE TABLE
spt_fallback_usg BASE TABLE
```

The query requests records from the view where the table name starts with SPT, is followed by an unspecified number of characters, has an underscore _ as part of its name, is followed by F, and ends with an unspecified number of characters. Because the underscore character has a special meaning as a wildcard character, it has to be preceded by the escape character /. As you can see, the set of SP_FALLBACK tables uniquely fits these requirements.

With a bit of practice, you can construct quite sophisticated pattern-matching queries. Here is an example: the query that specifies exactly two characters preceding 8 in the first part of the name, followed by an unspecified number of characters preceding 064 in the second part:

```
SELECT  bk_id
       ,bk_title
       ,bk_ISBN
FROM   books
WHERE  bk_ISBN LIKE  '__8%064%'
```

Note that the percent symbol (%) stands for any character, and that includes blank spaces that might trail the string; including it in your pattern search might help to avoid some surprises.

AND

AND combines two Boolean expressions and returns TRUE when both expressions are true. The following query returns records for the books with price over 20 and which titles start with S:

```
SELECT bk_id,
       bk_title AS Title,
       bk_price AS Price
FROM   books
WHERE bk_price > 20 AND bk_title LIKE 'S%'
```

Only records that answer both criteria are selected, and this explains why *no* records were found: The book has one and only one price, either/or logic. This query will search for the books priced at $29.99 *and* have the word *Functions* anywhere in the title:

```
SELECT bk_id,
       bk_title AS Title,
       bk_price AS Price
FROM   books
WHERE  bk_price = 26.39 AND bk_title LIKE  '%Functions%'
```

When more than one logical operator is used in a statement, AND operators are evaluated first. The order of evaluation can be changed through the use of parentheses, grouping some expressions together.

NOT

This operator negates a Boolean input. It can be used to reverse output of any other logical operator discussed so far in this chapter. The following is a simple example using the IN operator:

```
SELECT bk_id,
       bk_title AS Title,
       bk_price AS Price
FROM   books
WHERE  bk_price NOT IN (49.99, 26.39, 50, 40)
```

The query returned information for the books whose price does not match any on the supplied list: When the IN operator returns TRUE (a match is found), it becomes FALSE and gets excluded while FALSE (records that do *not* match) is reversed to TRUE, and subsequently gets included into the final result set.

OR

The OR operator combines two conditions according to the rules of Boolean logic.

Even a cursory discussion of the Boolean logic and its applications is outside the range of this book, but you can find more at www.wrox.com, *in Wiley's SQL Bible, or at* www.agilitator.com.

When more than one logical operator is used in a statement, OR operators are evaluated after AND operators. However, you can change the order of evaluation by using parentheses (an example of the usage of the OR operator is given earlier in this chapter in a paragraph discussing the IN operator). The following query finds records corresponding to either criterion specified in the WHERE clause:

```
SELECT bk_id,
       bk_title AS Title,
       bk_price AS Price
FROM   books
```

```
WHERE  bk_price = 39.99 OR bk_price = 26.39;
bk_id     Title                       Price
--------- --------------------------- -----
      6 SQL Bible                     49.99
      9 SQL Functions                 26.39
```

Assignment Operator

The *assignment operator* is one of the most intuitive to use. It assigns a value to a variable. The only confusion in using this operator might stem from its overloading. All RDBMSs overload this operator with an additional function: comparison. This is in contrast to some programming languages, such as Java or C# which use single equals for assignment and double for comparison.

The *equals operator* (=) is used as an assignment in the following SQL query that updates the price (`BK_PRICE`) column in the table:

```
UPDATE books
SET    bk_price = 18.88
WHERE bk_id = 1;
```

Note that the same operator wearing a different hat (something called *overloading* in programmer parlance) is used for comparing values (in the WHERE clause) and for assignment (the SET statement).

In some SQL procedural *languages, there are distinctions between assignment and comparison operators. Oracle PL/SQL uses := for assignment and = for comparison. Microsoft SQL Server's Transact-SQL uses only one operator for these purposes, =, as does DB2 SQL PL. See Chapter 4 for more information on procedural extensions.*

Bitwise Operators

Bitwise operators perform bit operations on integer data types. To understand the results of the bitwise operations, you must understand the basics of Boolean algebra, and this is outside the scope of this book.

Only Microsoft SQL Server provides bitwise operators. The DB2 dialect of SQL does not have bit operation support built into the language, and Oracle 11g has a `BITAND` *function that works identically to SQL Server's bitwise* AND.

Bitwise operations are not typical for a high-level, set-based language such as SQL, and one might be hard-pressed to come up with a usage example. One use is as a complex bit mask made for color; after all, RDBMSs now support more than just text and numeric data. Another use of the XOR (exclusive OR) operator is to encrypt data based on some numeric key.

Operator Precedence

Precedence refers to the order in which operators from the same expression are being evaluated. When several operators are used together, the operators with higher precedence are evaluated before those with the lower precedence.

In general, the operators' precedence follow the same rules as in high school math, which might be somewhat counterintuitive, and it can further be changed with addition of parentheses.

The order of precedence is indicated in Table 2-15.

TABLE 2-15: Operators Precedence

OPERATOR	PRECEDENCE
Unary operators, bitwise `NOT` (Microsoft SQL Server only)	1
Multiplication and division	2
Addition, subtraction, and concatenation	3
Logical comparison operators	4
Logical NOT	5
Logical AND	6
Everything else: OR, LIKE, IN, BETWEEN	7

The evaluation precedence can dramatically affect results of the query. One of the ways to remember the order of operation is this mnemonic: ***P***lease ***E***xcuse ***M***y ***D***ear ***A***unt ***S***ally (PEMDAS) — parentheses, exponents, multiplication, division, addition, and subtraction.

TRY IT OUT Demonstrating Order of Precedence

This simple exercise illustrates the importance of operators' precedence order. Let's do some math in SQL:

1. Open your SQL client and establish connection to your RDBMS.
2. Enter the statement (add "FROM dual;" if you use Oracle, or "FROM sysibm.sysdummy1" if you use DB2 9.7, at the end of the SELECT statement):

```
SELECT 10*9-8+7-6/3 AS result
result
-----------
87
```

3. Try changing the order by introducing brackets:

```
SELECT 10*(9-8)+(7-6)/3 AS result
result
-----------
10 [Looks like it would be 10 + 1/3? (though could be rounded by the RDBMS).]
```

How It Works

The order of operations will affect the results of the query because operators are applied in order of precedence. Parentheses break the predefined order and introduce one of their own — expressions in parentheses are evaluated before anything else.

If you compare this with results obtained by running the previous expression through the "standard" calculator just by typing in the numbers and operators as they come, the expression 10*9-8+7-6/3 would evaluate to 27.66. The Microsoft Calc utility supplied with every version of Windows demonstrates this behavior. In Scientific mode, it applies the order of operations rules, but in Standard mode it won't (the modes are toggled through the View menu of the program).

SUMMARY

To construct a relational database, a data modeling process is deployed. It goes through several elaboration phases wherein a conceptual idea is transformed into logical and then physical representations of the data.

The data in the relational database are constrained by data types; each column in the table being one and only one data type. This helps to maintain data integrity by disallowing incompatible data types from entering into the database. RDBMSs perform both implicit and explicit data type conversion when one data type is transformed into another. It is best practice to use explicit data type conversion. A special case of data type is NULL, which signifies absence of data and requires special handling.

The database structure is defined by a subset of the SQL called the Data Definition Language (DDL), while data operations are the domain of the Data Manipulation Language (DML). There are restrictions on the use of each, specific to particular RDBMS implementations. The DDL statements CREATE, ALTER, and DROP can be used to create, alter, or destroy database objects.

The DML includes INSERT, UPDATE, and DELETE statements; while Data Query Language (DQL) includes a single member: SELECT. All these statements can be used with SQL operators, and they employ additional clauses/keywords to limit affected records horizontally, and apply vertical limits through specifying columns.

Although not emphasized in SQL, operators serve their important roles by enabling you to manipulate output and to specify selection criteria and search conditions. Operators are generally uniform across all database vendors, although there are some exceptions. The precedence of operators is an established order in which RDBMSs evaluate expressions that contain more than one operator; it is very important to take into consideration the precedence order. Using parentheses, you can specify custom precedence in an expression (as opposed to the default precedence order).

3

A Thing You Can Relate To — Designing a Relational Database

You may have heard the term "database model," but you most definitely have used one. How so? Because one of the database models is a flat file familiar to anyone who ever used computer.

Flat files *per se* cannot be rightfully called databases as they do not have the properties associated with databases, as we've discussed in Chapter 1, but they are the foundation upon which a relational database management system (RDBMS) is built. They are used to persist the information — both data and metadata — comprising the physical layer; define conventions and structure, add an application that manages these files; and you would end up with a skeleton of a database. If one is to translate a LIBRARY relational data model into a flat file one, the tables could become files — *books.txt* and *authors.txt*, for example.

These files would contain a number of records, and an application would read the file sequentially, sifting through records until it found one that matched the search criteria (for a book, for example) and then use information to read through the other file to find the author's information.

Here's an idea: Why not combine these two files into a single file, call it *library.txt*, and search only one file instead of two? We are back to a bucket of data: one table, one column, one row; dumping everything together would make it harder to read and match the information. The worst thing of all is that every application that will use this database would have to have an intimate knowledge of the file structure, and would have to implement logic that allows finding and combining the records into a meaningful result set. This logic would have to be rewritten every time you change the file structure. Ouch! No wonder flat file databases never made it to the enterprise sunlight.

The evolution of the flat files model was the *hierarchical model*. The flat files were organized into a hierarchy, and each file in the system became a branch of a specific type — a node, in techspeak — of the hierarchy; the records in these files contained a pointer to related records in another file (node), which in turn had a pointer to another record/file, and so on. This model introduced the notion of a one-to-many relationship, in which a *parent* record (higher in the hierarchy) could have none, one, or many child records, but the "child" had one, and only one, "parent." This was a breakthrough concept. Hierarchical databases, and closely related, next-generation network databases, made it to the operating rooms of big business corporations and — believe it or not — some might be still in use.

Both hierarchical and network models offered performance and relative usability in handling data. Now an application that made use of the data did not have to know beforehand all the branches/nodes/entities/files that made up the database; every record either had a pointer to another record, or not. One could traverse the entire hierarchy just by knowing how to read these files and discovering relationships on-the-fly. Unlike hierarchical databases, the networking database required the relationship to be named, thus allowing a node to participate in multiple relationships. This provided a much greater degree of flexibility, albeit at the expense of the complexity of choosing your path through the database now that there were multiple ones from which to select. Yet it suffered from the same problem: a predefined number of relationships.

The database technologies really shot up with the advent of the next step in the evolution: the *relational model*. It started with the realization of the simple truth that because no one can predict how the data is going to be used in the future, there is no point to try. Let users decide how to navigate the model and combine data into sets; the relational model was born.

As you'll see in Chapter 12, the relational model was not the last word.

The relational model was a new idea because previous models processed records sequentially, one at a time. In 1970, Dr. E. F. Codd, an IBM researcher, combined all the ingredients: parent/child relationship, multitude of navigational paths, and set theory in his seminal paper titled "A Relational Model of Data for Large Shared Data Banks."

ENTITIES AND ATTRIBUTES REVISITED

The concepts of entities and attributes were briefly touched earlier in Chapter 2, and the preceding paragraph highlighted complexities facing implementations based on relation models.

On the most basic practical level, you could consider entities to be tables and attributes to be columns in these tables. One of the first steps taken when creating a data model is analyzing a particular business environment in need of a database. In our case, we are building a library to keep track of all the books you have, or may have in the future. Therefore, the first entity you'd think of would be BOOK. What are the attributes of a book? A title, an author, a publisher, a price tag, to name but a few; all these could become columns in your BOOKS table. As you will see later in this chapter, taken through a more rigorous normalization process, some of these attributes might become entities of their own, and some would disappear all together. There are but two keys to the proper design of a relational database: primary and foreign.

Keys to the Kingdom: Primary and Foreign

A *primary key* is a unique identifier for a row of data in a table. In its most basic form, a primary key would be a column in the table, though it could be a unique combination of the columns. The concept of a key in the relational database is simple yet powerful: It enforces integrity (see later in this chapter), and helps define relationships between the entities in your data model.

A uniquely identifying row in a table is more than a whim, it is absolutely essential for performance of the SQL query against this table, and constitutes the first line of defense in a data quality battle. In databases of yore, based on hierarchical and network models, the order in which a table was populated was of importance — records were added in specific sequence, and when this sequence had to be broken due to an error or a changing business rule, the whole table had to be reorganized. The relational model abolished the requirements, but the need remained; it was addressed with the *primary key*.

It is considered to be a best practice always to have primary key in a table.

There are several rules that make a column (an attribute, a field) a primary key.

- A primary key cannot be empty; more specifically, it cannot contain a NULL value (explained in the previous chapter).
- A primary key must be unique within the entire table.
- A new primary key is created when a new row of data is inserted.
- Once created, a primary key should not be changed.

From these rules, a set of best practices for selecting primary keys for your tables could be created.

First, make your primary key meaningless. It might be tempting to use some unique identifier such as phone number, e-mail address, or Social Security number (SSN) as a primary key; after all, they are guaranteed to be unique and could save some database space! Don't. Data that has meaning could change. A new e-mail address or phone number could be associated with a record representing a person; this would violate primary key rules and create a number of problems that would percolate through your database. In the database world, such artificial keys are known as *surrogate* keys (as opposed to *natural* primary keys).

Second, make your primary keys compact and (preferably) numeric. Computers are designed to manipulate numbers — this is what they are good at; alphanumeric values slow searches down. For example, many RDBMS have the equivalent of a global unique identifier (GUID) data type. It might seem to be an ideal candidate for a primary key: It is unique, not only within your little table, but globally, and it is absolutely a meaningless combination of numbers (e.g., `0xff19906f868b11d0b42d70c04fc964ff`). But too much of a good thing becomes a problem:

- This number occupies 16 bytes of storage, increasing space requirements (for instance, an INTEGER data type occupies only 4 bytes).
- It is assigned randomly, without which makes it impossible to produce a meaningful index, resulting in significantly slower queries.

- It is not suited for the applications relying on incrementing key values serially (business rules violation, performance problems, and so on).

There are two ways to create a primary key: embedding it into a CREATE TABLE statement, or altering an existing table with a PRIMARY KEY constraint. The syntax is virtually identical across all RDBMS, and is also part of SQL Standard. The CREATE TABLE syntax example is as follows:

```
CREATE TABLE books
(  bk_id      INTEGER       NOT NULL,
   bk_title   VARCHAR(50)  NOT NULL,
   bk_ISBN    VARCHAR(50),
        CONSTRAINT bk_pk PRIMARY KEY (bk_id)
);
```

Here's the ALTER TABLE syntax (which assumes that the table BOOKS is already created and that the [bk_id] attribute was defined as NOT NULL).

```
ALTER TABLE books
        ADD CONSTRAINT bk_pk PRIMARY KEY (bk_id);
```

One of the roles that a primary key plays in relational databases is enforcing entity integrity. The rule is rather simple: Every table should have a primary key. All modern databases enforce primary key constraint; an attempt to enter duplicate primary key will generate an error.

TRY IT OUT Violating Entity Integrity

In this activity, we create tables with a primary key constraint and see how RDBMS enforces it.

1. Open the SQL client of your choice (see Appendix D for information on universal SQL clients, or Appendix C for accessing RDBMS with built-in facilities).
2. If you have not yet created the database and BOOKS table, now would be a good time to do so (refer to Chapter 1 for the syntax or download the scripts from `www.agilitator.com`).
3. Once the table is created, populate it with data by running the INSERT statement. For this exercise, you might leave most of the columns to be populated with defaults (i.e., NULLs).

```
INSERT INTO books (bk_id, bk_title) VALUES (1, "SQL Bible")
```

4. Run the preceding query from step 3 once more, and compare the error message you get with one of those listed in Table 3-1. The exact text of the message is RDBMS specific but they all convey the same message - constraint violation.

How It Works

The integrity constraints in modern RDBMS are enforced on the database level: once defined it becomes the responsibility of the RDBMS. Any attempts to violate constraint would generate an error message similar to one you've seen in step 4.

This was not always the case, in early versions RDBMS relied upon client applications to perform the necessary checks; having constraints simplifies application logic, and ensures integrity of the data.

The text of the error message will be different for every RDBMS, but the meaning will be unmistakable: entity integrity violation. Table 3-1 lists the error messages and their codes for the RDBMS covered in this book.

TABLE 3-1: Primary Key Constraint Violation Messages

RDBMS	ERROR NUMBER	SAMPLE OF AN ERROR MESSAGE
Oracle 10g	ORA-00001	Unique constraint (<schema>.BOOK_PK) violated.
IBM DB2 LUW	SQLSTATE: 23505	NB: DB2 returns a verbose message spanning at least a page, with detailed explanation of the error, potential causes and suggestions for how to fix it.
Microsoft SQL Server 2008		Server: Msg 2627, Level 14, State 1, Line 1 Violation of PRIMARY KEY constraint pk_bk_id. Cannot insert duplicate key in object [books]. The statement has been terminated.
PostgreSQL 9.0	SQLSTATE: 23505	ERROR: duplicate key value violates unique constraint "BOOK_pkey".
MySQL 5.5	ERROR 1062 (23000)	Duplicate entry '1' for key 3.
Microsoft Access 2010	No error code returned to built-in SQL Query tool	Will warn you about inability to insert rows due to rule violation.
OpenOffice.org BASE	No error code returned to built-in SQL command utility	Violation of unique constraint SYS_PK_48: duplicate value(s) for column(s) "bk_id".

SQLCODE and SQLSTATE are there to help developers diagnose problems and provide meaningful message. They provide insight into outcome of the most recently completed SQL statement, and are generally consistent with SQL Standard.

Relationship Patterns

Foreign key is all about relationships. It works in tandem with the primary key; most likely it *is* a primary key taken from its parent table and inserted into the child table. To extend the parent/child analogy (not to be taken too far, though), the child table carries a FOREIGN KEY as the parent's genetic code.

Besides the primary key, the RDBMS also has a concept of the candidate key. Such a key also uniquely identifies a record in a table, and could have been designated as a primary key. There might be more than one candidate key in the pool but only one of them could be selected as primary (for example, there could be many princes but only one could be crowned a king).

Unlike the primary key, the foreign key does not have to be unique within a single table nor within your relational schema.

The primary/foreign key pair defines several flavors of relationships: one-to-one, one-to-many, and many-to-many. Table 3-2 presents a matrix of the possible combinations.

TABLE 3-2: Relationship Patterns Matrix

	ZERO	ONE	MANY
ZERO	N/A	N/A	N/A
ONE	A record in the parent table relates to zero or one record in the child table. Notation: 1:0	A record in the parent table relates to one and only one record in the child table. Notation: 1:1	A record in the parent table relates to one or many records in the child table. Notation: 1:N
MANY	A record in the parent table relates to zero or more records in the child table. Notation: N:0	While theoretically possible (and allowed in some RDBMSs), a many-to-one relationship, wherein a child table contains multiple foreign keys from multiple parents' tables, is not recommended because of increased complexity enforcing referential integrity (discussed later in this chapter). Notation: N:1	A many-to-many relationship requires an intermediate table that converts it to two one-to-many relationships. Notation: N:N

To illustrate the concept, let's take a look at our library data model, again. Figure 3-1 (Library data model) presents a normalized data model for our library database.

The table (entity) BOOKS is in a 1:1 (one-to-one) relationship with the table LOCATION, which means that for each book there will be one and only one location.

The tables BOOKS and AUTHORS are in N:N (many-to-many) relationship that needs to be resolved to prevent redundancy through the intermediate table BOOKS_AUTHORS. The many-to-many relationship means that one book could be written by many authors, but the same person could author more than one book. If not for the intermediary table, both tables would have to maintain additional redundant information, which would violate normalization rules.

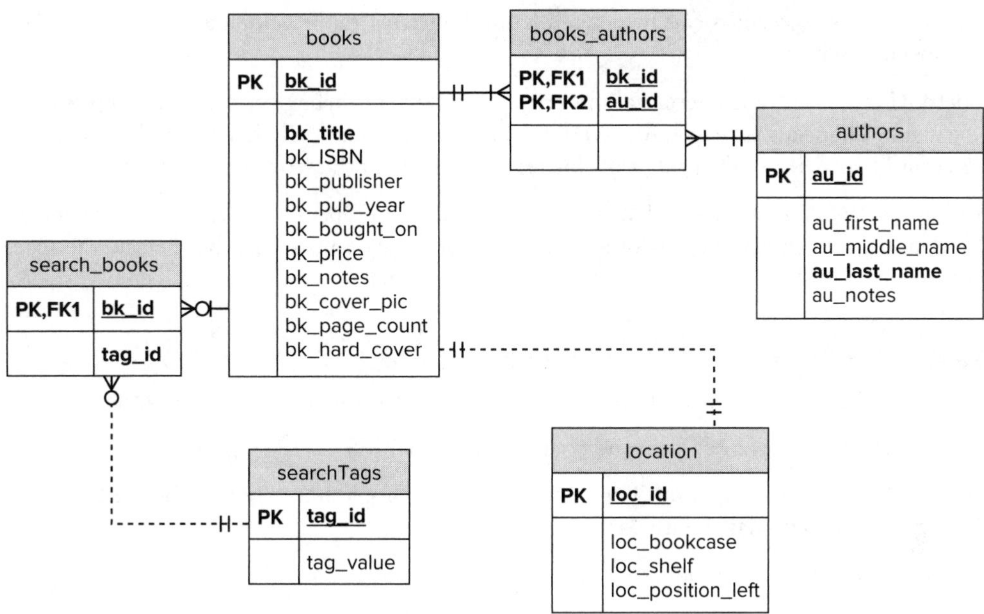

FIGURE 3-1

In the SQL syntax the relationships are established with primary and foreign key constraints. A parent table always has to have a primary key that it lends to the child table as its foreign key. As with the primary key, there are two ways to establish a relationship with a foreign key in the SQL: the CREATE syntax and ALTER syntax.

```
CREATE TABLE location
(      loc_id              INTEGER          NOT NULL,
fk_bk_id            INTEGER          NOT NULL,
loc_bookcase         VARCHAR(50)     NOT NULL,
loc_shelf            INTEGER         NOT NULL,
loc_position_left   INTEGER,
              CONSTRAINT fk_books FOREIGN KEY (bk_id)
                      REFERENCES books(bk_id)
);
```

Here's the ALTER TABLE syntax (which assumes that the table BOOKS is already created and that the [bk_id] attribute was defined as NOT NULL):

```
ALTER TABLE location
        ADD CONSTRAINT fk_books FOREIGN KEY (bk_id)
        REFERENCES books(bk_id);
```

The concept of referential integrity is all about maintaining and enforcing this relationship. In the early days of the RDBMS this relationship was purely logical — it was possible to delete a record in the parent table and leave the records in the child table orphaned. In the RDBMS world you must start with deleting a record from the child table and then proceed to deleting records from its parent table. Another important consequence of adding a referential integrity constraint is that it works both ways: no records could be added to a child table unless there is a corresponding parent table, just as no records can be deleted from the parent table as long as there is a child record associated with it.

All modern RDBMSs enforce referential integrity to prevent this behavior, and some implement sophisticated mechanisms such as CASCADE DELETE to automatically remove child records when parent's records are deleted (the syntax of this feature is beyond the scope of this book).

The desktop relational databases such as Microsoft Access and OpenOffice.org BASE provide visual tools for defining referential (and any other supported) integrity constraints, but behind the scenes these respective RDBMS assemble and execute SQL statements.

TRY IT OUT Violating Referential Integrity

In this activity we are going to create tables with primary key constraint and see how RDBMS enforces it.

1. Open the SQL client of your choice, and connect to an RDBMS.
2. Assuming that you followed all the Try It Outs, you now should have both the BOOKS and LOCATION tables populated with data.
3. Type in the following SQL command.

```
DELETE FROM books;
```

How It Works

Referential integrity constraint follows exactly the same rules as the entity integrity constraints we've tried to violate in the previous activity. It is enforced by the RDBMS itself, and an error will be raised whenever there is an attempt to violate it. In this case, we've tried to delete records from the parent table leaving potentially orphaned records in the child tables. The FOREIGN KEY constraint prevented the deletion.

The text of the error message will be different for every RDBMS, but the meaning will be unmistakable: referential integrity violation. Table 3-3 lists the referential integrity error messages and their codes for the RDBMS covered in this book.

TABLE 3-3: Foreign Key Constraint Violation Messages

RDBMS	ERROR NUMBERS	MESSAGE
Oracle 10g	ORA-02292	Integrity constraint (<constraint_name>) violated - child record found.
IBM DB2 LUW	SQLCODE: -532 SQLSTATE: 23504	SQL0532N A parent row cannot be deleted because the relationship <foreign_key constraint name> restricts the deletion.

RDBMS	ERROR NUMBERS	MESSAGE
Microsoft SQL Server 2008	SQL State: 23503	The DELETE statement conflicted with the REFERENCE constraint "<constraint name>." The conflict occurred in database "library," table "dbo.BOOK," column 'BK_ID.' The statement has been terminated.
PostgreSQL 9.0	SQL State: 23503	ERROR: update or delete on table <table_name> violates foreign key constraint <constraint_name> on table <table_name>.
MySQL 5.5	ERROR 1217	Cannot delete or update a parent row: a foreign key constraint fails.
Microsoft Access 2010	No error code returned to built-in SQL Query tool	Will warn you about inability to delete rows due to rule violation.
OpenOffice.org BASE	No error code returned to built-in SQL Query tool	Violation of refrential integrity constraint SYS_FK_##:.

There are many ways to enforce referential integrity besides the FOREIGN KEY constraint. For instance, before it was widely implemented, one could use triggers (a special sort of program executed on INSERT, UPDATE, or DELETE; more about these in Chapter 4). All major RDBMSs nowadays support foreign key constraints, and they should be used to enforce referential integrity.

Domain Integrity

Domain refers to the range of values that an attribute for an entity (okay, a column for a table) would accept. Domain integrity ensures that only valid data gets into the column.

There is no single CONSTRAINT that you can specify for the column. Data type declaration is a constraint, albeit an unreliable one if your RDBMS permits implicit data type conversions (see the note later in this chapter).

The length of the data type is another example of a domain integrity constraint. CHAR(10) will not accept strings 11 characters in length. Neither column declared as INTEGER will allow entry of decimal fractions.

The ability to enter NULL values into the column is a domain constraint: columns created with a NOT NULL qualifier — a requirement for a primary key field — will complain. This also relates to yet another type of domain constraint: DEFAULT. One could specify that if no value is supplied, a default would be inserted. The default value could be generated by a function, such as the GETDATE() function in Microsoft SQL Server, which would plug in the current date and time to your newly inserted record. This could come handy for tracing and auditing, and frees you from the necessity to supply a value.

A single column could have multiple constraints applied to it, not only those that we've discussed so far (for example, the declaration `bk_d INTEGER NOT NULL` implements two constraints: data type and NOT NULL) but also through custom rules and functions that some RDBMSs implement. For instance, Microsoft SQL Server has the CREATE RULE statement that it made part of its dialect of SQL. It allows you to specify expressions (range, patterns) to evaluate data upon insertion, and either allow or reject it.

Many RDBMSs allow for implicit data type conversions whereby compatible data types will be accepted and converted into required types without you ever knowing it. Most of the time this proves to be a very convenient feature, but sometimes it might yield unpredictable results. Therefore, it is recommended that you always use explicit conversion functions (more on this in Chapter 4) and not rely on the RDBMS engine to do the thinking.

TRY IT OUT Violating Referential Integrity

In this activity, we are going to try and break domain integrity rules.

1. Open the SQL client of your choice and connect to an RDBMS.
2. Assuming that you followed all the Try It Outs, you now should have the LOCATION table with all columns and constraints defined; alternatively, you can run this statement:

```
CREATE TABLE location
(      loc_id              INTEGER        NOT NULL,
       fk_bk_id            INTEGER        NOT NULL,
       loc_bookcase         VARCHAR(50)   NOT NULL,
       loc_shelf            INTEGER       NOT NULL,
       loc_position_left    INTEGER
);
```

3. Type in a SQL command:

```
INSERT INTO location VALUES (1,1,'first on the left',1,1)
```

The data will be inserted with a message acknowledging success.

4. Now let's try to break the rules:

```
INSERT INTO location VALUES (NULL,1,'first on the left',1,1)
```

It fails with a message that says something similar to "column does not allow NULLs."

5. Let's try and replace the INTEGER value for the LOC_ID column to a character value '2' — its character nature being manifested by single quotes around the character:

```
INSERT INTO location VALUES ('2',1,'first on the left',1,1)
```

If your database allows for implicit conversion (as Oracle and Microsoft SQL Server do, for instance), this statement will be executed without a single hiccup.

6. Now try something that is also a character but cannot be converted into a number:

```
INSERT INTO location VALUES ('A',1,'first on the left',1,1)
```

This time Oracle would complain "ORA-01722: invalid number", and SQL Server would acknowledge limits of its guessing power by stating that "Conversion failed when converting the varchar value 'A' to data type int."

How It Works

The constraints put in place when the table was created are enforced by the RDBMS, and a specific error is returned when there is an attempt to violate a constraint. The NOT NULL constraint has been violated in step 4, and the RDBMS has rejected the record, returning a specific error message.

Another constraint, INTEGER data type declared for LOC_ID column, was violated in step 6. Some RDBMS would allow SQL statement in step 5 because they would implicitly convert character data "2" into numeric data 2.

AM I NORMAL? BASICS OF RELATIONAL DATABASE DESIGN

Now that some ground rules have been covered, we can proceed to designing our database. A database design still remains more of an art than an exact science, but there are few simple rules to follow to organize raw data into a well-behaved relational data model. Traditionally, the process is called *database normalization*, and its steps are measured in forms: first normal form (1NF), second normal form (2NF), and so on up to fifth normal form (5NF).

The rules for the 1NF state that:

- Each row has to be unique.
- There should be no repeating groups of data.
- All columns have to contain only atomic values.

Atomic value refers to a singular indivisible piece of data. Hint: A column that contains a list of comma-separated values won't be considered atomic. Nothing helps more to achieve uniqueness than integrity — entity integrity. Every 1NF table must have a primary key.

The 2NF builds upon the predecessor, the 1NF, and adds an additional rule:

- No partial functional dependencies are allowed, or only columns with full dependency on the primary key are allowed.

Now, what *is* partial functional dependency? It's when nonkey columns do not have full allegiance to the primary key and might be dependent on others. For example, in the data model shown on Figure 3-1 the column BK_PUBLISHER in the BOOKS table does not really depend on the primary key BK_ID, and ought to be isolated into a table of its own; we leave it in the BOOKS table partially to illustrate the concept, partially because we've made an assumption that a book could have one and only one publisher, and decided not to store any information about publishers. One easy rule is to look for the records that have identical values in the columns.

The 3NF includes both 1NF and 2NF, and then imposes a new rule (which might appear to be a modification of the 2NF rule, but it is not):

- All nonkey columns in the table should be mutually independent.

The 2NF form asks whether a nonkey column relies fully on the primary key, and 3NF adds that it should also be absolutely independent of its fellow nonkey columns. The question to ask is this: What happens to other columns in the table if one of the nonkey columns gets updated? If the answer is nothing, the column stays; otherwise, it should be moved to a table of its own.

The other two forms, 4NF and 5NF, are better left alone for the duration of this book. In fact, unless you aspire to become a data modeler, the forms are better left alone, period. There are advantages as well as disadvantages to the highly normalized databases, and one needs to understand the ramifications fully before proceeding beyond 3NF. The more normalized the data model, the more JOIN statements one has to use to compile data (see the UNION and JOIN paragraph later in this chapter); in fact, denormalization might speed up the data retrieval process at the price of increased data storage redundancy.

Designing a database goes through a number of iterations. The same steps get repeated over and over again until you're satisfied with the results. There is, however, no such thing as a completely normalized database. For one thing, any database that goes beyond third normal form incurs a significant performance hit (as it struggles with all the additional joins needed to accommodate data stored in separate tables); for another, it can be difficult to determine clues for further separation of data into the fourth and fifth normal forms. Use your best judgment about where to stop normalizing your database.

With the rules of the game explained, let's start the normalization process and get to 3NF in no time.

First, let's think about a real-life situation we are trying to model with the LIBRARY database. It is all about books and where you keep them. These nouns have a good chance to be converted into tables (*entities* in data modeling parlance). Let's put them down and think about what defines these entities and what attributes they have. Table 3-4 summarizes the results of the brainstorming.

TABLE 3-4: Entities and Attributes Brain Dump

ENTITY	ATTRIBUTES	NOTES
books	Book title, number of pages, cover (hard/soft), publisher, author(s), ISBN number, cover picture, date of purchase, price, and so on.	Book will have but a single title, number of pages, and ISBN number. What about authors? There are tons of books (and publishers) that have more than one.
location	Type (bookcase, bookshelf, attic, garage), shelf (top, bottom, middle), position on the shelf (first, 35th)	The type seems to be a bit generic; all my books are ether in bookcases, or on loan to my friends. Let's keep track of books that are in the book-case. Now, how do I define *middle shelf*? A bookcase on the second floor has four... I'd better number my shelves, say from bottom to the top.

The preceding analysis has uncovered several potential problems, namely, authors, publishers and shelves. Maybe they deserve to be put into an entity of their own? Let's create three entities (tables), and try to sort out attributes (columns) according to the 1NF, 2NF, and 3NF rules, as shown in Table 3.5.

TABLE 3-5: Applying Normalization to Entities and Attributes

BOOKS	AUTHORS	LOCATION
bk_id (primary key)	au_id (primary_key)	loc_id (primary key)
Book title	First name	Bookcase
ISBN	Last Name	Shelf
Page count	Middle Name	Order/Position on the Shelf
Price		

The first field/column/attribute that goes into the table is primary key, which will make the entire record unique in the table.

Next, all data has to be atomic (1NF). This means that each identified attribute will have a field of its own, and cannot be separated into more attributes.

Next, what really belongs to the single entity, and what really belongs somewhere else. The most contentious attribute would be that of Author(s). Does a book have an author, or it is the author that has the book? This ambiguity is a sure indication that these ought to be separate (after all, the same cannot be plausibly said about title or page count). Moreover, if there is more than one author, we would violate rules of the repeating groups statement in the 1NF and 2NF rules. (The author does not really depend on the book, nor does the book depend on the author. There could be situations in which this weak dependency might be dissolved.)

One might argue that the price or page count could be also modified and that there might be correlation between the price and page count; but it would be a tenuous relationship at best, not a real-world common situation. This brings us to an interesting point: the way you apply normalization rules depends on the knowledge of the domain to which you're applying these rules. If you were to design a data model where price really depends on the page count, price might be better off belonging to a different entity.

Once the logical analysis is completed, you're ready to deal with the actual creation of the conceived database inside some RDBMS package. The process is by no means linear: you'll find yourself traveling back and forth between these two phases as you fine-tune your database requirements. For example, the decision not to model PUBLISHERS as a separate entity could be later revised, and the model would be updated with another table and relationships. This book presents the SQL syntax for creating database objects (see Chapters 1 and 2). The design of the database objects could be done completely independent of the particular RDBMS software, or it could be tied up to it. While one might argue that designing specifically for Oracle or Microsoft SQL Server would increase performance, sticking with a plain generic approach (when possible) makes your design more portable and spares you some of the maintenance and upgrading headaches.

Specifying Constraints

Once your entities and attributes are defined, there are a number of constraints to enforce the integrity of the database and the data it contains. As discussed earlier in this chapter, primary keys and foreign keys enforce referential integrity, which means that each record in the child table is linked to a record in the parent table (i.e., no orphaned records).

Primary key and UNIQUE constraints also enforce entity integrity. The concept of *entity integrity* refers to making sure that a row in the table is unique within the table; that is, its combination of column values is unique throughout the table (even though data might be repeated in some columns). The concept could be easily illustrated with real life examples: there might be quite a few people on this planet named "Alexander," there will be significantly fewer named "Alexander Kriegel," and in all probability there will be only one who's also an author of the Discovering SQL book; the combination of attributes makes it unique.

The NOT NULL constraint, while enforcing domain integrity, also has an indirect role in enforcing entity integrity because it is a prerequisite for every primary key.

Domain integrity refers to the data itself and is enforced by using the appropriate data type (for example, RULES and CHECK constraints) as well as DEFAULT constraints. CHECK constraints ensure that only specific data, in a range of values or formats, is entered into the column; while DEFAULT constraints specify default values for the column in case you do not have a value for it when inserting new records.

In addition to these built-in integrity constraints, it is possible to enforce custom constraints through the use of triggers, stored procedures, and other RDBMS-specific features (see Chapter 4 for more information).

Selecting a Flavor For Your Data Model

A data model does not exist in a vacuum, a thing unto its own; it serves some specific business purpose, which is, naturally, reflected in its design. General-purpose database types can be divided into two broad categories: operational databases and analytical databases. The operational database (*OLTP*, which stands for *online transaction processing*) handles day-to-day operations: recording data, printing payroll checks, and so on. The data in such a database accumulates quickly and changes rather frequently. While you might not be entering a new book into your Library database every minute, the overall purpose of the data model makes it suitable for OLTP and, with sufficient modifications and optimizations, could be used by a commercial book company.

Analytical databases (*OLAP*, which stands for *online analytical processing*) are used to store historical data, which is analyzed for reporting purposes, used to generate statistics, and so on. The information in such a database is mostly static; new data can be added, but the historic data cannot usually be modified. In addition, the information in the OLAP database is often stored in an aggregated, or de-normalized, state (see more about normalization earlier in this chapter), and there might be many levels of aggregation, depending on the particular purpose. Think of these data models when you need to answer questions such as this (admittedly convoluted), "What is the correlation between the frequency with which the book is being checked out at the local library with its page number and the region in which the publisher has its headquarters?" Some of the seemingly outlandish correlations might yield surprising insights.

The data model reflects the purpose for which the database was created. OLTP requires a highly normalized database to record every minute detail that the enterprise might require. In other words, OLTP is a recording database with a secondary reporting purpose. The very same design that allows for fast data capture is less than ideal when it comes to retrieving it. The normalized design might require numerous JOIN(s) and aggregation operations to combine the data before it can be displayed in a meaningful way. This business need, together with the ascending wave of business intelligence applications, implies a completely different database design: a data warehouse.

OLAP is, in theory, a read-only database, at least from the user's point of view. In order to provide fast performance, the data in an OLAP database is usually denormalized and often aggregated.

Data Warehouses and Data Marts

Judging by the fact that you are reading a book about SQL, you might have heard about data warehousing. A *data warehouse* is a database made up of a number of smaller, highly specialized, denormalized databases: data marts. A data warehouse provides the basis for the decision support. It contains data snapshots (mostly static historical data). The father of data warehousing, Bill Inmon, defines the data warehouse as follows:

- **Subject oriented** — All data contained in the database is organized around/related to some object/concept/event.
- **Time variant** — The data is tracked along the timelines, so that trends can be discovered.
- **Non-volatile** — The data collected into the warehouse should not be modified; it becomes essentially read-only.

- **Integrated** — The warehouse data is self-contained; it gathers data from a variety of sources and incorporates all necessary data into single locations.

Data marts are subsets of the data warehouses. The analogy follows the real-life warehousing operations in which product (information) is gathered at a single location (warehouse) and then distributed to smaller locations such as stores or marts. In a sense, a data warehouse is a generic storage whereas data marts are specialized databases, customized for a particular user or group of users.

Both data warehouses and data marts are designed around two basic schemas (model types): star and snowflake.

There is a battle simmering in the data warehousing field between the two paradigms, one pioneered by Bill Inmon, and another advocated by Ralph Kimball. The former considers the data warehouse but a part of the enterprise BI (business Intelligence) system; it stores normalized data in 3NF, and data marts are specialized subsets of the central data warehouse. The latter uses dimensional storage (see Star and Snowflakes schemas later in this chapter), and the data warehouse is the sum of the data marts (i.e. data is distributed, not centralized). There is no right or wrong here. Both implementations are found in the enterprise, and choosing one over another reflects competencies, business models and overall approach to data in corporate environment.

Star and Snowflake Schemas

Both star and snowflake schemas utilize the same relational principles upon which every RDBMS is built. They introduce the concept of fact tables and dimension tables. The fact table would contain some hard, quantifiable data; the dimension table would contain some qualitative, descriptive data. The former usually contains large amounts of data (millions of rows), while the latter would be much smaller. The designations *fact* and *dimension* are not cast in stone, but depend on particular circumstances. There is a simple rule of thumb to be applied when differentiating between the two: the fact table contains the "what" being analyzed, while the dimensions table contains what the fact data is being analyzed "by." The name *star* refers to the visualization — a fact table surrounded by the dimension tables, all of which are related to this fact table through primary/foreign key relationships.

A *snowflake* schema is a variation of the star schema where dimension tables can in turn have dimensions of their own. The diagram of the schema resembles a snowflake — hence the name. Snowflake schemas reduce data redundancy of the dimension tables, making the "analyzing by" process much more granular. The tradeoff is performance vs. aggregation level.

What Could and Does Go Wrong

As the saying goes: To the man with a hammer, every problem looks like a nail. Nothing could be truer with regard to the mistakes that people often make while trying database design.

Users with previous experience in nonrelational databases may tend to design databases that resemble hierarchical or network databases, or even flat files and spreadsheet designs, described earlier.

If you have the luxury of designing your database from scratch, consider yourself lucky and use every technique you can find in the database literature, subject to your project's schedule and resources. More often you will face the task of redesigning a database to fit new business requirements, improve performance, and so on. Whatever you do, don't try reusing existing database structures as a basis for a new database. If it is wrong for your particular task because its design cannot accommodate the new features you are trying to implement, take a fresh look without the limits imposed by the legacy stuff. If you seem to be able to reuse some parts and pieces, maybe there is no need for redesign. Maybe you need only to improve upon an existing database. Redesigning databases to preserve legacy data is not a small task and should be approached with caution.

Another common problem arises from the tendency to utilize every single feature offered by a particular RDBMS vendor. While improving performance — at least potentially, or most of the time — this approach could lock you into that vendor's product and might cost you dearly both in time and money if you move your database to a different vendor. Believe it or not, there were times when dBASE, Btrieve, FoxPro, and Clipper ruled the earth. Sticking to a few sound principles might not give you the very last drop of performance you could squeeze out of a database, but it will serve you well should you decide to go with a different RDBMS vendor down the road.

People spend their entire careers mastering the intricacies of data modeling, and this book will not turn you into a database design expert overnight. Instead, it provides you with a solid footing to take your next step down the road.

Working with Multiple Tables

Things were pretty straightforward when we only had a single table. Now we have several and still have to produce a single set of data. The solution? We could JOIN the UNION.

In a SELECT statement, the JOIN keyword, as the name implies, joins records from two (or more) tables, while UNION is used to combine records returned from two or more SELECT statements. We will talk about both in more details in Chapter 7; here we are going to restore faith in the sanity of the people who designed SQL and put down the normalization rules. Honestly, they did know what they were doing!

JOIN Syntax

Let's take a look at the two tables: BOOKS and AUTHORS, presented in Figure 3-2 and Figure 3-3.

Why can't we just run SQL query?

```
SELECT * FROM books, authors;
```

In fact, you can! Try it. See anything unusual? The returned data set contains every possible combination of the records from both tables — highly

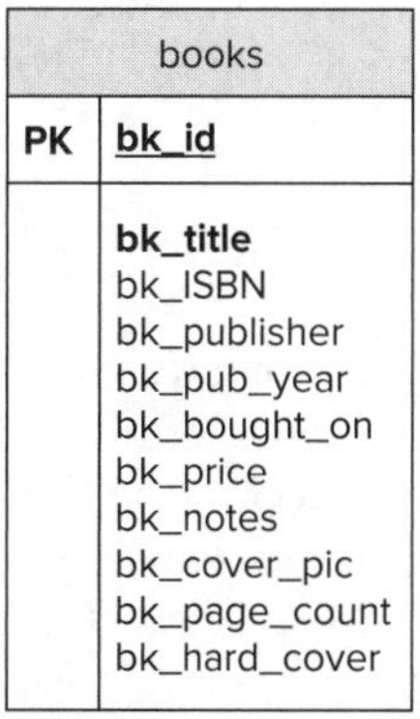

books	
PK	bk_id
	bk_title bk_ISBN bk_publisher bk_pub_year bk_bought_on bk_price bk_notes bk_cover_pic bk_page_count bk_hard_cover

FIGURE 3-2

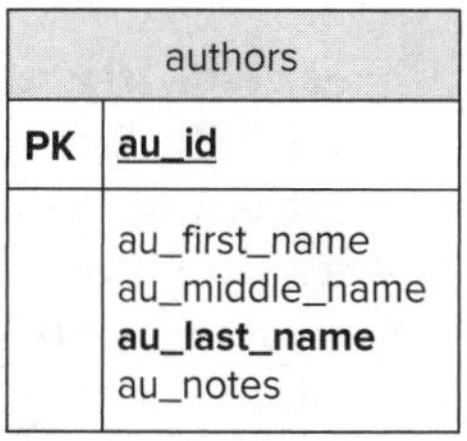

authors	
PK	au_id
	au_first_name au_middle_name **au_last_name** au_notes

FIGURE 3-3

confusing and utterly useless. Additionally, it uses obsolete syntax. The correct syntax for the previous query is the following:

```
SELECT * FROM books CROSS JOIN authors;
```

This syntax will yield the very same result, but at least you'll have the satisfaction that it was produced intentionally, not because you forgot to specify JOIN criteria. This is where primary and foreign keys shine.

Let's take a closer look at proper JOIN(s), but first a rule: Never use deprecated syntax in your SQL. The unintentional CROSS JOIN (or Cartesian product, as it is known) would never escape your attention with proper syntax; it is very easy to do with the old one (and things get worse as the number of tables in the JOIN increases). So to extract meaningful information from both BOOKS and AUTHORS, we should use the intermediary table: BOOKS_AUTHORS created to resolve the many-to-many (N:N) relationship (see Figure 3-4).

books_authors	
PK,FK1 **PK,FK2**	**bk_id** **au_id**

FIGURE 3-4

The SELECT statement that matches authors with the books they wrote using the JOIN syntax would look as follows:

```
SELECT authors.au_last_name, books.bk_title FROM books JOIN books_authors
ON (books.bk_id = book_authors.bk_id) JOIN authors
ON (book_authors.au_id = authors.au_id)
```

This code requires explanation. The purpose is to extract a list of authors' last names and the books they wrote in a single SELECT statement. Because of the potential N:N relationship, an intermediary table was introduced that matched the book's ID to the author's ID. The JOIN produced records from the BOOKS table that had matching IDs from the BOOKS_AUTHORS table, and combined them with records produced by matching authors' ID in the intermediary table with them in the AUTHORS table. The result was the correct list of authors and their respective masterpieces combined in a single happy data set.

UNION Operator

While JOIN "glues" data sets horizontally, the UNION operator appends data sets vertically. There is a catch; because the values combined in the resulting set go into the same column, they *have* to be of the same (or compatible, if implicit conversion is enabled) data type. Here is a query that combines BOOKS.bk_title with AUTHORS.au_first_name:

```
SELECT bk_title FROM books
UNION
SELECT au_first_name FROM authors
```

Predictably, the results do not have much use because semantically these are different attributes, and UNIONizing them produced meaningless albeit valid data; the single column takes whatever name is used in the first query of the UNION (yes, there might be more than two queries combined). There are cases in which concatenating data sets vertically is important; for instance, if you were scattering your books across different geographical regions, by author's country of residence, and needed to produce a combined inventory list. As long as data types in the queries are *vertically* compatible, the hypothetical query might just look like this:

```
SELECT bk_title FROM books_Europe
UNION
SELECT bk_title FROM books _Asia
UNION
SELECT bk_title FROM books_NorthAmerica
```

There is much more to JOIN(s) and UNION(s); the UNION operator and JOIN keyword will be revisited in Chapter 7 in much greater detail. For now, know that there are means to assemble the information into unified data sets even if it was broken into pieces and scattered around the relational model realm. There *is* a method to the madness.

Dynamic SQL

As with hierarchical and network database models, you might feel a bit constrained by the SQL requirement to spell out all tables and columns (entities and attributes) upfront. Why can't you define these during execution, on-the-fly, through parameters? It would make code so much more versatile. Just substitute a table name for a variable, and the same statement could be reused time and again for different tables, columns, or databases.

```
SELECT <list of fields> FROM <list of tables>
```

The truth is, you can do all of the above with dynamic SQL. Every time you craft an SQL query manually, you assemble it from the elements that did not exist before: table names, list of fields to be selected, and relationships between objects. With a bit of programming, using either external programming languages such as Java or C# or built-in procedural extensions such as Transact-SQL (Microsoft SQL Server) or PL/SQL (Oracle), you can automate this procedure. The following code in the Java programming language executes but a single statement against the Oracle 10g Express Edition database; the SQL statement is passed as a command line argument to the function `main()` of the *QueryOracle* class:

```
public class QueryOracle {
public static void main(String[] args)
throwsClassNotFoundException, SQLException
  {
// specific information on how to connect to Oracle 10g database
Class.forName("oracle.jdbc.driver.OracleDriver");
    String url = "jdbc:oracle:thin:@myhost:1521:xe";

//open the connection with authorized UserID("scott") and Password("tiger")
Connection conn =
DriverManager.getConnection(url,"scott","tiger");

// create Java-specific object for submitting SQL to RDBMS
Statement stmt = conn.createStatement();

//args[0] contains the query "SELECT * FROM books"
// submit SQL query to database
ResultSetrset = stmt.executeQuery(args[0]);

// scroll through collection of records
// returned by Oracle RDBMS
while (rset.next()) {
System.out.println (rset.getString(1));
    }
```

```
//clean up
stmt.close();
System.out.println ("finished");
   }
}
```

This is not a Java programming language book, so the preceding code is but a very basic example that sacrifices robustness for clarity in illustrating the concept.

It is easy to see how this code can be used to execute almost any type of SQL statement: SELECT, INSERT, UPDATE, DELETE; or even (assuming that the user has sufficient privileges) issue commands that would create and drop database objects such as tables and views.

An external program can be written in any programming language, and (as long as it can connect to the database and execute an SQL query), it can be used for dynamic SQL programming.

Dynamic SQL can also be used from within the RDBMS environment. This requires vendor-specific commands to be used. Table 3-6 lists the keywords implemented in different RDBMS to execute dynamic SQL from within RDBMS (usually as part of stored procedure code).

TABLE 3-6: Dynamic SQL Support across RDBMS

RDBMS	DYNAMIC SQL EXECUTION SYNTAX	NOTES
ORACLE	EXECUTE IMMEDIATE	Oracle also offers a possibility to execute an arbitrary SELECT query as part of its OPEN cursor PL/SQL statement.
Microsoft SQL Server	EXECUTE() EXEC() sp_executesql	The built-in system stored procedure takes two predefined parameters and an unlimited number of custom ones.
IBM DB2	EXEC SQL EXECUTE <statement> USING <parameters>; END-EXEC EXECUTE IMMEDIATE PREPARE and EXECUTE	There are limitations on what SQL statements can be used with dynamic queries.
PostgreSQL	EXEC SQL EXECUTE IMMEDIATE PREPARE and EXECUTE	Unless being reused within the same scope, the prepare statement needs to be deallocated.
MySQL	PREPARE and EXECUTE	Unless being reused within the same scope, the prepare statement needs to be deallocated.

Here is an example of a stored procedure using dynamic SQL that could be executed in a MySQL environment.

```
mysql> delimiter $$
mysql>
mysql> CREATE PROCEDURE getBookByISBN (inISBN VARCHAR(20))
    -> BEGIN
    ->   SET @sql=CONCAT(
    ->       "SELECT *
    ">          FROM books
    ">          WHERE bk_ISBN=",inISBN);
    ->     PREPARE s1 FROM @sql;
    ->     EXECUTE s1;
    ->     DEALLOCATE PREPARE s1;
    ->END$$
```

Now the procedure could be called multiple times with different ISBN values; alternatively, the entire SQL query could be passed into the stored procedure to be compiled and executed.

There are several common programming libraries for accessing RDBMS: Open Database Connectivity (ODBC), Java Database Connectivity (JDBC), Microsoft Active Data Objects for .NET(ADO.NET) Providers, and so on. We are going to touch briefly on the subject in Appendix D.

Both Microsoft Access and OpenOffice.org BASE allow for executing dynamic SQL from within their respective built-in programming environments: Visual Basic for Applications (VBA) and BASIC. The particulars of each programming interface are beyond the scope of this book, but examples can be found on the book's support site at `www.Wrox.com` and at `www.agilitator.com`.

Ultimate Flexibility, Potential Problems

RDBMSs are there to obey your command as long as the command is issued in syntactically correct SQL. The query you submit to the database engine, be it IBM DB2 or Microsoft Access, is in a human readable format; it is the engine's job to translate it into machine language understood by computers so that it can be executed and the results returned to you.

The process begins with parsing the query, a process of analyzing the text to determine its grammatical structure (it is a Structured Query Language, after all). Once the database engine recognizes it as a valid SQL (e.g., `SELECT * FROM`, not `FROM SELECT*`), it prepares an execution plan: which tables in which sequence to access, which filters at what state to apply, and so on. The idea is to optimize the query for the most efficient execution (we'll be discussing query execution plans more in Chapter 9). Then the database engine executes the query and returns results to the client that submitted the query.

There are significant differences in how the process and its steps are implemented across the RDBMS. The details of this are beyond scope of this (and most other) books on SQL.

Herein lay the dynamic SQL problems: vulnerability to security attacks and subpar performance.

First, security. Dynamic SQL is prime target for SQL injection attacks. Once you allow your SQL statement to be constructed, there is a real concern that it might not be constructed correctly, or will be maliciously mis-constructed. It is one thing for a web page to display results of `SELECT * FROM books`, and it would be quite different if the statement read `SELECT * FROM salaries`. There might not be just a lucky guess. With sufficient privileges, an intruder could just query INFORMATION_SCHEMA views to find which objects are in the database. An even scarier scenario might be passing a query DROP TABLE books (though you might be saved by the referential integrity constraints discussed earlier in this chapter).

Even if you use dynamic SQL in your stored procedures (stored procedures will be discussed in more detail in Chapter 4), or validate inputs in your code prior to submitting it to the RDBMS, the ability to execute an arbitrary SQL statement could potentially reveal sensitive data, modify database objects, or destroy data.

Second, performance. An SQL statement submitted to the database engine has to be compiled prior to execution. The compilation process takes human readable statements, such as SELECT, INSERT, UPDATE, or DELETE, and translates them into machine codes that your computer can understand. Part of the process is optimization, determining the plan on the most efficient way to fetch data. A big part of the optimization relies on specific objects and indices assigned to them. If these are only known at the execution time, the database engine cannot construct an efficient access plan; your dynamic SQL query could be running by an order of magnitude slower than the one that only substitutes parameters.

While details of implementation differ across various RDBMSs, the general idea for speeding up query performance is to hash the text query in the cache along with the execution plan while keeping parameters (WHERE clause) separate; thus the same plan could be reused with different parameters. With dynamic SQL, this is impossible as the query hash will be different (different tables, different columns, different JOINs) every time it is generated. Despite some advanced optimization features, dynamic SQL is inherently slower than a "conventional" static one.

Finally, some of the queries that you can use with conventional static SQL cannot be used in dynamic SQL. The limitations vary wildly across different implementations.

SUMMARY

Primary and foreign keys are essential to specifying relationships between tables in a relational database. They are used to enforce different types of integrity: entity integrity (primary key) and referential integrity (a combination of primary and foreign keys).

Database normalization is an iterative process that takes the data model through several refinement stages called normal forms; each subsequent stage includes the rules of the preceding one and then adds more. Usually, 3NF (the third normal form) is the desired outcome of the normalization process.

A normalized database produces data sets assembled from the tables with the help of the JOIN keyword and UNION operator.

Dynamic SQL allows for execution of SQL statements whose structure and content are not known prior to execution. It provides ultimate flexibility as the statements could be assembled in an ad hoc fashion. This flexibility comes at the price of reduced performance and increased vulnerability to security threats, however.

Overcoming the Limitations of SQL

Structured Query Language (SQL) is a set-based language. As such, it is poorly equipped to handle situations in which procedural thinking is required. A SELECT statement, with a little help from the database engine, would almost instantaneously comb through millions of records, perhaps perform JOIN, UNION and ORDER operations, filter the data according to precise search criteria, and more. Yet, as software developers have discovered, there would come a time when you need to pay closer attention to your data, and manipulate it row by row, field by field. This is where SQL functions, and especially procedural extensions, enter the scene.

SQL functions exist to make your life easier, and, to some extent, alleviate the procedural deficiency of set-based SQL. While a query is busy retrieving some data for you, the functions used within that query are validating, converting, calculating, getting system information, and more. Think of them as tools designed to accomplish a single well-defined task (calculating a square root or converting lowercase letters into uppercase, for example) and doing it for each and every row that the query fetches. Just call it by name and pass some arguments (or not), and see your data transformed.

The list of SQL functions available for use within a particular relational database management system (RDBMS) implementation grows with every new release, and some vendors are allowing users to define their own custom functions to perform nonstandard tasks. One of the problems arising from using nonstandard functions (and only a handful are defined in SQL Standard) is that of portability. Some functions are identical in name and usage, some are named differently, and some exist only within a particular RDBMS implementation; the most confusing are those that have similarly sounding names but radically different behavior.

Not all of these functions (some would say very few) are part of the SQL Standard — be it SQL-89, SQL-92 SQL:1999, SQL:2003, or even SQL:2008. In fact, all these standards specify only a handful of functions as a requirement for conformance to a specific level (entry, intermediate, or full). The old saying that you cannot program a standard still holds true.

A *function* is generally a named block of executable code that accepts parameters (variables) and returns values. Most of the time a function would return only a single value of a specific data type (a string, a number, a date), but there are also multivalued functions capable of returning collections of variables and even tables. A list of parameters passed into a function is called the function's *signature* in programming lingo.

In addition to functions, either built-in or user-defined, most RDBMSs allow the creation of a different type of executable code, stored procedures, and triggers. They differ from functions in that they do not return values, so they cannot be used in SQL statements. Representing a special type of a stored procedure that executes automatically upon the happening of some event, triggers are outside the scope of this book (though they will be briefly touched in Chapter 10 as one of the SQL security mechanisms). Only functions can be used in SQL queries.

Now, let's take a plunge and see what the functions could do for us.

Every vendor has its own classifications of the functions supported in its database product. IBM groups its DB2 9.7 functions into column functions, scalar functions, row functions, and table functions. Oracle uses terms such as single-row functions, aggregate functions, analytic functions, and object-reference functions. Microsoft sports the most detailed classifications of rowset functions, aggregate functions, ranking functions, and scalar functions. Other RDBMSs follow mix-and-match patterns.

IN NUMBERS, STRENGTH

Computers are good at keeping up appearances: text, pictures, sounds. Below the surface are electrons flowing through electronic circuits, participating in billions of calculations per second. In short, computers are all about math, and all programming languages were designed to take advantage of it. SQL is no exception. While it might not be as powerful in math as languages specifically designed for this purpose (for example, language "R" designed specifically for statistical calculations), the built in mathematical functions allow for rather sophisticated mathematical expressions to be inserted into your queries.

Let's take a look at SQL's most useful numeric functions. To illustrate the functionality we are going to use Microsoft SQL Server syntax; to make it work with your RDBMS you might need to make some modifications. SQL Server, Microsoft Access, and PostgreSQL allow you to execute a SELECT statement containing an expression without pointing to an actual table, but Oracle and IBM DB2 require you to SELECT from something (add "FROM dual;" and "FROM sysibm.sysdummy1" at the end of your query, respectively); MySQL would also want you to use DUAL pseudo-table; OpenOffice.org BASE does not allow free form expressions. Table 4-1 presents a matrix of the numeric (mathematical) functions for the RDBMSs discussed in the book.

Neither Microsoft Access nor OpenOffice implementations of the SQL contain all functions described in the chapter, even those considered standard by the SQL committee. Please see vendor's documentation to find out whether a specific function is implemented in your RDBMS.

While it is safe to assume that libraries will only deal with positive numbers, you might cross into a negative territory at some point. The SIGN function will tell you where you stand:

```
SELECT SIGN(5) AS positive, SIGN(-5) AS negative;
positive    negative
----------- -----------
1           -1
```

Interestingly enough, the sign indicator will change depending on the data type of the numeric values you're passing into the function: Integers will return simple 1,-1, but real numbers (FLOAT, DECIMAL, REAL) will display as many zeroes as there are decimal places in the number.

```
SELECT SIGN(5) AS positive, SIGN(-5.0001) AS negative;
positive    negative
----------- -----------
1           -1.0000
```

Sometimes you have to be sure that the numbers you deal with are always in positive territory, therefore you might need the ABS() function, which returns the absolute value of the number.

```
SELECT ABS(5) AS former_positive, ABS (-5.0001) AS former_negative;
former_positive    former_negative
----------------- ----------------
5                  5.0001
```

The other common mathematical functions help calculate the square root and evaluate the expression to a specific power.

```
SELECT POWER(2,2) as two_squared, POWER(2,3) as two_cubed;

two_squared   two_cubed
------------- -----------
4             8
```

The SQRT function will extract the square root from a number.

```
SELECT POWER(2,2) as two_squared, SQRT(POWER(2,2)) as square_root;

two_squared   square_root
------------- -----------
4             2
```

While there is no equivalent CURT function to extract cubic root, you can use fractional values in the POWER function to achieve the same result. Even though integer values worked in the previous examples, for fractional values we must use decimals (FLOAT).

```
SELECT CAST(POWER(27.0,1/3.0)AS FLOAT) as 3rd_root

3rd_root
----------------------
3
```

Generating random numbers could come in handy in many situations. The RAND() functions generate a pseudo-random number between 0 and 1. For most practical purposes, it could be considered "random enough," but keep in mind that its uniqueness is not guaranteed; sooner or later this function is bound to produce identical values. Some RDBMSs have implemented more rigorous functions to produce truly unique identifiers (for example, the SQL Server NEWID() function), but this functionality is nonstandard. The RAND() function accepts one optional argument: seed, of the INTEGER data type. If the argument is not specified, the MS SQL Server would assign the seed randomly, producing different results each time the function is called. With a seed specified, the value will always be the same. For example:

```
SELECT RAND() AS random, RAND(10) as seed10, RAND(10) as seed10more

random                 seed10                 seed10more
---------------------- ---------------------- ----------------------
0.182458908613686      0.713759689954247      0.713759689954247
```

In addition, many RDBMSs have implemented more sophisticated mathematical capabilities used in statistical analysis such as STDDEV(), which returns standard deviation of a sample; VAR(), which returns the variance of a sample; or VARP(), returning variance of a population. These are outside of the scope for this book, but give you an idea of the possibilities.

Rounding is an essential math operation. With a little help from the tree of available functions, CEIL[ING](), FLOOR(), and ROUND, quite a bit can be accomplished in SQL. For instance, you could round up or round down the price of the books in the LIBRARY database while selecting records by running this query:

```
SELECT bk_title
,CEILING(bk_price)
,FLOOR(bk_price)
,ROUND(bk_price, 1)
FROM books;
```

The output is two integers and a decimal rounded to one decimal place. Note that the calculations were performed per row. The CEIL function (short for CEILING; some RDBMSs require full name, some are content with the short version) returns an integer value that is closer to positive infinity; FLOOR returns an integer value that is closer to negative infinity, and ROUND just does what it was asked to do: round to the nearest number with one decimal place. Table 4-1 lists selected mathematical functions across the RDBMS servers.

TABLE 4-1: Select Mathematical SQL Functions

SQL FUNCTION	DESCRIPTION	RDBMS SUPPORT
ABS	Returns the absolute value of a numeric input argument.	All
POWER	Returns the argument X raised to the power Y.	Microsoft Access uses '^' operator, and SQL Server has both the function and the operator
SQRT	Returns the square root of the argument X.	Microsoft Access uses function SQR
RAND	Generates some random numbers between 0 and 1.	Microsoft Access uses function RND
FLOOR	Rounds numeric arguments *down* to the nearest integer value.	All
CEIL	Rounds numeric arguments *up* to the nearest integer value.	All; some support also CEILING synonym
ROUND	Returns the numeric argument rounded to the integer number of decimal places.	All

BUILDING CHARACTER

SQL functions excel at manipulating strings; for example, changing letter case, changing alignment, finding ASCII codes, extracting substrings, and so on. Usually, but not always, the output of such functions in RDBMS implementations is a string (even though SQL Standard mandates it to be *always* a string).

What can they do for us? Let's start with concatenation. The following query would return all records from `BOOKS` table concatenating values in `BK_TITLE` and `BK_ISBN` columns.

```
SELECT CONCAT(bk_title, bk_ISBN) FROM books;
```

There is a rather serious limitation of the CONCAT function. It can only accept two parameters, which means that only two fields can be concatenated at a time. To concatenate more strings together, you have to use some workarounds, such as staggering the functions or using more intuitive concatenation operators. Here is an example using the former trick:

```
SELECT CONCAT(CONCAT(bk_title, ','),bk_ISBN) FROM books;
```

The output of the inner CONCAT function serves as input for the outer CONCAT function, and the result is the list of titles and ISBN numbers separated by a comma. To alleviate burdens of this somewhat unintuitive syntax, the RDBMS came up with an alternative use of the operator, and some (such as MySQL) allow more than two arguments into their CONCAT functions. Oracle, IBM DB2, and PostgreSQL use || (two vertical lines) as their concatenation operator, while Microsoft SQL Server uses a plus sign (+). The following syntax will be valid for Oracle, DB2, PostgresSQL, and OpenOffice BASE (with some insignificant syntactical tweaking):

```
SELECT bk_title || bk_ISBN FROM books;
```

This one will work in Microsoft products:

```
SELECT bk_title +  bk_ISBN FROM books;
```

Most RDBMSs will perform implicit conversion when concatenating strings and, say, numbers. If any of the operands is a character data type, the result will always be a string.

```
SELECT bk_title +  bk_price FROM books;
```

Table 4-2 lists some of the useful character functions implemented by the RDBMSs discussed in this book.

TABLE 4-2: Select Character Functions for Server-Based RDBMD

ORACLE 11G	IBM DB2 9.7	MICROSOFT SQL SERVER 2008	POSTGRESQL	MYSQL	DESCRIPTION
`CONCAT` str1, str2) operator "II"	`CONCAT` (string1, string2)	operator +'	operator "II"	CONCAT	Returns the result of concatenation of two strings. It is overloaded for Microsoft SQL Server, where it also adds up numeric values. HSQLDB supports syntax identical to Oracle and DB2, while Microsoft Access uses concatenation operator "&"
`INSTR` (string, sub-string, start position, occurrence)	`LOCATE` (string1, string2, n) `POSSTR` (string1, string2, n)	`CHARINDEX` (string1, string2, n) `PATINDEX` (<pattern>, <string>)	POSITION STRPOS	INSTR POSITION	Returns the position of an occurrence of a substring within the string. The `POSSTR in IBM DB2` test is case-sensitive. HSQLDB has LOCATION function; Microsoft Access has INSTR and INSTRREV functions

ORACLE 11G	IBM DB2 9.7	MICROSOFT SQL SERVER 2008	POSTGRESQL	MYSQL	DESCRIPTION
`SUBSTR` (string,1,n)	`LEFT` (string, n)	`LEFT` (string, n)	SUBSTRING	LEFT	Returns *n* number of characters starting from the left. HSQLDB has SUBSTRING function Microsoft Access uses LEFT function
`LENGTH` (string)	`LENGTH` (string)	`LEN` (string)	CHARACTER_LENGTH CHAR_LENGTH LENGTH	CHAR-ACTER_LENGTH	Returns the number of characters in a string. HSQLDB uses LENGTH function Microsoft Access uses LEN function
`LPAD` (string1,n, string2)	`REPEAT` (char expression, n) `SPACE` (n)	`REPLICATE` (char expres-sion, n) `SPACE`(n)	LPAD	LPAD REPEAT	For `REPEAT` and `REPLICATE` func-tions, return the first argument replicated *n* times. For Oracle's LPAD, the function returns the first argument padded on the left with the third argu-ment *n* times. The `SPACE` function is used to replicate blank spaces *n* times *n* times. HSQLDB uses REPEAT function Microsoft Access uses SPACE function

continues

TABLE 4-2 *(continued)*

ORACLE 11G	IBM DB2 9.7	MICROSOFT SQL SERVER 2008	POSTGRESQL	MYSQL	DESCRIPTION
`LTRIM` (string, set)	`LTRIM` (string)	`LTRIM` (string)	LTRIM	LTRIM	Returns the string with leading blank characters removed. HSQLDB uses LTRIM function Microsoft Access uses LTRIM function
`REPLACE` (string1, string2, string3)	`REPLACE` (string1, string2, string3)	`REPLACE` (string1, string2, string3)	OVERLAY	REPLACE	Replaces all occurrences of `string1` within `string2` with `string3`. HSQLDB uses REPLACE function Microsoft Access uses REPLACE function
`RTRIM` (string, set)	`RTRIM` (string)	`RTRIM` (string)	RTRIM	RTRIM	Returns string with trailing blank characters removed. Additionally, the optional second argument in Oracle's implementation allows you to specify which characters are to be removed. HSQLDB uses RTRIM function Microsoft Access uses RTRIM function
`TO_CHAR` (expression)	`CHAR` (expression)	`STR` (expression)	CONVERT	CHAR	Converts the argument expression into a character string. HSQLDB uses CONVER ad CAST functions Microsoft Access uses CSTR function

ORACLE 11G	IBM DB2 9.7	MICROSOFT SQL SERVER 2008	POSTGRESQL	MYSQL	DESCRIPTION
`SUBSTR` (string, n, m)	`SUBSTR` (string, n, m)	`SUBSTRING` (string, n, m)	SUBSTR	SUBSTR	Returns a part of a string starting from the *n*th character for the length of *m* characters. HSQLDB uses SUBSTRING function Microsoft Access uses combinations of functions such as LEFT, MID, and RIGHT
`TRANSLATE` (string1, string2, string3)	`TRANSLATE` (string1, string2, string3) `INSERT` (works similar to `STUFF`)	`STUFF` (string1, start_position, length, string2)	TRANSLATE	REPLACE	Replaces all occurrences of `string1` within `string2` translated into `string3`. The `STUFF` (Microsoft) and `INSERT`(IBM) functions delete specified length of characters at the `start_position` and then insert `string2` in that place. HSQLDB uses REPLACE function Microsoft Access uses REPLACE function

continues

TABLE 4-2 *(continued)*

ORACLE 11G	IBM DB2 9.7	MICROSOFT SQL SERVER 2008	POSTGRESQL	MYSQL	DESCRIPTION
`TRIM ([BOTH|LEADING|TRAILING, [trim_character]] ,string)`	`STRIP (BOTH |LEADING| TRAILING, string)` `TRIM (BOTH |LEADING| TRAILING, string)` `LTRIM (RTRIM` (string))	`LTRIM (RTRIM` (string))	BTRIM	TRIM	Trims leading or trailing spaces off the string or both. Oracle's version also allows for trimming any arbitrary character off the string. HSQLDB uses combination of LTRIM,RTRIM functions Microsoft Access uses TRIM function
`UPPER` (string)	`UPPER` (string) `UCASE` (string)	`UPPER` (string)	UPPER	UPPER UCASE	Converts all characters of a string into uppercase. HSQLDB uses UCASE function Microsoft Access uses UCASE function

String functions are arguably the most widely used and the most confusing of the SQL functions. Examples of the most common uses are given later on in the chapter.

Because of the inherent capability of the databases to work with different sets of languages, almost every RDBMS either has an overloaded function to recognize a non-English character set, or separate functions to deal with this situation. Oracle, for instance, has NLS_versions of its most popular string functions, with an additional input parameter to specify locale. Some RDBMSs go by data type passed into the function (for example, NVARCHAR as opposed to VARCHAR).

"X" Marks the Spot: Finding the Position of a Character in a String

If you go back to Chapter 1 and revisit the rationale behind separating data into a set of columns, an argument could be made for single column design. Functions such as `INSTR`, `LOCATE`, `POSITION`, and `CHARINDEX` are used to determine the position of a specific character (or combination of characters) within a string. Based on this information, you can slice and dice text in a number of ways using other functions.

CHARINDEX

The CHARINDEX function will return a number: a position of a string within another string. Let's try to parse some of the strings together to see how this works. We'll use our initial "fridge" database to provide long unwieldy strings with which to work; for instance, this one:

```
Microsoft SQL Server 2000 Weekend Crash Course; 978-0764548406; HungryMinds;
2001;06.20.2002;19.99
```

If you don't have it, you could create it now by executing the following statement:

```
CREATE TABLE myLibrary (all_my_books VARCHAR(4000));

INSERT INTO myLibrary VALUES ('Microsoft SQL Server 2000 Weekend Crash Course;
978-0764548406; HungryMinds; 2001;06.20.2002;19.99')
```

The semicolons in the string are there to separate semantically separate chunks of data, and this is exactly what we are going to look for with the CHARINDEX function. (CHARINDEX has equivalents in other RDSMSs: INSTR, LOCATION, POSITION, and so on. For an equivalency chart of some of the useful functions, please see Appendix C.)

CHAR

The string you will work with has semicolons used as delimiters for the tokens; they mark the spots where the SUBSTRING function would chop the string into pieces.

While we could use the actual semicolon character as delimiter, the more reliable way is to use ASCII code 59 to specify the semicolon character. With the help of the `CHAR` function [for instance, CHR(59)], such syntax, with minor modifications, would be portable across all RDBMSs. The CHAR function (and corresponding CHR function in other implementations) returns a character while accepting an ASCII code number as an argument.

ASCII stands for the American Standard Code for Information Interchange. It is a character-encoding scheme based on the ordering of the English alphabet and represents text characters in computers — with each character, including non-printable characters such as carriage returns — being assigned a specific number.

The syntax of the functions in the RDBMS implementation varies wildly. The following example uses Microsoft SQL Server to illustrate the concept; most of the arguments for this function are optional.

This query, executed in SQL Server 2008, looks for an occurrence of the semicolon within the string starting with the first character:

```
SELECT CHARINDEX (CHAR(59),'Microsoft SQL Server 2000 Weekend Crash Course; 978-
0764548406; Hungry Minds') AS first_token_position;

first_token_position
--------------------
47
```

Now that you know the position, you could request the first token by its length in characters by using the SUBSTRING function.

Optional arguments are the arguments that have some default value assumed if the argument were not supplied. Because the order of arguments is fixed, you must enter all the arguments prior to the one that you decided to specify. In the previous example, we forgo specifying the starting point for our search, and 1 is assumed by the function.

SUBSTRING

The `SUBSTR` (`SUBSTRING` in Microsoft SQL Server) function returns part of a string passed in as an argument, designated by the starting position and the desired length of the substring, expressed in characters. Using input from the previous example, we could get our first token now:

```
SELECT
SUBSTRING('Microsoft SQL Server 2000 Weekend Crash Course; 978-0764548406;
HungryMinds',1,46)as first token
first_token
----------------------------------------------
Microsoft SQL Server 2000 Weekend Crash Course
```

Note that the length requested was 46 characters, not 47, because the last character would be a semicolon.

Before you'll be ready to tackle the parsing of the entire string, you need to get acquainted with one more function: the one that returns the length for the entire string.

LENGTH

In an argument, the function `LENGTH` (`LEN` for Microsoft SQL Server) returns a number of characters. (Not a number of bytes! See Chapter 3 for more details.) If an argument is not of a character type, it will be implicitly converted into a string in all three RDBMSs, and its length will be returned. To find the length of the string we've been using so far, you might run the following query (we are using Microsoft SQL Server syntax throughout this exercise):

```
SELECT LEN(all_my_books) as total_length
    FROM mylibrary;

total_length
------------
98
```

The function returns the number of characters in the string, including blanks and all nonprintables. There are different functions to help you determine the number of bytes in a string, which would be useful when determining the size of non–character data types such as dates. Refer to Appendix C for a comprehensive list of built-in SQL functions.

TRY IT OUT Parsing Text Using SQL Built-in Functions

We will put all these functions together and construct a query that would extract three tokens out of the string used to illustrate the string functions CHAR, CHARINDEX, SUBSTRING, and LENGTH. At the same time, the query will illustrate why SQL is not the best language for parsing the text, and why procedural extensions were introduced.

1. Start with the string, as it was used before:

```
'Microsoft SQL Server 2000 Weekend Crash Course;
978-0764548406; HungryMinds;'
```

2. Insert it into a table so you do not have to carry it around (skip this step if you already have it in the database):

```
DELETE myLibrary;
INSERT INTO mylibrary VALUES ('Microsoft SQL Server 2000 Weekend
Crash Course;978-0764548406;Hungry Minds;');
```

3. Run the query to determine the location of the first semicolon:

```
SELECT CHARINDEX(CHAR(59),book)) as first_token_position
FROM myLibarary;
```

   The query returns 49.

4. Use this calculated value to extract the first substring:

```
SELECT SUBSTRING(all_my_books, 1,CHARINDEX(CHAR(59),all_my_books )-1) as
first_token FROM mylibrary; first_token
-----------------------------------------------
Microsoft SQL Server 2000 Weekend Crash Course
```

5. Now, let's see what it takes to extract a second token in a generic way:

```
SELECT SUBSTRING(all_my_books, 1,CHARINDEX(CHAR(59),all_my_books )-1) AS first_
token, SUBSTRING(SUBSTRING(all_my_books,(CHARINDEX(CHAR(59),all_my_books)+1),
LEN(all_my_books))
,1,CHARINDEX(CHAR(59),SUBSTRING(all_my_books,(CHARINDEX(CHAR(59),all_my_books)+1)
,LEN(all_my_books)))-1) AS second_token
FROM mylibrary;

first_token                                      second_token
-----------------------------------------------  -----------------
Microsoft SQL Server 2000 Weekend Crash Course   978-0764548406
```

As you can see, things grow very hairy pretty quickly. The preceding code is extremely complex and error-prone, and is used only as an illustration of how text parsing functions could be used with your SQL queries, and how quickly you could get lost.

How It Works

Now, let's figure out how it works. The CHARINDEX function is used to find the position of the first occurrence of the semicolon delimiter. Using this value in the SUBSTRING function, we can now extract the first token from the string by instructing the function to start with the first character and go to the position of the delimiter. Because we do not want to include the delimiter, we subtract one from the value of the position.

Next, we need to figure how to extract the second token. One way to do it is to start counting with the first occurrence of the delimiter's position, 49, and repeat the same algorithm used to find the first token. Again, because we do not want to include the semicolon as the first character of the token, we start counting from the next character: the delimiter's position plus one. The first argument is the combination of functions returning the second part of the string. Then we supply argument: the number 1. We are counting from the first character again, only this time the first token chunk is already removed. Then comes the delimiter: CHAR(59) and the last argument is again the expression returning the second part of the whole string contained in the BOOK column of the MYLIBRARY table.

As you may have guessed, extracting the third token from the string with the same query will increase the complexity even more. The rule of thumb is *not* to have strings to parse in the first place. This is what first normal form is for. When you have to do it, use either built-in procedural extensions or general programming languages.

TRIM, LTRIM, and RTRIM

Although it might not be apparent, blank spaces in your data can be a major concern. Usually, blank spaces are not shown in the user interface when you type in some character values, which can easily cause mistakes. RDBMSs require absolute precision. The string 'user' and the string 'user ' (with a trailing blank space) are never the same.

The functions to use are TRIM, LTRIM, and RTRIM. The first removes trailing spaces from both sides of a string, while LTRIM and TRIM remove blank spaces from left and right sides, respectively. This might appear to be a bit redundant, having three functions when one would do. The explanation is the usual "implementation details": some RDBMSs implement one and some implement others.

The functions that help trim off blanks (and in some cases, other characters) act similarly in all three RDBMSs: they remove leading or trailing characters from a string expression.

Consider the following example that uses IBM DB2 syntax:

```
SELECT
LENGTH(LTRIM('   three_blanks')) ltrimmed,
LENGTH('   three_blanks') with_leading_blanks
FROM sysibm.sysdummy1
ltrimmed    with_leading_blanks
----------- -------------------
12          15
```

This would make all the difference when comparing strings. The syntax for trimming varies among the RDBMSs, so it is prudent to check which one is supported by your favorite database.

DATE AND TIME FUNCTIONS

Date and time functions are some of the most useful yet confusing functions ever provided by the RDBMS. The SQL Standard does not mandate which have to be implemented, so the vendors and organizations building RDBMSs, left to their own devices, implemented a huge variety of DATE and TIME functions.

What Time Is It?

Keeping a time track of the changes in the database requires access to the system's date and time settings. Oracle implemented the `SYSDATE` pseudo-column (which can be considered a function for our purposes), which returns the system's current date and time. Microsoft SQL Server has the `GETDATE()` function, and IBM DB2 9.7 consistently uses a `CURRENTDATE` special register in the `SELECT` part of the query. These functions (with a sample of their respective outputs) are listed in Table 4-3.

TABLE 4-3: Getting the Current Date from RDBMSs

RDBMS	SQL SYNTAX	OUTPUT
Oracle	SELECT SYSDATE [FROM DUAL];	08-OCT-10 7:47:01 PM
IBM DB2	SELECT CURRENT DATE [FROM SYSIBM.SYSDUMMY1]	10/8/2010
SQL Server 2008	SELECT GETDATE()	2010-10-08 19:27:11.364
PostgreSQL	LOCALTIME(), NOW(), CURRENT_TIME()	2010-10-08 19:25:19.264
MySQL	NOW(), CURRENT_TIME(), CURENT_DATE, UTC_DATE	2010-10-08 19:29:10.378
Microsoft Access	NOW(), DATE(), TIME()	10/8/2010 7:34:06 PM
OpenOffice BASE	CURDATE(), CURTIME()	10/8/2010

The date output can be formatted using various vendor-specific masks, arguments, or conversion functions; please refer to the RDBMS manual for more information on formatting. Knowing the date and time is half the battle; you need the capability to extract date parts, day, year, and months, to be able to manipulate them in your queries. One way to do it is to convert the date into a string and parse it using string functions, or you can use a shortcut and turn to the functions already implemented by the RDBMS.

For instance, the following query extracts DAY, MONTH, and YEAR from the current date returned by the Microsoft SQL Server function:

```
SELECT GETDATE()AS cur_date, DAY(GETDATE()) AS cur_day
, MONTH(GETDATE()) AS cur_month
, YEAR(GETDATE()) AS cur_year
```

```
cur_date                cur_day     cur_month   cur_year
----------------------- ----------- ----------- -----------
2010-10-08 17:01:25.827 8           10          2010
```

Substituting Microsoft's GETDATE in the previous example for equivalents from Table 4-3, your query would yield analogous results in IBM DB2, PostgreSQL, and My SQL. Unfortunately, this syntax does not work for every RDBMS because vendors have different ideas about how to implement this functionality. Oracle, for instance, prefers to use this syntax (and PostgreSQL supports it in addition to the previous example).

```
SELECT
      SYSDATE AS cur_date
, EXTRACT(DAY FROM SYSDATE)AS cur_day
, EXTRACT(MONTH FROM SYSDATE)AS cur_month
, EXTRACT(YEAR FROM SYSDATE)AS cur_year

cur_date                cur_day     cur_month   cur_year
----------------------- ----------- ----------- -----------
08-OCT-10               8           10          2010
```

As they might say in Lapland, there is more than one way to roast a reindeer. The RDBMS implemented a number of different date and time functions trying to anticipate every imaginable situation. There are no fewer than 20 date and time functions in every RDBMS, and most of them do things in their very own way. Please refer to vendor's documentation for a wider selection of functions for your SQL toolbox.

Date Arithmetic

Unlike the orderly world of numbers, dates are maddeningly difficult to work with. Think of it — a year has 365 days (except when it has 366), divided into 12 months (and don't forget quarters!). Adding insult to injury, each month could have either 30 or 31 days, except on one occasion when it has either 28 or 29. Then, we have 24-hour days; each hour contains 60 minutes, each minute contains 60 seconds, but each second contains 1,000 milliseconds. Try to explain this to a Martian!

The databases had to learn to deal with these complexities; no one can confidently add and subtract dates using date and time functions. Before we start manipulating dates, it is important to keep in mind that DATE and TIME are structured data types; that is, they have different parts. In case of a DATE, you will have MONTH, DAY, and YEAR (see the previous paragraph on how to extract these parts from a DATE). With some additional effort, a day of the month could be converted into either a day of the week or a day of the year. It goes similarly with TIME, where you have HOUR, MINUTE, and SECOND (with some RDBMSs providing ways to deal with milliseconds).

Let's start with adding months. It should come as no surprise to you that almost all RDBMSs implement it differently. Oracle and IBM DB2 use the ADD_MONTHS function and direct date arithmetic, while Microsoft decided on a Swiss Army knife approach with the DATEADD function found both in SQL Server and Access. The MySQL open source RDBMS sports function

DATE_ADD, while neither PostgreSQL nor OpenOffice provides a single function each to that effect. A compendium of the functions used in DATE and TIME math is shown in Table 4-4.

TABLE 4-4: Selected Functions for Manipulating DATE and TIME

RDBMS	FUNCTION	DESCRIPTION
Oracle	DATE_ADD MONTHS_BETWEEN Date arithmetic	Used with different parameters; could add days, months, or years. Returns number of months between two dates.
IBM DB2	Date arithmetic only	Uses arithmetic operators plus/minus with qualifiers.
Microsoft SQL Server	DATEADD DATEDIFF	Used with different parameters; could add days, months, or years. Calculates difference between two dates.
PostgreSQL	AGE	
MySQL	DATE_ADD PERIOD_ADD PERIOD_DIFF	Used with different parameters; could add days, months, or years. Adds time period in years. Calculates difference between two dates.
Microsoft Access	DATEADD DATEDIFF	Used with different parameters; could add days, months, or years. Calculates difference between two dates.
OpenOffice BASE/HSQLDB	DATEDIFF	Returns difference between two dates.

The following example query returns the date that is exactly two months from date 2010-10-10, supplied as literal and implicitly converted to a DATE data type:

```
SELECT DATEADD(month,2,'2010-10-10') months

months
-----------------------
2010-12-10 00:00:00.000
```

If no time specifics are provided, the function assumes midnight. The DATEADD function can also add days, hours, and minutes to a date by supplying an appropriate first parameter to the function. The very same function could be used to subtract the date: Just change the sign of the second parameter.

```
SELECT DATEADD(month,-2,'2010-10-10') months

months
-----------------------
2010-08-10 00:00:00.000
```

To find the difference, use the DATEDIFF function.

```
SELECT DATEDIFF(MONTH,'2010-10-10','2010-12-10')AS months

months
-----------
2
```

To accomplish the same feat with direct date arithmetic, just add MONTHS. This syntax, for instance, will be understood by IBM DB2 and, with slight modifications, by Oracle.

```
SELECT (CURRENT DATE + 2 MONTH) add_months
    FROM sysibm.sysdummy1

add_months
------------
  12/10/2010

SELECT (CURRENT DATE - 2 MONTH) subtract_months
    FROM sysibm.sysdummy1

subtract_months
------------
  08/10/2010
```

This pretty much illustrates the concept of date arithmetic: To add or subtract hours, minutes, and seconds, just use the corresponding expression. You can substitute the date value with that from a table in a query, or use a literal. Also, note that DAY/DAYS and MONTH/MONTHS are interchangeable.

TRY IT OUT Hunting for Leap Years

Some databases provide a convenient way to find whether a particular year is a leap year by providing functions that calculate numbers of days; some don't. Nevertheless, with date functions, you could make an educated guess by finding whether this particular year has a February 29.

The years 2008 and 2012 show up as leap years on my calendar, whereas 2009 and 2010 do not. Let's see whether my calendar is correct.

```
SELECT
    DATEADD(month,-8,'2008-10-29') AS year2008
   ,DATEADD(month,-8,'2009-10-29') AS year2009

year2008                year2009
----------------------- -----------------------
2008-02-29 00:00:00.000 2009-02-28 00:00:00.000
```

The function finds February 29 in 2008, but for 2009 it comes up with February 28. I think I'll keep my calendar for the time being.

How It Works

The month of February in a leap year contains 29 days; in a regular year it ends with 28. Taking day 29 of an arbitrary month of the year and using the difference in months between them, we subtract the exact number of months from the date to get to the date in February of that year. In a leap year, we receive February 29; in a regular year we get only February 28.

This might not be the most efficient or even most convenient way to find a leap year, but arguably it is the most fun.

A GLIMPSE OF AGGREGATE FUNCTIONS

Once you put numeric values into your database there is quite a lot you can do with them besides displaying them in reports. Wouldn't it be nice to find out how many books you have in your library? Or how much you've spent on them? What is the most or least expensive book you've ever bought? The SQL aggregate functions are there to help you. Table 4-5 lists some of the most commonly used aggregate functions.

Let's start with counting the books. The syntax is deceptively simple.

```
SELECT COUNT(*) AS total_count FROM books;
total_count
-----------
12
```

What we get is the row count in the BOOKS table; assuming that we have no duplicate copies in the table, we ought to be all right. The people who designed SQL were pretty smart and foresaw this situation, hence the DISTINCT keyword we can use to weed off duplicates. Just run this query and we'll be in business:

```
SELECT DISTINCT COUNT(*) FROM books; From Boris: Output?
```

Somehow, results are exactly the same, even though we know we have some duplicates. If you take a closer look at the query you'll see that we apply DISTINCT keyword to the results produced by function COUNT(), which, being but a single number, will be distinct by definition. We need to make sure that we are COUNTing DISTINCT records, but with this syntax we cannot use * for all fields, we have to spell actual fields to perform the count on:

```
SELECT COUNT(*) AS total_records, COUNT( DISTINCT bk_title)  AS distinct_titles
FROM books;
total_records distinct_titles
------------- ---------------
12            12

(1 row(s) affected)
```

Finally, we have an exact count of distinct titles and a total number of records.

Now, let's see how much we've spent on books. The function SUM will give us the result:

```
SELECT SUM(bk_price) AS total  FROM books;
total
---------------------
354.91
```

The column bk_price has numeric values, and they have been summed to bring us the total. If you try to sum values in the field in which the data type is non-numeric (for example, a VARCHAR or DATE), an error will be returned.

What was the most money you ever paid for a book? The MAX function can answer the question:

```
SELECT MAX(bk_price) AS max_price FROM books;
max_price
---------------------
69.26
```

With numbers it is all self-explanatory, but things get murkier if you try to find out MAX on text or date fields. Running this query on the DATE field will return the latest date, but evaluating VARCHAR might yield surprising results:

```
SELECT MAX(bk_title) AS max_title  FROM books;
max_title
-----------------------------------------------------
Wiley Pathways: Introduction to Database Management
```

The SQL defines MAX for a character field as the last in alphabetical order: If the title begins with *Z* it will be selected as the max from the list, regardless of the case; then it will consider next character, and *ZZ* will beat *ZA* in the race. The evaluation will continue until all characters in the string are accounted for. In our case, the 'W' is selected as the maximum value.

The function MIN is just the opposite of the function MAX, and the least expensive book in the library is the following:

```
SELECT MIN(bk_price) AS min_price FROM books;
min_price
---------------------
8.89
```

The last aggregate function we will take a look at in this chapter is AVG(). It stands for average, and calculates the average (or mathematical mean) of the values on the list:

```
SELECT AVG(bk_price) AS average  FROM books;
average
---------------------
29.5758
```

As with SUM, the AVG() function works only on numeric values and will throw an error if applied to an incompatible data type.

You might wonder how to calculate the median. Surely, there must be a MEDIAN() function! Unfortunately, no. There are ways to calculate the median, but not a single function, and each RDBMS will have a different answer.

There are many more questions to be asked about aggregate functions. For instance, do aggregate functions always return a single value? (It depends.) Can I use the AVG() function with the DISTINCT keyword? (Yes.) And what about NULL(s) in aggregate functions? These questions and more will be explored again in greater detail in Chapter 5.

TABLE 4-5: Selected Aggregate SQL Functions

SQL FUNCTION	DESCRIPTION	RDBMS SUPPORT
AVG	Calculates the arithmetic average of the series of numbers of its argument.	All
COUNT	Returns number of records for the table.	All
MAX	Returns MAXimum value in a set.	All
MIN	Returns MINimum value in a set.	All
SUM	Returns sum of all value in the column.	All

CONVERSION FUNCTIONS

Earlier in the book we discussed why all data cannot be just text and proposed specific data types as a solution. This presents a new problem: conversion between different data types. Sometimes it becomes necessary to convert one data type to another. For example, in some RDBMS implementations, the `CONCAT` function requires all members to be converted into strings before they can be concatenated. The permutations of the different data types need to be converted into each other before they can be manipulated: numbers to strings, and strings to numbers, dates to string and back, the applications are virtually endless. This is what conversion functions are good at. As it becomes clearer that English, while important, is not the only language on Earth, there is an ever-increasing demand for national character databases. Conversion functions might provide translation for English character–based data, so it can be correctly represented in the character set of other alphabets. Some of the most common conversion functions for three major RDBMSs — Oracle, SQL Server, and IBM DB2 — are listed in Table 4-6.

TABLE 4-6: Conversion Functions

ORACLE 11G	IBM DB2 9.7	MICROSOFT SQL SERVER 2008	DESCRIPTION
CAST (data type AS data type)	CAST (data type AS data type)	CAST (data type AS data type) CONVERT (into data type, value, format)	Converts one data type into another data type for which a meaningful conversion can be made. HSQLDB uses both CAST and CONVERT functions. Microsoft Access uses number of type specific functions such as CINT (convert to integer) or CDATE (convert to date) and so on.
TO_CHAR (expression)	CHAR (expression)	CAST [expression as VARCHAR/CHAR (N)]	Converts an expression of a compatible data type into a string of characters. HSQLDB uses CAST/CONVERT functions. Microsoft Access uses CSTR function.
TO_DATE (expression)	DATE (expression)	CAST (expression as DATETIME)	Converts an expression of a compatible data type/format into the DATE/DATETIME data type. HSQLDB uses TO_DATE function. Microsoft Access uses CDATE function.

Sometimes a RDBMS converts data implicitly from one type to another. While this feature might be convenient, it is also something to worry about. One example is the loss of precision when inserting the FLOAT *data type into a column that was declared as* INTEGER*. The number loses all decimal places because it is truncated when converted automatically into* INTEGER.

Conversion Between Different Data Types

There are two general SQL functions that perform conversion: CAST and CONVERT. These functions convert one data type into another. The CAST function is almost universal and used similarly across all RDBMSs. (PostgreSQL allows you to create your own versions of the CAST function. Microsoft Access uses the nonstandard FORMAT function.)

The CAST function syntax is as follows:

```
CAST (<expression> AS <into datatype>)
```

There are slight differences in the CAST function's capabilities among the three implementations: IBM DB2 9.7, SQL Server, and Oracle can cast any built-in data type into another built-in data type, whereas PostgreSQL and MySQL have some compatibility restrictions. If any of the conversions cannot be performed, the database will complain by throwing an error.

The following example demonstrates casting a string into DATE and a number into a string:

```
SELECT
     CAST ('10/10/2010' AS DATETIME) string2date
    ,CAST('01235' AS INTEGER) string2number
string2date              string2number
----------------------- -------------
2010-10-10 00:00:00.000 1235
```

CAST is not the only function to be used, but it is the most generic one you can use with the most portability. Many RDBMSs have created shortcuts: conversion functions that perform specific data type conversions. For instance, Oracle's TO_CHAR (and its equivalents in other implementations, such as CHR and STR) converts any data into character data, and TO_DATE would attempt conversion to data type (if possible).

Conversion Between Different Character Sets

There are between 3,000 to 8,000 spoken languages in the world, and approximately 100 have a unique writing system. Although the single-byte ASCII encoding system served well to store Latin-based characters, it fails to accommodate non-Latin characters. To address the situation, a new universal character set standard — Unicode — was introduced. The latest version of Unicode consists of more than 107,000 characters covering 90 scripts.

Of course, RDBMSs must be able to perform translations among different character sets to be considered international players.

For instance, Microsoft SQL Server uses the NCHAR and UNICODE functions for converting among character sets. The NCHAR function returns the UNICODE character being given an integer code (defined by the Unicode standard), and the UNICODE function returns a number corresponding to the Unicode character.

The following operations take the Scandinavian character Ø to find a UNICODE number for it:

```
SELECT UNICODE('Ø') uni_code
uni_code
----------
216
```

We could then display the character again by passing this number into the `NCHAR` function:

```
SELECT NCHAR(216) uni_character
uni_char
--------
Ø
```

Similar functions exist in all other RDBMSs. If you deal with non-Latin scripts, such as Russian, Hebrew, Arabic, or Chinese, you'll need to find out more about these capabilities.

Every RDBMS provides a number of functions used to access information about the database. By definition, these functions are not part of SQL Standard because of fundamental differences in various RDBMS implementations. In fact, they are mostly provided for the Database Administrator (DBA) to use. Some of these will be discussed in Chapter 8.

MISCELLANEOUS FUNCTIONS

With every classification there are always some functions that do not fit into a single well-defined category. Some of the functions implemented by the major commercial RDBMSs are shown in a "Miscellaneous" category in Table 4-7.

TABLE 4-7: Miscellaneous Functions

ORACLE 11G	IBM DB2 9.7	MICROSOFT SQL SERVER 2008	DESCRIPTION
`COALESCE` (expression1, expression2, expression3...)	`COALESCE` (expression1, expression2, expression3...) `VALUE`	`COALESCE` (expression1, expression2, expression3...)	Returns first argument on the list that is not `NULL`. HSQLDB uses COALESCE function. Microsoft Access could use combination of IIF and IsNULL functions.
`CASE` (expression) `WHEN`<compare value>`THEN`<substitute value>`ELSEEND` `DECODE` (expression, compare value, substitute value...)	`CASE` (expression) `WHEN`<compare value>`THEN`<substitute value>`ELSEEND`	`CASE` (expression) `WHEN`<compare value>`THEN` <substitute value>`ELSEEND`	Compares an input expression to some predefined values and outputs a substitute value, either hard-coded or calculated. HSQLDB uses CASE statement. Microsoft Access could use hierarchy of IIF functions.

ORACLE 11G	IBM DB2 9.7	MICROSOFT SQL SERVER 2008	DESCRIPTION
NULLIF (expression1, expression2)	NULLIF (expression1, expression2)	NULLIF (expression1, expression2)	Compares two expressions; if they are null, returns NULL; otherwise. The first expression is returned. HSQLDB uses NULLIF function. Microsoft Access uses combination of IIF and IsNull functions.
NVL (expression, value)	COALESCE (expression, value)	ISNULL (expression, value)	Checks whether an expression is null; if it is, returns a specified value. HSQLDB uses IFNULL function. Microsoft Access uses IsNULL function.

MAKING THE CASE

Conditional execution is not easy in SQL, and some implementations recommend using a custom function to format a conditional output of a query. Some rudimentary capabilities were introduced to remedy the situation, however. In 1999, the SQL Standards committee introduced the CASE statement.

Not everybody came onboard with it, at least not immediately. Oracle was very fond of its own DECODE function that (Oracle claimed) was more versatile and powerful. Without disputing the claim, we want to note that it finally relented, and introduced CASE expressions in version 10g (yet its beloved DECODE function is still supported, if only for backward compatibility).

Oracle's DECODE function allows you to modify the output of the SELECT statement depending on certain conditions (IF . . . THEN . . . ELSE logic). It compares an expression (usually a column value) to each search value one by one. If a match is found, the function returns the corresponding result; otherwise, it returns the default value. If no match is found and no default is specified, the function returns NULL. In addition to DECODE, Oracle 11g also has a CASE statement that is identical in usage to that of the other RDBMSs discussed here.

The CASE statement produces similar results using much less cryptic syntax, and no function is involved.

For example, in our LIBRARY database table BOOKS, the column BK_PUB_YEAR could be used to sort out "new" and "old" titles.

While it is in the eye of the beholder, such a report might require additional information on how to interpret the somewhat cryptic `Y` and `N`. The query that would resolve the problem in Oracle (using DECODE function) is the following:

```
SELECT
nk_title,
DECODE(BK_PUB_YEAR, '2000', 'old',
'2011', 'recent', 'undefined') AS
FROM books;
```

In plain English, the `DECODE` statement in this query means: If the value in the column `BK_PUB_YEAR` is `2000`, then replace it in the output with the `"recent"` string; if the value is `2011`, then put `"recent"` in its place; if it is neither `2000` nor `2011`, replace it with `undefined`. The maximum number of components (including expression, search criteria, matches, and defaults) for the function is 255.

This example produces identical results in SQL which conforms to the standard, now understood by virtually every RDBMS:

```
SELECT
bk_title,
    CASE bk_pub_year
        WHEN < 2000 THEN 'old'
        WHEN > 2010 THEN 'recent
        ELSE 'undefined'
    END
FROM books;
```

The query becomes much more readable, with an added benefit of being portable across all three RDBMSs. The `CASE` statement is not limited to the SELECT query only; it can also be used in an UPDATE query, in a WHERE clause, and several others.

For every function that substitutes one value for another, it is important to specify data of compatible data types: The substitute value must match that of the column.

Some RDBMSs would implicitly convert numeric value into character data based on the assumptions they make when analyzing operands. For instance, if all operands appear numeric, even when some of them represent years and some represent book price, SQL Server would simply add them together because they all could be cast as numbers, and the first operand is a number.

```
SELECT 1 + '2009' + '098765432' AS total

total
-----------
98767442
```

The result is different if you change the order of the operands or enclose 1 in quotes, indicating that you want to treat it as a character, not a number.

```
SELECT '1' + '2009' + '098765432' AS total

total
--------------
12009098765432
```

While automatic conversion makes your life easier, it is also leads to sloppy code. Because the behavior differs from RDBMS to RDBMS and is not guaranteed to be supported in any future releases, you should not rely on it.

SQL PROCEDURAL EXTENSIONS

If you are familiar with other programming languages, such as Java, C/C#, Visual Basic, PHP, or JavaScript, you will immediately notice the difference among any of these languages and set-based SQL.

The majority of general-purpose programming languages out there are procedural. A *procedural program* is essentially a list of step-by-step instructions that tell the computer what to do (for example, repeatedly read user's input, multiply it by some predefined constant, and store the result in a database table). A procedural program can be instructed to evaluate input and branch into different execution paths, depending on the outcome; it can recover from an error or use subroutines. Most importantly, it does not need an SQL engine to run.

The first RDBMS implementations did not have procedural language capabilities. All procedural database processing was done using embedded programming. All major procedural languages that were popular back then (C, COBOL, Pascal) had (and still have) special extensions (precompilers) that allowed the programmer to embed SQL statements directly into programming language code to be compiled together. The work of precompilers was to translate SQL into appropriate language constructs that could later be compiled into binary code.

As relational databases became increasingly sophisticated, and more internal control was delegated to RDBMSs, the idea arose to store procedural programming modules inside RDBMSs in compiled (binary) format. Off-loading most of the processing to a server makes a lot of sense. As a result, each vendor implemented its own version of internal RDBMS procedural modules.

Before the introduction of the SQL/PSM (Persistent Storage Module) in the evolving SQL Standard there were no facilities in SQL to deal with these issues, so RDBMS vendors filled the gap by introducing hundreds of proprietary functions and whole new languages into their respective databases. Virtually every database vendor today provides procedural extensions for use with its database products. Oracle has built-in PL/SQL, Microsoft uses its own dialect of Transact-SQL (which shares its roots with Sybase, another RDBMS vendor), and DB2 9.7 uses SQL PL. The open source RDBMS PostgreSQL allows for virtually any procedural language to be used with its SQL engine and PL/pgSQL. MySQL has added limited support for stored procedures in version 5, using its own unnamed yet dialect. Both Microsoft Access and OpenOffice BASE allow for their respective versions of Basic to be used inside the database. Unlike set-based SQL, these procedural extensions allow for creating full-fledged programs within their respective host environments. Custom UDFs are usually created using one of their procedural languages (more on stored procedures later in the chapter).

A special type of stored procedure, a *trigger*, was mentioned earlier in this chapter. It is associated with a database object (usually a table, but some RDBMSs allow triggers on databases and instances) and executes upon a change event happening to that object, such as an UPDATE, INSERT, or DELETE for a table; or an ALTER or DROP event for the objects inside RDBMS. This is an advanced topic and is outside the scope of the book.

Some vendors allow for general-purpose languages such as Java or C# to be used for procedural programming within their RDBMS. Microsoft SQL Server allows for procedures and functions to be created in C#; while Oracle, DB2, and PostgreSQL support the Java programming language.

SQL proper lacks procedural constructs. Specifically, it lacks the capability to perform operations in (optionally named) hierarchical logical blocks that can accept and return values, perform iterations, execute conditional statements, and so on. To some extent this deficiency is alleviated with SQL functions, but to be able to manipulate data on a row by row basis one has to use procedural extensions, or, as is the case with Microsoft Access and OpenOffice BASE with HSQLDB, some variations of a built-in scripting language. Table 4-8 lists the procedural extensions supported by the respective RDBMSs.

TABLE 4-8: RDBMS and Procedural Extensions

RDBMS	PROCEDURAL LANGUAGES SUPPORTED	SUPPORTED TYPES
Microsoft SQL Server	Transact-SQL, .NET languages (C#, VB.Net)	Stored procedures, functions, triggers
Oracle	PL/SQL, Java, .NET languages (C#, VB.Net)	Stored procedures, functions, triggers
IBM DB2 LUW	SQL PL, Oracle's PL/SQL, Java, .NET languages (C#, VB.Net)	Stored procedures, functions, triggers
PostgreSQL	PL/pgSQL, PL/Perl, PL/Python, PL/TCL, as well as ability to plug in other procedural languages	Stored procedures, functions, triggers
MySQL	MySQL Stored Procedure Language	Stored procedures and functions
Microsoft Access	Visual Basic For Applications (VBA)	Programming modules; queries
OpenOffice BASE	OpenOffice BASIC	Programming modules; queries

Although the basic syntax elements of these three languages are similar, the advanced features differ significantly. For simplicity sake, we are going to stick with one flavor of RDBMS procedural language: Transact-SQL implemented by Microsoft SQL Server (also found in Sybase). Versions for other RDBMSs are available for download from the book's site at www.wrox.com and at www.agilitator.com.

Happy Parsing: Stored Procedures

The mechanics of creating a stored procedure is simple:

```
CREATE PROCEDURE <procedure name> (procedure arguments>)
<procedure body>
```

Because stored procedures cannot be used in a SELECT statement, there is no easy way to pass in a field name (well, there are ways, like dynamic SQL, or the hitherto unmentioned CURSOR, but they do not change the fundamental fact that a stored procedure is an outsider in the set-based world).

The body could contain declared variables, conditional statements, loops, and error-handling routines — everything you came to expect from a procedural language. Let's apply these basic concepts to see how a stored procedure can be used to help the situation with the insanely convoluted parsing algorithm introduced earlier in the chapter.

TRY IT OUT

We will create a stored procedure to parse a string into three tokens according to delimiters found in the string, and return it to the calling client. We will use Microsoft SQL Server Transact-SQL, but the same principles are applicable to every other procedural language implemented in RDBMSs.

1. First, let's create a table to collect output of the parsing routine. Run the following statement from the Query Analyzer window:

   ```
   CREATE TABLE tokens (id INT IDENTITY(1,1), token_value VARCHAR(max))
   ```

   The IDENTITY column will automatically insert incremental numbers into the ID column to keep track of the tokens.

2. Enter the text of the stored procedure (you can download scripts from the book site); we'll discuss how it works later in this chapter:

   ```
   CREATE PROCEDURE usp_ParseString(@string2parse VARCHAR(max)
   , @delimiter CHAR(1))
   AS
   BEGIN
   DECLARE @remainder VARCHAR(max)
   DECLARE @token VARCHAR(100)
   DECLARE @position INT
   SET @remainder = @string2parse

      WHILE CHARINDEX(@delimiter,@remainder)> 0
      BEGIN
       --- find position of a delimiter in the string
       SET @position = CHARINDEX(@delimiter,@remainder)
       --- extract token from the string
       SET @token = SUBSTRING(@remainder, 1,@position-1)
       --- save the token into [tokens] table
       PRINT @token
       PRINT @remainder
   ```

```
        INSERT INTO tokens VALUES(@token)
        --- afterremiving token,
        --- assign new string to the @remainder variable
        SET @remainder = SUBSTRING(@remainder,@position+1, LEN(@remainder))
      END
    END
```

3. Compile the stored procedure by highlighting the entire text and clicking Execute at the top toolbar of the Query Analyzer (with the red exclamation mark on the left of the Execute caption).

4. Run the stored procedure while supplying the necessary arguments. The EXEC keyword is used in Microsoft SQL Server:

```
execusp_ParseString 'Microsoft SQL Server 2000 Weekend Crash Course;
978-0764548406;Hungry Minds;', ';'
```

   Note that the semicolon appears three times in the body of the string; the algorithm of the preceding stored procedure relies on this fact (the logic would have been slightly different if this semicolon were not present).

5. After the execution completes, run the SELECT query on the TOKENS table:

```
SELECT * FROM tokens
id        token_value
--        --------------------------------
1         Microsoft SQL Server 2000 Weekend Crash Course
2         978-0764548406
3         Hungry Minds
(3 row(s) affected)
```

How It Works

The stored procedure accepts two arguments: the string to parse and a delimiter separating tokens in the string. Several variables were declared to hold intermediate values as we proceed at chopping the string. The WHILE loop will continue to execute as long as there is a single semicolon in the string. The expression (CHARINDEX(@delimiter,@remainder)> 0) evaluates to TRUE. Inside the WHILE loop, the steps are as follows: first find the position of the semicolon in the string and chop off the token, starting from the first character up to the semicolon position, and then insert it into the TOKENS table; the remainder of the string, starting with the second character (excluding the semicolon) until the end, is assigned back to the variable @remainder, and the cycle repeats until no semicolons remain.

Keep in mind that the code of the procedure is used only to illustrate a concept, and as such contains no error handling or assumption validations. The code providing this functionality would have to be more robust to be considered production quality.

User-Defined Functions (UDFs)

The ability to extend built-in functionality is a double-edged sword. It is extremely satisfying to be able to step outside limits imposed by people and organizations implementing the RDBMS, but there is a price to pay. Besides understanding basic syntax and programming constructs, one also has to consider the ramifications of using custom functions: portability, security, and performance. Always read the RDBMS documentation: There is a good chance that a function you need is already there.

The syntax is straightforward:

```
CREATE FUNCTION <function name> (<arguments>)
RETURN <data type>
<function body>
RETURN <return value>
```

In this code snippet, the <arguments> are the values that the function takes in, and the return <data type> spells out the data type of what the function is supposed to return when execution reaches the RETURN statement. The return is what differentiates a UDF from a stored procedure. There is another important distinction: A function can be used in a SELECT statement, but a stored procedure cannot.

In addition to the expected discrete data types, such as characters and numbers, some RDBMSs allow for returning tables, so you could SELECT from a function. A detailed discussion of UDFs is outside the scope of this book, but the reader is encouraged to refer to other titles, such as *SQL Functions* or *SQL Bible, 2nd Edition*, found in the sample data in our Library database, both published by Wiley with Alex Kriegel as one of co-authors.

TRY IT OUT

We will create a custom function to return the price of the book in pounds sterling and Euros in addition to the U.S. dollars you've entered. This would require us to create a table to hold exchange rates. Throughout this example, we will use Microsoft SQL Server Transact-SQL syntax. The data type used in the example — SMALLMONEY — is Microsoft-specific referring to a numeric data type used to store monetary data values from -214,748.3648 through +214,748.3647, with accuracy to a ten-thousandth of a monetary unit.

1. Create an exchange rates table in the LIBRARY database and insert data (the exchange rates will have to be updated to reflect the current status, of course):

```
USE library
CREATE TABLE exchange_rates(currency  VARCHAR (15), rate_to_dollar MONEY)

INSERT INTO exchange_rates VALUES ('euro',0.728)
INSERT INTO exchange_rates VALUES ('pound',0.639 )
```

2. Create a UDF to convert the rates:

```
CREATE FUNCTION ufn_Exchange(@price SMALLMONEY, @currency VARCHAR(15))
RETURNS SMALLMONEY
AS
BEGIN
    DECLARE @return SMALLMONEY
    SELECT @return = @bprice/rate_to_dollar
        FROM exchange_rates
          WHERE currency = @currency

RETURN (@return)
END;
```

3. Construct an SQL query listing all titles in the BOOKS table with prices in U.S. dollars, British pounds, and Euros.

```
SELECT
bk_title
, bk_price AS dollars
, dbo.ufn_Exchange(bk_price,'pound') AS pounds
, dbo.ufn_Exchange(bk_price,'euro') AS euros
FROM books;
```

How it works

The custom function accepts two parameters: the numeric value to be converted and the currency indicator specifying which exchange rate to use. The first value is selected from the BOOKS table; the second is hard-coded into the query. The function dbo.ufn_Exchange is executed twice for each row returned by the SELECT statement. For the five records contained in our table, this means 20 function calls, and each call performed a SELECT query of its own. Think about it from a performance point of view.

Why Use Procedural Extensions?

Stored procedures, UDFs, and triggers can be used in many different ways and for many different reasons, both valid and otherwise. The main benefits include performance improvement, network traffic reduction, increased database security, and code reusability.

These benefits of performance improvement, network traffic reduction, increased database security, and code reusability affect the RDBMSs discussed in this book differently. For instance, network traffic is not much concern for users of desktop databases such as Microsoft Access and OpenOffice BASE.

Performance and Network Traffic

Stored routines can be used to improve application performance. By virtue of being compiled — that is, translated into machine code stored inside the RDBMS — they generally execute faster than SQL statements, which have to be compiled every time they're submitted to the database. Compilation is an expensive process in terms of CPU cycles and memory.

Network traffic can also be significantly reduced by referring to a stored procedure and passing the arguments into it. Such a process is much more concise than sending verbose SQL statements. Each individual statement is probably not large enough to improve the overall network performance, but in a large system with thousands of users and hundreds of thousands of SQL statements, it can make a difference.

Database Security

Stored procedures, functions, and triggers can be used to improve database security. A stored procedure (or function) is a separate database object that could have a separate set of privileges. In theory, this procedure could be the user's only gateway to the data in database functionality. A user could be only allowed to connect to the RDBMS and execute this procedure.

Triggers could be even more useful for security implementation. A trigger for a table could validate input, preserve modified data, and record changes made to a table by different users for audit purposes; triggers declared on a database level would be able to intercept database-wide events such as creating, altering, and dropping database objects.

Code Reusability

Another important benefit of stored routines is code reusability. Once designed and compiled, a stored procedure or UDF can be used over and over again by multiple users (or applications), saving time on retyping large SQL statements and reducing the probability of human errors. Also, when a persistent module needs to be changed, the change won't affect the client programs that access the module, as long as all the calling parameters (procedure's signature) remain the same. In contrast, such a change would require updating every application that uses this database if it were using dynamic or embedded SQL.

It's not all icing on the cake; there are veritable drawbacks to using procedural extensions. First, it affects the portability of your code. Any custom function or procedure would have to be translated when you move from one RDBMS to another. While some databases such as IBM DB2 would allow you to run Oracle's PL/SQL code, others will not. Second, consider the potential effects on database performance. Your custom procedure will never be as optimal as a built-in one and is much likely to contain bugs (test your code thoroughly).

SUMMARY

SQL's built-in functions complement inherent deficiencies in the nonprocedural language. They perform many useful tasks, ranging from rounding numbers to string manipulation to conversion of data types to the sophisticated processing logic of substitute functions.

While the number of functions defined in SQL92/99 standards is relatively small (although expanded in SQL:2003), every RDBMS vendor has added its own set of these useful tools well in excess of hundreds. Therefore, it should not come as a surprise that functions differ across the vendors — by capability, implementation details, syntax, or simply by being included or excluded from the implementation. Never assume that an SQL function found in one implementation would exist in another.

To enhance RDBMS functionality and alleviate some deficiencies inherent in SQL, the early RDBMSs have introduced procedural extensions to the language. These extensions allow for creating programs running inside the RDBMS, which implement procedural logic and allow for structured programming techniques to be used. They also offer the benefits of increased efficiency, enhanced security, and code reusability.

Grouping and Aggregation

Having your data delivered in minute detail works fine until you need to look at the bigger picture. How many books have you accumulated in your library? What is the total cost? How much do you spend on average? These questions, and more, are addressed in SQL with aggregate functions.

We touched on aggregate functions briefly in Chapter 4 as part of the discussion of SQL functions in general and promised to answer a few questions about them; now's the time.

AGGREGATE SQL FUNCTIONS REVISITED

SQL Standard includes a surprising number of advanced statistical functions (more than 20!) that you might never encounter solving day-to-day problems, and most enterprise-class RDBMSs added a few of their own. A detailed discussion of these SQL functions belongs in an advanced book. A list of the most common functions can be found in Table 5-1, later in this chapter.

Aggregate functions return a single value based on a specific calculation within a set (group) of values. In the most basic case, the group is the entire table data set.

AVG()

There is a line in a humorous essay by Stephen Leacock that describes a particular kind of library: "There are, of course, all the new books, the new fiction, because there is a standing order with Spentano to send up fifty pounds of new fiction by express once a week." Supposing that we maintained our library in the same fashion, how would our accountant handle it?

```
SELECT
        AVG(bk_price)        AS average_price
       ,AVG (bk_page_count) AS average_pages
FROM books;

average_price     average_pages
----------------  --------------------
29.5758           597
```

This is how much we spent on books on average (depending on your data you might have spent more or less, on average, per book), and there are an average of 597 pages per book. Put in context, this data might even be useful to track your book spending habits, for instance.

Of course, depending on our needs, we may put conditions on our query to narrow down the data set for which the average is being calculated. For instance, to find the average price per book of only those books that cost more than $30, we can run this query:

```
SELECT
    AVG(bk_price) AS average_price
FROM books
   WHERE bk_price > 30;

average_price
-------------------
50.4875
```

The AVG function takes into consideration only records for which data exist. It is a good idea to ignore the record and not implicitly convert NULL into zero.

TRY IT OUT Counting NULL(s) and Zeroes

In order to explore how AVG function treats NULL, we will update some of our records with NULL values and then calculate averages. We will use Microsoft SQL Server 2008 to run the queries, but the behavior is identical across all RDBMSs in this book.

1. Open Microsoft SQL Server Management Studio and connect to your database using Windows authentication.
2. In the upper-left corner click the New Query button.
3. In the opened query window (the middle pane), enter the following SQL query:

```
SELECT AVG(bk_price) AS average_price FROM books;

average_price
----------------
29.5758
```

4. Update the BK_PRICE column for one of the records; for example, record with BK_ID=12 to NULL:

```
UPDATE books SET bk_price = NULL
WHERE bk_id = 12;
```

5. Run the query from Step 3 again by pressing the Execute button on the toolbar of SQL Server Management Studio:

```
SELECT AVG(bk_price) AS average_price FROM books;

average_price
----------------
31.3372
```

6. Let's update the same record (BK_ID=12) with zero value:

```
UPDATE books SET bk_price = 0
WHERE bk_id = 12;
```

7. Run the query from Step 3 again:

```
SELECT AVG(bk_price) AS average_price FROM books;

average_price
----------------
28.7258
```

8. Restore the original value for the record 12:

```
UPDATE books SET bk_price = 10.20
WHERE bk_id = 12;
```

How It Works

The mathematical average is calculated as the sum of all values, divided by their count. When all 12 records have numeric values in the BK_PRICE column, the average is 29.5758.

When the BK_ID = 12 record is updated with NULL value, it gets excluded both from the sum of the values (dividend) and from the record count (divisor); only 11 records and their values will be used to calculate the average. The result is therefore is bit higher (31.3372) because the price taken out of the equation is relatively small ($10.20).

When we update the record with the zero value, both the zero and the record are counted toward the averages. The result is different because now this book IS counted. In fact, it is counted as having cost nothing, which brings the average down some.

Finally, if we tried to compute the AVG on a column where there were no data in ANY rows (all NULLs, all the way down), we would get a NULL as our result. No data means no data!

This behavior is identical across all RDBMSs.

COUNT()

Counting the number of records in your data set is easy with the COUNT function. There are two primary ways this function can be used: counting everything or just specific columns:

```
SELECT COUNT(*) AS records_count
FROM location;

record_count
--------------
12
```

Used in this way, the function allows us to compute the number of rows in the table. The asterisk symbol (meaning "all") can be substituted for a specific column name, say, BK_ID:

```
SELECT COUNT(bk_d) AS records_count
FROM location;

record_count
--------------
12
```

The results are identical because every row in the column BK_ID has a value in it. This is not the case when the column contains NULL ("no data here"), but if we NULL-out some column value in the BOOKS table and run our COUNT on it, the results would be quite different:

```
UPDATE books SET bk_price = NULL where bk_id = 12;

SELECT COUNT(bk_price)AS counting_prices
FROM books;

counting_prices
------------------
11
```

Now we have a different result! What's the difference? This time we have asked the function to compute the number of rows, where there is a value in the given column (bk_price in this case; don't forget to restore the value as in Step 8 of the first Try It Out in this chapter).

Use of aggregate functions is not limited to the SELECT, UPDATE, and INSERT lists; they just as successfully can be used in the WHERE clause, though additional restrictions apply. (This is discussed later in this chapter.)

Again, we can put conditions on this query: for instance, how many books do we have in the right-most bookcase in the living room?

```
SELECT COUNT(*) AS counting_books
FROM books
  WHERE  (bk_price  > 30);

counting_books
-----------------------
4
```

Looks like only four out of 12 books cost more than 30 dollars, which might indicate that either we do not buy expensive books or we just forgot to enter the prices. Remember that the NULL value is not counted.

MAX()

This function returns the highest value in the specified column:

```
SELECT MAX(bk_price) AS max_price FROM books;

max_price
------------------
69.26
```

What would happen if there were several books with identical prices? Only one number will be returned regardless of how many there might be. When the column is the numeric data type, the greatest number will be returned and applied to a text field. It will return the value that sorts last in the alphabetical order, and it cannot be applied to either binary or XML data type columns. For instance, consider the following query:

```
SELECT MAX(bk_title) AS max_title FROM books;

max_title
-------------------------------------------------------
Wiley Pathways: Introduction to Database Management
```

The title was returned because it is last on the alphabetically sorted titles list.

MIN()

This function returns the lowest value in the specified column:

```
SELECT MIN(bk_price) AS min_price FROM books;

min_price
------------------
8.89
```

Applied to a text field, it will return the value that sorts first in the alphabetical order:

```
SELECT MIN(bk_title) AS min_title FROM books;

min_title
-------------------------------
A La Recherche du Temps Perdu
```

As with every other aggregate function, columns containing NULL values are simply ignored.

Both MAX and MIN functions work on single-value columns, and you cannot ask them to return, say, a greatest/least number from a list of numbers; you would have to use a different function. Both Oracle and MySQL offer GREATEST and LEAST functions; for instance, the following query would be perfectly legal in Oracle (but would not work in IBM DB2, SQL Server, Microsoft Access, or PostgreSQL):

```
SELECT
    LEAST(1,2,3,4,5,6,7,8)    AS min_num
   ,GREATEST1,2,3,4,5,6,7,8) AS max_num
FROM dual;

min_num   max_num
--------- ---------
1         8
```

There are ways to emulate this functionality in other RDBMSs: by creating custom functions or by delving into advanced SQL data manipulation, which is outside the scope of this book.

SUM()

To calculate totals, SQL supplies the SUM function; this function returns the total of all numeric values in a column:

```
SELECTSUM(bk_price) total_costs
FROM  books

total_costs
------------------
354.91
```

Similar to AVG, any rows without data in the given column (showing NULL in it) are ignored. An attempt to SUM the column that has no data in any row results in NULL. If you try to run SUM on a non-numeric (text) column, you will get an error.

Table 5-1 shows common aggregate functions in use.

TABLE 5-1: Commonly Used Aggregate Functions

SQL FUNCTION	DESCRIPTION
AVG	Returns the calculated average of the list of numbers; NULL values are ignored.
COUNT	Returns the number of rows retrieved by the query; NULL values are ignored.
MAX	Returns a single maximum value for a given column ; NULL values are ignored.
MIN	Returns a single minimum value for a given column ; NULL values are ignored.
SUM	Returns the sum of the numeric values in a column; NULL values are ignored.

TRY IT OUT Constructing an AVG Function of Our Own

The SQL is very flexible to allow you to combine several functions in a query (SELECT, UPDATE, and INSERT) to produce the desired result. Here, we are going to try to reproduce the AVG() function's functionality:

1. Open Microsoft SQL Server Management Studio and connect to your database using Windows authentication.
2. In the upper-left corner, click the New Query button.
3. In the query window, enter the following query:

```
SELECT
     SUM(bk_price)/COUNT(bk_price) AS average_price
   , SUM(bk_price)                 AS total_price
   , COUNT(bk_price)               AS books_count
FROM books;

average_price    total_price    books_cout
---------------- -------------- --------------
29.5758           354.91         12
```

How It Works

Calculating averages is simple: get the total of all values and divide it by the number of the values in the set. Using the SUM() function to produce the former and COUNT() for the latter, we can instruct the database engine to calculate the average from the dynamic values produced by these two functions.

All the rules applied to individual functions fully apply to their quotients (NULLS, zeroes, and so on).

ELIMINATING DUPLICATE DATA

The full syntax for the aggregate functions discussed in this chapter follows the same pattern:

```
FUNCTION (DISTINCT | ALL)
```

Here's an example:

```
AVG(DISTINCT | ALL)
```

The default is ALL, meaning that all values in the set will serve as input to the function. Using the DISTINCT keyword, the duplicate values will be ignored. For instance, we can count all the books published by Wiley:

```
SELECT
    COUNT(bk_publisher) AS pub_count
FROM books
WHERE bk_publisher = 'Wiley';

pub_count
------------------
4
```

The result is 4, which is how many Wiley books are in our library. The results will be quite different if we ask for a DISTINCT record count:

```
SELECT COUNT(DISTINCT bk_publisher)  AS pub_count
FROM books
WHERE bk_publisher = 'Wiley';

pub_count
----------------
1
```

The four values have collapsed into one because we have exactly one occurrence of the value in the data set. Of course, both variants could be used within the same query:

```
SELECT
  COUNT(bk_publisher)              AS pub_count
, COUNT(DISTINCT bk_publisher)     AS distinct_count
FROM books;

pub_count   distinct_count
----------- ---------------
12          9
```

The preceding results show 9 distinct publishers in our table, out of a total of 12.

It matters where you insert your DISTINCT keyword. Used within an aggregate function, it produces aggregated results for the set of distinct values; used outside it makes the return result distinct. Consider these two queries and their respective outputs:

```
SELECT
    DISTINCT COUNT(bk_publisher) AS pub_count
FROM books;

pub_count
----------------
12


SELECT
    COUNT(DISTINCT bk_publisher) AS pub_count
FROM books;

pub_count
----------------
9
```

The results are different because in the first query the DISTINCT keyword made sure that only distinct *results* of the COUNT function were returned. In this case, it is redundant because an aggregate function without the GROUP BY clause (see later in this chapter) always returns only a single record. In the second query, it makes sure that only distinct values are *counted* prior to the result being returned.

Even though some aggregate functions can be used with character data (or date and time data types), they are really designed for numbers. They accept neither XML nor binary data types as input.

GROUP BY: WHERE YOUR DATA BELONGS

By now, you might be wondering how you would go about selecting data based on the aggregated values. For instance, how do you find all publishers whose average book price is above $20? Surely, you could use the trusty WHERE clause, right? Uh, no. Try executing a query like this:

```
SELECT bk_publisher
FROM books
    WHERE AVG(bk_price) > 20;
```

You get an error message that in the context of Microsoft SQL Server 2008 reads as follows:

```
An aggregate cannot appear in the WHERE clause unless it is in subquery contained
in a HAVING clause or a select list, and the column being aggregated in an outer
reference.
```

Yet there is a way to ask the database engine such a question, and get a result, by using the GROUP BY clause (with the HAVING clause not far behind), but let's get the basics nailed down first.

Aggregating results by rolling them up to a single value is useful, as is having all the data stored in the individual records, but sometimes a middle ground is needed. Using the WHERE clause with an aggregate function allows us to aggregate a subset of the results. For example, we can count books published by a particular publisher. To do the same for all publishers, we would have to run as many queries as there are distinct publishers in our table; moreover, we would need to know the publishers by name to ask for them, and we may not know the names of all the publishers. If only we could ask the database for aggregated information grouped by some criterion without supplying hard-coded values. Here's where the GROUP BY clause comes in.

The GROUP BY clause only works in tandem with aggregate functions and appears after all the SELECT, WHERE, and JOIN keywords in the query. To produce an aggregated price list by publisher (to discover how much you have spent buying books from this particular publisher) without ever knowing what publishers are in the table, use the following query:

```
SELECT
    bk_publisher
  , SUM(bk_price) AS books_total
FROM books GROUP BY bk_publisher;

bk_publisher                 books_total
---------------------------- ---------------------
Ace Trade                    16.29
Broadway                     18.48
Gallimard                    69.26
Greenbook Publications       8.89
MacMillan                    38.88
Microsoft                    24.99
Orb Books                    16.29
Picador                      10.20
Wiley                        151.63
```

We know that there are exactly nine distinct publishers in our BOOKS table, so nine records were returned. Only for one publisher, Wiley, have we multiple books in the table, and the prices of these books were summed up and attributed to Wiley — along with other publishers and their summaries, respectively. All of this was provided in a single query, without having to spell names of the specific publishers. This is the beauty of the declarative nature of SQL.

The returned results in the previous query are sorted alphabetically by BK_PUBLISHER, in descending order; this is the default. To sort it in a different order, you would need to use an additional ORDER BY clause, which is covered later in this chapter.

Every aggregate function, or combination thereof, could be used with GROUP BY clause. For example, to calculate not only SUM, but also AVG, MI, MAX, and COUNT, you could include it all in a single query:

```
SELECT
    bk_publisher
    , SUM(bk_price) AS books_total
    , AVG(bk_price) AS avg_price
    , MIN(bk_price) AS min_price
    , MAX(bk_price) AS max_price
    ,COUNT(bk_price) AS book_count
FROM books
    GROUP BY bk_publisher;
bk_publisher          books_total  avg_price    min_price  max_price    book_count
--------------------  -----------  ------------ ---------  ------------ -----------
Ace Trade             16.29        16.29        16.29      16.29        1
Broadway              18.48        18.48        18.48      18.48        1
Gallimard             69.26        69.26        69.26      69.26        1
GreenbookPublications  8.89         8.89         8.89       8.89        1
MacMillan             38.88        38.88        38.88      38.88        1
Microsoft             24.99        24.99        24.94      24.99        1
Orb Books             16.29        16.29        16.29      16.29        1
Picador               10.20        10.20        10.20      10.20        1
Wiley                151.63        37.9075      26.39      55.26        4
```

The results are predictable. With the exception of Wiley books, all other publishers are represented by a single book (output of the COUNT() function) and their total, min, max, and average prices are identical across the board. The differences are shown in Wiley's case, where the product of the aggregate functions over prices for its four books is calculated.

It is possible to GROUP BY more than one column, but you need to understand how the set logic works to be able to formulate a question. Adding an additional column to your GROUP BY when selecting from a single table would produce a result set requiring additional manual steps to make sense of. For example, simply adding BK_TITLE to BK_PUBLISHER in the query asking to summarize BK_PRICE will give you results indistinguishable from a standard SELECT query:

```
SELECT
    bk_publisher   AS publisher
  , SUM(bk_price)  AS books_total
FROM books
GROUP BY bk_publisher, bk_title;

publisher                  books_total
-------------------------- ---------------------
Gallimard                    69.26
Broadway                     18.48
Microsoft                    24.99
MacMillan                    38.88
Greenbook Publications        8.89
Wiley                        29.99
Orb Books                    16.29
Wiley                        39.99
Wiley                        26.39
Picador                      10.20
Ace Trade                    16.29
Wiley                        55.26
```

The order appears to be wrong. Should it not be ordered by BK_PUBLISHER? No, by default it is ordered by the last column specified in the GROUP BY clause; in this case, by BK_TITLE (even though the column itself is not on the select list). The column BK_TITLE does not have to appear on the select list to be included in the GROUP BY clause, but the opposite is not true: all columns listed in the GROUP BY clause must be included in the SELECT list (with the exception of the aggregated function column).

You won't be able to use an aggregate SUM() function in the standard SELECT query which includes non-aggregated columns on the list because the database engine would get confused by being asked to produce both record-level and aggregate results without a GROUP BY, but sum of a single value is, by definition, this value.

If your question involves data from another table JOIN(ed) together, the results are much more interesting. To find the total price of the books published by a particular publisher per shelf in your bookcase, you might use the following query:

```
SELECT
    SUM(bk_price) AS books_total
  , bk_publisher AS publisher
FROM books INNER JOIN location
    ON bk_id = fk_bk_loc
        GROUP BY bk_publisher, loc_shelf;
books_total          publisher
-------------------- ----------------------------------
69.26                Gallimard
8.89                 Greenbook Publications
10.20                Picador
16.29                Ace Trade
38.88                MacMillan
16.29                Orb Books
18.48                Broadway
24.99                Microsoft Press
151.63               Wiley

(9 row(s) affected)
```

A total of nine records were returned, a sign that we have grouped the results by nine distinct publishers. In addition, we can see price distribution by shelf, with all Wiley books being stored on shelf #5, totaling $151.63.

GROUP BY could be used all by itself without any aggregate functions to support. A query, such as the following, would return a list of publishers grouped by, well, publisher:

```
SELECT bk_publisher AS publisher
FROM books
GROUP BY bk_publisher

publisher
--------------------------
Ace Trade
Broadway
Gallimard
Greenbook Publications
MacMillan
Microsoft
Orb Books
Picador
Wiley
```

Each publisher now appears only once on the list, and the result is sorted alphabetically, in default ascending order. If you're saying that the same could be achieved by simply selecting BK_PUBLISHER with the DISTINCT keyword, you are absolutely correct. In fact, there is a good chance that behind the scenes RDBMSs would treat both statements in the same way, preparing the same execution plan (see Chapter 9 for more information on execution plans and query optimization).

GROUP BY with HAVING Clause

With all the power a GROUP BY clause brings to the table it lacks the selectivity afforded by the WHERE clause. When all data is aggregated, how do you select a set with an average greater than $20 (a question we had asked at the beginning of the section)? One way is to use a subquery (covered in the next chapter), another way is to create a view (see Chapter 7), and then there is the HAVING clause. Let's find the publishers of the books in our library with average book prices over $20:

```
SELECT
    bk_publisher AS publisher
  , AVG(bk_price) AS avg_price
FROM books
   GROUP BY bk_publisher
      HAVING AVG(bk_price) > 20;

publisher                 avg_price
------------------------- --------------------
Gallimard                69.26
MacMillan                38.88
Microsoft Press          24.99
Wiley                    37.9075
```

The AVG() function is used both in the SELECT list and in the HAVING clause, but it does not have to be. It was included only to show that the average prices were indeed in the specified range. At the same time, should you decide to include the BK_PRICE column in the SELECT list, it can only appear as an argument for some aggregate function.

Being able to use aggregate functions as a filtering criterion certainly adds to the selectivity of the query, but, again, you don't have to. If you decide to select records with simply BK_PRICE > 20, you can do that, although you would have to include the BK_PRICE in both the SELECT list and GROUP BY clauses, with very little to show up for the effort. The two following queries produce almost identical results on our data set:

```
SELECT
    bk_publisher
   ,bk_price
FROM books
  GROUP BY bk_publisher,bk_price
    HAVING bk_price > 20;

bk_publisher                      bk_price
--------------------------------- ---------------------
Gallimard                         69.26
MacMillan                         38.88
```

```
Microsoft Press                  24.99
Wiley                            26.39
Wiley                            29.99
Wiley                            39.99
Wiley                            55.26

SELECT
    bk_price
   ,bk_publisher
FROM books
    WHERE bk_price > 20;

bk_price              bk_publisher
--------------------- -----------------------
39.99                 Wiley
55.26                 Wiley
29.99                 Wiley
26.39                 Wiley
69.26                 Gallimard
24.99                 Microsoft Press
38.88                 MacMillan
```

In both cases, seven records were selected, and the only difference is that with GROUP BY you get the result set to be ordered by BK_PRICE. This brings us to the next section: sorting the output.

ORDER BY Clause: Sorting Query Output

The default order of a query's results is usually the order in which the records were entered into the table; queries with the GROUP BY clause return results in ascending order for the value in the last column on the GROUP BY list. There is a way to force the order; we are referring to the ORDER BY clause introduced in Chapter 2.

There are two ways to order the result — ascending and descending — and with ordering by multiple columns you can have both. Consider the following query:

```
SELECT
     bk_publisher  AS publisher
    ,bk_price      AS price
FROM books
    ORDER BY bk_publisher ASC;
publisher                                 price
----------------------------------------- ---------------------
Ace Trade                                 16.29
Broadway                                  18.48
Gallimard                                 69.26
Greenbook Publications                     8.89
MacMillan                                 38.88
Microsoft Press                           24.99
Orb Books                                 16.29
Picador                                   10.20
Wiley                                     39.99
Wiley                                     55.26
Wiley                                     29.99
Wiley                                     26.39
```

Predictably, we see results organized by publisher in ascending order (the default in all RDBMSs, but the ASC modifier is added to demonstrate the point). Now, by adding BK_PRICE DESC to the ORDER BY clause we instruct the database engine to organize the returned records *first* in ascending order by publisher and *then* in descending order by price:

```
SELECT
     bk_publisher  AS publisher
    ,bk_price      AS price
FROM books
    ORDER BY   bk_publisher ASC
, bk_price DESC;
publisher                                price
---------------------------------------- ----------
Ace Trade                                16.29
Broadway                                 18.48
Gallimard                                69.26
Greenbook Publications                    8.89
MacMillan                                38.88
Microsoft Press                          24.99
Orb Books                                16.29
Picador                                  10.20
Wiley                                    55.26
Wiley                                    39.99
Wiley                                    29.99
Wiley                                    26.39
```

If you notice familiarity with the results produced by the GROUP BY clause, you are absolutely right: the records are grouped by the columns, cascading from the first on the list through the last. The use of the ORDER BY clause with GROUP BY is no different, with one important exception: in this case, it can be used with aggregate functions. Because it is the last filter to be applied after all other processing had been done, it must go at the very end of a query.

In Chapter 2, we introduced the TOP and LIMIT keywords as a means to restrict the number of records returned by a query (known as the "top N queries" problem). When using SQL aggregated functions without the GROUP BY clause, we naturally receive but a single record; when there is a need to limit output of a query that does use the clause, LIMIT and TOP could be used just as you would use them in a standard SELECT query.

An important thing to keep in mind is that the more clauses you pile onto your query, the more complex interactions become, and the results might not be quite what you might have expected.

Here is the query that reverses the default ascending order by BK_PUBLISHER imposed by the GROUP BY clause:

```
SELECT
   bk_publisher  AS publisher
  ,AVG(bk_price) AS avg_price
FROM books
    GROUP BY bk_publisher
```

```
        ORDER BY bk_publisher DESC;

Publisher                avg_price
----------------------- --------------
Wiley                   37.9075
Picador                 10.20
Orb Books               16.29
Microsoft               24.99
MacMillan               38.88
Broadway                18.48
Greebook Publications    8.89
Gallimard               69.26
Ace Trade               16.29
```

If we want to order the results by BK_PRICE, which is not on the SELECT list, we'd have to add BK_PRICE to GROUP BY clause list. Note that ORDER BY overrides the sort order imposed by GROUP BY, and now we have 12 records returned instead of 9, as it was the case in the previous example, because now we are GROUP(ing) by the *combination of both* publisher and price.

```
SELECT
   bk_publisher  AS publisher
  ,AVG(bk_price) AS avg_price
FROM books
    GROUP BY bk_publisher,bk_price
        ORDER BY bk_price DESC;
publisher                              avg_price
-------------------------------------- ---------------------
Gallimard                              69.26
Wiley                                  55.26
Wiley                                  39.99
MacMillan                              38.88
Wiley                                  29.99
Wiley                                  26.39
Microsoft Press                        24.99
Broadway                               18.48
Ace Trade                              16.29
Orb Books                              16.29
Picador                                10.20
Greenbook Publications                  8.89
```

To use the full power of aggregate functions, we could order the final result set by a product of an aggregate function; for example, by average book price for that publisher in descending order:

```
SELECT
    bk_publisher  AS publisher
   ,AVG(bk_price) AS avg_price
FROM books
    GROUP BY bk_publisher
        ORDER BY AVG(bk_price) DESC

publisher                       avg_price
------------------------------- ---------------------
Gallimard                       69.26
MacMillan                       38.88
```

```
Wiley                        37.9075
Microsoft Press              24.99
Broadway                     18.48
Ace Trade                    16.29
Orb Books                    16.29
Picador                      10.20
Greenbook Publications        8.89
```

Comparing the results with the almost identical query used earlier, you can see that ORDER BY overwrote the order introduced by the GROUP BY clause; additionally, the GROUP BY collapsed BK_PUBLISHER columns into groups (9 versus 12 in the previous example), which did not happen when both BK_PUBLISHER and BK_PRICE were employed. The reason behind this behavior is that grouping by publisher yields 9 distinct groups in our table; grouping by publisher *and* price makes it 12 distinct groups.

TRY IT OUT Bringing It All Together

You've learned about aggregate functions and the GROUP BY, HAVING, and ORDER BY clauses. Let's bring all them together to extract information from our tables, which would require tedious manual effort to produce without SQL and relational databases. In this exercise, we will find the lowest-priced book on the fourth shelf of our bookcase using Microsoft SQL Server 2008 as our RDBMS database engine.

1. Open Microsoft SQL Server Management Studio and connect to your database using Windows authentication.
2. In the upper-left corner click the New Query button.
3. In the query window, enter the following query and click the Execute button, located on the same toolbar as the New Query button:

```
SELECT
   bk_publisher  AS publisher
 , MIN(bk_price) AS cheapest_book
FROM BOOKS
    INNER JOIN location ON bk_id=fk_bk_loc
        GROUP BY bk_publisher, loc_shelf
            HAVING loc_shelf = 4
                ORDER BY MIN(bk_price)

publisher            cheapest_book
-------------------- --------------------
Microsoft             24.99
Broadway              18.48
```

How It Works

The task of finding the cheapest book would definitely involve an aggregate MIN() function that returns the least value found in the column for all records. The additional constraint was to find the cheapest book, not in the entire collection, but on the fourth shelf of our bookcase. This means that we would need data from two tables (BOOKS and LOCATION). The final requirement was to find the cheapest book for every publisher whose books are on this shelf.

The records were selected from BOOKS and LOCATION joined on the PRIMARY/FOREIGN key relationship, GROUP(ed) BY the two columns BK_PUBLISHER and LOC_SHELF. The results were narrowed down to only these on the fourth shelf by imposing HAVING loc_shelf = 4 limit, and ordered in default ascending order on the least price with the ORDER BY clause.

While not the only way to produce the desired results, it certainly allowed us to utilize all concepts introduced in this chapter.

SUMMARY

Grouping and aggregation in SQL provide a user with a 10,000-foot view of the data, as opposed to the minute details of individual records. The aggregated data is returned as a single record, regardless of how many individual records there might be in the table. SQL aggregate functions are mostly used with numeric data, and some could work with other data types (such as characters and dates). Aggregate functions could employ additional DISTINCT keywords to filter data prior to aggregation.

More than a single record could be returned with aggregate SQL functions when used in conjunction with the GROUP BY clause, which groups aggregate values based on criteria specified in the clause. To allow for an additional selection filter based upon aggregated values, a special HAVING clause is used, which acts as a WHERE clause for the GROUP BY data sets.

The returned records could be further ordered using the ORDER BY clause, which is the final filter applied to the records returned by a query.

When One Is Not Enough: A Query Within a Query

SQL allows for nesting queries, putting a SQL statement within another SELECT statement. Readers familiar with programming concepts might compare it to a nested loop structure, or you can visualize a telescopic tube with nested segments.

WHAT YOU DON'T KNOW MIGHT HELP YOU

A *subquery* is an answer to several questions rolled up into a single statement. It is a variation on the concept "I do not know, but I know someone who does."

Subquery in the WHERE Clause

The subquery can be used almost anywhere in the SQL statement, but the most common use is in the WHERE clause.

To illustrate the concept, let's try to find what books we might have on the top (fifth) shelf in the bookcase: "The one in the living room to the right":

```
SELECT bk_title, bk_publisher FROM books
    WHERE bk_id IN (SELECT fk_bk_loc FROM location
        WHERE loc_shelf = 5)
bk_title                                             bk_publisher
---------------------------------------------------- -------------------
SQL Bible                                             Wiley
Wiley Pathways: Introduction to Database Management   Wiley
Microsoft SQL Server 2000 Weekend Crash Course        Wiley
SQL Functions: Programmers Reference                  Wiley
```

All we knew in this case (no pun intended!) was that we wanted books stored on shelf #5, and the relation between the BOOKS and LOCATION tables specified by primary/foreign keys, respectively. The subquery was executed first; it returned all the values (book ID(s)) associated with shelf #5 (LOC_SHELF column) in the bookcase with the unwieldy name 'The one in the living room to the right':

```
SELECT fk_bk_loc FROM location WHERE loc_shelf = 5
fk_bk_loc
---------------
1
2
3
4
```

Then the outermost query matched the BK_ID values with the returned list and made the selection from BOOKS table.

A subquery is also called an *inner query* or *inner select*, while the statement containing a subquery is also called an *outer query* or *outer select*. The SELECT query of a subquery is always enclosed in parentheses.

EXISTS Operator

The IN operator allows for undefined search criteria; any of the values on the list returned by the subquery would work; the same goes for the EXISTS operator, as well as the opposites NOT IN and NOT EXISTS. Additionally, the latter does not require any fields to be listed in the WHERE clause; it just checks that at least a single record was returned by the subquery:

```
SELECT bk_title, bk_publisher FROM books
    WHERE EXISTS (SELECT * FROM location
        WHERE loc_shelf = 5)
bk_title                                             bk_publisher
---------------------------------------------------- ----------------------------------
SQL Bible                                            Wiley
Wiley Pathways: Introduction to Database Management  Wiley
Microsoft SQL Server 2000 Weekend Crash Course       Wiley
. . .
A Short History of Nearly Everything                 Broadway
Steppenwolf                                          Picador

(12 row(s) affected)
```

You might expect that the preceding query would return results identical to the query that uses the IN operator, but you got all 12 books instead — not just those located on the fifth shelf. The reason is simple: The subquery always returns TRUE because there are four books on the shelf, and the outer query returns the records from the BOOKS table WHERE "there is always something on fifth shelf" (which there is). Therefore, all 12 records were returned. In each of these cases, there is no practical limit on the number of rows returned by the subquery.

It is possible to impose exact conditions on the result returned by the subquery with the equal (=) operator; this in turn requires limiting the subquery results to exactly one row. This is known as a *scalar subquery*, a subquery that returns only a single value. If we re-run the query after replacing the IN operator with =, we'll get an error saying that the subquery returned more than one value.

One way to avoid this is to force the query to return exactly one record, as in the following query, which uses Microsoft SQL Server syntax (refer to Chapter 2 for RDBMS-specific limits):

```
SELECT bk_title, bk_publisher FROM books
    WHERE bk_id = (SELECT TOP 1 fk_bk_loc FROM location
        WHERE loc_shelf = 5)
bk_title                                             bk_publisher
---------------------------------------------------- -------------------
SQL Bible                                             Wiley
```

Note that we must specify a column in the subquery to be matched exactly to that in the WHERE clause of the outer query; inequality comparison operators (!=,<,<=,>,>=) can be used in the preceding query as well.

ANY Operator

Using additional operators such as ANY helps to introduce some flexibility. This query matches BK_ID against any value returned by the subquery. Notice that we do not have to limit the number of rows, and that the results are identical to the query which uses IN operator:

```
SELECT bk_title, bk_publisher FROM books
    WHERE bk_id = ANY (SELECT fk_bk_loc FROM location
        WHERE loc_shelf = 5)
bk_title                                             bk_publisher
---------------------------------------------------- -------------------
SQL Bible                                             Wiley
Wiley Pathways: Introduction to Database Management   Wiley
Microsoft SQL Server 2000 Weekend Crash Course        Wiley
SQL Functions: Programmers Reference                  Wiley
```

ALL Operator

Using the ALL operator requires matching all BK_ID(s) returned from the subquery, which is impossible; a single value cannot match more than a single one. Inequality operators such as < and > work well here. For instance, to ask for all records where BK_ID is less than all the values on the list, we would use the following:

```
SELECT bk_title, bk_publisher FROM books
    WHERE bk_id < ALL (SELECT fk_bk_loc FROM location
        WHERE loc_shelf = 5)
bk_title                                             bk_publisher
---------------------------------------------------- -------------------
```

Not a single record. Why? Just recall from Chapter 2 that the ANY operator will evaluate the expression to TRUE if any of the values on the list complies with the condition, while ALL requires every value on the list to do the same. Since one of the books on the fifth shelf has BK_ID=1 (*SQL Bible*), the outer query has to find something that is less than 1, so the recordset is empty.

Another way to ensure that one and only one record is selected is to use aggregate functions such as MAX, COUNT, or AVG.

This behavior is consistent across all RDBMSs discussed in the book.

The SELECT query of a subquery is always enclosed in parentheses. It cannot include a COMPUTE or FOR BROWSE clause, and may only include an ORDER BY clause when a TOP (LIMIT) clause is also specified.

Subquery in the SELECT List

As mentioned before, a subquery can be used virtually anywhere in an SQL statement; the usual suspects are components where expressions are used. The following example demonstrates how a subquery is being used in a SELECT list of a SELECT query:

```
SELECT bk_title, bk_publisher,
(SELECT TOP 1 au_last_name FROM
    authors a JOIN books_authors ba
ON (a.au_id=ba.au_id)
      JOIN books b ON(ba.bk_id=b.bk_id))AS author
FROM books ;
bk_title                                   bk_pu                     author
------------------------------------------ ----------------------    -------
SQL Bible                                  Wiley                     Kriegel
Wiley Pathways: Introduction to Database...  Wiley                   Kriegel
Microsoft SQL Server 2000 Weekend...       Wiley                     Kriegel
SQL Functions: Programmers Reference       Wiley                     Kriegel
A La Recherche du Temps Perdu              Gallimard                 Kriegel
After the Gold Rush: Creating...           Microsoft Press           Kriegel
Letters From Earth                         Greenbook Publications    Kriegel
Mindswap                                   Orb Books                 Kriegel
Stranger in a Strange Land                 Ace Trade                 Kriegel
Jonathan Livingston Seagull                MacMillan                 Kriegel
A Short History of Nearly Everything       Broadway                  Kriegel
Steppenwolf                                Picador                   Kriegel
```

A full 12 records are returned, but every single row returned to the client is stamped with the same author's last name — whoever happened to come at the top of the list (it can be changed using the ORDER BY clause in the subquery). Not a result we've been looking for.

To remedy this situation, you can use correlated query *(discussed later in the chapter).*

In noncorrelated subqueries, it is more common to use aggregate functions to add the same value to all records returned by the outer query. Here is a query demonstrating this concept (at the expense of stretching usability limits; the same result can be achieved using just the MAX function, without wrapping it in a subquery):

```
SELECT bk_title,
    (SELECT MAX(bk_price)FROM books) AS max_price
FROM books;
bk_title                                             max_price
-------------------------------------------------   ---------------
SQL Bible                                            69.26
Wiley Pathways: Introduction to Database Management  69.26
Microsoft SQL Server 2000 Weekend Crash Course       69.26
. . .
A Short History of Nearly Everything                 69.26
Steppenwolf                                          69.26

(12 row(s) affected)
```

Of course, the same MAX value will be in every row returned by the query (but this is what we asked for). The rules for subqueries in the SELECT list are the same as for scalar subqueries used in the WHERE clause, and they can be used, with slight modifications, across all RDBMSs we're discussing here.

Only a single column can appear in the single subquery on the SELECT list. If you need more than one, use separate subqueries or concatenate fields:

```
SELECT bk_title
     , bk_publisher
     , (SELECT MAX(bk_price)FROM books) AS max_price
     , (SELECT MIN(bk_price)FROM books) AS min_price
FROM books;bk_title                                     max_price       min_price
-------------------------------------------------   --------------- ---------
SQL Bible                                            69.26           8.89
Wiley Pathways: Introduction to Database Management  69.26           8.89
Microsoft SQL Server 2000 Weekend Crash Course       69.26           8.89
. . .
A Short History of Nearly Everything                 69.26           8.89
Steppenwolf                                          69.26           8.89

(12 row(s) affected)
```

TRY IT OUT Finding the Highest-Priced Book on the Shelf

Let's apply what we've learned so far to a practical exercise for finding the highest-priced book on the fourth shelf of our library's bookcase.

1. Open your favorite SQL client to connect to the RDBMS.
2. Switch the context to the LIBRARY database:

```
USE library;
```

3. Execute the following SQL statement:

```
SELECT TOP 1
    bk_title AS Title
 , bk_price AS max_price
 FROM books
    WHERE bk_id IN (SELECT fk_bk_loc FROM location
       WHERE loc_shelf = 4
          AND loc_bookcase ='The one in the living room to the right')
ORDER BY bk_price DESC

Title                                                  max_price
--------------------------------------------------   ----------------
After the Gold Rush: Creating a True Profession....    24.99
```

How It Works

The subquery in the WHERE clause returns all ID(s) for the books located on the fourth shelf of the bookcase with the somewhat unwieldy name 'The one in the living room to the right,' and the outer query matches these IDs to select records from the BOOKS table.

The final step is sorting these records in descending order by BK_PRICE, ensuring that the highest-priced book is on top of the list, and then selecting the TOP 1 record from this list.

Note that this is not the only way to get the desired outcome. A query with the GROUP BY . . . HAVING clause might be a better choice.

Subquery in the FROM Clause

A subquery can appear virtually anywhere in the SQL statement. The WHERE and HAVING clauses are the most popular examples, but you are not limited to them. A subquery can serve as the ad hoc view (see Chapter 7), also called an *inline view*. For example, the following query allows for selecting from an inline view named AdHoc. It ties together AUTHORS, BOOKS, and the intermediate BOOKS_AUTHORS table, joined with a LOCATION table to produce a combined result with the AUTHORS table (supplying the author's first name), the BOOKS table (book title) and LOCATION table, and the "name" for the bookcase:

```
SELECT
FirstName
, BookTitle
, BookID
,location.loc_bookcase
FROM
(SELECT DISTINCT
a.au_first_name AS FirstName
,b.bk_title AS BookTitle
```

```
,b.bk_id AS BookID
FROM authors a
INNER JOIN books_authors ba ON a.au_id = ba.au_id
INNER JOIN books b ON ba.bk_id=b.bk_id ) AdHoc
INNER JOIN location ON location.fk_bk_loc = AdHoc.BookID;
FirstName     BookTitle                                 BookID  loc_bookcase
------------- ----------------------------------------- ------- -----------------------
Alexander     SQL Bible                                 1       The one in the living...
Alexander     Introduction to Database Management       2       The one in the living...
Alexander     SQL Server 2000 Weekend Crash Course      3       The one in the living...
Alexander     SQL Functions: Programmers Reference      4       The one in the living...
. . .
```

We get back 23 records, even though there are only 12 books listed in our BOOKS table. The reason is that some books have more than one author, and they all have a row of their own. While the query can be easily re-created with a four-way JOIN, it makes the query more readable because of logical separation. An important nuance: The inline view must be named (AdHoc, in our case) even if you do not intend to JOIN it with any other view or table.

We are using aliasing of the tables because of a possible ambiguity in the table names appearing both in outer and inner queries. The SQL engine cannot guess our intentions; it must be told exactly what to do.

Subquery in the HAVING Clause

The HAVING clause in GROUP BY implements the same idea as the WHERE clause used in the standard SELECT statement: it narrows down selection criteria used for aggregation.

The books are getting pricier by the year, and if you set an average list price at about $20, it might be interesting to find out which of the books you own are above (or below) the average. Let's narrow our search even further — to the top shelf of our bookcase — using one of the previous examples:

```
SELECT
    bk_title AS Title
 ,  bk_price
 FROM books
     WHERE bk_id IN (SELECT fk_bk_loc FROM location
       WHERE loc_shelf = 5
          AND loc_bookcase ='The one in the living room to the right')
GROUP BY bk_price, bk_title
HAVING bk_price > 20
Title                                                       bk_price
----------------------------------------------------------- ------------
SQL Functions: Programmers Reference                        26.39
```

```
Microsoft SQL Server 2000 Weekend Crash Course                    29.99
SQL Bible                                                         39.99
Wiley Pathways: Introduction to Database Management               55.26
```

We have four books with list price above average. But guessing the average price, and using it as a hard-coded value, are not the best coding practices though; it would be much better to be able to calculate the average price of all the books you own and compare it to the book prices on the fifth shelf:

```
SELECT
    bk_title AS Title
 ,  bk_price
 FROM books
     WHERE bk_id IN (SELECT fk_bk_loc FROM location
       WHERE loc_shelf = 5
          AND loc_bookcase ='The one in the living room to the right')
GROUP BY bk_price, bk_title
HAVING bk_price >(SELECT AVG(bk_price) FROM books);
Title                                                  bk_price
------------------------------------------------------ ---------------------
Microsoft SQL Server 2000 Weekend Crash Course         29.99
SQL Bible                                              39.99
Wiley Pathways: Introduction to Database Management    55.26
```

Apparently our guess was wrong; the average of all the books we've accumulated on the shelf must be higher than $20 because we see two books disappearing from the list. Indeed, running a quick query confirms it; our average price is above $28:

```
SELECT AVG(bk_price) AS AvgPrice
     , MIN(bk_price) AS MinPrice
     , MAX(bk_price) AS MaxPrice
  FROM books;
AvgPrice              MinPrice              MaxPrice
--------------------- --------------------- ---------------------
29.5758               8.89                  69.26
```

A subquery in the HAVING clause can use aggregate functions on both sides of the expression, with all operators (IN, ANY, ALL, and so on) except the EXISTS operator.

TRY IT OUT Using the Subquery in the GROUP BY ... HAVING Clause

How do you get a list of titles and publishers located on a bookshelf with the goofy name 'The one in the living room to the right' containing only books published in 2005 or later? One way is to use a GROUP BY with HAVING clause. The following exercise uses Microsoft SQL Server syntax, but it can be adjusted to any other RDBMSs discussed in the book.

1. Open your favorite SQL client to connect to the RDBMS.
2. Switch the context to the LIBRARY database:

   ```
   USE library;
   ```

3. Execute the following SQL statement:

   ```
   SELECT loc_shelf
       , bk_publisher
   ```

```
     , bk_title
    FROM books b JOIN location l ON (b.bk_id=l.fk_bk_loc)
GROUP BY
    loc_shelf
  , bk_title
  , bk_publisher
       HAVING loc_shelf IN
          (SELECT loc_shelf FROM location
             WHERE fk_bk_loc IN (SELECT bk_id FROM books
                                      WHERE bk_published_year  >= 2005
                   AND loc_bookcase='The one in the living room to the right'))
loc_shelf   bk_title                               bk_publisher
----------- -------------------------------------- ------------------------------
2           A La Recherche du Temps Perdu           Gallimard
2           Letters From Earth                      Greebook Publications
2           Steppenwolf                             Picador
3           Jonathan Livingston Seagull             MacMillan
3           Mindswap                                Orb Books
3           Stranger in a Starnge Land              Ace Trade
4           A Short History of Nearly Everything    Broadway
4           After the Gold Rush                     Microsoft
5           SQL Server 2000 Weekend Crash Course    Wiley
5           SQL Bible                               Wiley
5           SQL Functions: Programmers Reference    Wiley
5           ..Introduction to Database Management   Wiley

(12 row(s) affected)
```

How It Works

As in the examples throughout the chapter, the subquery contained in the HAVING clause executes first, replacing the expression with a list of book ID(s) published on or later than the year 2005. Then the outer query gets executed, assembling records from values found in both BOOKS and LOCATION, and grouping them by the shelf number for all the shelves holding the books with ID(s) found in the subquery.

Subqueries with INSERT

Inserting values into a table returned by a SELECT statement might come in handy when transferring data between compatible table structures. The data can come from a different table, a view, or even from the very same table. For instance, if you just bought a second edition of a book and want to transfer most, but not all, values from the first edition, you can run the following query:

```
INSERT INTO books(
    bk_id
  , bk_title
   ,bk_publisher)
    SELECT 100, bk_title, bk_publisher
WHERE bk_id = 1;
```

The preceding statement will transfer the book title and the publisher name for a single record, leaving every other column to be filled with default values. As you can see, the mix-and-match approach works here. The hard-coded values can also be used alongside the column names in the SELECT statement.

The requirement is that the number of the values and the respective data types must match the list of columns in the INSERT statement. For instance, we can supply hard-coded values only, and can still insert values:

```
INSERT INTO books(
    bk_id
  , bk_title)
    SELECT 100,'Some book title';
```

More than one record can be inserted at once — an example of the set-based language power — although you cannot get around constraints placed on the table. In the previous example, the primary key constraint will prevent you from entering records with duplicate BK_ID, but it will work with an empty table.

TRY IT OUT INSERTing Records with a Subquery

To transfer all, or a subset of, records into a table, one can use a subquery with an INSERT statement, selecting records from an existing table. If the table were constrained by a UNIQUE or PRIMARY KEY constraint, it must be empty to avoid violating the constraint.

Let's create a separate table and transfer to it only books located on the fifth shelf of our bookcase.

1. Open your favorite SQL client to connect to the RDBMS.
2. Switch the context to the LIBRARY database:

   ```
   USE library;
   ```

3. Create an empty table with a PRIMARY KEY constraint, with a basic syntax, using all default options:

   ```
   CREATE TABLE MyBooksonFifthShelf(
       bk_id                bigint          NOT NULL
      ,bk_title             varchar(100)    NULL
      ,bk_ISBN              varchar(50)     NULL
      ,bk_publisher         varchar(100)    NULL
      ,bk_published_year    int             NULL
      ,bk_price             smallmoney      NULL
      ,bk_page_count        int             NULL
      ,bk_bought_on         smalldatetime   NULL
      ,bk_hard_cover        bit             NULL
      ,bk_cover_pic         varbinary(max)  NULL
      ,bk_note              xml             NULL
    CONSTRAINT PK_MyBooks PRIMARY KEY CLUSTERED
   (
     bk_id ASC
   ))
   ```

4. Transfer all records from BOOKS table to the MyBooks table for the books located on the fifth shelf of the bookcase:

   ```
   INSERT INTO MyBooksonFifthShelf
       SELECT * FROM books
   ```

```
WHERE bk_id IN (SELECT fk_bk_loc FROM location
       WHERE loc_shelf = 5
          AND loc_bookcase ='The one in the living room to the right')
```

5. Verify that correct records were transferred:

```
SELECT bk_id, bk_title from MyBooksonFifthShelf;
bk_id                bk_title
-------------------- ---------------------------------------------------
1                    SQL Bible
2                    Wiley Pathways: Introduction to Database Management
3                    Microsoft SQL Server 2000 Weekend Crash Course
4                    SQL Functions: Programmers Reference

(4 row(s) affected)
```

How It Works

The SELECT statement takes everything found in the BOOKS table, including the values for the BK_ID column, which has a PRIMARY KEY constraint placed on it; it will not accept duplicate values. Since we are inserting all unique values into BK_ID column as part of our overall query, there are no conflicts, and all rows are transferred successfully.

The restriction can be bypassed if we do not try to insert values into a primary key column, but declare it as an IDENTITY column instead (or its equivalent in RDBMSs other than Microsoft SQL Server). The IDENTITY constraint will take care of creating unique values for each record inserted. Of course, this would allow you to insert rows that would only differ in the BK_ID values.

Subqueries with UPDATE

A subquery can be used as an assignment value in an UPDATE statement as long as the subquery returns a single value at a time. If no rows are returned, the NULL value will be assigned to the target column in the outer UPDATE statement. Both noncorrelated and correlated subqueries can be used (discussed later in the chapter), and the values from different columns can be concatenated.

Getting a little bit ahead of ourselves, we can use a correlated subquery to update the BK_NOTES column in the BOOKS table with information based upon the very values already contained in the columns in an XML string (see Chapter 11 for more information on XML and semistructured data):

```
UPDATE books SET bk_notes =
    ( SELECT '<books><book><title>'+ bk_title + '</title>'
        + '<authors><author></author></authors>'
        + '<publisher>' + bk_publisher +' </publisher>'
        + '<price>' + CAST(bk_price AS VARCHAR(10))
        + '</price></book></books>'
FROM books sub
    WHERE sub.bk_id = books.bk_id)
```

Here we use a correlated subquery (see the next section) because we want to update each record with relevant information, specific to this particular book, not the same value for all the records in the table. The noncorrelated version would simply use the same value for all rows of the column.

To verify the inserted values, run a SELECT statement on the column (the BK_Notes value wrapped to the next line due to constraints of the page):

```
SELECT bk_id, bk_notes FROM books
WHERE bk_id= 1;
bk_id   bk_notes
------- ------------------------------------------------------------------------------
1      <books><book><title>SQL Bible</title><authors><author/></authors>
<publisher>Wiley </publisher><price>39.99</price></book></books>
1      <books><book><title>Wiley Pathways: Introduction to Database
Management</title><authors><author/></authors><publisher>Wiley
</publisher><price>55.26</price></book></books>
```

We have a basic XML document that can be further updated and expanded using techniques described in Chapter 11 of this book.

The XML string has to be well formed, meaning that each element must have an opening tag and a corresponding closing tag in order to be entered into the XML data type field as a string (it will be parsed and converted into XML upon UPDATE). The Microsoft SQL Server will warn you if your XML string violates this rule. For example: removing but one opening tag <author> would result in an error.

```
Msg 9436, Level 16, State 1, Line 1
XML parsing: line 1, character 55, end tag does not match start tag
```

Subqueries with DELETE

Suppose you removed a book from your collection and now you need to clean up your tables from the obsolete records. With relational databases, there is quite a bit of cleaning to do, unraveling all the relationships starting with the "childmost" table. In the preceding scenario, you need to remove a record from LOCATION, SearchTags, SearchBooks, and BOOKS_AUTHORS; and only then you can delete it from the BOOKS and AUTHORS tables. This is quite a bit of work to be performed, and most likely you will have to use more than one DELETE statement wrapped inside a transaction (to maintain the integrity of the database; see Chapter 3 for more information on integrity and Chapter 10 for transactions information).

To demonstrate the use of a subquery in a DELETE statement, you will remove a record from the LOCATION table based only on a fuzzy recollection that it was on the fifth shelf and had the word "Gold" in its title (*After the Gold Rush*: *Creating a True Profession of Software Engineering*).

Deleting a record based on assumption is never a good idea because you might inadvertently delete records you didn't want to delete. Always make sure that precise criteria uniquely identifying the records are specified.

The following query will remove BK_ID associated with the book from the LOCATION table:

```
DELETE location
    WHERE fk_bk_loc =
        (SELECT bk_id FROM books WHERE bk_title LIKE'%Gold%')
```

Once the query is executed, the record is gone, and the BOOKS table will contain a book without an assigned location on the shelf in the bookcase. You can restore it by inserting the data back.

```
INSERT INTO location (
    loc_id
   ,fk_bk_loc
   ,loc_bookcase
   ,loc_shelf
   ,loc_position_left)
VALUES(5,6,'The one in the living room to the right',4,1)
```

Or if you run it within a transaction, roll back the changes (see Chapter 10 for information on transactions). Another option is drop and re-create the entire table from the scripts posted on `www.wrox.com` and `www.agilitator.com`.

CORRELATED QUERY

Normally, a subquery has no awareness of the outer query of which it is a part. It executes as if it were a stand-alone SELECT statement and could not care less what and how it was invoked. A correlated subquery changes this. In the case of a "standard" subquery, the statement is evaluated once, and the results are passed on to serve as a filter for the outer query. In correlated mode, the outer query must be invoked multiple times, once for each record returned by the inner query.

A *correlated subquery* (one in which the WHERE condition depends on values obtained from the rows of the containing query) executes once for each row. A *noncorrelated subquery* (one in which the WHERE condition is independent of the containing query) executes once at the beginning. The SQL engine makes this distinction automatically.

The classic use of the correlated subquery is in the WHERE clause. Let's consider the query we created earlier:

```
SELECT bk_title, bk_publisher FROM books
    WHERE EXISTS(SELECT * FROM location
        WHERE location.loc_shelf = 5 and location.fk_bk_loc = books.bk_id )
bk_title                                              bk_publisher
----------------------------------------------------------------------------
SQL Bible                                             Wiley
Wiley Pathways: Introduction to Database Management   Wiley
Microsoft SQL Server 2000 Weekend Crash Course        Wiley
SQL Functions: Programmers Reference                  Wiley

(4 row(s) affected)
```

By using the EXISTS operator, we now do not have to specify BK_ID in the WHERE clause of the outer SELECT statement. Even though it might appear counterintuitive, a subquery still executes first with values from the LOCATION table; then the outer query (the one that SELECTS data from the BOOKS table) gets executed with BK_ID, satisfying the expression with the EXISTS operator. This makes a correlated query rather an expensive affair, though not in every case. Some query optimization and well-selected indices might improve performance dramatically (see Chapter 9 for information on optimization techniques).

TRY IT OUT Listing Book Titles and Corresponding Authors with a Correlated Subquery

Previously we wrote a query that returned book titles and authors using a subquery in a SELECT statement SELECT list and it only worked for the first record on the list. Every other record was matched with the same author. A correlated query can remedy this situation.

1. Open your favorite SQL client to connect to the RDBMS.
2. Switch the context to the LIBRARY database:

```
USE library;
```

3. Execute the following SQL statement (to shorten the list, we added ellipses to signify omitted records):

```
SELECT bk_title, bk_publisher,
(SELECT TOP 1 au_last_name FROM
    authors a JOIN books_authors ba
ON (a.au_id=ba.au_id)
      JOIN books b ON(ba.bk_id=b.bk_id)
WHERE b.bk_id= outer_b.bk_id ORDER BY au_last_name ASC)AS author
FROM books outer_b ;
bk_title                                bk_publisher                  author
--------------------------------     ---------------------------  --------------
SQL Bible                               Wiley                         Kriegel
. . .                                   . . .                         . . .
SQL Functions: Programmers Reference    Wiley                         Garrett
A La Recherche du Temps Perdu           Gallimard                     Proust
. . .
Letters From Earth                      Greebook Publications         Twain
Mindswap                                Orb Books                     Sheckley
. . .                                   . . .                         . . .
Steppenwolf                             Picador                       Hesse

(12 row(s) affected)
```

How It Works

The correlated subquery executes 12 times, once for each record in the outer query, because each time it is tied to a specific BOOK_ID, the one matching the outer query as requested in the (WHERE b.bk_id= outer_b.bk_id) condition. A matching author's last name is returned by the subquery to be joined to the final result set.

There is a caveat: this approach will only work with books that have one and only one author. The TOP 1 will cut off everybody but the topmost on the list of the returned values. The problem of pivoting columnar values to represent them as rows is an advanced subject, outside of the current book scope.

The correlated subqueries can be used everywhere noncorrelated subqueries can, with the very same restrictions and conditions. As you can imagine, there is a penalty to pay for the selectivity afforded by the correlated subquery. In the preceding example, the subquery would have to be executed 12 times: once for each row in the outer query; noncorrelated subqueries would execute only once.

HOW DEEP THE RABBIT HOLE GOES: NESTING SUBQUERIES

The subquery can host a subquery of its own, the sub-subquery can do the same, and the sub-sub-subquery...you get the picture. They are called *nested subqueries*: a query within a query within a query.

The following is an example of a nested query that tries to find information about books that we tagged as containing SQL references:

```
SELECT bk_id, bk_title FROM books
    WHERE bk_id IN
        (SELECT bk_id FROM search_books
            WHERE tag_id in
                (SELECT tag_id FROM searchTags
                  WHERE tag_value LIKE 'SQL%'))
bk_id    bk_title
-------- -------------------------------------------------------
1        SQL Bible
2        Wiley Pathways: Introduction to Database Management
3        Microsoft SQL Server 2000 Weekend Crash Course
4        SQL Functions: Programmers Reference

(4 row(s) affected)
```

Let's unravel the three queries. A subquery executes first. That is, the innermost query executes first, and the statement works up from there. In the previous example, the following query was executed first, and it returned a list of tag IDs associated with the books that have a title starting with *SQL*:

```
SELECT tag_id FROM searchTags WHERE tag_value LIKE 'SQL%'
tag_id
--------------------
1

(1 row(s) affected)
```

There is but one token (out of 28) which has "SQL" as its value. This could be verified by running a SELECT query against the SearchTags table. The next-level query now looks like this:

```
SELECT bk_id FROM search_books WHERE tag_id in (1)
bk_id
--------------------
1
```

```
2
3
4

(4 row(s) affected)
```

The tag ID 1 from the SearchTags table corresponds to four book ID(s) in there, and the result of this query is to produce yet another list of values: the BK_IDs from the SEARCH_BOOK table. The final query to be executed now looks like this:

```
SELECT * FROM books WHERE bk_id IN (1,2,3,4)
bk_id    bk_title
-------- ---------------------------------------------------
1        SQL Bible
2        Wiley Pathways: Introduction to Database Management
3        Microsoft SQL Server 2000 Weekend Crash Course
4        SQL Functions: Programmers Reference
```

This outermost query finally returns the results to you (or rather to the client application you are using).

There is no theoretical limit in SQL Standard on the nesting level (the number of times there can be a query within a query), but keep in mind that an SQL statement is a string that has a hard physical limit of a data type the operating system could handle, and RDBMS vendors might impose limits of their own.

The actual nesting level (how many subqueries you can have within one another) and exactly where the subquery appears in the statement are limited by the RDBMS capability. Microsoft SQL Server, for instance, used to put a hard limit of 32 nesting levels, which was lifted in version 2005, and it is unlimited now. Even now, the actual limit is based upon the complexity of the query and hardware configuration, and might be significantly lower (anything is smaller than infinity).

In its current version, Oracle supports up to 255 levels in the WHERE clause and allows unlimited nesting in FROM clause. DB2, PostgreSQL, and MySQL do not impose limits on the number of subqueries you can use, though all other restrictions, such as length of a SQL statement, still apply. The desktop RDBMSs such as Access and OpenOffice BASE do not specify how many levels you can go, but you are sure to get "the query is too complex" error once you approach 40 subqueries in one statement.

The correlated subqueries (discussed earlier in this chapter) impose additional complexity, and it is reasonable to expect that the nesting level would be reduced further.

A SUBQUERY OR A JOIN?

Subqueries in general (and nested subqueries in particular) can be alternatively formulated as JOIN statements. Other questions can only be answered with subqueries. Normally, there won't be any performance difference between a statement that includes a subquery and an equivalent JOIN version that does not. Nevertheless, in some cases, especially where an EXISTS operator is used, a JOIN yields better performance. A correlated subquery will almost always perform worse than a semantically equivalent JOIN, even though modern RDBMS's optimizers would likely create identical execution plans (see Chapter 9 for more information on query optimization) for either query type.

There is another important distinction. Unlike when using a JOIN, you cannot return a value retrieved in a subquery to your client; it's for internal consumption only.

The next chapter is dedicated to a detailed discussion of JOIN. While the syntax of a JOIN query is no less verbose, it can better optimize performance and is more readable than a nested subquery (though some RDBMSs internally convert subqueries into JOINs).

SUMMARY

A query within a query is a powerful mechanism to retrieve additional information. The subquery can appear in any type of SQL statement, including SELECT, INSERT, UPDATE, and DELETE. It can be used in any part of SQL statement clauses, including WHERE, FROM, and SELECT list.

There are two types of subqueries: correlated and noncorrelated. The former refers to a syntax in which the subquery references the outer query, and the latter represents a subquery that is independent of the outer query. A number of operators can be used to evaluate results returned by the subquery to the outer query, such as IN, EXISTS, ANY, SOME, and ALL. Subqueries can be used with the GROUP BY... HAVING clause in conjunction with aggregate functions.

Often, a subquery can be replaced with an equivalent JOIN syntax, which might result in performance gain. There is no practical limit on the nesting level for the subqueries, either correlated or noncorrelated, although some RDBMSs do impose limits.

7

You Broke It; You Fix It: Combining Data Sets

Let us recall from Chapter 3 that *normalization* of a relational database is the process of arranging the data with maximum precision and minimum duplication. This is largely achieved by establishing *relationships* between several tables that contain data. The relationships are established through the use of special values, called *keys*, which are unique to every record in the entire database.

Formal terminology of the relational theory could be quite confusing. Throughout the book I use friendly terms such as table, row, (record) and column, while the corresponding formal terms would be relation, tuple, and attribute.

This approach is good for maintaining data and minimizing inconsistencies, but it is not exactly user-friendly when it actually comes to *using* data. A cook would normally have all the ingredients lined up before she embarks on creating a dish, and then combining them according to certain rules. A user of the database must do something similar: Figure out the blocks of the data she wants to access and then fetch all the necessary data from various tables into one temporary structure, or *data set.* This is a job for the JOIN keyword, briefly touched on in early chapters.

JOINS REVISITED

The data in RDBMSs reside in tables which are linked via parent-child relationships, and the number of such links grows as the data model is taken through the normalization process.

Usually, the tables from which data are fetched (the source tables) are linked, or *joined*, in order to produce related data. In one of the tables, say, table BOOKS from our Library database, every row must have a unique key value (every row must be uniquely identified); in another table, LOCATION, there is a column where the keys from table BOOKS are stored. This column is said to contain the *foreign keys* for table BOOKS.

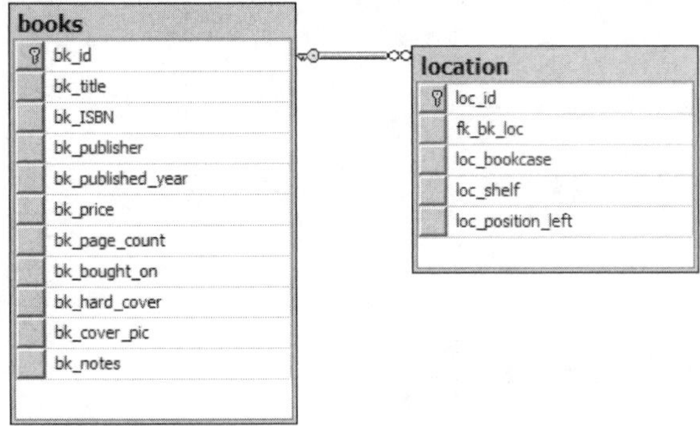

FIGURE 7-1

The diagram in Figure 7-1 is further explored in Figure 7-2, where it presents actual values, and the lines point out the relationship between the tables (because no orphaned records are allowed, every row in the table LOCATION will have a corresponding row in the table BOOKS. The reverse is not true, however, parent tables can have rows without corresponding rows in the child table. According to the best practices rule, each table also has a primary key: BK_ID and LOC_ID respectively. Table LOCATION also has foreign key: FK_BK_LOC.

	bk_title	bk_ISBN
1	SQL Bible	978-0470229064
2	Wiley Pathways: Introduction to Database Managem...	978-0470101865
3	Microsoft SQL Server 2000 Weekend Crash Course	978-0764548406
4	SQL Functions: Programmers Reference	978-0764569012
5	A La Recherche du Temps Perdu	978-2070754922
6	After the Gold Rush: Creating a True Profession of So...	978-0735608771
7	Letters From Earth	978-1617430060
8	Mindswap	978-0765315601
9	Stranger in a Strange Land	978-0441788385
10	Jonathan Livingston Seagull	978-0075119616
11	A Short History of Nearly Everything	978-0307885159
12	Steppenwolf	978-0312278670

	loc_id	fk_bk_loc	loc_bookcase	loc_shelf	loc_position_left
1	1	1	The one in the living room to the right	5	1
2	2	2	The one in the living room to the right	5	2
3	3	3	The one in the living room to the right	5	3
4	4	4	The one in the living room to the right	5	4
5	5	6	The one in the living room to the right	4	1
6	6	11	The one in the living room to the right	4	2
7	7	8	The one in the living room to the right	3	1
8	8	9	The one in the living room to the right	3	2
9	9	10	The one in the living room to the right	3	3
10	10	5	The one in the living room to the right	2	1
11	11	7	The one in the living room to the right	2	2
12	12	12	The one in the living room to the right	2	3

FIGURE 7-2

In the preceding example shown in Figure 7-2, the relation is established through BK_ID (the primary key) and FK_BK_LOC (the corresponding foreign key). There is one to one correspondence between the rows in the table BOOKS and the rows in the table LOCATION. This is not always the case. One or *more* rows in LOCATION table may contain the same key value for BOOKS, if we have multiple copies of the book, and, of course, there may be some rows in BOOKS for which there would be no matching data in LOCATION at all (for example, a new book, not yet assigned permanent location on the bookshelf), so they contain no value in that column (we say they contain NULL in that column). It is also worth noting that table LOCATION may contain foreign keys for several different tables.

In the preceding examples we assumed, for simplicity's sake, that a PRIMARY KEY consists of only one column. As mentioned before, this is not always the case. There could be composite primary and foreign keys comprising several columns. As long as the combination is unique within the table, and none of the columns contains NULL values, this would be a perfectly valid primary key candidate.

For example, the table BOOKS_AUTHORS from our Library database contains the foreign keys for both BOOKS and AUTHORS tables. Table 7-1 shows the resolution of a many-to-many situation through an intermediary table.

TABLE 7-1: Resolving a N:N Relationship

BOOKS		BOOKS_AUTHORS		AUTHORS	
bk_title	bk_id	bk_id	au_id	au_id	au_last_name
SQL Bible	1	1	1	1	Kriegel
...		1	2	2	Trukhnov

In a normalized database, there is a price to be exacted for reducing data redundancy. It was paid in increased navigational complexity for the normalized database. In order to associate an author with a book, we have to go through an intermediary table, with PRIMARY and FOREIGN keys as our only guidance to assemble our data set out of two (or more) tables.

There are several ways in which tables may be joined, discussed in the following section.

INNER JOIN

This is the most ubiquitous JOIN in the RDBMS world, and the sharpest tool in your toolbox. It combines data from several tables, and returns a subset where the data overlaps, as shown in Figure 7-3.

The tables are represented by the respective circles, and the shaded area represents the data set where JOIN conditions were satisfied. The records from either side are "glued" together horizontally (as opposed to a UNION operator; see later in this chapter, which appends data sets vertically).

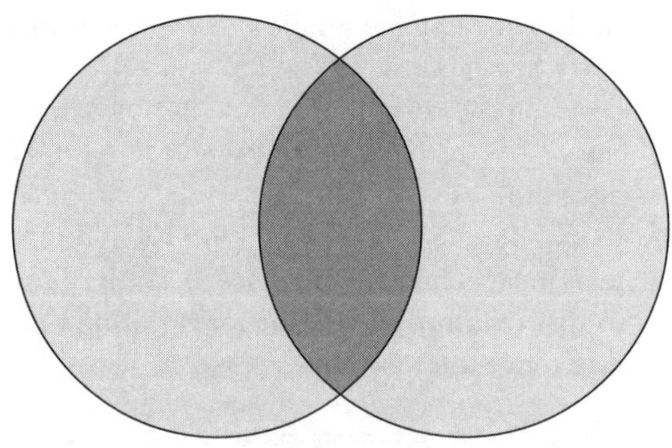

FIGURE 7-3

In RDBMSs, the data are stored in a format understood best by computers, the questions are being asked by humans; the SQL is the middle ground where both parties meet.

The Library database is designed so that one location (space on a bookshelf) may contain no more than one book, but one book may reside in several locations (presumably, different copies or different editions of the same book). Say we need to produce a list of book titles stored on each shelf of our bookcase. Part of the data can be found in the BOOKS table, and part of it is in the LOCATION table. A pair of keys, BK_ID and FK_BK_LOC, will join them together. The SQL query to do so could be as follows:

```
SELECT
    loc_bookcase        AS bookcase
  , loc_shelf           AS shelf
  , loc_position_left   AS position
  , bk_title             AS title
  FROM location INNER JOIN books
    ON location.fk_bk_loc = books.bk_id;
```

The results of the query are presented in Table 7-2.

TABLE 7-2: INNER JOIN Output Results

BOOKCASE	SHELF	POSITION	TITLE
The one in the living room to the right	5	1	*SQL Bible*
The one in the living room to the right	5	2	*Wiley Pathways: Introduction to Database Management*
The one in the living room to the right	5	4	*SQL Functions: Programmers Reference*
The one in the living room to the right	4	1	*After the Gold Rush: Creating a True Profession of Software Engineering*
The one in the living room to the right	3	1	*Mindswap*
The one in the living room to the right	3	2	*Stranger in a Strange Land*
The one in the living room to the right	3	3	*Jonathan Livingston Seagull*

BOOKCASE	SHELF	POSITION	TITLE
The one in the living room to the right	2	1	*A La Recherche du Temps Perdu*
The one in the living room to the right	2	2	*Letters From Earth*
The one in the living room to the right	2	3	*Steppenwolf*

The INNER JOIN keyword instructs the database engine to prepare the data set based on data from both tables, and JOIN them on a specific relationship: the primary key BK_ID from table BOOKS and foreign key FK_BK_LOC from the LOCATION table, matched against each other in what in database terminology is called an *equijoin* (a JOIN that uses an equality operator to match the key).

While equijoin is the most-often-used type of JOIN, the logical extrapolation from the existence of equijoins would be that non-equijoins must be somewhere in the toolbox, too. Indeed, SQL provides it; this type of JOIN(s) would use non-equality operators (greater-than, less-then, not-equal) to JOIN records into a single data set.

Non-equijoins could produce surprising albeit not entirely un-anticipated results. For instance, had we replaced equijoin with non-equijoin using the greater-than operator in the preceding query, we would get 66 rows back, and using the not-equal operator would yield 132 rows. Close examination of the data would reveal the logic behind these results, and it might not be what you were after. This type of JOIN could be useful, but most of the time identical results could be achieved with more transparent methods, and you'd be well advised to abstain from using them until later, when you become more familiar with SQL.

The qualifier INNER is not a required part; a simple JOIN keyword would be sufficient. At the same time, it is highly recommended for better maintainability and readability of your SQL code. As we proceed exploring OUTER joins, this will come in handy. Some RDBMSs allow for substituting NATURAL for INNER or OUTER (the NATURAL JOIN is a special case of the the equijoin when columns from the joined tables have identical names), and some allow additional keywords, such as EQUI, to be used. Stick to the most common INNER JOIN syntax, and your queries will have a much better chance to be executed across different RDBMSs.

The important point in our INNER JOIN example is that, if there are any books in the database that have not yet been placed on the shelf, or any unoccupied shelf space, neither those books nor that shelf space will appear in the result.

Let's take it step by step:

```
SELECT loc_bookcase, loc_shelf, loc_position_left, bk_title
```

These are the data items we want delivered:

```
FROM location INNER JOIN books ON location.fk_bk_loc = books.bk_id
```

We get the data from two tables, LOCATION and BOOKS, and only from the rows that match. The INNER JOIN with an equality operator means "only from the rows that match." The matching rule: Each LOCATION row has to have the same value in FK_BK_LOC column as the BOOKS row does in *BK_ID* column.

TRY IT OUT Extracting JOIN(ed) data from RDBMSs

Let's try to perform some keyword searches on the books we have in the database. Currently, we have the table Search Tags containing all kinds of keywords that we've created when books were added to the database, and an intermediate table SEARCH_BOOKS to establish relationships between the books and the search keywords. A JOIN would help us to find out what books in our database were tagged with the "SQL" keyword. We will be using the Microsoft SQL Server database engine for this activity, but it will work for any other RDBMSs.

1. Open Microsoft SQL Server Management Studio, and connect to your database using Windows authentication.
2. In the upper-left corner, click the New Query button and enter the following SQL query:

```
SELECT
    bk_title AS title
FROM books bk INNER JOIN search_books sb
    ON bk.bk_id = sb.bk_id
INNER JOIN searchTags st
    ON sb.tag_id = st.tag_id
        WHERE st.tag_value = 'SQL'
```

3. Click the Execute button on the toolbar and observe the returned results:

```
title
----------------------------------------------------------
SQL Bible
Wiley Pathways: Introduction to Database Management
Microsoft SQL Server 2000 Weekend Crash Course
SQL Functions: Programmers Reference

(4 row(s) affected)
```

How It Works

The query has two JOIN statements. One JOIN combines data sets from tables BOOKS and SEARCH_BOOKS, and the second JOIN combines SEARCH_BOOKS with the SEARCH TAGS table.

The matching records were pulled from all the table pairs and joined together in a single data set, and then the filtering on condition tag_value = 'SQL' was applied. Then, all qualified records are returned to the client.

The same results could be achieved in a variety of ways. Here's an example using nested subqueries:

```
SELECT bk_title as title FROM books where bk_id IN
     (SELECT bk_id FROM search_books WHERE tag_id IN
            (SELECT tag_id FROM searchTags where tag_value = 'SQL'));
```

You be the judge as to which code is easier to understand: the code with JOIN(s), or that with subqueries. My bet is on the former.

We will come back to this in the next section, and examine the ways to include empty shelves or unplaced books in our result, but first, let's see how we could get more data into our final data set following the same basic JOIN rules.

The JOIN syntax is a relatively new phenomenon. While endorsed for years by the RDBMS, it was eschewed by the vendors in favor of more "familiar" WHERE clause syntax. Any query used in this chapter could be rewritten using this syntax, and it could still be understood by the RDBMS. For instance:

```
SELECT
    loc_bookcase
  , loc_shelf
  , loc_position_left
  , bk_title
FROM location
WHERE location.fk_bk_loc = books.bk_id
```

Where's the incentive to use the new syntax? First of all, the new syntax is endorsed by the SQL Standards Committee and is now supported by all RDBMSs discussed in this book. Second, the old syntax is only supported for backward compatibility and might be deprecated in the later releases. Arguably, the new syntax increases readability of the code and might even prevent some common SQL errors such as unintended Cartesian product queries, discussed later in the chapter.

N-way INNER JOIN

What happens when there is no direct relationship between the two tables? Why, you get more tables involved! You saw it in action in the exercise included in the preceding section on INNER JOIN.

For instance, we would like to list all the books and their respective authors. Remember that a book does not know where in the database its authors are (meaning, there is no information in a row in the BOOKS table about the book's authors), nor does an author know where his books are. Rather, there is in the database a table, BOOKS_AUTHORS, which contains the knowledge about which book was written by which authors and which author has written which books. Each row in that table contains a foreign key for the BOOKS table and a foreign key for the AUTHORS table. If a book was written by several authors, there are several rows in that table, each containing the same book ID and different author ID(s), and vice versa for any author who has written several books.

Since a BOOKS row has no foreign keys for AUTHORS or an AUTHORS row for BOOKS, we have no way of JOIN(ing) those two tables together. Nevertheless, we can JOIN each of them to BOOKS_AUTHORS:

```
SELECT
books.bk_title AS Book
, authors.au_last_name AS Author
FROM books INNERJOIN books_authors
ON books.bk_id = books_authors.bk_id
           INNER JOIN authors
    ON authors.au_id = books_authors.au_id;
```

The result is shown in Table 7-3. As you might have expected, if a book has more than one author, it will be listed as many times as there are authors.

TABLE 7-3: Listing Books and Their Respective Authors

BOOK	AUTHOR
SQL Bible	Kriegel
SQL Bible	Trukhnov
Wiley Pathways: Introduction to Database Management	Gillenson
Wiley Pathways: Introduction to Database Management	Ponniah
Wiley Pathways: Introduction to Database Management	Taylor
Wiley Pathways: Introduction to Database Management	Powell
Wiley Pathways: Introduction to Database Management	Miller
Microsoft SQL Server 2000 Weekend Crash Course	Kriegel
Wiley Pathways: Introduction to Database Management	Trukhnov
Wiley Pathways: Introduction to Database Management	Kriegel
SQL Functions: Programmers Reference	Kriegel
SQL Functions: Programmers Reference	Jones
SQL Functions: Programmers Reference	Stephens
SQL Functions: Programmers Reference	Plew
SQL Functions: Programmers Reference	Garrett
Mindswap	Sheckley
Stranger in a Strange Land	Heinlein
Jonathan Livingston Seagull	Bach

BOOK	AUTHOR
Steppenwolf	Hesse
A Short History of Nearly Everything	Bryson
A La Recherche du Temps Perdu	Proust
After the Gold Rush: Creating a True Profession of Software Engineering	McConnell
Letters From Earth	Twain

There may be repeating book titles in the resulting data set, as well as repeating author names, but each *combination* of a book title and an author name appears only once.

Let us deconstruct the logic behind the data set returned by the query. Here is the first part, the SELECT list:

```
SELECT
books.bk_title AS Book
, authors.au_last_name AS Author
```

Nothing mysterious here; we let the query engine know what data we are interested in, as well as asking for some prettier column names than the default (the AS alias). Note that we don't have to request data from each of the tables we are querying. In this case, we want something from the BOOKS table and from the AUTHORS table, but nothing from BOOKS_AUTHORS:

```
FROM books INNER JOIN books_authors
ON books.bk_id = books_authors.bk_id
```

This is where we define the first INNER JOIN. We specify which tables are to be joined and how they are to be joined. In this case, we match the values of the BK_ID column in one table and BK_ID field in the other table (the column names need not be the same, although it is convenient when they are):

```
INNER JOIN authors ON authors.au_id = books_authors.au_id
```

Here we define the second INNER JOIN. Note the difference from the first. In the first case, we specified two tables, `books INNER JOIN books_authors`, while here we only specify one table: `INNER JOIN authors`. We don't need to specify the other table. It's bound to be one of the two that have been mentioned already, and the row-matching rule will define which one (in this case, "match the values of the AU_ID column in the AUTHORS table with the values of the AU_ID column in the BOOKS_AUTHORS table").

If we run this query, and if our BOOKS table has some books that are not mentioned in the BOOKS_AUTHORS table, no such books will be included in the resulting data set or any authors from the AUTHORS table, if no mention of them exists in the BOOKS_AUTHORS table.

TRY IT OUT Using the Four-way JOIN

How do you find which books from which authors you have stored on the top shelf of your bookcase with a title beginning with "SQL"? By JOIN(ing) the LOCATION, BOOKS and AUTHORS tables, of course. Because there is a many-to-many relationship between the books and their respective authors, we'll have to include the BOOKS_AUTHORS intermediate table to resolve the complexity. We are going to use Microsoft SQL Server to demonstrate this functionality, but the script will run without any changes in every other RDBMS discussed in the book. Let's get started:

1. Open Microsoft SQL Server Management Studio and connect to your database using Windows authentication.
2. In the upper-left corner click the New Query button and enter the following SQL query:

```
SELECT
    au_last_name AS author
  , bk_title AS title
FROM books bk INNER JOIN books_authors ba
  ON bk.bk_id = ba.bk_id
INNER JOIN authors au
  ON ba.au_id = au.au_id
INNER JOIN location loc
  ON bk.bk_id = loc.fk_bk_loc
    WHERE loc.loc_shelf = 5
       AND bk.bk_title LIKE 'SQL%'
```

3. Click the Execute button on the toolbar and observe the returned results:

```
author           title
---------------- ----------------------------------------------
Kriegel          SQL Bible
Trukhnov         SQL Bible
Kriegel          SQL Functions: Programmers Reference
Jones            SQL Functions: Programmers Reference
Stephens         SQL Functions: Programmers Reference
Plew             SQL Functions: Programmers Reference
Garrett          SQL Functions: Programmers Reference

(7 row(s) affected)
```

How It Works

As in the previous examples, the evaluation of JOIN(s) leads to ever-dwindling choices until the data set is fully conformed to the specified criteria. In this case, the database engine matched records from all tables' pairs (BOOKS/BOOKS_AUTHORS, BOOKS_AUTHORS/AUTHORS, and BOOKS/LOCATIONS) joined on the keys of the JOIN statements. Then final filtering was applied, reducing the data set to only records that have LOC_SHELF = 5 and BK_TITLE starting with "SQL" (recall that pattern matching with the LIKE predicate).

LEFT OUTER JOIN

While it is not stated upfront, there are always two tables to each JOIN and true to our anthropomorphizing nature, we visualize them as being either on the LEFT or on the RIGHT, regardless of where and how the database keeps them. The idea of an OUTER join is built upon this notion. For example, the LEFT OUTER JOIN is used when we want to see the full list of things that interest us on the LEFT, along with any additional features that some items on the list may have on the RIGHT side. If none is present, unmatched rows on the LEFT are complemented by the NULL(s) on the right. Figure 7-4 presents the concept of the LEFT OUTER JOIN.

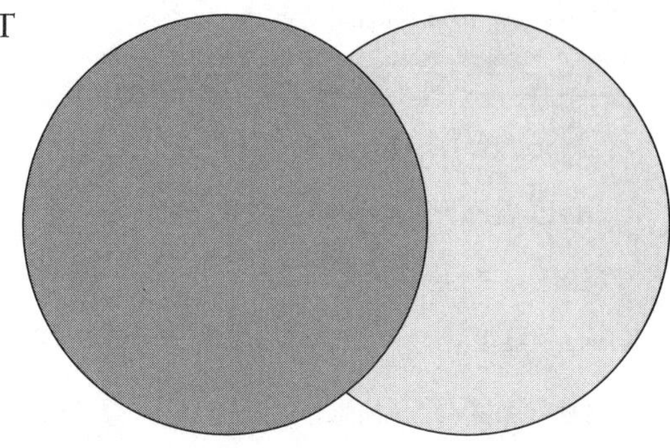

FIGURE 7-4

Let us, for instance, list all the shelf space we have, along with whatever books we may have on our bookshelves. Now, we do want *all the books*, even those that were not yet placed on the shelf. Since all our books have their rightful place in the bookcase already, we'll have to create unmatched rows in the BOOKS table. It will becomingly be assigned BK_ID = 13:

```
INSERT INTO books (bk_id, bk_title)
    VALUES (13,'LEFT JOIN EXAMPLE')
```

The rest of the columns will be filled in with default NULL.

Now, we can use the book-placement query from a few paragraphs earlier. Only now, we'll change the JOIN type from INNER to LEFT OUTER:

```
SELECT
      bk_title
    , loc_shelf
    ,loc_position_left
  FROM books LEFT OUTER JOIN location
    ON location.fk_bk_loc = books.bk_id
```

We are asking for all records from the BOOKS table, and everything else, including unmatched rows from the LOCATION table. The newly inserted record (the last row in the table) has no corresponding location on the shelf, so it was complemented with NULL(s) for the values. Had we run the INNER JOIN operation now, the thirteenth record would be simply excluded as one without match. Table 7-4 presents result of the previous query.

TABLE 7-4: Results Returned by LEFT OUTER JOIN Query

TITLE	SHELF	POSITION
SQL Bible	5	1
Wiley Pathways: Introduction to Database Management	5	2
SQL Functions: Programmers Reference	5	4
After the Gold Rush: Creating a True Profession of Software Engineering	4	1
Mindswap	3	1
Stranger in a Strange Land	3	2

continues

TABLE 7-4 *(continued)*

TITLE	SHELF	POSITION
Jonathan Livingston Seagull	3	3
A La Recherche du Temps Perdu	2	1
Letters From Earth	2	2
Steppenwolf	2	3
LEFT JOIN EXAMPLE	**NULL**	**NULL**

At least we know now what books have not been placed yet. Had we used INNER JOIN, this "book" would not have showed up.

RIGHT OUTER JOIN

This is a mirror image of the LEFT OUTER JOIN. Now we are after the information supplied by the right side of the pair. We still have unmatched records in the BOOKS table. By moving the table to the right side and deploying the RIGHT OUTER JOIN, we could get an identical result. Figure 7-5 illustrates the concept.

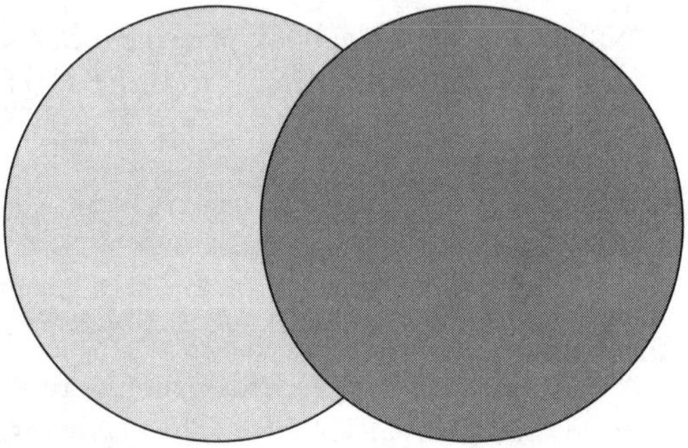

FIGURE 7-5

We get the same result as in the LEFT OUTER JOIN example; only this time the records are matched with NULL(s) to the right:

```
SELECT
loc_shelf
  , loc_position_left
  , bk_title
FROM location RIGHT OUTER JOIN books
ON location.fk_bk_loc = books.bk_id
```

The results of the query are displayed in Table 7-5.

TABLE 7-5: Results Returned by the RIGHT OUTER JOIN Query

SHELF	POSITION	TITLE
5	1	*SQL Bible*
5	2	*Wiley Pathways: Introduction to Database Management*
5	4	*SQL Functions: Programmers Reference*
4	1	*After the Gold Rush: Creating a True Profession of Software Engineering*
3	1	*Mindswap*

SHELF	POSITION	TITLE
3	2	*Stranger in a Strange Land*
3	3	*Jonathan Livingston Seagull*
2	1	*A La Recherche du Temps Perdu*
2	2	*Letters From Earth*
2	3	*Steppenwolf*
NULL	**NULL**	**LEFT JOIN EXAMPLE**

FULL JOIN

The FULL JOIN is a combination of the LEFT and RIGHT OUTER JOINs, as shown in Figure 7-6.

FIGURE 7-6

The next query gives us the data set with *all* our books and *all* our locations, with *some* of them on the same row. The query would be the same, only FULL JOIN will be applied:

```
SELECT
loc_shelf
  , loc_position_left
  , bk_title
FROM location FULL JOIN books
ON location.fk_bk_loc = books.bk_id
```

Since the records are now returned from either side, the position of the tables in the query does not matter anymore. Table 7-6 reflects the change.

TABLE 7-6: Results Returned by FULL JOIN Query

TITLE	SHELF	POSITION
SQL Bible	5	1
Wiley Pathways: Introduction to Database Management	5	2
SQL Functions: Programmers Reference	5	4
After the Gold Rush: Creating a True Profession of Software Engineering	4	1
Mindswap	3	1
Stranger in a Strange Land	3	2
Jonathan Livingston Seagull	3	3

continues

TABLE 7-6 *(continued)*

TITLE	SHELF	POSITION
A La Recherche du Temps Perdu	2	1
Letters From Earth	2	2
Steppenwolf	2	3
LEFT JOIN EXAMPLE	**NULL**	**NULL**

In the preceding example, the LOCATION table could not have unmatched records because of the referential integrity constraints (see Chapter 3 for more details on referential integrity), so we had to switch the tables and apply different types of JOIN(s). There are plenty of situations where the JOIN criteria are not the same as the primary/foreign key relationships, and you will have sets with matched and unmatched records from both sides.

If, for instance, you'd JOIN the tables on a column that is neither the primary nor the foreign key (for example, BK_ID = LOC_POSITION_LEFT), the result would be lots of NULLS from unmatched LOCATION records because we have only four distinct values for the LOC_POSITION_LEFT versus 13 for the BK_ID (yes, exactly nine NULL(s) will be returned). While a valid SQL operation, this query would not make much sense from the logical point of view, but demonstrates the concept of the OUTER JOIN rather nicely.

Now that we do not need this superfluous record, we could safely remove it from our BOOKS table:

```
DELETE books WHERE bk_id=13;
```

The keyword OUTER in the preceding JOIN examples is optional. Simply using LEFT, RIGHT, or FULL would suffice. The same goes for INNER JOIN. The RDBMS figures out that a JOIN without any qualifiers is of the INNER type. Nevertheless, using these qualifiers is considered a good practice, as it contributes to better maintainability of your SQL code by leaving nothing to be guessed.

Self JOIN: Looking Inside for an Answer

Here's a novel concept: JOIN(ing) a table to itself. You may wonder why you would want to do that. Don't we have all we need right there? Yes and no. For example, try this: List the books that were published in the same year in the order in which they were added to the database.

Here's a self-join query to answer this question:

```
SELECT
    fst.bk_id
  , fst.bk_title
  , snd.bk_id
  , snd.bk_title
FROM books fst JOIN books snd
    ON fst.bk_published_year = snd.bk_published_year
```

```
        WHERE fst.bk_id < snd.bk_id;
bk_id     bk_title                      bk_id  bk_title
-------- ---------------------------- --------------------------------5          A
La Recherche du Temps Perdu  12    Steppenwolf
7        Letters From Earth              11    A Short History of Nearly…
(2 row(s) affected)
```

First, you will notice that the tables have to be aliased because otherwise the database engine won't be able to distinguish which table we are referring to in other parts of the statement. It was a good practice before; now it is a necessity. Next, we JOIN the table by the year of publishing and then indicate that we want different records for the same year (otherwise, we would get the same book from each of the tables).

The important thing to remember is that despite JOIN(ing) the table with itself, you are still dealing with *two instances* of the table, separate from each other for all intents and purposes. There is no practical limit to how many times the table could refer to itself in a query.

While the above results could potentially be achieved with subqueries and GROUP BY statements, it would be difficult to list two book titles on the same row.

The self JOIN is not some special type of a JOIN; it is but a demonstration of the flexibility afforded by SQL syntax.

CROSS JOIN (aka Cartesian Product)

Finally, let us take a look at a different sort of JOIN. So different, in fact, that its syntax does not even allow for a row-matching condition!

```
SELECT
    loc_bookcase
, loc_shelf
, loc_position_left
, bk_title
  FROM location CROSS JOIN books
(144 row(s) affected)
```

How could this have happened: 144 rows? We only have a dozen records in either of the tables! What sort of JOIN is this? It has another name: *Cartesian product*. Recall the Cartesian coordinate system, with two axes at right angles to each other, and numbers going up each axis from the 0 point at the intersection. One common example of this system is the chess board, except that, along one of the axes, the numbers are replaced by letters.

If we want to name every single square on the chess board, we will use its coordinates: A1, A2, E4, E5, and so on. In other words, we match every single value from one axis with every single value from the other. This is the Cartesian Product (it's almost like we "multiply" Ax1, Ax2, and so on).

The CROSS JOIN does the same thing with the tables: it pairs up every row of one table with every row of the other table. As you might expect, the result is usually quite big. The output from just two tables in the preceding example will result in 144 rows returned (each table has 12 rows), and the more tables that are added to the query, the bigger the result gets.

What's so "join" about it? Not much, really, and old SQL syntax makes this rather obvious. You just list the tables to select from without any JOIN criteria:

```
SELECT
    loc_bookcase
  , loc_shelf
  , loc_position_left
  , bk_title
FROM location,books
```

In other words, we dispense with the word JOIN altogether, and just list the tables. Herein lies the predicament; omitting the WHERE clause creates a Cartesian product query, and makes it very easy to do. Results might be more than you have asked for. Table 7-7 shows the progression of the resulting data set from including increasing numbers of the tables contained in the Library database.

TABLE 7-7: Cartesian Products in the Library Database

TABLES LISTED IN FROM CLAUSE	RECORDS RETURNED
location, books	144
location, books, authors	2,736
location, books, authors, books_authors	62,928
location, books, authors, books_authors, search_books	3,901,536
location, books, authors, books_authors, search_books, searchTags	109,243,008

Our tiny Library database, with but six tables, none of which contained more than 12 records, produced truly astronomical results. Imagine what would happen in a production database comprising dozens, even hundreds of tables with millions of rows! This is the surest way to grind your database to a halt and make your DBA very unhappy.

Using CROSS JOIN with a WHERE clause would limit the number of the records returned. For example, the Cartesian product of the following query

```
SELECT  loc_bookcase, loc_shelf, loc_position_left, bk_title
FROM location CROSS JOIN books
WHERE bk_id = 1
```

would only return 12 records, and not 144 as in the example at the beginning of this paragraph.

Fortunately, the new syntax requires that you explicitly declare your intentions upfront, and would not allow queries with an accidental Cartesian product. You must use the CROSS JOIN keyword or supply join criteria. It pays to head your DBA warning: Using old join syntax might be harmful for your database. Mercifully, many RDBMSs stopped supporting the old syntax in their respective databases. Unless you need to work with legacy code, you'd be better off never to use this old syntax in your queries.

One might wonder, if a CROSS JOIN is a bad thing to be avoided why even bother providing the keyword? The truth is that there are legitimate uses for CROSS JOIN. For instance, it offers a fast and easy way to produce huge data sets for testing. Another scenario might include joining the data set produced by a CROSS JOIN to select rows which neither LEFT nor OUTER JOIN(s) could produce by themselves such as including customers who had zero total sales for a given product (the library scenario might ask for patrons who never borrowed a specific book within a year.)

CROSS JOIN could be a very powerful tool, and as such it must be approached with caution. Processing huge data sets will consume system resources. One of the best practices in SQL is to be as selective as possible, and minimize the amount of data accessed in a query.

Is there a limit on how many JOIN(s) an SQL query could have? There is a practical limit after which the complexity of preparing execution plans, let alone executing them, brings a server to its knees. The actual number would depend on the RDBMS and the hardware on which it is running, but if you find yourself using more than a dozen, you might want to recheck your assumptions.

STATE OF THE UNION

The Library database does not offer us much reason to use UNION, but let's pretend that you want the full list of book titles and author names combined. Perhaps you want to create a master directory, in which you can look up a book either by its title or author, all in one list:

```
SELECT
    books.bk_title AS title
FROM books
UNION
SELECT
    authors.au_last_name
FROM authors
```

UNION does not establish a link, or a connection, between tables; it simply jams them together, one atop another. Note that the syntax of a UNION operation is different from that of a JOIN. UNION reflects the fact that tables are not connected, but merely "glued" together, as shown in Table 7-8.

TABLE 7-8: Result of a UNION Query

TITLE
A Short History of Nearly Everything
After the Gold Rush: Creating a True Profession of Software Engineering
Bach
Bryson

continues

TABLE 7-8 *(continued)*

TITLE
Garrett
Gillenson
Heinlein
Hesse
Jonathan Livingston Seagull
Jones
Kriegel
Letters From Earth
McConnell
Microsoft SQL Server 2000 Weekend Crash Course
Miller
Mindswap
Plew
Ponniah
Powell
Proust
A La Recherche du Temps Perdu
Sheckley
SQL Bible
SQL Functions: Programmers Reference
Stephens
Steppenwolf
Stranger in a Strange Land
Taylor
Trukhnov
Twain
Wiley Pathways: Introduction to Database Management

Note that the book titles and the author names are all in the same single column of the resulting data set, and they are ordered alphabetically, without paying attention whence the record came. Your results might be different, as not all RDBMSs support this ordering feature. Use ORDER BY clause if you need the result set to be in specific order.

If you are using ORDER BY with queries glued together by the UNION operator, keep in mind that the ordering is done on the entire set. You can't use ORDER BY within the queries, only with the entire statement.

The important consideration is the data compatibility: We can build a list of book titles and author names because each of them is a text string. We can't combine things of different types, such as dates from one table and prices from another. What sort of sense would such a list have? (Of course, we can build a query that would put dates in one column of the resulting data set and prices in another column, such as quarterly sales results. That would be a fine job for a JOIN, but UNION combines data from different tables into a *single column* of the result, so all the data must be of the same data type.) The compatibility principle applies not only to the data types but also to the structure of the data set. The number of columns specified in the SELECT list of each query must be the same, and their respective data types must be compatible.

UNION may be useful when there is a need to combine similar data from several different tables. Sometimes, the designers of a database may present a single logical data table as several physically distinct tables, perhaps for faster access, or easier distribution among separate pieces of hardware. In those cases, UNION will help bring the data from the several tables back together into a single data set.

Though our data does not have duplicates, the UNION takes care of eliminating the duplicate entries on the list. If there were more than one author with the same surname, only one would make it to the list. If your intent is to include *all* records, you must use the UNION ALL operator.

Let's add a record for an author: John M. Bryson, author of *Strategic Planning for Public and Nonprofit Organizations: A Guide to Strengthening and Sustaining Organizational Achievement* (no relation to Bill Bryson, who is already in our database. As with the superfluous record added to our BOOKS table, we will insert only the absolute minimum data required: AU_ID and AU_LAST_NAME:

```
INSERT INTO authors (au_id, au_last_name)
    VALUES (20, 'Bryson')
```

Now we can run exactly the same query we introduced at the beginning of this section, and see that it yields the very same results, with only one Bryson appearing on the list:

```
SELECT
    books.bk_title AS title
FROM books
UNION ALL
SELECT
    authors.au_last_name
FROM authors;
```

The picture is quite different when we run UNION ALL. Not only do we get two authors named *Bryson* on the list but we also lose our ordering. Each piece of the UNION comes back in its original order from each query (notice the *Bryson* at the end of the data set), and the results of the second query are simply appended to the first, as shown in Table 7-9.

TABLE 7-9: Result of a UNION ALL Query

TITLE
SQL Bible
Wiley Pathways: Introduction to Database Management
Microsoft SQL Server 2000 Weekend Crash Course
SQL Functions: Programmers Reference
A La Recherche du Temps Perdu
After the Gold Rush: Creating a True Profession of Software Engineering
Letters From Earth
Mindswap
Stranger in a Strange Land
Jonathan Livingston Seagull
A Short History of Nearly Everything
Steppenwolf
Kriegel
Trukhnov
Gillenson
Ponniah
Taylor
Powell
Miller
Jones
Stephens
Plew
Garrett

TITLE
Sheckley
Heinlein
Bach
Hesse
Bryson
Proust
McConnell
Twain
Bryson

Sometimes the data are, in fact, different. Yet, there is an aspect of similarity. Imagine organizations with many roles for the members to play: a school, where a person may be a teacher, a student, a custodian, or the principal; a factory, with workers, managers, support personnel, and sales people. You get the idea. Each of these roles will have its own table in the database, yet the master list of "people" can be constructed by using the UNION on all those tables and asking only for the last name and first name — *every* member of every role is bound to have them!

Where a JOIN adds more and more relevant details from many connected tables to the result, the UNION takes disparate tables, cuts out irrelevancies, and reduces the tables to some narrow, but common view.

There is no practical limit to how many UNION(s) a single query can have, but there is practical evidence that the number runs into the thousands. The actual number depends on hardware (CPU, RAM) and particular RDBMS implementation.

A POINT OF VIEW

As you have seen, the SQL queries could grow quite large, and at some point their complexity could become overwhelming. Moreover, after spending hours to get your query, complete with JOIN(s), UNION(s), functions and other things afforded by SQL syntax, you might want to save the resulting scripts for future use.

This is where SQL VIEW comes into the picture. To paraphrase Goethe, a VIEW is frozen query.

Johann Wolfgang von Goethe, an early nineteenth-century German writer and philosopher who is considered by many one of the most important thinkers of the Western Civilization, once remarked, "I call architecture frozen music." *He might have been paraphrasing his compatriot Friedrich Wilhelm Joseph von Schelling, who expressed a similar idea 30 years earlier.*

Like every object in the database, a view is created as part of a Data Definition Language (DDL) statement (see Chapter 2 for discussions on DDL, DML, and DQL). Unlike them, however, the CREATE VIEW syntax also contains Data Query Language (DQL), the query to extract data. Most of the books introduce VIEW(s) along with TABLE(s) due to the similarity of the CREATE syntax. When on the discovery journey, the logical place to find them is in multitable data extraction as a means to manage all the complexity. Let's take a look.

CREATE VIEW

In its most basic form, converting a query into a view is a snap; just add a CREATE VIEW statement, along with the name for the newly created object. For instance:

```
CREATE VIEW vwBooksONshelves
AS
    SELECT
        loc_bookcase      AS bookcase
      , loc_shelf         AS shelf
      , loc_position_left AS position
      , bk_title          AS title
  FROM location INNER JOIN books
    ON location.fk_bk_loc = books.bk_id;
```

The view is created, and now you can query it with simple SELECT * syntax, as demonstrated in the following example:

```
SELECT * FROM vwBooksONshelves;
```

The results in Table 7-10 are identical to those produced by the query itself.

TABLE 7-10: Results of Two Table JOIN Queries Wrapped in a VIEW

BOOKCASE	SHELF	POSITION	TITLE
The one in the living room to the right	5	1	*SQL Bible*
The one in the living room to the right	5	2	*Wiley Pathways: Introduction to Database Management*
The one in the living room to the right	5	4	*SQL Functions: Programmers Reference*
The one in the living room to the right	4	1	*After the Gold Rush: Creating a True Profession of Software Engineering*

BOOKCASE	SHELF	POSITION	TITLE
The one in the living room to the right	4	2	*A Short History of Nearly Everything*
The one in the living room to the right	3	1	*Mindswap*
The one in the living room to the right	3	2	*Stranger in a Strange Land*
The one in the living room to the right	3	3	*Jonathan Livingston Seagull*
The one in the living room to the right	2	1	*A La Recherche du Temps Perdu*
The one in the living room to the right	2	2	*Letters From Earth*
The one in the living room to the right	2	3	*Steppenwolf*

VIEW(s) can be put to many uses, encapsulating complexity, enforcing security, and so on. Some of these options will be discussed in greater detail later in the chapter. There are quite a few RDBMS-specific options that might go along with the CREATE VIEW statement, but the preceding syntax is universal, and will work identically across every RDBMS we're discussing in this book.

Almost any SQL query (of the DQL variety) in this book can be converted into a view, but there are a few exceptions. In some RDBMSs, a query with the ORDER BY clause cannot be used in a VIEW (but a GROUP BY clause can). Consequently, some RDBMSs disallow the use of the keywords that cause "ordering" (DISTINCT, FIRST, and so on). Hyper Structured Query Language Database (HSQLDB) and MySQL, for instance, allow ORDER BY; Oracle, Microsoft SQL Server, Microsoft Access, PostgreSQL, and IBM DB2 do not. None of the RDBMSs allows a view to refer to itself (a *circular reference*) or any transient structures, such as temporary tables (see Chapter 8 for more information).

Being an integrated environment that combines both database and programming constructs, Microsoft Access can be used as a front end for other RDBMSs. This capability comes with many restrictions. For instance, in the context of this chapter, the Microsoft Access database engine does not support the use of CREATE VIEW (or any of the DDL statements, for that matter) with non–Microsoft Access database engine databases.

If a view or a table with the same name already exists in the database, the RDBMS will throw an error. Some RDBMSs (Oracle, PostgreSQL, and MySQL) provide alternative REPLACE keyword to address the situation (in others, a view must be dropped before another view with the same name could be created). For example:

```
CREATE OR REPLACE VIEW vwbooksONshelves
AS
    SELECT
        loc_bookcase      AS bookcase
      , loc_shelf         AS shelf
      , loc_position_left AS position
      , bk_title          AS title
  FROM location INNER JOIN books
    ON location.fk_bk_loc = books.bk_id;
```

One could easily construct views limiting the user to a subset of data, either vertical (by restricting columns exposed by the view), or horizontal (by limiting the number of records returned).

It is considered to be a good practice to name your database objects according to a naming convention. For instance, you can prefix views with vw to differentiate them from tables.

The following view returns titles of the three most expensive books that could be found on the top shelf (#5) of our bookcase. It uses Microsoft SQL Server syntax (which allows for the ORDER BY clause to be used in a view):

```
CREATE VIEW vwTop3booksOn5thShelf
AS
    SELECT TOP 3
        loc_position_left AS position
      , bk_title          AS title
      , bk_id
  FROM location INNER JOIN books
    ON location.fk_bk_loc = books.bk_id
       WHERE loc_shelf = 5
       ORDER BY bk_price DESC;
```

Running the SELECT statement on the view returns a subset of data: only two columns, limited to only three top records, ordered by BK_PRICE (even though the column BK_PRICE is not accessible through the view):

```
SELECT * FROM vwTop3booksOn5thShelf;
position    title                                                 bk_id
----------- ----------------------------------------------------- -----------
2           Wiley Pathways: Introduction to Database Management   2
1           SQL Bible                                             1
3           SQL Functions: Programmers Reference                  3

(3 row(s) affected)
```

Abstracting data with views not only makes it more user friendly by hiding the complexity of the underlying data model but it also serves as a security mechanism by denying access to the rows and columns not explicitly exposed through a view. For example, if your intention was to give the user the ability to find the three most expensive books on the fifth shelf without divulging actual prices, the view in the above example would do just that. Even though BK_PRICE exists in the underlying table, a person having only privilege to query the view [vwTop3booksOn5thShelf] would never be able to see the price, or even find out what would be the fourth most expensive book.

TRY IT OUT Wrapping Complexity in a VIEW

Let's try to construct a relatively complex query containing several JOINS and the GROUP BY clause to find books tagged with a search tag such as *SQL,* and group them by the year of publishing. We'll wrap the query into a VIEW afterward to see how the complexity could be hidden from the users. The examples are created in Microsoft SQL Server, but should work without any modification on other RDBMSs.

1. Connect to the RDBMS, and open New Query window.
2. In the query window type in the following code, and click Execute.

```
CREATE VIEW vwOneComplexView
AS
SELECT bk_title AS title
    , bk_published_year AS pub_year
    , loc.loc_shelf
FROM books bk INNER JOIN books_authors ba
    ON bk.bk_id = ba.bk_id
INNER JOIN authors au
    ON ba.au_id = au.au_id
INNER JOIN location loc
    ON bk.bk_id = loc.fk_bk_loc
INNER JOIN search_books sb
    ON sb.bk_id = bk.bk_id
INNER JOIN  searchTags st
    ON st.tag_id = sb.tag_id
WHERE loc.loc_shelf = 5
AND st.tag_value IN ('SQL')
GROUP BY
  bk_published_year
, bk_title
, bk_price
,loc_shelf
```

3. Confirm that the command executed successfully, and that the view was indeed created.
4. Delete the code from the query window. Type in and execute a new query.

```
SELECT * FROM vwOneComplexView
ORDER BY title;

title                                                pub_year    loc_shelf
---------------------------------------------------- ----------- -----------
Microsoft SQL Server 2000 Weekend Crash Course       2001        5
SQL Bible                                            2008        5
SQL Functions: Programmers Reference                 2005        5
Wiley Pathways: Introduction to Database Management  2007        5

(4 row(s) affected)
```

How It Works

This view ties together six tables using INNER JOIN syntax. Additionally, it imposes two restrictions, searching only for books tagged with "SQL," and only these located on the top (fifth) shelf. The results are grouped by the BK_PUBLISHED_YEAR column from the BOOKS table (as well as three more columns). By wrapping all this complexity in a single view, we have the ability to simplify queries run by business users, imposing certain business and security rules at the same time. If a user only was granted SELECT privileges to this view, he or she would never be able to view books outside the specified search criteria. Only books tagged with SQL and only those on the fifth shelf will appear in the result set. The user has control over sorting the records with the ORDER BY clause, referring to aliases exposed by the view. In the preceding query the ORDER BY clause ordered records by TITLE, overriding the default order imposed by GROUP BY used in the view syntax.

ALTER VIEW

When a change you wish to apply to an existing view does not warrant the view's complete rewrite, you could use the ALTER VIEW syntax. There are quite a few differences between RDBMSs in regard to what this statement could alter, and some (HSQLDB, MS Access) do not support it at all.

Oracle's ALTER VIEW statement cannot change the VIEW definition (add columns, rename columns, and so on). Instead, it uses this statement to add constraints to the existing DDL definitions (see Chapter 8 for more information on constraints). Apparently, Oracle figures that CREATE OR REPLACE would take care of the rest.

IBM DB2 uses ALTER VIEW only to add columns to the existing query definition. The rest of the RDBMSs use ALTER VIEW as a synonym for REPLACE, with the important distinction that using ALTER does not affect security permissions you might have created for this view (see Chapter 10 for more information on security).

DROP VIEW

Unlike a query, a VIEW is a permanent database object, and must be disposed of as such. It follows the very same syntax you might use when destroying other database objects:

```
DROP VIEW vwBooksONshelves;
```

Depending on the RDBMS, there might be some additional options that could be specified with the statement. The two keywords, CASCADE and RESTRICT, instruct the RDBMS either to drop all other objects dependent on this view or prevent the statement from being executed whenever such objects exist. Not every database supports these statements, though. Once the VIEW is dropped, all other objects depending on this view will be invalidated. Dropping a view does not affect data in the underlying objects.

Updatable VIEW

It was not long ago that VIEW(s) were just that: read-only windows into your data. Some RDBMSs have loosened the restrictions somewhat, and you can INSERT, UPDATE, or DELETE using VIEW(s). Currently, only Oracle, MySQL, Microsoft SQL Server, and IBM DB2 offer this capability. Even with them, there are conditions to be satisfied before a view could become an updatable one.

The biggest restriction is that an updatable view cannot include more than one table. Other restrictions preclude the use of the GROUP BY and ORDER BY clauses, the DISTINCT keyword, no aggregate functions or subqueries, and no calculated columns. The list goes on and on. Some SQL statements might require additional specific conditions. For example, in order to use the INSERT statement on a view, all NOT NULL columns must be included in the SELECT statement used to create this view.

TRY IT OUT INSERTing, UPDATEing, and DELETEing through a VIEW

Let's create a view that allows users to add new records to the database, but restricts them to being able to UPDATE only two columns in the underlying table. We are going to use Microsoft SQL Server for this activity, but it will work in other RDBMSs supporting updatable views.

1. Open Microsoft SQL Server Management Studio and connect to your database using Windows authentication.
2. In the upper-left corner, click the New Query button.
3. In the opened query window (the middle pane), enter the following SQL query:

```
CREATE VIEW vwBookPrices
AS SELECT
   bk_id
 , bk_title
 , bk_price
FROM books;
```

4. Insert a new record by executing the following query, supplying only BK_ID value:

```
INSERT INTO vwBookPrices (BK_ID) VALUES (100);

(1 row(s) affected)
```

5. Verify that the record is indeed inserted into the BOOKS table by running this query:

```
SELECT
    bk_id
  , bk_title
  , bk_price
FROM books;

bk_id   bk_title  bk_price
------  -------   ---------
100     NULL      NULL
```

6. Update the newly inserted record with the book's title and price by running the following query:

```
UPDATE vwBookPrices
    SET bk_title= 'Faust'
      , bk_price = 11.90
WHERE bk_id = 100

(1 row(s) affected)
```

7. Verify that the record is indeed inserted into the BOOKS table by running this query:

```
SELECT
    bk_id
```

```
   , bk_title
   , bk_price
FROM books
WHERE bk_id = 100
;

bk_id   bk_title  bk_price
------  -------   ---------
100     Faust     11.90
```

8. Finally, delete the record:

```
DELETE vwBookPrices WHERE bk_id = 100;
(1 row(s) affected)
```

How It Works

This view is based on a single table (BOOKS) and allows for UPDATE(ing) the columns BK_TITLE and BK_PRICE, as well as INSERT(ing) new records, because, with the exception of BK_ID, the primary key on the column, all other columns allow NULL(s). We are also allowed to delete the record; in fact, we would be allowed to DELETE all records from the BOOKS table if not for referential integrity constraints that do not allow "orphaned" records in a *childmost* table.

WITH CHECK OPTION

The ability to add, modify, and delete data through a view opens a whole new can of worms. How can you ensure consistency between the data that can be *entered* through the view and the data that can be *displayed* through it?

Let's say that in the previous exercise we've added additional constraints when creating our view, limiting the number of the records displayed to the first 12:

```
CREATE VIEW vwBookPricesFirst12
AS SELECT
   bk_id
 , bk_title
 , bk_price
FROM books
WHERE bk_id <= 12
```

As it is, nothing prevents us from entering new records following the very same steps outlined in the above exercise, inserting a record with BK_ID=100. Seeing the very same records through the view is a different story, since the view definition only displays records with BK_ID <= 12.

Unless you've implemented this behavior intentionally, you'd probably want to see the data going into your table or prevent invalid data from going through the view in the first place. Enter CHECK OPTION.

Added to the VIEW definition, this statement will throw an error whenever data the view won't be able to display is entered. Here's how Microsoft SQL Server would react:

```
CREATE VIEW vwBookPricesFirst12
AS SELECT
```

```
   bk_id
 , bk_title
 , bk_price
FROM books
WHERE bk_id <= 12
WITH CHECK OPTION;

INSERT INTO vwBookPricesFirst12(bk_id) VALUES (100);

Msg 550, Level 16, State 1, Line 1
The attempted insert or update failed because the target view either
specifies WITH CHECK OPTION or spans a view that specifies WITH CHECK OPTION
and one or more rows resulting from the operation did not qualify under
the CHECK OPTION constraint.
The statement has been terminated.
```

Note that there would be no problem updating the BOOKS table directly. Only the view imposes the restriction because it cannot display records with BK_ID greater than 12.

Checking data upon entry carries a heavy performance hit price tag and should be used judiciously.

CHECK OPTION is part of the SQL Standard and is supported by all RDBMSs with updatable VIEWS capabilities: Oracle, MySQL, Microsoft SQL Server, and IBM DB2.

Hierarchical Views

For most practical purposes, a view is just another table in the database and therefore could be used to serve as a base for another view. In fact, you can JOIN views with other views and tables in the same query and then create a view on top of all this.

If we decide to figure out who the authors are for the "top three books on the shelf," we could use a view created earlier in the chapter and add data from the AUTHORS table as follows:

```
CREATE VIEW vwTop3BooksWithAuthors
AS SELECT
    vw.bk_id
   , vw.title
  , au.au_last_name
FROM vwTop3booksOn5thShelf vw JOIN books_authors ba
    ON vw.bk_id = ba.bk_id
        JOIN authors au
    ON ba.au_id = au.au_id;

SELECT * FROM vwTop3BooksWithAuthors;

bk_id    title                                                   au_last_name
-------- ------------------------------------------------------  ----------------
1         SQL Bible                                               Kriegel
1         SQL Bible                                               Trukhnov
2         Wiley Pathways: Introduction to Database Management     Gillenson
2        Wiley Pathways: Introduction to Database Management      Ponniah
2        Wiley Pathways: Introduction to Database Management      Taylor
2        Wiley Pathways: Introduction to Database Management      Powell
2        Wiley Pathways: Introduction to Database Management      Miller
```

```
2        Wiley Pathways: Introduction to Database Management      Trukhnov
2        Wiley Pathways: Introduction to Database Management      Kriegel
4        SQL Functions: Programmers Reference                     Kriegel
4        SQL Functions: Programmers Reference                     Jones
4        SQL Functions: Programmers Reference                     Stephens
4        SQL Functions: Programmers Reference                     Plew
4        SQL Functions: Programmers Reference                     Garrett

(14 row(s) affected)
```

In the preceding example, we joined a view (vwTop3booksOn5thShelf) with two tables and created another view. Now the data could be extracted with a single SELECT without worrying about business rules encapsulated in both views, conditions limiting the data set only to the top shelf (you don't even need to know that the top shelf is #5), and to only three books with the highest price.

This opens a whole world of possibilities. Imagine building a finely tuned hierarchy of views, abstracting data ever more from the data model, and giving your data users nothing more than a single SELECT to extract information without worrying about underlying complexity! Yet there is a price to pay in server performance terms. Being dynamic in nature, VIEW(s) cannot be optimized in the same way as tables can, and can never be as fast for data retrieval. Adding yet another level will negatively affect performance of your database even more. There are valid business scenarios when hierarchical views are indicated, but ramifications of this decision should not be taken lightly.

Benefits and Drawbacks

When pondering the question whether to use underlying tables or abstract data with views, you always are balancing performance against complexity abstraction. You need to understand the ramifications of going either way and find a perfect balance.

VIEW(s) are good for the following:

- **Abstracting data model complexity** — For the end user.
- **Code reuse** — An SQL query is a transient thing unless you persist it in the client's code (embedded SQL), in a stored procedure, or in a VIEW.
- **Enhanced security** — VIEW can be used to limit users' access to data.
- **Personalization** — Several different VIEW(s) can be based upon the same data set, exposing different fields, having same fields renamed differently for different users, and so on.

The main drawbacks of using VIEW(s) are as follows:

- **Performance hit** — A VIEW is only as fast as the query it is based upon; it can never be optimized for data access the same way a table can.
- **Code portability** — Implementations differ significantly across RDBMSs.
- **Complexity** — Hidden from the end user, but it is still there. It has to be maintained, and with source code hidden from the average user it might increase maintainability costs.

You might have wondered what happens to the SQL source code for the view after you execute the CREATE VIEW statement. It is stored in the database along with other DDL statements, and can be retrieved through RDBMS system catalogs, system stored procedures, or INFORMATION_SCHEMA views. For more information, see Chapter 10.

BUT WAIT; THERE'S MORE!

So far, we were JOIN(ing) and UNION(ing) our data sets in every way imaginable, but set theory as implemented in SQL has a few more tricks up its sleeve: INTERSECT and EXCEPT. Both of these were endorsed by the SQL Standard and most RDBMSs.

INTERSECT

The INTERSECT operator is used on the results of two queries to include only the records produced by the first query that have the matching records in the second query. If you notice a similarity between *subqueries* and the EXISTS operator discussed in Chapters 2 and 6 you are absolutely correct. In many ways, they are the same.

For instance, to find out which books have been allocated places on a shelf in our bookcase, we could run the following query:

```
SELECT bk_id FROM  books
    INTERSECT
SELECT fk_bk_loc FROM location;
bk_id
--------------------
1
2
3
4
5
6
7
8
9
10
11
12

(12 row(s) affected)
```

The result is 12 records: the exact number of books we have in the BOOKS table, all assigned to some place in the bookcase. Had we entered a new book into the table and not created a record for it in the LOCATION table, this new book would not show up in the tally (in fact, we will try this out at the end of this section).

The reasons for using INTERSECT is code maintainability. The intent is clearer when using the operator as opposed to the subquery. For all we know, RDBMSs might treat them both in exactly the same way behind the scenes.

EXCEPT and MINUS

The goal that is the Holy Grail of database programming is to minimize the volume of data transfer over the network and eliminate unnecessary processing on the client. This means asking the RDBMS for the data you need and leaving everything else untouched. Just as INTERSECT gives us the ability to include the matching records from combined query, EXCEPT allows us to exclude them.

The INTERSECT and EXCEPT operators are mere convenience and can be replaced with INNER and OUTER JOIN(s), respectively (plus some additional tweaking to eliminate duplicate records).

Substituting EXCEPT for INTERSECT in the preceding example would show us BK_ID(s) for all books that do not have a place allocated to them in the bookcase (no corresponding record in the LOCATION table):

```
SELECT bk_id FROM  books
    EXCEPT
SELECT fk_bk_loc FROM location;
bk_id
--------------------

(0 row(s) affected)
```

Only records from the BOOKS table that do not have corresponding records in the LOCATION table will be returned. You will try out these operators along with INTERSECT in the activity section at the end of the chapter.

The NOT EXISTS operator with a correlated subquery could be used instead of the EXCEPT(MINUS) keyword. While not officially endorsed by the SQL Standards Committee, this syntax is supported in all RDBMSs (with the exception of HSQLDB used as embedded RDBMSs in OpenOffice).

The keyword EXCEPT is implemented in DB2, Microsoft SQL Server, and PostgreSQL. Whereas Oracle uses the MINUS keyword, MySQL, and HSQLDB recognize both EXCEPT and MINUS. Microsoft Access does *not* support either one.

TRY IT OUT Subtracting Data Sets

To take a closer look at the data set operations such as INTERSECT and EXCEPT, we need to introduce some data in our perfectly matched data. We already did this when discussing LEFT OUTER JOIN earlier in this chapter and we can use the same record again.

We will add an unmatched record to the BOOKS table and then take it for a spin applying both operators:

1. Open Microsoft SQL Server Management Studio and connect to your database using Windows authentication.

2. In the upper-left corner, click the New Query button.

3. In the opened query window (the middle pane), enter the following SQL query:

```
INSERT INTO books (bk_id, bk_title)
    VALUES (13,'UNMATCHED RECORD')
```

4. Now that we have a book without a corresponding shelf location, let's see what we can find using the INTERSECT and EXCEPT operators. First, execute a query with the INTERSECT operator:

```
SELECT bk_id FROM  books
    INTERSECT
SELECT fk_bk_loc FROM location;
```

5. Predictably, it brings in only 12 records — those matched from both tables.

6. Running the EXCEPT query gets us different results:

```
SELECT bk_id FROM  books
    EXCEPT
SELECT fk_bk_loc FROM location;
bk_id
--------------------
13

(1 row(s) affected)
```

How It Works

After a new record was inserted into the BOOKS table, it contained 13 rows, but only 12 of them are matched by a record in the LOCATION table. This models the situation when you got a new book, but haven't assigned it a place in the bookcase. INTERSECT returns matching records only from both tables. As a result, the record with BK_ID = 13 is not included.

When we run the EXCEPT query, the matching records were subtracted from each other, and only unmatched records were returned — in this case, the newly inserted "UNMATCHED RECORD."

SUMMARY

Hosting your data in a relational data model has both benefits and drawbacks. Since your data now is spread across many tables, the data must be constructed into a data set to be of use. The JOIN operator provided by SQL facilitates the process. It allows joining data sets gathered from the tables on some meaningful criteria, often primary and foreign keys.

Each JOIN operator involves two tables, and there is no practical limit on how many JOIN(s) a query could contain or how many tables could be JOIN(ed) in a query. The standard JOIN types are

INNER JOIN, LEFT and RIGHT OUTER JOIN, and FULL JOIN. They refer to the way the data sets from participating tables are matched.

While JOIN(s) combine data sets horizontally, the UNION operator combines them vertically, producing a single list of records from the different queries.

When JOIN and UNION operators are used in a query, in addition to a variety of clauses, the query could quickly become complex. This complexity could be abstracted using the VIEW construct; a VIEW is a frozen query. In addition to hiding complexity, they also could be used to address data security, as well as data access customization.

The concepts introduced and elaborated in this chapter are, by and large, part of the SQL Standard, yet there are significant differences between different RDBMS implementations.

8

What Else Is There, and Why?

The hardest task of trying to put together an introduction to a complex and convoluted subject such as SQL is deciding which concepts and features to include and which to leave out. The SQL Standard maintained by the International Standards Organization (ISO) lists hundreds of features grouped in nine sections, and RDBMS vendors and organizations add hundreds more. This chapter introduces some concepts normally left for more advanced books because we believe that you need to be aware of their existence even when you are just learning the ropes.

AN INDEX FOR ALL SEASONS

One of the best ways to improve database performance is through effective indices. Without an index, the database engine will search in the dark, methodically scanning each and every record in the table until it finds the set satisfying the search criteria. With an index, it first asks for directions and then gets what's needed much faster (in most cases). As you will see in Chapter 9, indices are very important in helping the RDBMS figure out an execution plan (how to find and combine the data requested). While speeding up the retrieval, indices are detrimental for INSERT and UPDATE queries. It pays to slow down and think about how your data will be used before creating an index.

An index is an auxiliary object; it does not exist separate from a table. The basic syntax is identical across RDBMSs. Here's a statement to create an index named IX_BK_ID on column BK_ID for the table BOOKS:

```
CREATE INDEX ix_bk_id
   ON books (bk_id);
```

An index can be created for an empty table or for one that already contains data. In the latter case, some restrictions might apply, as you will see later in the chapter.

The basic CREATE INDEX syntax is deceptively simple, but rest assured that as you start digging, the complexity quickly mounts. Oracle's CREATE INDEX statement, for example, taking into consideration attributes, logging, and partitions, can span several pages of code and might easily become a subject for a book of its own.

If you run a SELECT statement on the BOOKS table before and after executing the previous statement, you'll notice no difference in performance. There are several reasons for this:

- **Data set is too small** — In small tables, a full table scan might be faster than using an index. Consider a book analogy: If you are asked to find a certain word in a 400-page book, you'd be well advised to use an index to find the numbers of the pages containing this word first. But if you have only a single paragraph, going to the index is a waste of time.
- **Not all indices are created equal** — If the column for which you've created an index is not part of your search criteria, the index will be useless at best and detrimental at worst.

A table can have more than one index, and an index can contain more than one column. For example, we can add BK_TITLE for an index to be used in queries that search by both fields:

```
CREATE INDEX ix_bk_combined
   ON books (bk_id,bk_title);
```

The rule of thumb is to create indices on the columns you are using in the WHERE clause of your query. For example:

```
SELECT * FROM books
    WHERE bk_price > 20;
```

The index on the BK_PRICE column speeds up queries on a sufficiently large data set; the same goes for columns used in the GROUP BY and HAVING clauses. If you find yourself running repeated queries in which two or more columns are always used as a group in the search criteria, a composite index might be a better choice than several single indices.

The most effective indices are created on columns with a small percentage of duplicate values. An index on a primary key column is an example where there are no duplicate values, and RDBMSs automatically create an index on a column declared with PRIMARY KEY constraints. At the same time, there can be too much of a good thing. Creating an index on a column containing the global unique identifier (GUID) data type is not recommended, even though GUID values are virtually guaranteed to be unique. The reason is the drastically increased storage needs (GUIDs take up 16 bytes), and larger index sizes as a result.

Indices on numeric columns work much better than on columns that contain character data: after all, computers were designed to work with numbers, while character searches, besides needing to compare multiple characters (the shorter, the better) involve additional things such as collation considerations.

In the composite indices, one has to pay attention to the order in which the index columns are listed: The first column provides the most performance boost, while others are considered in the second and third turn, and so on. If your search is on a column that is a part of composite index and is not the first on the list, some RDBMSs will not use this index at all, and will perform a full table scan (an expensive operation that indices are supposed to prevent).

UNIQUE Index

An index can be used to ensure the uniqueness of the values in a column, in which case it is created with the UNIQUE keyword:

```
CREATE UNIQUE INDEX ix_bk_id
   ON books (bk_id);
```

Such an index would be used to enforce the integrity of the table, and is implicitly created for the column (or set of columns) declared as PRIMARY KEY; by definition a column with UNIQUE INDEX cannot contain NULLs.

This feature is being deprecated in many databases in favor of the UNIQUE constraint. This seems to be logical development; indices should have no business enforcing integrity.

CLUSTERED Index

The data entered into the table comes in randomly. We don't buy books in alphabetical order; normally we enter them as they come. Consequently, the indices created for these columns are but pointers to the records; the actual records can be scattered all over the place; this is the default non-clustered index. With CLUSTERED index, the data in the table is organized according to the index, which results in faster performance. Physical data blocks are "clustered" together just as index entries pointing to these blocks are. This significantly speeds retrieving the records as there is no need to spin the disk to get to the needed data. In Oracle RDBMSs, clustered indices are known as *index organized tables* (*IOTs*).

There is only one way data can be physically organized on the disc, so only one clustered index can be created per table. In Microsoft SQL Server, creating a column(s) with PRIMARY KEY constraint automatically creates a unique clustered index on this column (or set of columns, in the case of a composite index). In other RDBMSs, you must specify whether the index is clustered.

Oracle supports IOTs; they are part of the CREATE TABLE definition and can grow quite complex. The most basic table organized by the index on the primary key might look as follows:

```
CREATE TABLE books (
    bk_id INTEGER
  , bk-title
  , ...
    PRIMARY KEY (bk_id)
        ORGANIZATION INDEX;
```

Creating Oracle IOTs with advanced options is beyond the scope of this book.

To create a clustered index on a column other than the primary key in Microsoft SQL Server, you must specify the CLUSTERED keyword:

```
CREATE CLUSTERED INDEX ix_bk_id
   ON books (bk_id);
```

The IBM DB2 syntax falls in between the two. It creates an index and then issues the CLUSTER command. For example:

```
CREATE INDEX ix_bk_id
   ON books (bk_id)
     CLUSTER;
```

PostgreSQL uses Oracle's notion of an IOT, which is reflected in its syntax; it clusters the table, not the index. Here's an example of the syntax:

```
CLUSTER books USING ix_bk_id;
```

The index, of course, has to exist before this command will have any effect.

When selecting candidates for a clustered index, it is highly recommended to select columns with the most static data. Every change in this column will require reordering the entire table, as the RDBMSs will have to move the index entry. It can be an expensive operation and can cause performance problems. This explains that while primary keys are the prime candidates for a clustered index, key values are as static as they come.

In MySQL, clustered indices are only supported with the *InnoDB* storage engine and are created on primary key columns only. (MySQL provides several different types of storage, each providing some specific capability.)

Neither the Hyper Structured Query Language Database (HSQLDB) nor Microsoft Access supports clustered indices with its native storage engine. When used as a front end for other RDBMSs, the other RDBMS rules apply.

There are several more exotic indices introduced by RDBMSs to address specific needs; two of them are worth mentioning here: the function-based index and XML index.

We will be discussing XML data types in greater detail in Chapter 11, which deals with unstructured and semistructured data. The idea behind the index is to speed up queries on the XML data type, which takes into consideration its structure. The syntax is complex and proprietary; every RDBMS supporting XML data types came up with its own. An XML index can significantly improve the search on XML documents stored in the database. Please be sure to check vendors' documentation for specifics.

The idea behind a *function-based index* (*FBI*) is to speed up queries where the search criterion uses a function. Instead of creating an index for the value contained in the column, the FBI contains function output values. Let's say you perform a search for a book title and decide to compare values converted into uppercase to make a case-insensitive search. In Oracle, such a query would look as follows:

```
SELECT * FROM books
   WHERE UPPER(bk_title) = 'SQL BIBLE';
```

Now, the presence of the UPPER() function in the WHERE clause will slow the query down because RDBMSs cannot use an index defined on the BK_TITLE column. The solution is to create an index on UPPER(bk_title):

```
CREATE INDEX ix_bk_title_upper
    ON books(UPPER(bk_title));
```

This is an advanced feature found in Oracle, and it can be emulated in some other databases (for example, Microsoft SQL Server supports indices on computed columns — those that use functions for values).

An INDEX Destroyed

While *basic* syntax for creating indices is almost identical across the RDBMSs (this is not true of the complete syntax, which includes all optional clauses), it is different when it comes to altering or dropping an index. Details of ALTER INDEX are very RDBMS-specific and are outside the scope of this book. Besides, it is much easier to drop an index and re-create one (although there might be situations when you do not want this).

Oracle 11g R2 has a new feature called "invisible indexes" which could be an example of when ALTER is preferable to DROP. The syntax "ALTER INDEX <index_name> INVISIBLE;" instructs the optimizer (see Chapter 9 for more information on query optimization) to ignore the index, so the consequences of dropping an index could be tested without impacting the system's performance (and this action can be limited to session scope only).

The Oracle and IBM DB2 syntax is rather straightforward:

```
DROP INDEX ix_bk_id;
```

In Microsoft SQL Server, you have to add the table name along with the index name:

```
DROP INDEX books.ix_bk_id;
```

In MySQL, dropping an index means altering a table for which this index was created:

```
ALTER TABLE books
    DROP INDEX ix_bk_id;
```

Not to be outdone, Microsoft Access comes up with its own version:

```
DROP INDEX ix_bk_id ON books;
```

OpenOffice BASE with HSQLDB follows Oracle's syntax, with an optional clause that prevents an error message if you attempt to drop a non-existent index:

```
DROP INDEX ix_bk_id IF EXISTS;
```

TABLE REVISITED

A table is the most fundamental concept in a relational database. CREATE TABLE was introduced in Chapter 1 and used in every chapter ever since, yet it still holds some tricks up its sleeve.

When you create a table, its permanence is assumed; after all, we are going to store data, right? When you need to store data permanently, you create a table; when you need to store temporary data, you create a temporary table.

If your data processing is too complex to be accomplished in one single sweep, you might want to consider a place to store intermediate results to be used further down the line. Once the processes using this intermediate data are completed, the temporary storage area, along with the intermediate data, simply goes away. This is the idea behind the *temporary table.*

SQL syntax for creating temporary tables varies across the RDBMSs, and some, like Microsoft Access, while supporting the idea in principle, do not include it as part of SQL implementation.

There are lots of gotchas and important details you need to master to count this object type confidently as part of your SQL toolbox, yet some basics will help you to get started.

A temporary table normally has a scope, it can be global or local, and its behavior depends on the RDBMS and context. As you might expect, there is some confusion in terms. For example, Oracle defines all temporary tables as GLOBAL, but they can only be transaction-specific or session-specific (see Chapter 10 for more information). Either way, they are visible only to the user who creates them. In Microsoft SQL Server, the local temporary table is used in the same way, in context of a session that created them, while the global temporary table will be shared across sessions. The important point shared across all RDBMSs is transience, not only of data but also of the table structure definition.

Here's the SQL syntax for creating a local temporary table in Microsoft SQL Server:

```
CREATE TABLE #my_temp_table(
    column1 INT
  , column2 VARCHAR(10)
    );
```

The hash sign (#) indicates that the table is both temporary and local; it can only be accessed from the same session that created it and will disappear once the session (connection) is closed. Things are a bit different with a global temporary table, created with a double hash prefix:

```
CREATE TABLE ##my_temp_table(
    column1 INT
  , column2 VARCHAR(10)
    );
```

Now, the table will be visible across the entire instance of your SQL server (for example, if you open yet another concurrent connection to your database) and will disappear when the *last* session referencing this table closes.

Oracle's temporary tables are only local (in a Microsoft SQL Server sense). They are not shared across different sessions, yet they are created with keyword GLOBAL.

```
CREATE GLOBAL TEMPORARY TABLE my_temp_table(
    bk_id    INT
  , bk_title VARCHAR(10)
    ) ON COMMIT PRESERVE ROWS;
```

The difference is in the last clause. If you instruct Oracle to PRESERVE ROWS, the data will be preserved for the duration of the session; with ON COMMIT DELETE ROWS, the data will be blown away once the transaction (a unit of work (UOW), discussed in Chapter 10) is completed.

PostgreSQL treats its temporary tables as views, SQL query being part of the CREATE TEMP TABLE syntax and the base table from which data are gathered must exist. The query executes only once: to fill the newly created table with data. From this moment on, any changes to the original base tables will not be reflected in the temporary table:

```
CREATE GLOBAL TEMP TABLE my_temp_table ON COMMIT DROP
    AS SELECT * FROM books;
```

There are quite a few options that can be specified and are beyond the scope of this book. The basic syntax in the preceding example will create a temporary table, MY_TEMP_TABLE, as a snapshot of the BOOKS table and will be destroyed automatically once the transaction (see Chapter 10) is committed. Other options are similar to those found in Oracle: PRESERVE ROWS and DELETE ROWS, with the former being the default option. The keyword GLOBAL (and its opposite LOCAL) are optional and are safely ignored by PostgreSQL. The temporary table exists only within context of the session. The documentation simply states that they are "ignored for compatibility." We'll leave it at that.

In order to create an empty temporary table structure in PostgreSQL, you can specify an impossible condition that returns an empty data set, for example:

```
CREATE GLOBAL TEMP TABLE my_temp_table ON COMMIT DROP
    AS SELECT * FROM books WHERE bk_id < 0;
```

MySQL supports only session-scoped temporary tables, pretty much along the lines of Microsoft SQL Server single-hash prefixed tables:

```
CREATE TABLE my_temp_table(
    column1 INT
  , column2 VARCHAR(10)
    );
```

There is no transaction-controlled behavior in MySQL temporary tables, both data and the table will disappear once connection to the database is terminated.

While you can be almost assured that a temporary table will disappear upon termination of the database connection (Oracle, for example, preserves temporary table definitions between sessions), it is considered a best practice to use DROP TABLE explicitly.

Both DB2 and Open Office BASE/HSQLDB treat temporary tables as variables to be declared within a batch with DECLARE keyword. The similarity ends there. For instance:

```
DECLARE GLOBAL TEMPORARY TABLE my_temp_table
(
    column1 INT
  , column2 VARCHAR(10)
) ON COMMIT DELETE ROWS;
```

Temporary tables are usually created as part of a batch within the session and are not visible to other concurrent sessions though some vendors might have implemented different sets of rules.

There are a number of RDBMS-specific details governing the lifecycle of temporary tables. Most of them are way beyond scope of this book; please refer to the RDBMS specific documentation for more information.

VIEW REVISITED

In the previous chapter, we defined a VIEW as a frozen query, emphasizing that unlike a table it stores no data. Here we introduce views that do just the opposite: *materialized views*.

The idea behind a materialized view is to combine benefits of a VIEW and a TABLE into a single database object, usually for performance reasons. An SQL view offers ultimate flexibility; the data can be pulled in from several tables, aggregated, ordered, and otherwise made user-friendly. Yet, there is a price to pay; even with advanced RDBMS optimization, a query might be executed once for each request, and you cannot index dynamic data. With the table, on the other hand, you have all the advantages of index optimization, but to use data from more than one table, you have to run an SQL query.

A materialized view offers you the best of both worlds. As a query it collects the data from different tables, and as a table it persists it in the database. The catch? You sacrifice concurrency. Materialized views have to be updated periodically. The usage scenarios for materialized views are those when large amounts of relatively stable data need to be queried by a large number of users, and persisting the query would offer an increased performance; the data can be refreshed during off-peak hours, along with rebuilding the indices. You get fast and simple SELECT, even though the data are as up to date as the last refresh.

Materialized views were introduced by Oracle, and adopted by a number of RDBMS vendors. Details of implementation differ widely. Microsoft SQL Server introduced what it calls *indexed views*, which allow for creation of an index on a view as you would on an ordinary table. IBM DB2 provides a Materialized Query Table (MQT), whose definition is based upon a query.

Materialized views functionality can be duplicated with a table and a scheduled process, either inside or outside the RDBMS. This is the path taken by PostgreSQL and MySQL. Performance gains afforded by materialized views concepts would be negligible in desktop databases such as Microsoft Access and OpenOffice BASE/HSQLDB, even though it can be mimicked with built-in programming facilities.

BY ANY OTHER NAME: ALIASES AND SYNONYMS

People invent different names for the same things all the time. The English word "Sun," French "le Soleil," and German "die Sonne," all look and sound distinctly different, yet they still refer to the same object. The same concept applied to RDBMSs becomes synonyms and aliases.

Throughout the book, we have used aliasing to rename columns and tables inside an SQL query for convenience reasons, to shorten fully qualified names. These aliases were short-lived, surviving only for the duration of the query. Other queries could have used the same name or come up with its own. Creating synonyms and aliases as *database objects* allow for creating an alternate reality.

In its most generic meaning, a SCHEMA in RDBMS context is a way to group database objects logically inside a database. The SQL Standard defines schema *as a "named group of related objects," yet different RDBMSs implement it differently. In Oracle, for instance,* schema *is almost identical to* user, *while Microsoft SQL Server and DB2 are both closer to its standard meaning. Like other database objects, schemas can be created, altered, and dropped. A detailed discussion of schema is beyond the scope of this book.*

Consider Oracle RDBMS. An Oracle database concept is quite different from a database notion of Microsoft SQL Server, for instance: Each Oracle user has his own set of tables, indices, or views (in Oracle, USER and SCHEMA are often interchangeable). To allow one SCHEMA/USER to access objects stored in another SCHEMA/USER, assuming that one has sufficient privileges assigned by the database administrator (DBA), a fully qualified name must be specified. For example, for USER_1 to query the BOOKS table created in the SCHEMA belonging to USER_2, he might use the following query:

```
SELECT * FROM user2.books;
```

A two-part name ensures that the data are selected from the correct table, and not from the BOOKS table, which might happen to be in the USER_1 schema. For a one-time query it might be okay to type the fully qualified name, but if this table is used on regular basis, you might want to shorten it a bit. You can do it by creating an Oracle SYNONYM:

```
CREATE OR REPLACE PUBLIC SYNONYM bks
    FOR USER_2.books;
```

Better yet, you've just hired a French team to work on your database and would like to provide them with descriptive names for the database objects in French. Here's one way to do it:

```
CREATE OR REPLACE PUBLIC SYNONYM livres
    FOR USER_2.books;
```

In Oracle, you can create synonyms for virtually any database object: tables, views, functions, stored procedures, packages, and so on. You can even create a synonym for another synonym already defined in the RDBMS!

Once a synonym is created, you can use it as any RDBMS object it represents: SELECT from a table or view a synonym, execute a synonym created for a stored procedure, and so on. For example:

```
SELECT * FROM livres;
```

A similar principle applies to IBM DB2, except that you'd use ALIAS instead of SYNONYM:

```
CREATE ALIAS livres
    FOR USER_2.books;
```

Microsoft SQL Server introduced SYNONYMs in its version 2005 as a way to shorten multipart names (for instance, if you have several databases defined in your SQL Server installation and want to run a query that ties together tables from these different databases). Instead of using a three- or four-part name, you can create a synonym:

```
CREATE SYNONYM livres
    FOR library.dbo.books;
```

The database owner (DBO) schema is the default schema that will be used when none is specified.

You might have noticed a similarity between VIEW and SYNONYM. Both can be used to refer to database objects by another name, but the similarity ends there. Views cannot be used to replace multipart naming, SCHEMA.TABLE or SERVER.DATABASE.SCHEMA.TABLE because a view residing in the database must also be addressed by a multipart name.

MySQL does not support synonyms as database objects; neither does PostgreSQL (though it is on the to-do list and is actively discussed in the community). Microsoft Access and OpenOffice BASE/HSQLDB also do not support them, reserving the ALIAS keyword for different purposes altogether.

AUTO-INCREMENTED VALUES

Almost every table in the Library database has a primary key of a numeric data type, and the INSERT statements include the actual values for each record. The purpose of the numbers is to enforce referential integrity and possibly to keep track of the records because the numbers increase with every new book added. These values are not used anywhere else; in fact, it is considered to be a best practice to use meaningless (in context of the table's data) unique values for the primary key columns, as have pointed out in Chapter 3. Keeping track of these numbers to know exactly what to insert next is a nuisance in small single-user databases and can be a major headache for large multiuser systems.

How can you find out what the next number will be? You can query the table for the maximal number; this is how it used to be in the days of yore (Microsoft SQL Server syntax):

```
SELECT @next_value = MAX(book_id)+1 FROM books;

INSERT INTO books (bk_id, bk_title)
    VALUES (@next_value, 'NEXT BOOK IN SEQUENCE')
```

There are several major problems with this approach, though. The first problem arises in multiuser environments. However brief the time it takes for the query to get executed, there is no guarantee that somebody else's query would not grab the same value and thus try to insert the same value as you. This can be addressed with locking down the table in a transaction (see Chapter 10 for more information on transactions), which would negatively affect performance.

Another problem is a query itself. The insertion of a new value is performed as a batch in two steps, which requires additional processing: Declaring the variable NEXT_VALUE (in the earlier example, we used Microsoft SQL Server syntax, hence the @ sign, differentiating the declared variable from the SQL keyword), assigning the MAX value from the column BK_ID to this variable, incrementing it by 1, and then inserting it back into the same table. Add it to the inconsistencies across RDBMSs, and it begins to sound like a lot of hassle. Wouldn't it be nice to offload all this business of figuring the next value along with ensuring its uniqueness to the RDBMS? It sure would! The approach taken by the relational databases developers is split along two concepts: *sequences* and *identity columns*.

Identity Columns

The idea of an IDENTITY column is to let the table alone keep track of the values. It is defined as part of the Data Definition Language (DDL) statements, usually CREATE, and can be added later on with the ALTER statement (in those RDBMSs that support IDENTITY columns, that is). Unfortunately, the syntax for an IDENTITY column is different for every RDBMS that supports such a notion. Table 8-1 presents a matrix of the SQL syntax for creating IDENTITY columns across the database.

TABLE 8-1: IDENTITY Column SQL Syntax Across RDBMSs

RDBMS	BASIC SQL CREATE SYNTAX	NOTES
Microsoft SQL Server	CREATE TABLE <table> (<column> BIGINT IDENTITY(seed, increment))	Does not guarantee sequential gap-free values
IBM DB2	CREATE TABLE <table> (<column> GENERATED ALWAYS AS IDENTITY (START WITH seed, INCREMENT BY increment)	Different options available
PostgreSQL	CREATE TABLE <table> (<column>SERIAL);	Merely a shortcut to creating sequence
MySQL	CREATE TABLE <table> (<column> BIGINT NOT NULL AUTO_ INCREMENT=seed)	The seed value is optional; omitted defaults to 1
Microsoft Access	CREATE TABLE <table> (<column> COUNTER)	Defaults to seed=1, increment 1
OpenOffice BASE/ HSQLDB	CREATE TABLE <table> (<column> BIGINT IDENTITY)	Defaults to seed=1, increment 1

Neither Oracle nor PostgreSQL supports IDENTITY columns; instead they implement sequences *to generate sequential numbers.*

Microsoft SQL Server

If we chose to create our BOOKS table declaring BK_ID an identity column, the following would be a valid SQL syntax in Microsoft SQL Server:

```
CREATE TABLE books
(
            bk_id BIGINT IDENTITY(1,1)
         , bk_title TEXT
         , . . .
 )
```

The IDENTITY establishes the initial value and by how much this value will be incremented; the initial value is called *seed* and the incremental value is called *increment*. In the preceding example, the seed is 1, and the increment is also 1. Here we have chosen seed 100 and increment 50:

```
CREATE TABLE books
(
            bk_id BIGINT IDENTITY(100,50)
         , bk_title TEXT
         , . . .
 )
```

From this moment on, every record inserted into this table will get a unique BK_ID value — unique within the table, that is — assigned automatically. The numbers will grow sequentially by the increment specified in the column definition, 100, 150, 200, 250 and so on, for every record INSERT(ed) into the table.

The identity column can be defined when a table is initially created or added later on with an ALTER statement.

Normally IDENTITY columns can't be inserted into directly or updated through an SQL statement. To override this default behavior, you must modify the setting in your session with the SET IDENTITY_INSERT ON statement for this specific table. It is a good idea to turn it OFF after you do so.

Keep in mind, though, that the SQL Server makes no guarantees about sequential gap-free values in identity columns. The gaps in sequence can be introduced intentionally (for example, by deleting rows) or unintentionally (a database crash, for instance).

TRY IT OUT Adding Records to a Table with an IDENTITY Column

At the beginning of this book, we created the BOOKS table in our Library database. The inserted data had value for each column in the table, including BK_ID, which contains unique sequential numeric data. As such, it is a prime candidate to be re-created as an IDENTITY column. Let's try to implement this using Microsoft SQL Server 2008:

1. Open the SQL Client to connect to your RDBMS (please see Appendix C for information on how to do this). We will use Management Studio Express.

2. Connect to the Microsoft SQL Server instance (using either Windows Integrated Security or SQL Server Security).

3. Type in the following DDL statement to re-create the BOOKS table with a different name and an IDENTITY column; this is the most basic syntax:

```
CREATE TABLE identity_books(
   bk_id                    bigint  IDENTITY(1,1) NOT NULL,
   bk_title                 varchar(100) NULL,
   bk_ISBN                  varchar(50) NULL,
   bk_publisher             varchar(100) NULL,
   bk_published_year        int NULL,
   bk_price                 smallmoney NULL,
   bk_page_count            int NULL,
   bk_bought_on             smalldatetime NULL,
   bk_hard_cover            bit NULL,
   bk_cover_pic             varbinary(max) NULL,
   bk_notes                 xml NULL,
)
```

4. The next step would be to insert values. Note that we do not insert anything into the BK_ID column; it is not even on the list:

```
INSERT INTO identity_books
           (bk_title
           ,bk_ISBN
            )
     VALUES
           ('SQL Bible'
           ,'978-04700229063'
            )
```

5. Press the Execute button to run the query.

6. Repeat Step 5 (using exactly the same values) several times.

7. Issue the following SELECT statement against the IDENTITY_BOOKS table:

```
SELECT bk_id, bk_ISBN
   FROM identity_books;

bk_id                    bk_ISBN
--------------------     ------------------
1                        978-04700229063
2                        978-04700229063
3                        978-04700229063
4                        978-04700229063
5                        978-04700229063

(5 row(s) affected)
```

8. Try to add BK_ID onto the insert list and add a value to the VALUES list, as shown in the following DDL statement:

```
INSERT INTO identity_books
           (
```

```
          bk_id
         ,bk_title
         ,bk_ISBN
          )
   VALUES
         (
          100
         ,'SQL Bible'
         ,'978-04700229063'
          )
```

9. Click the Execute button and observe the following error message:

```
Msg 544, Level 16, State 1, Line 1
Cannot insert explicit value for identity column in table 'identity_books'
when IDENTITY_INSERT is set to OFF.
```

10. Drop the table so it won't clutter the database by typing in this SQL query and then pressing the Execute button:

```
DROP TABLE books;
```

How It Works

We have created a copy of the BOOKS table with IDENTITY for the BK_ID column. The IDENTITY was declared with seed 1 and increment 1, meaning that we want the sequence to start with 1 and be incremented by 1 for all additional sequential values.

The INSERT statement excluded the BK_ID because even though it has NOT NULL constraint defined, now it has default value supplied by the IDENTITY.

All other columns that are not on the list and for which no values were supplied will be populated with default NULL(s).

Running the same statement five times inserted duplicate values in every column except BK_ID, which was populated with a new sequential value for each new record inserted.

An attempt to insert value into the BK_ID column as part of the INSERT statement failed because it violated the IDENTITY convention used that, by default, does not allow values to be inserted directly by default.

The table was removed from the database at the end of the exercise.

IBM DB2

DB2 supports both identity columns and sequences. It requires a numeric data type: SMALLINT, INTEGER, or DECIMAL (with a scale of zero).

The following is a basic example of defining an identity column on the CREATE TABLE statement:

```
CREATE TABLE books (
   bk_id INT  NOT NULL
```

```
        GENERATED ALWAYS
        AS IDENTITY (START WITH 1, INCREMENT BY 1 CACHE 10)

)
```

The BK_ID is declared as an IDENTITY column with seed value of 1, incremented by 1. The qualifier GENERATE ALWAYS means that the value will always be generated upon insertion — no exceptions. The alternate allowable value GENERATE BY DEFAULT means that the value will be generated only if none is supplied.

By specifying CACHE 10, we are instructing the database to fetch ten values and store them for faster retrieval in fast-paced environments. This option "reserves" the next ten values and stores them in somewhere in the local cache. This feature might result in unintentional gaps in numbering because, if the database crashes, the cache is gone, and a new cache is created. If strictly sequential numbering is important, you might specify NO CACHE to avoid this situation.

The identity column in IBM DB2 can be created as part of the table definition or by using the ALTER statement.

PostgreSQL

There is no support for identity columns in PostgreSQL (it uses *sequence* objects instead, as discussed later in the chapter), though there is a shorthand that makes it appear like one. The following statement will create a sequence called "book_id_seq" and assign it as default value to the BK_ID column of the INTEGER data type:

```
CREATE TABLE books (bk_id SERIAL);
```

There is also the BIGSERIAL pseudo–data type, which would create column of the BIGINT data type. As with all shortcuts, you trade control for expediency. The autocreated sequence will have all the default settings (see the ALTER SEQUENCE statement later in the chapter).

MySQL

The identity column in MySQL is defined with the AUTO_INCREMENT keyword, as shown in the following code snippet:

```
CREATE TABLE table_name  (
   bk_id INTEGER NOT NULL AUTO_INCREMENT
   , . . .
)
```

The number sequence by default will start with 1 and will be incremented by 1. To change the default seed of 1, you can specify AUTO_INCREMENT = 10 in the table's DDL or ALTER the table's AUTO_INCREMENT setting later. In the latter case, the increment by 1 still stays, so do the previously generated numbers.

The identity column in MySQL can be created as part of the table definition or by using the ALTER statement.

Microsoft Access

In Microsoft Access, you normally create an auto-increment column visually, as part of the table design, as seen in Figure 8-1 showing MS Access data type for the auto-increment field, and Figure 8-2 showing field properties for the Auto-Increment data type.

If you need to create an auto-increment column in Microsoft Access SQL, the syntax is as follows:

```
CREATE TABLE books
(
        bk_id COUNTER
      , bk_title TEXT
      , . . .
)
```

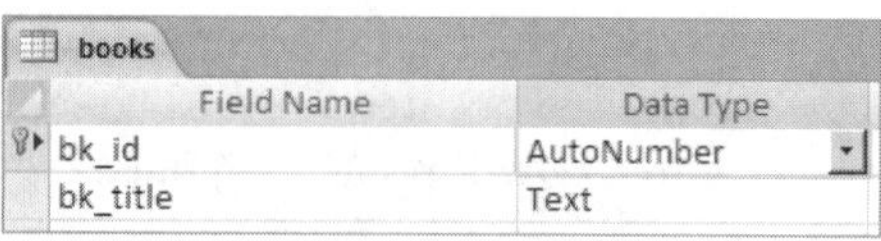

FIGURE 8-1

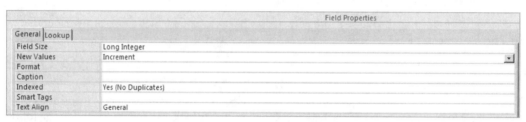

FIGURE 8-2

Unlike the other RDBMSs supporting auto-increment fields, MS Access makes implicit assumptions about auto-increment values: start with 1 and increment by 1.

The other built-in data type, a synonym, really is an AUTO-INCREMENT; substituting it for COUNTER will work exactly the same way.

When used as a front end for another RDBMS, MS Access will obey the rules imposed by this particular RDBMS.

OpenOffice BASE with HSQLDB

The auto-increment columns in the OpenOffice BASE are created in essentially the same way as in Microsoft Access with the exception of data type. What MS Access defines as a LONG INTEGER is BIGINT in HSQLDB, as shown Figure 8-3 (creating a column of the auto-increment-compatible data type).

On the graphical interface, this is the only data type that allows for the "AutoValue" option to be specified, as shown in Figure 8-4 (setting the AutoValue for the HSQLDB column).

Field Name	Field Type
bk_id	BigInt [BIGINT]
bk_title	Text [VARCHAR]

FIGURE 8-3

The SQL syntax behind it translates it into something like this:

```
CREATE TABLE books
(
```

```
        bk_id BIGINT IDENTITY
      , bk_title TEXT
      , . . .
)
```

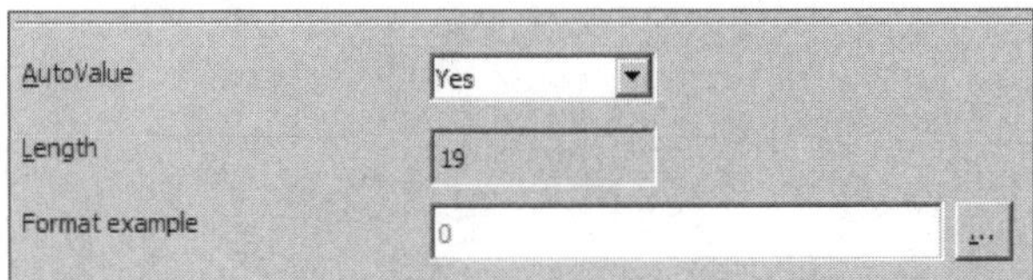

FIGURE 8-4

As with MS Access, there are assumptions made to start your numbering from 1 and incrementing by 1.

HSQLDB supports both sequence and identity columns. When used as a front end for another RDBMS, the OpenOffice BASE, like MS Access, will obey the rules imposed by this particular RDBMS.

Who Am I: Finding One's IDENTITY

When inserting a record with an identity column, you rely on the RDBMS to come up with the next number to fill in the identity, but how do you find the value for the identity that had been assigned? You can query the table immediately after insertion to find the MAX() value, but it might not work in multiuser environments where the table can be inserted into by more than one concurrent user (you can lock other users out while performing the operation, but this would hardly be a recipe for a high-performance database).

Each RDBMS deals with the problem in its own way, all of them proprietary and nonstandard. Table 8-2 lists the SQL functions used to retrieve inserted identity values for each of the RDBMSs.

TABLE 8-2: Retrieving Inserted Identity Values

RDBMS	SQL FUNCTION
Microsoft SQL Server	SCOPE_IDENTITY
IBM DB2	IDENTITY_VAL_LOCAL
MySQL	LAST_INSERT_ID
HSQLDB	IDENTITY

Some of the functions might not be accurate in multiuser environments when records in the table might be inserted by a number of concurrent users. For instance, Microsoft SQL Server's function operates within a session's scope and will return values inserted by the processes running within this session, even though other sessions might have inserted more records. Others, such as MySQL, do not guarantee it because of the global scope of their SQL functions.

All tables that use autogenerated sequential numbers for values are susceptible to identity gaps. The gaps can be introduced with deletions of the rows, database crashes, resetting identity column values, and so on. There is no easy way to deal with these gaps other than going back and modifying the data.

SEQUENCES

Unlike identity columns, sequences are independent RDBMS objects, not tied to a specific table. They have been implemented in Oracle, IBM DB2, PostgreSQL, and HSQLDB/OpenOffice BASE. More importantly, they have made it into the SQL Standard Committee.

The basic syntax for creating a sequence is identical across those RDBMSs supporting sequences (some might insist on adding the SCHEMA name as the first part of the sequence name). To create a generator that begins with 1, and generates sequential values in increments of 1, all you have to do is to issue this statement:

```
CREATE SEQUENCE seq_books;
```

Of course, there are quite a few optional clauses that can go with this statement: You can specify initial value, increment value, max and minimum values, the order (descending or ascending), and so on. Once a sequence is created, it can be referenced from an SQL statement by name, and its properties provide access to the current, next, and previous values.

Here are some examples of how the sequence created in the previous example can be used:

```
SELECT seq_books.NEXTVAL as next_value
FROM dual;

next_value
-----------------
1

SELECT seq_books.CURRVAL as current_value
FROM dual;

current_value
-----------------
1


SELECT seq_books.NEXTVAL as next_value
FROM dual;

next_value
-----------------
2
```

The DUAL table is provided by Oracle to SELECT from when you really do not need any data. IDB DB2 is even more forthright; it wants you to select from SYSIBM.SYSDUMMY1 so you'll never forget that you are selecting from nothing at all. All other RDBMSs discussed in this book are not as literal and allow you to drop the FROM clause altogether:

```
SELECT seq_books.NEXTVAL as next_value
    FROM SYSIBM.SYSDUMMY1;

next_value
-----------------
1
```

The older version of IBM DB2 might require different syntax:

```
SELECT NEXTVAL FOR seq_books as next_value
    FROM SYSIBM.SYSDUMMY1;

next_value
-----------------
1
```

PostgreSQL prefers notation of SQL function. To fetch NEXTVAL from a sequence SEQ_BOOKS created in PostgreSQL you might use the following syntax:

```
SELECT nextval('seq_books') AS next_value;

next_value
-----------------
1
```

CURRVAL and NEXTVAL are standard methods to access the values generated by the sequence. Only IBM DB2 also provides PREVVAL, which is one step behind NEXTVAL.

Once the sequence is created, it can be used as part of an SQL statement: INSERT, UPDATE, and DELETE, though primarily it is used with INSERT(s). For example, in an IBM DB2 database you might have used the following query:

```
INSERT INTO BOOKS (
    bk_id
  , bk_title)
    VALUES (seq_books.NEXTVAL, 'NEW BOOK TITLE');
```

To replicate identity column behavior, a sequence can be tied to a table's columns as a DEFAULT value constraint (as PostgreSQL does) or through a trigger (in case of Oracle and IBM DB2; see more about triggers later in this chapter) that would examine inserted records and add NEXTVAL to the list of the values to be inserted.

Let's take a quick look at some generic useful options that can be specified while creating a sequence. The more complete syntax, though not full, would look like the following:

```
CREATE SEQUENCE seq_books
    START WITH 1
    INCREMENT BY 1
    MAXVALUE 100
    MINVALUE 1
    CYCLE
    CACHE 10;
```

The sequence created in this way would start with 1 and would be incremented sequentially by 1 up to a maximum value of 100 (alternatives would be NOMAXVALUE constant). After that, it would be CYCLEd and begin from 1 again. (If you do not want your sequence to cycle, specify NOCYCLE instead.) The CACHE 10 option would "reserve" the next 10 values and store them somewhere in local cache for faster retrieval; this is an optimization technique for fast-paced environments.

Like any other database object, a sequence can be ALTERed. For example, here we are resetting the sequence with all new values:

```
ALTER SEQUENCE seq_books
    RESTART WITH 100
    INCREMENT BY 5
    NOMAXVALUE
    NOCYCLE
    NOCACHE;
```

A sequence can be destroyed following the same format as all other RDBMS objects:

```
DROP SEQUENCE seq_books;
```

There are optional CASCADE and RESTRICT keywords that can be added at the end to deal with potential dependencies. For example, if a sequence is referred to as a default constraint on a column, the RESTRICT keyword would prevent the sequence from being dropped.

TRY IT OUT Using Sequence Object-Generated Values

The sequence object in RDBMSs is used to generate sequential numeric values. The object exists within the database schema, and (unlike IDENTITY columns) is independent of other objects (unless explicitly stated). Here you will see how a sequence object can be used with IBM DB2 LUW 9.7 to generate values for the BOOKS table in the Library database.

1. Open your favorite SQL Client to connect to a DB2 Library database. Here we use Squirrel SQL Client (for configuration details, see Appendix D or visit us online at `www.agilitator.com`).

2. Create a sequence by running the following SQL query: Type it into the SQL tab of the Squirrel Client and press the Run button (Ctrl+Enter):

```
CREATE SEQUENCE seq_books
    START WITH 100
    INCREMENT BY 1
    MAXVALUE 10000
    MINVALUE 1
    NOCYCLE;
```

3. Next, type in the following INSERT statement:

```
INSERT INTO identity_books
           (
            bk_id
           ,bk_title
           ,bk_ISBN
            )
     VALUES
           (
            seq_books.NEXTVAL
```

```
        ,'SQL Bible'
        ,'978-04700229063'
         )
```

4. Check the current value of the SEQ_BOOKS sequence by running the following query:

```
SELECT seq_books.CURRVAL AS current_value
FROM sysibm.sysdummy1;

current_value
-----------------
100
```

5. Check the previous value of the SEQ_BOOKS sequence by running the following query:

```
SELECT seq_books.PREVVAL AS previous_value
FROM sysibm.sysdummy1;

current_value
-----------------
100
```

6. Verify that the newly inserted record indeed contains the value supplied by SEQ_BOOKS sequence object in the BK_ID column:

```
SELECT bk_id, bk_ISBN
   FROM books
WHERE bk_id > 99;

bk_id                  bk_ISBN
-------------------- ------------------
100                    978-04700229063
```

How It Works

We have created a sequence object to generate sequential numbers beginning with 100, running up to a maximum value of 1,000 with increments by 1.

We have used the method of the sequence object NEXTVAL to supply a valid value for the INSERT statement. Steps 4 through 6 verified that the current value for the SEQ_BOOKS object was incremented by 1 and now contains 101, that the previous value was 100, and that the record inserted into the BOOKS table indeed contains the value supplied by the sequence object.

Note that both CURRVAL and PREVVAL hold the same value, while NEXTVAL will acquire a value only when called upon. That is, neither CURRVAL not PREVVAL will have any value until NEXTVAL is called at least once.

COMPARING IDENTITY COLUMNS AND SEQUENCES

While there are similarities between identity columns and sequences, there are also differences. The major difference is that the sequence object is independent of any particular table and can be used by multiple tables; another distinction is that a sequence can be used in any SQL statement, including SELECT, UPDATE, and DELETE; whereas an identity column cannot.

Both sequences and identity columns generate unique numbers within their respective scopes, sequence objects, and tables. What if you need to generate a sequence of identities that are truly unique globally (the scope of the RDBMS or even the world)? Some databases provide built-in facilities; some leave you on your own to cobble up a solution. GUID values are represented in a hexadecimal string (for example, {780B9621-F5FB-4C31-8698-C92C9FFC7D37}) and, at least in theory, should never be generated twice. There are 3.4 × 10^38 total unique keys that can be generated (by comparison, there are only 1.33 × 10^50 atoms on Earth), which makes it highly unlikely (though not impossible) that the same number can be produced more than once. By their very nature, GUIDs are not sequential, and therefore are not the best choice for primary keys despite their assured uniqueness. The functions to generate GUIDs, also known as Universally Unique Identifiers (UUIDs) are vendor-dependent. Oracle provides SYS_GUID(), Microsoft SQL Server provides NEWID, MySQL has UUID(), and PostgreSQL has at least five(!) different functions to return GUID values. Microsoft Access calls a GUID a ReplicationID data type, which only applied to auto-increment fields; IBM DB2 or HSQLDB do not have built-in GUID generators (though one can be created using built-in programming facilities).

Once created, a GUID value can be stored in a specific "GUID"-data type or in a VARCHAR data type column.

TRIGGERS

We have already mentioned SQL procedural extensions in Chapter 4. Being a set-based language, the SQL lacks when it comes to dealing with single records: It has very little support for conditional execution, no looping, and complete absence of all other features that are implemented in procedural languages such as Java or C#. The ability to create stored procedures inside the RDBMS provides the best of both worlds.

Stored procedure is a persistent named module containing procedural code, and trigger is a stored procedure that is executed automatically in response to certain events on a particular database object. Traditionally, triggers were tied to the database tables and would file on events such as INSERT, UPDATE, and DELETE. Later on, the concept was extended to include database-wide events such as dropping and creating database objects. One of the most obvious uses for a trigger in the context of the preceding paragraph would be to use trigger to populate identity values based upon a sequence object.

With the exception of Microsoft Access, all RDBMSs discussed in this book support the *notion* of triggers (and a trigger-like functionality can be simulated using MS Access built-in programming language). The devil is, of course, in the details. Every vendor and organization had implemented it differently. This is a powerful feature; unfortunately, it is beyond scope of this book.

ONE HAPPY FAMILY: WORKING IN HETEROGENEOUS ENVIRONMENTS

So far, we've been working within the confines of a single database. All objects were created and managed by a specific RDBMS, be it Oracle, IBM DB2, Microsoft SQL Server, PostgreSQL, MySQL, MS Access, or HSQLDB. What if you have several different RDBMSs in your environment and need to use data from all of them?

One way is to transfer data among different RDBMSs in a process called extract, transform, and load (ETL) in database parlance. First, the data are extracted from the source database(s); second, it is transformed according to some rules; and third, it is loaded to a different RDBMS for querying. This is the bread and butter of a data warehousing operations. Some RDBMS vendors bundle ETL capabilities into their products (for example, Microsoft SQL Server); some rely on third-party companies, both open source and proprietary, to assist with the process.

Another approach is to use distributed querying capabilities offered by some RDBMSs. For instance, Microsoft SQL Server allows you to create a "linked server" from a variety of heterogeneous data sources (including Oracle, DB2, and MySQL, among others) that then can be included into an SQL query. The complexity of executing queries across these databases and returning a single result set is hidden in the layers of functionality built into the software.

There is a thriving market specializing in software to make distributed heterogeneous queries possible. Chances are that if you need such a query there will be a DBA somewhere around to help you with the process.

There is a relatively recent phenomenon that turns the traditional ETL model upside down. The idea is to bypass the intermediary staging area, load data directly into the target database tables, and then transform it there, in-situ, so to speak. There are advantages and disadvantages of both approaches, and expert advice is highly recommended.

SUMMARY

Learning SQL is easy, mastering it is hard. Every object created in the RDBMS and every query can have dozens of different options and clauses. The concepts introduced in this chapter span the entire spectrum, from basic to advanced.

Indices can be used to optimize query performance and, ultimately, the database application. There are different types of indices, and significant differences exist between SQL syntaxes implemented by various RDBMSs.

Temporary tables are used as workbenches to store and manipulate intermediate results; they can differ in scope and different lifecycle options, depending on implementation.

Materialized view is a concept introduced by several vendors to combine the advantages of views and tables into a single SQL object; the primary objective is to speed data retrieval by caching output of the query upon which the view is based and refresh it periodically.

The fully qualified names in the RDBMS are used uniquely to identify objects in multiuser, multi-schema environments; aliases and synonyms allow you to shorten these names for better readability and code maintenance.

The ability to generate numeric sequences automatically is a very useful feature provided by every RDBMS discussed in the book. There are two different approaches: identity columns (implemented in Microsoft SQL Server, IBM DB2, Microsoft Access, MySQL and OpenOffice BASE HSQLDB), and sequences (favored by Oracle and PostgreSQL). Some RDBMSs, such as IBM DB2, support both.

The sequences can be used with yet another feature of RDBMSs, triggers, to emulate the identity columns' functionality. Other uses of triggers include help in maintaining entity integrity and referential integrity in legacy applications.

The ability to query data across different RDBMSs is supported both with ETL processes and distributed heterogeneous queries. In the former case, the data are being extracted from one RDBMS, transformed, and loaded into another for querying; this is standard data warehousing practice. In the latter case, the implementation complexity is hidden behind a consistent interface that allows for execution of an SQL query without worrying about in which RDBMS the actual data resides. There are numerous concerns that need to be addressed with both approaches such as performance, security, and so on.

Optimizing Performance

If your database lives past infancy, and is deployed into a production environment and starts accumulating sizable amounts of data and users, sooner or later you will begin to worry about whether it performs at the optimal level. Being able to tell the RDBMS what you need is one thing, making sure that your order is executed in the most efficient way is another. The SQL is very good in abstracting your data needs from actual execution; all you need to say is *what* and let the RDBMS figure out *how*.

As your comfort level with the language grows, and you gain more knowledge into the relational databases world, you might begin to question the authority. Why does it take so long? Are my queries executing at the "as good as it gets" level, or are there ways to speed them up? Does my database perform at optimal level?

These and many more questions are bound to pop up should you stay in SQL land long enough.

DATABASE PERFORMANCE

What is RDBMS optimal performance? How do you define optimal performance? The people in the organization responsible for answering these questions are usually database administrators (DBAs), network administrators, or server administrators. At some level, this team might include software architects and software developers. It is not uncommon to see one person wearing some (or all) these hats, and at some advanced level it is as hard as it sounds (there is a reason for the big bucks paid to DBAs!).

Understanding what is involved in optimizing RDBMS performance would allow you to see possibilities for improvement and the limitations thereof. The ability to know one from the other comes with experience.

Performance Benchmarks

There are a few benchmarks that allow one to make an educated guess about whether your database server performs at top speed. Some of them are published by the vendors (and understandably should be taken with a grain of salt); some of them can be found on the Internet, published by aficionados of a particular RDBMS under unrepeatable conditions (and also should be taken with a pinch of salt); and your DBA can come up with some custom benchmarks, specific for your database.

Fortunately, there is an independent organization dedicated to benchmarking RDBMS performance: the Transaction Processing Performance Council or TPC for short.

According to the TPC, "the TPC is a non-profit corporation founded to define transaction processing and database benchmarks and to disseminate objective, verifiable TPC performance data to the industry." It was founded in 1998 as a nonprofit organization and is currently a recognized standard for database transaction processing performance. The TPC benchmarks are the gold standard for high-performance enterprise class RDBMSs. It measures peak performance achieved when an RDBMS and all its structures are tuned up for perfection, and costs are not an issue.

The TPC benchmarks come in three current flavors: TPC-C, -E, and -H (with a number of obsolete benchmarks such as A, B, D, as you might have guessed).

TPC-C is measured in transactions per minute (tpmC). It was created to test performance of an online transaction processing (OLTP) database. The benchmark simulates workload with a mix of five concurrent transactions of different types and complexity, either executed online or queued for deferred execution, on a database with nine types of tables with a wide range of record and population sizes.

Two other benchmarks measure performance under different scenarios: TCP-E, to model a brokerage firm with customers who generate transactions related to trades, account inquiries, and market research; and TCP-H for decision support, with its heavy use of ad hoc queries and concurrent data modifications.

IBM DB2 9.7 leads the roster with an impressive score of 10,366,254 tpmC benchmark (transactions per minute, close to 200,000 transactions per second!), at a cost of $1.38 per transaction; followed closely by Oracle 11g with 7,646,486 at a price of $2.36; and Microsoft SQL Server 2005 (the latest version for which the benchmark results were published) trailing at 1,807,347 tpmC at a price of 49 cents.

Keep in mind that such performance comes at a price, requires serious investment into hardware and tuning, and is usually an exclusive domain of the big players who need such performance and can afford it: large financial institutions, companies, and governments. The numbers give you an idea about how much this might cost: Just multiply the benchmark by the cost per transaction. In the case of IBM, it comes to a cool $14,000,000 (that's 14 *million*). Setting up and optimizing an RDBMS for such a performance requires a very advanced level of expertise, for which this book is but a tiny step.

Order of Optimization

While you cannot expect that your database will perform at the levels clocked by the TPC, the good news is that you will get a decent performance out of your database with but a minimal tuning and optimization because many RDBMSs automated many tasks that previously required DBA intervention. In many small-to-medium-size scenarios, the default options and automatic administration features will work adequately; large-scale deployments require advanced professional expertise.

Yet there are steps you can take to ensure that your database, your queries, and your applications perform at top levels. Database performance tuning and optimization is notoriously difficult because there are so many moving parts, a few of which are listed here:

- **Your application (the one that you use to access your data)** — It can be a desktop, mobile, or web-based, each environment coming with its own, very specific optimization options; additionally, your application can be partitioned across different domains, and include third-party components (such as ODBC/JDBC drivers, the translation layer between general programming languages and RDBMSs).
- **The network performance** — How fast is your network; what else is going over this wire?
- **The server environment where your RDBMS is installed (might not apply to desktop databases such as Microsoft Access)** — Includes the operating system (Windows, UNIX, Linux, MacOS, and so on) and OS-specific optimization tricks, amount of RAM (the computer memory), CPU speed, your hard-drive disk's speed, and amount of free space.
- **RDBMS configuration options** — Is your database optimized for OLTP or online analytical processing (OLAP); are vendor-specific options enabled (for example, Java, C# processing); are you using proper settings for your database?
- **The database schema** — Is your database highly normalized; are your tables properly indexed; do they have primary keys; are you using partitioning or triggers on the tables?
- **The SQL queries** — Are your queries constructed correctly (for example, overlooked Cartesian JOIN); are you using too many JOINs; are you using subqueries, stored procedures, custom functions, and so on?

Each of the previous components in any combination might affect database performance that would translate into poor user experience. Before you rush to optimize every one of these, take a deep breath and recall the Pareto Principle.

Vilfredo Pareto was an Italian engineer, sociologist, economist, and philosopher who lived between 1848 and 1923. After many years working as a civil engineer for the Italian Railway, he became a professor of economics at the University of Lausanne, Switzerland. The principle bearing his name was formulated in 1906, and came from an observation that 80 percent of Italy's wealth is owned by 20 percent of the population. This observation, also known as the 80/20 rule, applies to virtually every aspect of our lives. The very same Pareto noticed that 80 percent of his pea harvest is produced by 20 percent of the pea pods; the more modern examples include assertions that 80 percent of software crashes are caused by 20 percent of the software bugs, and so on.

While the exact ratio is open for discussion (80/20, 90/10 or 99/1), there is no doubt that effort efforts to target strategically important areas yield the most overall results. Database optimization is no different. Therefore, it would make the most sense to focus on what would bring you the most bang for the buck (figuratively speaking).

Hardware Optimization

The standard sequence for optimization starts with the server on which your RDBMS is running, followed closely by network performance optimization. These have to be verified before anything else because you need a solid foundation to build upon. Make sure that you get the best CPU you can afford, and that your RDBMSs have sufficient amounts of RAM and free disc space (see the recommended requirements for each respective RDBMS discussed in this book).

Operating System Tune-up

Next is your operating system. Some RDBMSs will run in different operating systems. Oracle, IBM DB2, PostgreSQL, MySQL, and HSQLDB can run on either UNIX/Linux or Microsoft Windows platforms, while SQL Server and Microsoft Access are Windows-only software. Each RDBMS has OS-specific configuration options to include its best performance. Make sure that your OS is patched to the level recommended by the RDBMS, no more, no less (we are speaking from performance point of view, but there is also a security perspective that needs to be balanced for *optimal* performance).

Optimizing RDBMSs

The RDBMS setup is your next frontier. There are many configuration parameters that need to be set depending on intended use. If you refer to the basic RDBMS installation steps (see Appendix B, as well as corresponding decks of slides, PowerPoint, PDF, or ODF formats, available for download from `www.wrox.com` or at `www.agilitator.com`), there are different options you can select to optimize your database for OLTP or OLAP use during setup. These can have a dramatic effect on your database performance, especially as the amount of data stored in your databases increases. Some configuration parameters can be modified after the setup; some require careful planning because they can be next to impossible to change.

Optimizing Database/Schema

Once your RDBMS is set up and running, you need to configure your application-specific database. As mentioned before, there is a fair amount of confusion in the terminology between different RDBMSs; schemas, databases and even users can refer to the same thing. Understandably, any potential optimization in these areas has to be performed on the vendor's terms. Please refer to the RDBMS-specific documentation for information on your particular database configuration options.

Still, we are getting closer to the subject of this book: SQL. The database and most (if not all,) of the objects it contains can be created using a Data Definition Language (DDL) statement, and herein lies your opportunity to affect performance. Chapter 3 discussed normalization techniques. Taking your data model to a fifth degree of normalization might be a Holy Grail for some applications and a performance hog for the others. Ultimately, it's your business objectives that will define the type of data model you will use: An analytics database would normally require a lower degree of normalization than a transaction processing one.

Denormalizing your data model might speed one, and slow down the other; it might increase data redundancy and add to data maintenance headaches. The primary reason for denormalizing the data model is to speed up SELECT queries, as denormalization reduces the number of JOIN(s) required to gather the data into a resultset.

For instance, suppose that when creating our LIBRARY data model we decided to keep publishers as part of the BOOKS table, and not separate them into a PUBLISHERS entity as normalization rules would normally require. There were two reasons behind the decision: We were not interested in collecting data about publishers, and we stated a one-to-many relationship between a book entity and a publisher entity (one book can be published by one and only one publisher; a publisher can publish one or many books). By including the publisher as an attribute into BOOKS table, we created a slightly denormalized schema (and increased the amount of data redundancy in the table; instead of a numeric key we'll store full publisher name). At the same time, we eliminated the need for a JOIN to fetch a publisher name into the SELECT statement as shown in Figure 9-1. This is the tradeoff we made to increase the performance of the query.

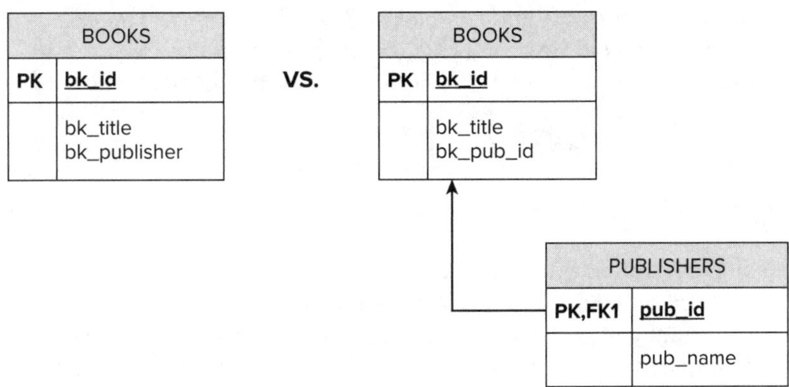

FIGURE 9-1

To produce a result set that includes a book title and corresponding publisher would only take a simple SELECT in one case and a JOIN between two tables in the other:

```
SELECT bk_title, bk_publisher FROM books;
```

versus:

```
SELECT bk.bk_title, pub.pub_name FROM books bk INNER JOIN publishers pub ON
bk.bk_pub_id = pub.pub_id;
```

The results of both queries will be identical while the query plans (see later in the chapter) prepared by the RDBMS will differ significantly. The second query will consume more memory and more CPU cycles than the first. While these additional resources might be very small, they might add up if the workload on your database, or the amount of data, increases (thousands of concurrent users or millions of rows).

Some might argue that because the BK_PUBLISHER column is a character data type and not an integer, it might slow down the index search on the column (see later in the chapter). Again, this would be something to be verified through an examination of your actual RDBMS query plans that estimate costs for each step in the query execution and then weigh the cost of a JOIN against the cost of an index search.

Other optimizations that can be performed at this level include data storage optimization, spreading actual data files across several drives to address potential contention issues.

Managing concurrency is another area where you can look for performance gains by specifying appropriate locking granularity level or selecting appropriate transaction isolation level.

In its enterprise incarnation, optimization might be taken to an entirely new level: the creation of massive parallel database clusters and the type of search engines that Google might be using. On these, queries from different users might run on different instances of RDBMSs, or even parts of the same query can be farmed out to different servers for processing to be combined into a final result set on output.

Application Optimization

This is an often forgotten component of every system that includes RDBMS data storage. Known at different times as a graphical user interface (GUI), a front end, an interface, a business layer, or a data access layer, these are important components that make the data available to the users, allows them to interact with it, and ultimately justifies the existence of the RDBMS in the first place.

Many Hoops to Go Through

It's a long way from data stored in your RDBMS to an application such as Microsoft Excel. There are layers upon layers of translation that stand between the familiar spreadsheet interface and data files managed by the RDBMS.

Before a single SQL statement is executed, an application such as Excel needs to establish connection to the RDBMS, the gateway to the data. There are several ways to do so: use the RDBMS native interface (the one provided by the vendor), use Open Database Connectivity (ODBC) drivers, Microsoft OLE DB Providers, Java Database Connectivity (JDBC) drivers, or a combination of these.

Once the connection is established, the application can submit requests to the RDBMS, and hopefully get results back. These results need to be interpreted, processed, and presented to the user. As the Greek legend of Samian King Anaeus recorded (see a Note later in the chapter), there is much between the edge of the cup and the lip, and there is much that can be done along the way: Application logic can be streamlined, better drivers can be bought, and so on. Remember the

80/20 rule: Check your system performance through the entire system and identify bottlenecks prior to any optimization.

Never Underestimate the Power of Perception

A slow query might appear to run fast if it gives a user what he or she needs upfront, while continuing to run in the background fetching the rest of the data. By designing for parallel tasks execution, you might win the prize.

Consider the following scenario: John's plan for today is to go through sales figures for the last quarter, line by line. Your application can try to get all the data he would need at once or it can fetch it in chunks of one week. If a company has lots of sales, the amount of data accumulated for the quarter can be significant. On the other hand, it might take John some time to go record by record and check the numbers. Your choice: Make him wait 15 minutes while your query fetches the data and your application processes and displays it, or limit the query to a week's worth of data to give John something on which to work right away while pulling the rest of the data into an application on a background thread. Which approach is likely to make John happier? Same query; vastly different performance perception.

Make sure that your application is tuned up before trying to squeeze out the last bit of performance from the RDBMS. This is an iterative process, and one should expect to make adjustments over and over until the desired level of performance is achieved.

The Samian King Aneaus planted a vineyard, but a seer warned him that he would not live to taste its fruit. The vineyard was grown, the first wine was made, and the king was raising the first cup of the young wine. He laughed at the words of the prophet, who contented himself with the saying, "There is much between the edge of the cup and the lip," when word came that a wild boar was ravaging the royal fields (these were the simple times!). King Anaeus set down the goblet, untasted, *grabbed his boar spear, rushed out, and was subsequently killed by the wild boar. The prophecy was fulfilled.*

SQL Optimization

Once you are reasonably sure of the foundations, you can start (or continue) with optimizing SQL queries.

SQL is a declarative language; it tells the RDBMS what needs to be done without going into details on how to do it. The syntax of the queries returning the same result can differ significantly because of a variety of options available within the language: *subqueries*, JOIN, and ordering and grouping can be used in different combinations.

Yet there is a method to the madness; behind the scenes, RDBMS is procedural at heart and it will employ the same bag of tricks that your average C#, Java, or PHP program would (parsing, looping, matching, and joining), all while relying on the environmental options available to it. Your set-based SQL query is translated into procedural chunks of code, and results are assembled just in time for return. The query parsing and rewriting is beyond the scope of this book (and a couple more levels beyond this book, frankly), but you can get some valuable insights into how an RDBMS "thinks" by examining the SQL query execution plan. The ultimate goal of SQL tuning is to improve the execution plan, and this is where you need a tool to understand what's going on.

A Peek Under the Hood: Query Optimizers

Assuming that you have the query logic all figured out; that is, that you do not ask for more data than absolutely needed and you do not have unintended gaffes in your syntax (such as Cartesian JOIN(s)), there is one more thing you can do: Rewrite your query to improve the execution plan, minimizing database access and data operations as much as possible. To do so, you need to understand how your RDBMS prepares your query for execution — how it plans to access the data. This requires an advanced understanding of how SQL in general and your RDBMS in particular works (and is, by and large, outside our scope). Nevertheless, taking a quick peek into the kitchen might help.

Every RDBMS we're discussing in this book has implemented an internal optimizer as part of its SQL interpretation and execution process, and some are better than others in providing a user-friendly access to the facility. In general, there are two types of optimizers: rule based optimizers (RBOs) and cost based optimizers (CBOs). The former is based on a set of predefined rules and crafts execution plans inferred from the statement syntax and existence of indices; the latter adheres to RBO-style rules, but can modify these rules on the fly based upon statistics collected from the tables's actual use to create a data access plan uniquely adapted for the query. The statistics (a name as good as any) represent volatile data about the table, and is collected in RDBMS system tables. Here's a sampling of what kind of information is collected, to mention but a few:

- Number of distinct values in the compound index columns
- Number of rows in a table
- Number of columns in a table
- Average length of a column's data
- Number of NULLs in a column
- Percentage of distinct values in a column
- CPU performance and utilization
- Input/output (I/O) operations

This information is processed into histograms, detailed information on how values are distributed over columns, and the columns are then used to create query execution plans.

There are a number of graphical tools, both built-in and available from third parties, to analyze the results and present them in a hierarchical diagram, with costs assigned to each note. Let's take a look at one example: cost based optimization for Microsoft SQL Server.

TRY IT OUT A Quick Look at Execution Plans in Microsoft SQL Server

Let's take a look at the execution plan for one of the subquery examples from Chapter 6.

1. Open SQL Server 2008 Management Studio.
2. Connect to your instance of SQL Server, and open a query window by clicking the New Query button in the upper-left corner of the program's window.

3. Run the following batch query:

```
use library;

SELECT bk_title, bk_publisher FROM books
    WHERE bk_id IN (SELECT fk_bk_loc FROM location
        WHERE loc_shelf = 5);
```

4. To have the execution plan prepared by the optimizer displayed, click the toolbar button on the right of the Execute button, as shown in Figure 9-2.

5. Run the query by clicking the Execute button on the toolbar. The execution plan for this query in Microsoft SQL Server 2008 will be displayed in the Execution plan tab of the output pane, as shown in Figure 9-3.

FIGURE 9-2

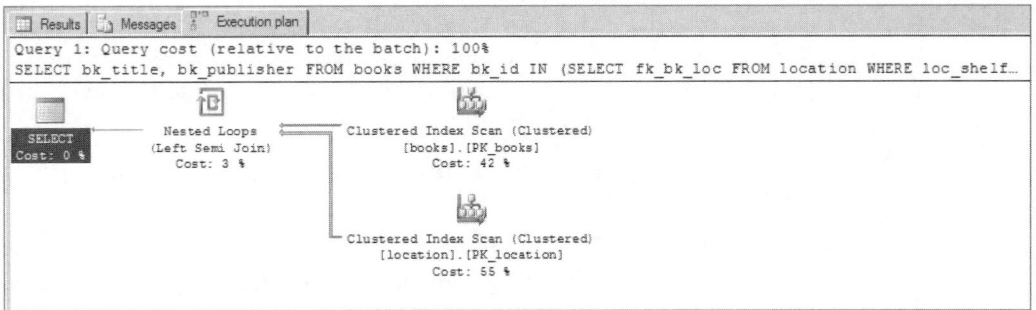

FIGURE 9-3

6. As you can see, the query optimizer ordered scans of two clustered indices on the BOOKS and LOCATION tables, with a 42/55 percent cost split, and then joins the records before returning the results.

7. Add a nonclustered index on the LOC_SHELF column (a bare-bones syntax):

```
CREATE INDEX ix_loc_shelf ON location
(
Loc_shelf ASC
);
GO
```

8. Rewrite the query with a JOIN and run it with the Execute button:

```
SELECT bk_title, bk_publisher FROM books bk INNER JOIN location loc
    ON bk.bk_id = loc.fk_bk_loc
        WHERE loc.loc_shelf = 5;
```

9. The costs of scanning the respective tables is now split 47/53, and there is no cost for merging the records. Additionally, the optimizer has decided to use a new index (IX_BK_LOC instead of the previously used clustered primary key index PK_LOCATION), as shown in Figure 9-4.

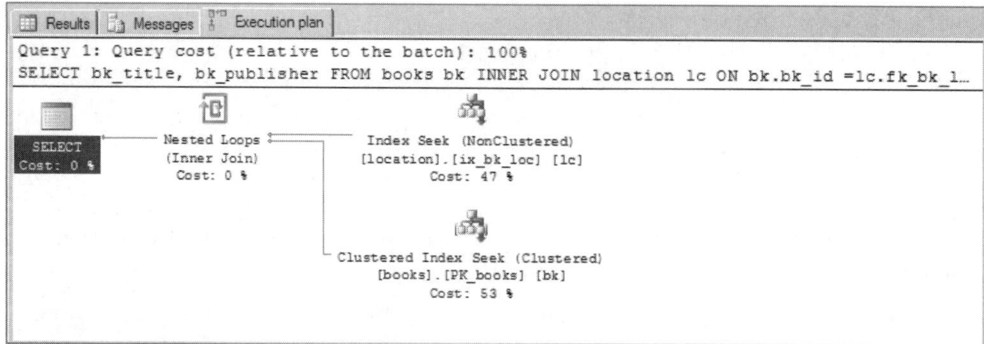

FIGURE 9-4

10. Create a copy of the LOCATION table by executing the following query:

```
SELECT * INTO location_copy FROM location;
```

This statement creates a copy of LOCATION table, albeit no constraints were copied over, just the structure and the data. Since the structure of the table is the same, including column names, we could can run the same query with only minimal changes

```
SELECT bk_title, bk_publisher FROM books bk INNER JOIN location_copy lcopy
    ON bk.bk_id = lcopy.fk_bk_loc
        WHERE lcopy.loc_shelf = 5;
```

11. As shown in Figure 9-5, the cost of finding records in the table LOCATION_COPY increased dramatically, to 52 percent, even though it is identical to LOCATION in every respect, with the exception of not having a primary key defined.

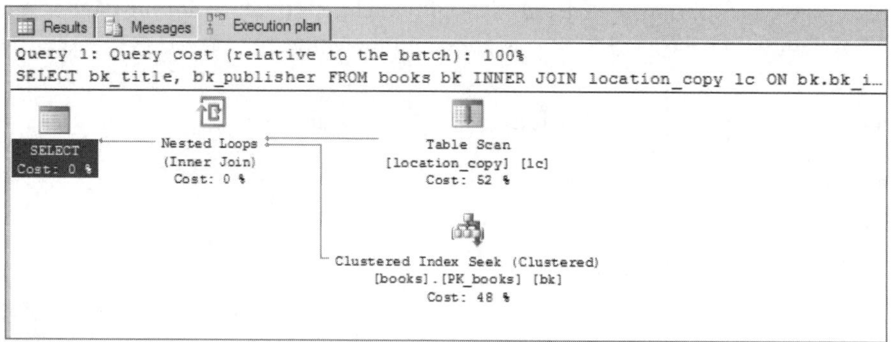

FIGURE 9-5

How It Works

The query optimizer prepares the execution plan based on the least relative costs for a given operation. The index scan operation was performed in the subquery example, which was replaced with the index seek operation for the second query. It used the JOIN syntax, and a full table scan was performed on a LOCATION_COPY table that did not have primary key defined.

The differences between index seek and index scan are subtle. The former is performed when the existing index is not selective enough (among other reasons), and the latter is just the opposite, used when there is an index on the search column (that is, the one specified in the WHERE clause). A full table scan, the third scenario, is performed when there is no index defined for the table and the optimizer has no clue where to look for the requested values. The last operation, the full table scan, is the most expensive and should be optimized first, with an index added, for example. There is an exception to the rule, though. For relatively small tables (100 rows or so), a full table scan might be faster than index scan.

Since our LIBRARY tables contain very little data, the difference in query execution times might be almost imperceptible among these three scenarios, but it will make a huge difference with large amounts of data in more complex queries.

As you can imagine, updating statistics is quite expensive in terms of computer memory and CPU cycles. Because of this, the statistics update does not happen automatically but has to be run manually or scheduled by a DBA familiar with the usage patterns of the database.

Table 9-1 lists information on types of optimizers implemented by the RDBMS, commands for obtaining data access plans, and commands for updating statistics used by the query optimizer.

TABLE 9-1: Query Optimizers

RDBMS	OPTIMIZER	DATA ACCESS PLAN	STATISTICS UPDATE
IBM DB2	CBO	EXPLAIN	RUNSTATS
Microsoft	CBO	EXPLAIN	UPDATE STATISTICS
MySQL	RBO	EXPLAIN	ANALYZE TABLE
Oracle	CBO	EXPLAIN PLAN FOR	ANALYZE
MS Access	RBO	SHOWPLAN	n/a
HSQLDB	RBO	EXPLAIN PLAN	n/a

Optimization Rules of Thumb for SQL Queries

Create your optimization strategy for the database type you have. There is no such thing as one size fits all. Follow the optimization order, get a better understanding of the query execution plan, and apply the 80/20 rule at each step.

The following sections contain lists of optimization tips which might help you speed up query execution and help overall database performance. Not all of these may apply to your particular situation. When in doubt, remember that your DBA is your friend (or drop me a line at `www.agilitator.com`). Some of these steps might be rendered obsolete by rapid advances in RDBMS technologies; some have been automated and need no manual intervention anymore; and some should be performed by a DBA. Still, there is value in familiarizing yourself with what's involved.

Indexing

- Always have a PRIMARY KEY in your table, preferably of the numeric data type.
- Always have an index on any FOREIGN KEY in your table.
- Create one clustered index per table (usually on the PRIMARY KEY column; keep in mind differences between implementations - the equivalent of clustered index in MS SQL Server or PostgreSQL would be index-organized tables (IOT) in Oracle).
- Create highly selective indices and composite indices with the most restrictive column first.
- Decide on ASCENDING or DESCENDING order based on the type of data and actual business usage pattern.
- Define indices on all searchable columns in the order they appear in the following part of the query:
    - WHERE clause
    - JOIN clause
    - ORDER BY clause
    - SELECT list
- Do not overdo indices: The wrong indices used by the query optimizer will slow down your query. Every index *increases* time spent on INSERT, UPDATE, and DELETE statements; and might speed up the SELECT statement.
- Indices on small tables might be detrimental to query performance.
- Indices on numeric data type columns perform better than indices on character data type columns.
- Keep composite indices as narrow as possible,; the fewer columns, the less reading time for the RDBMS.
- Indexing your NULL columns with a function-based index or a composite index including a non-null NULL column might speed queries relying on NULL and NOT NULL searches.
- Rebuild your indices periodically.
- When in doubt: use, use query execution plans.
- Update statistics for the tables on regular basis (normally, a DBA task).

Syntax

- Minimize the use of functions in your query, especially in WHERE clause filters.
- Avoid using custom User Defined Functions (UDFs).
- Avoid using hierarchical views (views based upon views).

- Replace NULL and NOT NULL comparisons with (not)equal operators whenever possible.
- Replace LIKE and NOT LIKE predicates with equality whenever possible.
- Use CASE statements for conditional transformation and aggregation.
- Minimize the use of HAVING clauses in your aggregate queries.
- Minimize the use of pattern matching in WHERE clauses.
- Watch out for implicit conversions in filtering the data; always use implicit conversions to prevent ambiguity about your intentions.
- Watch out for Cartesian JOIN (also known as cross-join), a situation in which no JOIN criteria is specified. The result is a data set of all possible permutations of the rows in the selected tables.
- Rewrite subqueries as JOIN(s) whenever possible; it *usually* improves performance.
- Rewrite EXISTS subqueries using MINUS and EXCEPT operators; as part of the set-based logic, they usually perform better.
- Minimize number of table and views references in the query.

Miscellaneous

- Select only what you need; this refers to setting both horizontal and vertical limits for the data sets returned (refer to Chapter 2 for more information). Always consider specifying lists of columns in the SELECT statement as opposed to using the asterisk (*) for "everything and his cousin."
- Consider partitioning the data into separate tables horizontally and off-loading less frequently used data to separate tables.
- Consider denormalizing and pre-aggregating data for some of the most actively used queries.
- Consider using stored procedures instead of ad hoc queries.
- Use constraints instead of custom triggers for your tables to enforce the rules.
- Pay attention to locking in your database and locking escalation rules for your RDBMS.
- Use RDBMS-specific optimization judiciously; the optimization facility and/or RDBMS might change without notice.

RDBMS-SPECIFIC OPTIMIZATION

Besides generic optimizations which by and large are applicable to every relational database system, there are quite a few vendor-specific optimizations which utilize concepts and facilities available only in this particular RDBMS. Of course, there is a price to pay in terms of reduced portability of the system, but sometimes the tradeoff might be justified.

Oracle 10g/11g

In version 10g, Oracle shipped with SQLAccess advisor (part of the DBMS_ADVISOR package, which was replaced with SQL Performance Analyzer in version 11g). The focus of the tool is to scan your database schema objects, and come up with recommendations for best indices and materialized views (refer to Chapter 8 for more information).

One of the most controversial issues is using Oracle SQL hints in your queries. A hint is not a suggestion for the Oracle optimizer to consider; it is a direct order to cease and desist, and just do as told. (I would add "if possible" to this sentence; there is a reason why it's called "hints" – not every hint is implementable.) There is a number of hints that can be used with Oracle that deal with JOIN orders and operations, access plans and query transformations, index utilization strategy, and more. Here is an example of Oracle forcing the query optimizer to use index IX_BK_ISBN created on bk_ISBN column:

```
SELECT /*+ index(bk ix_bk_ISBN) */
    bk_title
   ,bk_publisher
FROMbooksbk;
```

As you can see, the syntax has nothing to do with SQL proper, has arcane syntax, and makes your code Oracle-only and nonportable.

There are justifiable uses for hints in very fast–paced environments when data characteristics change so rapidly that statistics for the table become outdated very quickly. Nevertheless, using SQL hints requires advanced knowledge of Oracle and should be used as a last resort.

Oracle offers materialized views as a way to speed some SELECT queries (refer to Chapter 8 for more information) and table partitioning support.

With your DBA's help, look into various caching techniques for query plans and adjustment of various Oracle environmental parameters.

IBM DB2 LUW 9.7

IBM offers a number of tools to help with RDBMS performance analysis, including visualizers for the EXPLAIN facility (see earlier in the chapter): Visual Explain and command-line utility db2exfmt.

Additional tools include the following:

- **Design Advisor** — Generates a set of recommendations for a given set of SQL statements and a workload: indices, materialized views, Materialized Query Tables (MQTs in IBM parlance), physical tables reshuffling, table partitioning advice, and so on.
- **Query Patroller** — A tool to manage users, groups, and queries by balancing RDBMS resources across the submitted queries: boosting priority for some, and holding back the others.

DB2 also allows for SQL hints to be used, wrapped up as an optimization profile (an XML file containing instructions to the DB2 query optimizer), and activated for a duration of a session (see Chapter 10 for information on sessions) with a SET CURRENT OPTIMIZATION PROFILE (some RDBMS initialization parameters need to be set prior to being able to invoke the statement). The same warnings as with Oracle's hints apply: Know what you're doing and understand the ramifications of nonportable code.

Microsoft SQL Server 2008

Besides the execution plan visualizer, the Microsoft SQL Server offers additional tools such as Database Tuning Advisor (an updated version of the Index Tuning Wizard that shipped with SQL Server 2000). The advisor will consider tradeoffs offered by different options (for example, indices or partitioning), with a support for "what-if" scenarios testing, session monitoring facilities and more. Talk to your DBA, or refer to the vendor's documentation.

Microsoft SQL Server 2008 offers a number of SQL hints that can be used to force the optimizer to choose one specific query execution plan over another. Unlike Oracle or DB2, the SQL Server hints are part of the SQL proper, or rather Transact-SQL dialect. For instance, the following query:

```
SELECT bk_title, bk_publisher FROM books bk INNER JOIN location loc
    ON bk.bk_id = loc.fk_bk_loc
        WHERE loc.loc_shelf = 5;
```

can be rewritten with a hint to use a specific JOIN type, say a HASH join, as follows:

```
SELECT bk_title, bk_publisher FROM books bk INNER HASH JOIN location loc
    ON bk.bk_id = loc.fk_bk_loc
        WHERE loc.loc_shelf = 5;
```

In the query execution plan, you'll see that the preceding query will force the optimizer to perform an unnecessary HASH join, consuming a whopping 72 percent of the query execution costs (as opposed to 0 percent for the regular INNER JOIN with the least expensive LOOP type, as was shown earlier in the chapter).

Materialized views in SQL Server are called indexed views. They come with a few advanced features, such as view-specific SQL hints and support for .Net family of programming language data types. Keep in mind that this is an advanced feature, and there are a lot of limitations and prerequisites for this type of object.

When processing XML (see Chapter 11), it is recommended that you minimize the number of concurrent OPENXML statements and avoid using this statement on large XML files altogether.

Setting up server parameters, such as increasing the size of TEMPDB (SQL Server performs most of its sorting using this "workbench" database) and adjusting some parameters such as AUTO_CREATE_STATISTICS or AUTO_SHRINK. Using any of these requires an advanced level of understanding and is most likely to be performed by a DBA.

PostgreSQL

Using the EXPLAIN ANALYZE statement, along with other accoutrements, such as setting statistics levels for a column, will give you additional insight into your query optimizer work.

Tuning RDBMS server parameters can yield significant performance gains. Setting up maximum database connections, allocating memory to data caching and many other configuration parameters can make a big difference.

Maintain your database tables by running the VACUUM statement (compacting the database tables after any DELETEs and UPDATEs). Other useful commands are ANALYZE, for database and database objects; and EXPLAIN ANALYZE, for SQL queries.

Materialized views are not supported natively by PostgreSQL, though a number of workarounds have been proposed and implemented with PL/pgSQL triggers (see Chapter 4 for information on triggers).

The supported version of PostgreSQL, EnterpriseDB, has additional tools, such as Tuning Wizard, to help with optimal configuration.

MySQL

MySQL has two different main storage engines: MyISAM and InnoDB, each with its own performance optimization techniques. Usually you would use MyISAM, a default engine, for mostly read-type data because it offers no transactional support whatsoever and is optimized for SELECT queries.

The InnoDB storage engine takes MySQL one step closer to an enterprise class RDBMS. It adds support for referential integrity (refer to Chapter 3), as well as transactional support with COMMIT and ROLLBACK (see Chapter 10) to ensure data consistency in multiuser environments and row-level locking.

The basic syntax for creating MyISAM and InnoDB storage tables is very similar. For instance, the following query creates a table with InnoDB storage (and omitting the TYPE clause will default it to MyISAM):

```
CREATE TABLE authors (
    au_id                bigint NOT NULL PRIMARY KEY
  , au_first_name        varchar(50) NULL
  , au_middle_name       varchar(50) NULL
  , au_last_name         varchar(50) NULL
  , au_notes             text NULL
) TYPE=innodb;
```

Choosing the right table format based on intended table usage will yield real gains, although not always performance-related. If you expect the table to be used with INSERT, UPDATE, and DELETE statements, InnoDB might be a better option; you sacrifice speed for consistency. With mostly SELECT queries, MyISAM provides better performance.

Just as with Oracle, you can use SQL hints to override the optimizer's own plans for query execution, and the same caveats apply. Here is an example of a hint instructed MySQL to use a specific index

```
SELECT bk_title
      ,bk_publisher
FROM books USE INDEX (ix_bk_ISBN);
```

MySQL does not offer materialized views out of the box, but it is relatively easy to simulate with tables and triggers, just as in PostgreSQL.

Other optimization techniques include fine-tuning MySQL startup options, placing tables into memory, along with proper maintenance of the tables (with commands such as *myisamchk*, OPTIMIZE TABLE), and use of custom extensions (a blessing and curse of open source's protean nature).

Desktop RDBMSs

The desktop RDBMSs are in a league of their own and should be approached differently. Normally, they are designed for a single user and lack most of the advanced features that their full-featured RDBMS server-based peers have. In an attempt to capture a bigger market segment and answer a need for "something in-between," the rules were relaxed, and desktop databases were allowed to live on a network and be accessed by a number of simultaneous users.

Some of the optimization strategies discussed earlier in this chapter would still apply to the desktop databases. Take them on a case-by-case basis.

Microsoft Access

One of the most popular desktop database management systems, Microsoft Access enjoyed a long history of success, all the way from clunky version 1.0 released in November 1992. Being a mix of relational engine (Microsoft JET Database Engine, updated to ACE in later versions), GUI, and built-in language (Visual Basic for Applications [VBA]) to create applications, it has unique characteristics unknown to full-blown relational database servers.

Microsoft Access was not the first desktop database on the market. For years, the desktop market was dominated by Borland's dBASE and Paradox systems, as well as FoxPro and Clipper (which started as a compiler for dBase III). FoxPro was bought by Microsoft in 1992, and some of its technologies (especially query optimization) made it into Microsoft Access. Another popular desktop database management system is FileMaker, a cross-platform RDBMS now owned by Apple, evolved from the 1982 version developed originally by Nashoba Systems.

First of all, Microsoft Access database is not a server. It is a file — a complex structured file — but a file nevertheless. Even if you host this file on the network to enable simultaneous user access, a fair chunk of this file has to be copied over to a user machine before you can even start. As a result, Microsoft Access in a multiuser environment chokes when the number of concurrent users reaches a limit of more than a couple dozen (the official limit for concurrent connections is 255).

The other limitations include limits on the number of tables that can be referenced to in a query (32), the number of fields in a query (255), the number of JOIN(s) permitted (16), the number of AND operators in a WHERE or HAVING clause (99), and so on. Keep in mind that these limits might be much lower, depending on actual syntax and combinations. When MS Access reaches its limits, you'll see a message complaining of "too many" this or "too complex" that, which might simply be a red herring; do not expect it to diagnose the problem.

MS Access shares some optimization techniques with full-fledged RDBMSs; others are MS Access–specific. The former include the use of indices, return of limited data sets and limited number of fields, and the preferred use of JOIN(s) over subqueries. The latter include the following:

- Use of SQL functions over equivalent VBA (for example, use of the IS NULL operator instead of the ISNULL function; the function necessitates a call to VBA)
- Use of subqueries instead of MS Access Domain Aggregated functions (DLookup, DSum)
- Avoid ORDER BY on computed fields
- Use of FIRST with GROUP BY
- Use of stacked queries (a saved query used as an input to a query)

Like its grownup counterparts, MS Access JET Engine has a query plan analyzer named ShowPlan. It was added to Jet 3.0 (shipped with Microsoft Access 95 and enhanced in the current 2010 version). Even with its numerous limitations (for instance, it does not analyze subqueries), it will help you to analyze performance of your database and pinpoint bottlenecks. Using this utility goes beyond the scope of this book

One of the ways to scale MS Access is to use it as front end for enterprise-level RDBMSs such as Microsoft SQL Server or Oracle. This involves creating a GUI for using MS Access and linking remote server tables so they appear to be local. MS Access then serves as a pass-through, and actual query execution is performed on the linked servers.

OpenOffice BASE with HSQLDB Backend

Unlike Microsoft Access, the OpenOffice BASE does not have data storage of its own; instead, it ships with embedded open source HyperSQL RDBMS, which is also available in a server version. Additionally, it can connect to a number of other full-featured RDBMSs for which there is a suitable JDBC/ODBC driver.

When used as a front end to any of these RDBMSs, all optimization tips and techniques discussed earlier apply in full. When using HSQLDB, which is "almost" SQL-92 Standard–compliant (plus some core features of the SQL:2008 standard) according to the maintainers of the project, the optimization will be that of the HSQLDB (see more at `www.HSQLDB.org`). Using the SQL rule-of-thumb tips (see earlier in the chapter) might help, especially the indexing and syntax-related optimization.

The embedded version shipped with OpenOffice 3.2 is not the latest (2.0, as of the time of this writing) but the previous 1.8. The older version of HSQLDB has less efficient optimization schema, and lacks several multiuser-specific features, including some outdated locking mechanisms that might allow "dirty reads" (that is, reading uncommitted data; see Chapter 10 for more information).

YOUR DBA IS YOUR FRIEND

In a medium to large enterprise, it is highly likely that you will have a dedicated or part-time DBA. The DBA role is particular to each organization; some organizations would give developers and power users access to query execution plans; some would put it squarely in DBA domain. Your DBA will be your last resort after you checked all your application logic (nested loops, recursive functions, memory leaks, and so on), optimized the returned data sets, helped users to clean up computers from CPU hogging adware, and checked your SQL code for Cartesian JOIN(s) and unnecessary functions.

DBAs worth their salt will have intimate knowledge of the RDBMS your application is using. They know what an Oracle extent is and how to use DBCC in SQL Server. They will talk to your network guy, discussing things like double hops, DNS configurations, and excessive network collisions. They will set up traces on the processes running on the server and will help you figure out possible culprits. They will adjust database privileges, check query execution plans, resolve transaction deadlocks, and, if needed, help you with advanced optimization such as query caching and memory pinning.

In short, your DBA is your friend, be nice to her or him, as the case may be.

SUMMARY

Optimizing RDBMS performance requires a holistic approach because it involves many moving factors: network performance, server performance, software tune-up, and so on.

Before attempting to optimize logically and syntactically correct SQL statements, make sure that other parts of the system are on solid ground: client application, network, server, RDBMS software installation, and your database model. Any SQL query tune-up should start with examining the query execution plan to pinpoint bottlenecks, and focus on optimizing these first; the 80/20 rule will help you to stay focused.

Proper indexing of the table is absolutely crucial for the SQL performance in your database. Indexes can improve some queries and negatively affect others. Selecting an indexing strategy will ultimately depend on your business needs and intended usage scenarios.

Each RDBMS comes with a number of proprietary, database-specific, optimization tools and techniques. Using them might improve performance; the tradeoff is potential vendor lock-in as it will reduce portability of your code.

DBAs perform an important role, being an expert in particular technologies, and having a firm grasp of the issues surrounding relational database setup and operations. Any optimization quest must involve consulting a DBA at some point, the earlier the better.

10

Multiuser Environment

No database is an island. It is possible to imagine a scenario where a database is accessed by one and only one user, all changes are made and saved in a proper order, and nobody forgets to floss. Back on Earth, databases are usually created to be shared. Even the desktop databases, Microsoft Access and OpenOffice BASE, can potentially be shared on the network, and RDBMS servers were specifically designed from the ground up to support multiuser environments.

When more than one user accesses the same set of data, a new set of problems arises: What data should be visible to each of the users? Whose modification should take precedence? What is the guarantee that the data changes will not be lost during the execution of a lengthy database procedure? The answer to these (and many other problems) comes with the introduction of sessions, transactions, and locks.

Let's rephrase the preceding questions in the RDBMS vocabulary:

- *Transactions* offer solutions to potential data consistency problems.
- *Locks* deal with data concurrency problems.
- *Sessions* represent the context in which transactions and locks live.

SESSIONS

Whatever happens in terms of communication between an RDBMS server and a user accessing it happens in the context of a *session*. Think of it as a unique channel open for you, and you only, to access the data; or in the case of desktop databases such as Microsoft Access and OpenOffice BASE, your very own copy of the data file. A session is created for you automatically when you connect to a database and get authenticated.

In a multiuser environment, one of the primary concerns is data integrity. When a client application establishes a connection to an RDBMS server, it is said to *open a session*. The session becomes this application's private communication channel. The user may change some preferences within the session (for example, default language or default date format); these settings would affect only this particular user environment and would remain valid for the duration of the session only. The details of the implementation and default behavior of the sessions might differ among the RDBMSs, but these basic principles remain the same.

The tools we used throughout the book are the examples of clients accessing RDBMS servers in context of a session. In the case of desktop databases, things are a bit different. Microsoft Access files, for instance, can be used as just data storage or can contain more objects normally associated with an application: forms, reports, and so on (and there are ways to split the functionality into front-end and back-end files). As such, the "session" becomes a local copy of the open mdb/accdb file, which would have to be merged back into the "master" file (please refer to Microsoft Access–specific publications for more information on the subject).

OpenBase has different architecture from Microsoft Access. It was designed to be essentially a pass-through desktop front end, providing a front end for any database supported by Java Database Connectivity (JDBC) drivers; its built-in Hyper Structured Query Language Database (HSQLDB) database engine is a default choice, and the embedded version was not designed for a multiuser environment.

The command-line utilities provided by the RDBMS for their respective RDBMS servers were selected as the least common denominator. All RDBMSs provide a graphical user interface (GUI) in addition to numerous third-party utilities. For more information, please refer to Appendices C and D.

The SQL Standard specifies a number of parameters that can be used to connect to a database and also manipulated in a session, and most of them are implemented by the RDBMS, although some elements made it into proprietary syntax, ditching the letter, and preserving the spirit.

In Oracle, a user must have a system privilege `CREATESESSION` in order to establish a database connection and an ALTER SESSION privilege to change the session's parameters. Initially, all the default parameter values for the session are loaded from a special Oracle configuration file; the file can be modified only by a database administrator or someone who has the necessary privileges. Once the connection is established (a session is created), a user can alter the session according to his or her preferences and job requirements.

IBM DB2 provides surprisingly little control for the user over the session environment. It has a SET SESSION AUTHORIZATION statement (in compliance with SQL Standard) and a SET SESSION_USER equivalent that can be used to change a session's context.

The closest it comes to providing session control is with the `SETPASSTHRU` statement, which opens and closes a session for submitting SQL data directly to the database. Also, a global temporary table created during the session may be qualified with the `SESSION` component as a schema. (It is used to prevent ambiguity in accessing the table when the temporary table name is the same as some persistent table and in some other equally obscure cases.)

When a client terminates a session — either voluntarily or abnormally — all values set for various session parameters disappear. In addition, for all pending transactions, an implicit commit will be issued in the case of voluntary termination or rollback when the session has terminated abnormally.

The session can be killed or disconnected by a database administrator (DBA); syntax for the statements varies among RDBMSs.

TRY IT OUT Modifying a Session Parameter

Microsoft SQL Server 2008 has a number of statements that you can specify to alter the current session. These statements are not part of SQL Standard; instead they are part of the Transact-SQL dialect. Here we will change one of the settings, ANSI_NULLS, and see how it affects the outcome.

1. Bring up Microsoft SQL Server 2008 Management Studio Express, and connect to the Library database.
2. The following statement is supposed to bring all the records from the PHONE table of the LIBRARY database when the BK_PRICE field is not NULL:

```
SET ANSI_NULLS ON
GO
SELECT bk_title
FROM   books
WHERE  bk_price <> NULL
GO

(0 row(s) affected)
```

3. The query returns zero records despite the fact that there are supposed to be records satisfying this criterion; all books in the Library database have the price value.
4. Clear the query pane, and enter the new batch of SQL statements as follows:

```
SET ANSI_NULLS OFF
GO
SELECT bk_title
FROM   books
WHERE  bk_price<> NULL
GO

BK_TITLE
--------------------
SQL Bible
. . .
Steppenwolf
```

How It Works

Because NULL is not a specific value but a "placeholder in absence of thereof," it has to be treated differently. The SQL-92 standard mandates that the comparison operations involving NULL always evaluate to FALSE, and turning this parameter ON would force the database to follow this standard. Neither Oracle 10/11g nor IBM DB2 9.7 has such a setting as ANSI_NULLS.

This situation can be completely avoided if the more standard ISNULL syntax is used:

```
SELECT bk_title
FROM   books
WHERE  bk_price IS NOT NULL
```

The preceding query would return correct results in all RDBMSs.

Orphaned Sessions

Orphaned sessions occur when a client application terminates abruptly without the ability to terminate its open session to the RDBMS server. Usually, it is the responsibility of the operating system to detect that the client exited and notify the server. (In some implementations, the server would query the client whether it is still present after some period of inactivity.) Certain situations, however, might prevent a proper client exit (for example, sudden network failure). If the session were active (for example, the RDBMSs were processing some command at the time), it would detect dropped connections automatically and terminate the session. On the other hand, if the session were inactive, waiting for a command from the client, such a session would remain valid for the server.

Such sessions consume system resources and should be cleaned up. Usually it is done automatically after a certain interval configured for the server or is resolved manually by a DBA.

Transactions

A *transaction* is one of the mechanisms provided within SQL to enforce database integrity and maintain data consistency. The idea of the transaction is to provide a mechanism for ensuring that a multistep operation is performed as a single unit. If any of the steps involved in a transaction fails, the whole transaction is rolled back; if all the steps have been completed successfully, the transaction can either be committed (all the changes are saved into the database) or rolled back (all changes are undone).

The details of implementation differ among the RDBMS vendors, though the spirit of the SQL Standard is generally preserved. The desktop databases handle transactions in the code embedded within the database (Visual Basic for Applications (VBA) for Microsoft Access). The rest of the RDBMSs — Oracle, IBM DB2, Microsoft SQL Server 2008, and PostgreSQL — have robust transactional support. MySQL has implemented a unique feature, the ability to specify storage engines for its tables. InnoDB and IBMDB2I storage engines are capable of supporting transactions natively.

What Is a Transaction?

A transaction complements the concept of the session with additional granularity; it divides every operation that occurs within the session into logical units of work. In this way, database operations — those involving data modifications — are performed step by step and can be rolled back at any time, or committed if every step is successful.

Data Definition Language (DDL) structure modifications involving the creation and destruction of the database objects might *not be transactional and might not be rolled back. This depends on the RDBMS as well as some additional parameters (such as isolation levels, discussed later in this chapter).*

SQL Standard defined transactions at the very beginning and enhanced the concept during subsequent iterations. According to the standard, a transaction is started by the RDBMS, and continues until a `COMMIT` or `ROLLBACK` statement is issued; the details were left for the RDBMSs to implement. The SQL Standard transaction management statements are listed in Table 10-1.

TABLE 10-1: SQL Standard Transaction Management SQL Statement

SQL STATEMENT	DESCRIPTION
START (BEGIN) TRANSACTION	Starts an SQL transaction and sets its characteristics.
SET TRANSACTION	Sets the characteristics of the next SQL transaction for the SQL agent.
SET CONSTRAINTS	If an SQL transaction is currently active, sets the constraint mode for that SQL transaction in the current SQL session. If no SQL transaction is currently active, sets the constraint mode for the next SQL transaction in the current SQL session for the SQL agent.
SAVEPOINT	Establishes a savepoint.
RELEASE SAVEPOINT	Destroys a savepoint.
COMMIT	Terminates the current SQL transaction with commit.
ROLLBACK	Terminates the current SQL transaction with a rollback, or rolls back all actions affecting SQL data and/or schemas since the establishment of a savepoint.

A transaction must pass the ACID test in order to be qualified as such. The acronym stands for the following:

- **Atomicity** — Either all the changes are made or none. If any of the statements in the batch fail, all the changes, if any, must be reversed.
- **Consistency** — All the data involved in an operation must be left in a consistent state upon completion or rollback of the transaction; database integrity cannot be compromised.
- **Isolation** — One transaction should not be aware of the modifications made to the data by any other transaction unless it was committed to the database. Different isolation levels can be set to modify this default behavior.
- **Durability** — The results of a transaction that has been successfully committed to the database stay in the database.

One of the classic real-life examples of a transaction involves an ATM (bank machine) withdrawal operation. Suppose you need money, and you decide to withdraw this money from the nearest bank machine. You put in your bank card (user ID) and enter your personal identification number (PIN) to initiate the session. Once the bank confirms your identity, you are allowed to proceed; you can ask for a money withdrawal operation for a specific amount. That's where a transaction begins. There are several operations involved: The machine will have to check your account to verify that you have enough money to cover the transaction, it will subtract the money from your account, and then release the bills to you. If any of these steps (and some others, depending on the given bank policies) fails, the transaction must be aborted, and everything must revert to a state where it was before the transaction even began. This means that you cannot get your cash unless it was subtracted from your balance; the bank cannot subtract the money from your balance unless you have enough money to cover the transaction, and you actually got your cash. If any of these steps fails for whatever reason (you cancel the operation, the bank machine malfunctions), all changes would be rolled back.

The transaction model, as it is defined in the ANSI/ISO SQL Standard, utilizes the implicit start of a transaction, with an explicit `COMMIT`, in the case of the successful execution of all the logical units of the transaction, or an explicit `ROLLBACK`, when the noncommitted changes need to be rolled back (for example, when the program terminates abnormally); most RDBMSs follow this model.

Explicit and Implicit Transactions

An *implicit transaction* has been chosen as the default behavior in SQL Standard, which means it's better to err on the side of a caution. Whenever certain DDL and Data Manipulation Language (DML) statements are executed within a session, they start (or continue) a transaction. A transaction is terminated by issuing either a `COMMIT` statement or a `ROLLBACK` statement.

An *explicit transaction* is started by the client application with a `BEGIN TRANSACTION` statement and is terminated in a manner similar to the implicit transaction protocol. Such a transaction can optionally have a name, which helps with maintaining better code.

Microsoft SQL Server 2008, for example, provides the `SETIMPLICIT_TRANSACTIONS{ON|OFF}` *statement to configure the default behavior of the transaction. When the option is* `ON`*, the SQL Server automatically starts a transaction when one of the following statements is specified:* `ALTER TABLE`, `CREATE`, `DELETE`, `DROP`, `FETCH`, `GRANT`, `INSERT`, `OPEN`, `REVOKE`, `SELECT`, `TRUNCATETABLE`, *and* `UPDATE`*. The transaction must be explicitly committed or rolled back. A new transaction is started once any of the listed statements is executed. Turning the* `IMPLICIT_TRANSACTIONS` *option* `OFF` *returns the transaction to its default autocommit transaction mode.*

While not required by the SQL Standard, in most RDBMSs `COMMIT` is issued implicitly before and after any DDL statement.

COMMIT and ROLLBACK Transactions

The `COMMIT` statement ends the current transaction and makes all changes made to the data during the transaction permanent. The syntax is virtually identical for all RDBMSs that support transactions natively, as well as for the SQL Standard, and is very straightforward.

COMMIT [WORK]

The keyword `WORK` is not required, though it might be added for clarity. A simple `COMMIT` usually does the trick.

Some RDBMSs have crammed tons of additional options into COMMIT. For example, a somewhat simplified Oracle 10g/11g syntax looks as follows.

```
COMMIT [WORK] [COMMENT (<text>)[WRITE]] [FORCE (<text>), [<int>]] ;
```

Here the `COMMENT` *clause enables you to specify a comment (up to 255 bytes long) that is recorded for every pending transaction and can be viewed through the* `DBA2_PC_PENDING` *dictionary view (see later in this chapter for more information on system catalogs).*

The IBM DB2 9.7 syntax for transactional control statements follows SQL Standard. In IBM terminology, a transaction is a unit of work (UOW) that always starts implicitly when the SQL statement is issued against the database. No authorization is required to issue the statement; all locks held by the transaction are released afterward, and named transactions are not supported.

The following syntax will work for every RDBMS discussed in the book, with the exception of Microsoft SQL Server and PostgreSQL. This behavior is possible because a transaction is started implicitly with these RDBMSs:

```
UPDATE books
SET bk_price = 22.99
WHERE bk_id=1;

COMMIT;
```

Only `COMMIT` is required. Everything else is optional. Alternatively, `COMMIT WORK` can be used; this syntax is identical to COMMIT TRANSACTION.

No changes take place until the last `COMMIT` is executed, thereby allowing you to roll them back. There are some significant differences among RDBMSs. For instance, when `COMMIT` is executed, Microsoft SQL Server 2008 must start a transaction either implicitly or explicitly for another `COMMIT` to execute successfully; if no transaction is started, issuing this command will result in an error.

```
Server: Msg 3902, Level 16, State 1, Line 1
The COMMIT TRANSACTION request has no corresponding BEGIN TRANSACTION.
None of the other databases would complain, no matter how many times you execute
COMMIT (though some, like PostgreSQL, might warn you that there are no pending
transactions to commit).
```

Microsoft SQL Server 2008 does support the SQL Standard syntax in addition to its own. The Microsoft syntax allows for committing named transactions, whereas the Standard syntax does not.

```
COMMIT [ TRAN [ SACTION ] [<transaction name>]]
```

Nested Transactions

Named transactions are especially handy for nested transactions. The idea behind nested transactions is to have a transaction within a transaction within a transaction (each implementation imposing its own limits on how many levels one can have), and each "child" transaction is aware of the higher-level "parent" transaction. Only two of the RDBMSs discussed, Microsoft SQL Server 2008 and PostgreSQL, provide built-in support for nested transactions.

Only explicit transactions can be nested. Nested transactions in Microsoft SQL Server 2008 are for readability purposes only. Committing an internal transaction does not really commit anything; only the outermost `COMMIT` actually commits the changes. All other commits just decrement the transaction counter, but you can use SAVEPOINT(s) to be able to roll back changes.

Here is an example illustrating the concept in Microsoft SQL Server, using its built-in function @@ TRANCOUNT to keep track of the number of transactions initiated:

```
BEGIN TRANSACTION trans1
-- the transaction counter @@TRANCOUNT = 1
INSERT INTO <table> VALUES <values>
BEGIN TRANSACTION trans2
-- the transaction counter @@TRANCOUNT = 2
INSERT INTO <table> VALUES <values>
BEGIN TRANSACTION trans3
-- the transaction counter @@TRANCOUNT = 3
INSERT INTO <table> VALUES <values>
COMMIT TRANSACTION trans3
-- Nothing committed at this point but the transaction
-- counter is decremented by 1; @@TRANCOUNT = 2
COMMIT TRANSACTION trans2
-- Nothing committed at this point but the transaction counter
-- is decremented by 1; @@TRANCOUNT = 1
COMMIT TRANSACTION trans1
-- All INSERTs are committed to the database
-- the transaction counter is decremented by 1; @@TRANCOUNT =0
```

In this case, three transactions were initiated to insert three records into a table; only the very last `COMMIT` actually made the changes to the table permanent.

ROLLBACK

When changes made to the data in the databases need to be "undone," the `ROLLBACK` should be used. It may be issued any time before the last `COMMIT` and results in the automatic rollback of all changes made since the controlling transaction started.

The syntax is identical in all RDBMSs and in the SQL Standard except for user-named transactions in Microsoft SQL Server 2008 and some optional clauses. The following statement will attempt to update column `BK_PRICE` in the `BOOKS` table of the LIBRARY database, but all changes will be rolled back:

```
UPDATE book
SET    bk_price = 9.99
WHERE bk_id= 1

ROLLBACK WORK
```

As with a COMMIT statement, all the locks are released if the ROLLBACK command is issued. Vendor-specific ROLLBACK statements are shown in Table 10-2.

TABLE 10-2: Vendor-Specific ROLLBACK Statements

RDBMS	ROLLBACK SYNTAX
Oracle 10g/11g	`ROLLBACK[WORK][TOSAVEPOINT<savepointname>]|[FORCE<text>]`
IBM DB2 9.7	`ROLLBACK[WORK][TOSAVEPOINT<savepointname>]`
Microsoft SQL Server 2008	`ROLLBACK[TRAN[SACTION]][<transactionname>] [<savepointname>]`
PostgreSQL 9.0	`ROLLBACK [WORK	TRANSACTION]TO [SAVEPOINT] savepoint_name`
MySQL 5.1	`ROLLBACK [WORK] TO [SAVEPOINT] savepoint_name`

The WORK clause is optional, and the TOSAVEPOINT clause is explained later in this chapter. The FORCE clause pertains to distributed transactions, acting very much the same as in the COMMIT transaction statement. Microsoft SQL Server has an optional <transaction name> clause.

Because certain statements (such as DDL) automatically issue a COMMIT *before and after the statement's execution, every change to data that happened prior to the DDL statement would be committed as well.*

SAVEPOINT

Usually, a transaction consists of more than one SQL statement that you may want to COMMIT or ROLLBACK. To add granularity to the transaction processing, the SAVEPOINT concept was introduced. It allows you to specify a named point within the transaction, usually after some important milestone in the query. If any error occurs after that, all the changes are rolled back, not to the beginning of the transaction, but to that particular SAVEPOINT. An explicit (or implicit — like the one issued after a DDL statement) COMMIT releases all SAVEPOINTs declared within a transaction.

Here is an example of using SAVEPOINTS in an SQL batch statement:

```
UPDATE books
SET    bk_price = 22.88
WHERE  bk_id = 1;

SAVEPOINT first_update;

DELETE books
WHERE  bk_id = 2;

SAVEPOINT first_delete;
```

```
DELETE books
WHERE  bk_id = 10;

ROLLBACK first_update;

COMMIT;
```

In the preceding example, after the COMMIT statement is issued, only `UPDATE` gets committed to the database, all `DELETE`s are rolled back, the `SAVEPOINTfirst_delete` is erased, and all resources held by the query get released.

The SAVEPOINT name must be unique within the current transaction. If a new SAVEPOINT is declared using the same name, the previous SAVEPOINT will be destroyed.

Microsoft SQL Server 2008 has added the keyword TRAN syntax, when it comes to establishing the `SAVEPOINT`s.

```
SAVE TRAN[SACTION] <savepoint name>
```

To make the preceding code work in Microsoft SQL Server, just replace the keyword TRANSACTION with SAVE TRANSACTION.

Transactions that involve more than one database are referred to as distributed transactions. *Such transactions are by their very nature complex and require advanced skills and knowledge. Distributed transactions involve the use of the two-phase commit, which allows heterogeneous sources to participate in a transaction. A distributed transaction must minimize the risk of data loss in case of a network failure. The two-phase commit protocol is employed in distributed transactions, and while details of the implementation are different among the RDBMSs, they generally follow the same phases.*

Transaction Isolation Levels

There are different transaction isolation levels. *Isolation levels* refer to the capability of the transaction to see the world (data) outside its own scope (data modified by any other transaction). The SQL Standard isolation levels are listed in Table 10-3.

TABLE 10-3: SQL Standard Isolation Levels

ISOLATION LEVEL	RDBMS	DESCRIPTION
`READ UNCOMMITED`	DB2 (UR), MySQL, PostgreSQL, Microsoft SQL Server	This level is the lowest of all isolation levels, permitting *dirty reads* (uncommitted data can be seen). No locks are issued, and none are honored.

ISOLATION LEVEL	RDBMS	DESCRIPTION
READ COMMITED	Oracle, DB2 (CS), PostgreSQL, Microsoft SQL Server	This level specifies that shared locks will be held while data are being read. No *dirty reads* (containing uncommitted data) are permitted; though *phantom reads* (when row numbers change between the reads) may occur.
REPEATABLE READ	DB2 (RS), PostgreSQL, Microsoft SQL Server	No changes will be allowed for the data selected by a query (locked for updates, deletes, and so on), but phantom rows may appear.
SERIALIZABLE	Oracle, DB2 (RR), PostgreSQL, Microsoft SQL Server	The highest level of transaction isolation; places a lock for the whole data set; no modifications from outside are allowed until the end of the transaction.

Oracle 10g/11g has implemented three transaction isolation levels: SERIALIZABLE, READ COMMITED, and READ ONLY.

There is some terminology confusion in how DB2 9.7 defines transaction isolation levels. What SQL Standard specifies as SERIALIZABLE, it names REPEATABLEREAD (RR), which is the highest isolation level in DB2 9.7. The SQL Standard's keyword is supported as a synonym for RR; SQL Standard's REPEATABLEREAD becomes READSTABILITY (RS); and a new level, CURSORSTABILITY, is introduced.

The last one, CURSORSTABILITY (CS), is the default for IBM DB2 9.7 and resembles the READCOMMITTED level of the SQL Standard (essentially, it guarantees that a row of data will remain unchanged).

The UNCOMMITEDREAD (UR) level is the same as it is defined by the standard: no locks are acquired, so dirty reads are possible. (A *dirty read* refers to reading data that are being modified, so the results are unpredictable.)

Microsoft SQL Server 2008 supports all four levels of isolation plus a SNAPSHOT isolation level that guarantees that the data read during the transaction will be consistent with the data at the beginning of the transaction. The isolation level is set for the whole session, not just a single transaction.

Table 10-4 lists the four isolation levels and the behavior displayed under each. Dirty read refers to the ability to read data still uncommitted to the database; nonrepeatable read means that the data might change since your transaction accessed it; and a phantom read relates to a nonrepeatable read, and describes a situation in which identical queries executed against the same set of data return different results for each query.

TABLE 10-4: Transaction Isolation Levels in SQL

ISOLATION LEVEL	DIRTY READ	NONREPEATABLE READ	PHANTOM READ
Read Uncommitted	Yes	Yes	Yes
Read Committed	No	Yes	Yes
Repeatable Read	No	No	Yes
Serializable	No	No	No

Understanding Locks

Concurrency is one of the major concerns in a multiuser environment. When multiple sessions write or read data to and from shared resources, data might lose its integrity. To prevent this from happening, every RDBMS worth its salt implements concurrency control mechanisms. In the case of RDBMS servers, the concurrency is managed through various locking mechanisms. All RDBMSs (including Microsoft Access) have implemented sophisticated mechanisms for concurrency management. Locking is neither part of SQL nor is it a standard (though it does specify locking for cursors, a special construct used for row-by-row access).

Oracle has probably the most evolved and complex locking schema. It follows the rule that reading and writing processes cannot block each other, even if working on the same (or close) set(s) of data. Each session receives a read-consistent snapshot of the data. Thus, even if some other process has begun modifying data in the set, but has not committed the changes, every subsequent session will be able to read the data just as it was before; once the changes are committed in the first session, every other session is able to see it. The locks are acquired only when the changes are being committed to the database. Oracle automatically selects the least-restrictive lock. Users can choose to lock a resource (a table, for example) manually. In this case, other users still might be able to access the data, depending on the type of lock deployed.

IBM DB2 9.7 and Microsoft SQL Server 2008 both employ locks that can enable a reader to block a writer, and vice versa. The problem of concurrent access to the data is somewhat alleviated by the granularity of the locking (table, page, column, row). There are locks acquired by read-only queries, DDL statements, DML queries, and so on. Most of the time, a user does not have to worry about locking, as RDBMSs automatically select the most appropriate lock (or locks) for a particular operation. Only if this programmed logic fails should you attempt to specify the locks manually by using the SQL statements.

MySQL does lock data natively only on the table level, and relies on the InnoDB (or IBMDB2I) storage engine which support transactions, and add-on for row-level locking and transactional support; PostgreSQL has robust table and row-level locking mechanisms, each with fine granularity.

Locking Modes

There are two broad categories of concurrency: optimistic and pessimistic. The names are self-explanatory. Transactions with *optimistic* concurrency work on the assumption that resource conflicts, when more than one transaction works on the same set of data, are unlikely (though possible, leaving to the database to sort out any potential mess). Optimistic transactions check for potential conflicts when committing changes to a database, and conflicts are resolved by resubmitting data (in this case, the last commit takes precedence). *Pessimistic* transactions expect conflicts from the very beginning and lock all resources they intend to use. While ensuring the highest level of consistency, pessimistic locking is also the most expensive and can bog down a database. Usually, RDBMSs employ both optimistic and pessimistic transactions, and sometimes users can instruct their transactions to use either; pessimistic mode provides better consistency, but you pay a price.

Locking granularity has a significant effect on system performance. Row-level locking increases concurrency (it does not block other transactions from accessing a table), but it usually incurs overhead costs of administration that slows down the database. A full table lock is much less expensive in terms of system resources, but comes at the price of concurrency and performance. This is something to keep in mind when designing database applications.

Locks are used to implement pessimistic transactions, and each RDBMS has its own levels of locking, though there are some similarities. In general, there are either share locks or exclusive locks, which refer to the way a resource is being used.

For example, the following statement locks the `books` table of the Library database in exclusive mode:

```
LOCK TABLE books IN EXCLUSIVE MODE;
```

The transaction that issues this statement will attempt to lock the table for its exclusive use, although allowing for SELECT; if any other process keeps a lock on the table, the transaction will be put in a queue, and the lock will be acquired in priority received. The lock will be in place for the duration of the transaction (until `COMMIT` is executed). The actual syntax might vary with RDBMSs, but not by much.

Locking presents a potential issue: A deadlock situation might occur (see the next paragraph) if the transaction that already holds a lock on the table attempts to acquire a lock on a resource that the second transaction has a lock on.

Some databases, notably Microsoft SQL Server 2008 and IBM DB2 9.7 implement something called lock escalation. *This term refers to a process of converting many finely grained locks into "coarser," higher-level locks, thus reducing the system's overhead. Oracle 10g/11g never escalates its locks, preferring better concurrency over system resources. Neither MySQL (with InnoDB add-on) nor PostgreSQL use it.*

All other locks are at the discretion of the RDBMS (they are not user-configurable). Default locking is row-level, and a lock can escalate to a table-level lock. The lock escalation may be avoided using the previous `LOCKTABLE` statement. The escalation thresholds are configurable by a DBA.

There is a penalty to pay for the high granularity (row-level locking) because it degrades performance as SQL Server allocates more resources for row-level locking operations; it also increases the possibility of deadlocks occurring.

For a comparative matrix of the different lock types available in the respective RDBMSs, please check out the book's website at www.wrox.com, or go to www.agilitator.com.

Dealing with Deadlocks

The classic deadlock situation arises when two (or more) sessions are waiting to acquire a lock on a shared resource, and none of them can proceed because a second session also has a lock on some other resource that is required by the first session. Imagine a situation in which Session 1 holds resource A while trying to access resource B, and Session 2 holds resource B while trying to access resource A.

Usually RDBMSs resolve situations like these automatically by killing one of the processes and rolling back all the changes it may have made.

Oracle implements a sophisticated mechanism enforcing this rule: "Reader and writer processes cannot block each other." The idea behind this rule is to present each process with a consistent image of data without noncommitted changes. Nevertheless, deadlocks do occur in Oracle and usually are resolved by the RDBMS; in some rare cases, a manual resolution — choosing the deadlock "victim" process — is required. The most common deadlock types are ORA-00060 (*en queue* deadlocks) and ORA-04020 (library cache deadlocks). It is possible to specify the `NOWAIT` clause or set up session timeouts to avoid deadlocks, while some other techniques involve explicit locking and use of the isolation levels within the transaction. A deadlock may also be resolved manually through Oracle interfaces.

IBM DB2 runs a background process, Deadlock Detector, to find and resolve the deadlock situation. The session chosen as a deadlock victim is rolled back, and a special error is generated (`SQLCODE-901`, `SQLSTATE40001`). The read-only process is a prime candidate for the deadlock victim, and beyond that, DB2 employs "least cost" criteria to select the session to be killed. If deadlocks ever become a problem, IBM recommends using system-monitoring tools to collect information about the deadlock situations and either optimize the system or redesign any applications involved.

Microsoft SQL Server 2008 employs a proprietary algorithm for detecting deadlocks and resolves them in a way similar to that implemented by other RDBMSs: Deadlocks are resolved automatically or manually through the Enterprise Manager Console. It is possible to volunteer a session to become a deadlock victim by setting the `DEADLOCK_PRIORITY` parameter within that session (refer to the discussion of sessions earlier in this chapter).

Both PostgreSQL and MySQL try to resolve deadlock situation by aborting one of the competing transactions.

In all cases, the best practices call for avoiding deadlock situations in the first place by running smaller transactions, running frequent commits, refactoring your logic for accessing tables, using less explicit locking directives, and so on.

SQL Security

As a language, SQL provides only limited security mechanisms, relying on the actual RDBMS software to implement a more robust security framework. Security starts with the operating systems that host the RDBMS. UNIX, Windows, and Linux each implement their own mechanisms to protect files and communications, and end up with the users safeguarding their user ID(s) and passwords. The RDBMS application is subject to the same security rules as every other application you may run on the computer, only more so. It runs under some operating system account, and while its storage files might be encrypted, the operating system also can manage access to these files. This applies to the simple desktop databases or enterprise class RDBMSs running on "big iron" mainframes and computer clusters.

For the user, the security starts with initiating connection to the database, whereas the RDBMS verifies user credentials and grants access. After that, the RDBMS enforces privileges that a specific user has to the database objects.

Basic Security Mechanisms

Database security is an enormous topic, and exploring the ways in which leading database vendors implemented its various aspects is even larger. Security was not invented with the relational database; the password authentication, locks, audit, and other security concepts are as ancient as human history, and SQL just added a new twist. Following SQL Standard's lead (and customers' demand), all RDBMSs comply in establishing the security procedures. There are several levels of security common to all RDBMSs; what differs is the way each of these RDBMSs implement these levels.

Identification and Authentication

The first line of defense is authentication. Before you even access an RDBMS, you must submit sufficient information validated either by the RDBMS itself or by the operating system within which this database is installed. Once the identity is authenticated, you may proceed with the attempt to access the database resources, objects, and data.

Authorization and Access Control

Once the user is authenticated and granted access to the database, the RDBMS employs a complex, finely grained system of privileges (permissions) for the particular database objects. These privileges include permissions to create, access, modify, destroy, or execute relevant database objects; as well as add, modify, and delete data.

Encryption

Encryption provides an additional security layer that protects the data from unauthorized viewing. Even if access to the database is obtained, it will not be easy to decipher encrypted data into a human readable form without the help of a particular software client or a password.

Integrity and Consistency

While security is mostly based on authentication and authorization procedures, data integrity plays a certain role in protecting data from unintentional or malicious manipulation. For example, even if a user gains access to the database (by stealing a password, for example), he or she still has to follow relational rules for data manipulation, that, among others, do not allow orphaned records. The user won't be able to delete records from a parent table without understanding database relationships (though some RDBMSs had implemented the CASCADE feature that instructs RDBMSs to remove child records upon deletion of the parent), won't be able to insert a duplicate record into a column protected by the `UNIQUE` constraint, or won't be able to insert invalid data that would violate CHECK constraints.

Auditing

Auditing provides ways to monitor database activity, both legitimate and unauthorized. It preserves the trail of database access attempts — either successful or failed — data deletions and inserts (in case one has to find out what had happened), and so on. It is a necessary component in order to be considered for security certification, discussed later in this chapter.

Defining a Database User

The concept of the user, while being plain and simple in an intuitive layman way, is one of the most confusing concepts across the RDBMS implementations. SQL Standard does not specify any special syntax (or even a way) to create a user in the database). Left to their own devices, the database vendors have managed to create some ingenious solutions. For example, Oracle 10g makes very little distinction between a user and the database schema, and allows for both RDBMS password, and operating system account authentication. IDB DB2 LUW only uses operating system-defined users (or those defined by some external security framework); Microsoft SQL Server combines both approaches, using Windows accounts and special system procedures for adding users to a database; and PostgreSQL and MySQL both favor creating users authenticated directly by the database (with PostgreSQL also providing support for OS/network based authentication).

There are additional authentication methods, including LDAP and Kerberos protocols; these are intended for network based authentication, and are beyond the scope of this book.

Microsoft SQL Server differentiates between LOGIN and USER: the former is used for authentication (logging into the database), while the latter is used for authorization (assigning privileges to database objects).

A user can be an RDBMS user, an operating system user, a role, or an application role, defined on the database level. To allow for fine-grained security, an object in the database belongs to a schema and is owned by the user. This also addresses the problem of controlling access to the database objects through granting or revoking access privileges.

By definition, a database user is someone who makes use of the services provided by the RDBMS server. It can be an application, a database administrator, or just anyone who happens to access the database at any given moment. To facilitate administration, users are often assigned to groups or roles; a privilege granted or revoked from a role immediately takes effect for all users who belong to this role.

User authentication is the first line of defense when it comes to security issues, and the most basic syntax works across almost every RDBMS (with few variations):

```
CREATE USER LibraryUser
IDENTIFIED BY 'letmein';
```

In Oracle and DB2 such syntax would leave a lot to defaults, which is hardly a recipe for production database security. MySQL requires the user to be tied to the IP address of the database (*LibraryUser@localhost* for a default user), and PostgreSQL creates the user WITH PASSWORD "letmein."

Microsoft Access also allows for creating users using SQL statements similar to those just mentioned. OpenOffice BASE and its embedded HSQLDB database do not provide this capability.

Microsoft SQL Server 2008 syntax for creating a user is somewhat different; it requires LOGIN to be created first. Here's the most basic syntax to create both:

```
CREATE LOGIN libUsers WITH PASSWORD 'letmein';
GO;

CREATE USER LibraryUser FOR LOGIN libUsers
GO;
```

There are many more options for the syntax in every RDBMS, and selecting the right one requires a thorough understanding of both business domain and security issues; this is why creating user hierarchy is better left to your database administrator.

Once the user is created, it can be ALTERed or DROPped altogether. The basic syntax is virtually identical across all RDBMSs, but using ALTER is more database-specific:

```
DROP USER LibraryUser;
```

Oracle has an additional clause in the DROP USER syntax, CASCADE, which specifies that all objects in the user's schema should be dropped before dropping the user. Oracle does not allow dropping a user whose schema contains any objects unless this clause is specified.

The `ALTER USER` statement specifies a number of changes for a user, and since changes differ from RDBMS to RDBMS, there is no single syntax to be used across all of them. MySQL does not support the ALTER keyword, while Oracle lists more than a dozen options available. Microsoft SQL Server alters LOGIN and then remaps the USER, and DB2 alters user mapping with optional parameters set at the same time. So although it is SQL, it is extremely dialect-specific and requires advanced knowledge of a particular RDBMS.

IBM DB2 LUW uses a combination of external security services and internal access controls. IBM DB2 does not provide authentication services, relying instead on external services. This means that a user cannot be created unless he or she also has an operating system account: Windows, UNIX, or any other operating system (OS). As such, all user authentications are managed outside of the DB2 database. Microsoft SQL Server 2005 introduced the `CREATE USER` *statement; together with ALTER USER and DROP USER, it has become the standard user management mechanism. In addition, there is also a mechanism for user management through system stored procedures inherited from the previous version of SQL Server. Please note that while still supported, user management procedures might be deprecated in the future releases of Microsoft SQL Server.*

Managing Security with Privileges

An RDBMS is essentially a collection of objects (schemas, tables, views, procedures, and so on) and the processes that manage these objects. Restricting access to these objects is an essential security mechanism implemented on the SQL level through the *privileges* system.

Privileges represent the rights of a particular user to access, create, manipulate, and destroy various objects inside a database; as well as perform administrative tasks. Privileges can be granted to a user, `role`, or both (the concept of `ROLE` is discussed in the next paragraph).

All the privileges can be divided into two broad categories — *system privileges* and *object privileges* — and they vary widely among different database vendors. For a more detailed look, see the section on specific RDBMS implementations later in this chapter.

GRANT Statement

The SQL Standard defines privileges as the types of actions a user is authorized to perform on the objects and in the system to which he or she is granted access. All these privileges are consistent across the RDBMSs discussed in this book.

A privilege can be granted either to an individual user or to a role. The `GRANT` statement can be used for granting either system privileges or object privileges. The basic syntax for granting the privilege is fairly consistent across all RDBMS packages (though there are significant differences in advanced options), and multiple privileges can be granted in a single statement, such as the following:

```
GRANT [ALL [PRIVILEGES]] | <privilege,...>
[ON <object_name>]
TO <user> | <group> | <role>
[WITH GRANT OPTION]
```

Granting System-Level Privileges

System privileges allow users to perform some administrative tasks within a given RDBMS (creating a database; creating and dropping users; creating, altering, and destroying database objects; and so on). You need a sufficiently high level of authority within the RDBMS to be able to exercise or grant system privileges. The features that distinguish these system privileges from object privileges are their scope and sometimes the types of activities they allow the user to perform.

System privileges are strictly database-specific; each vendor implements its own set of system privileges and some system privileges may have different meanings for different RDBMSs. Some systems, Microsoft SQL Server, for instance, do not even define system privileges. They use privileges (permissions) for so-called *securables* that, on different levels, can be servers, databases, and schemas.

Here are some examples based in the LIBRARY database. The following code creates LibrarayUser, then grants the user a privilege to create a table in the database and pass it on to others:

```
CREATE USER LibraryUser
IDENTIFIED BY letmein;

GRANT CREATE TABLE
```

```
TO LibraryUser
WITH ADMIN OPTION;
```

Assuming that you have sufficient privileges, the user LibraryUser identified by the password `LETMEIN` will be created, but you cannot use this user ID and password to connect to the Oracle database if the user `NEW_USER` has not been granted the `CREATESESSION` system privilege, which it would need to access the database. The error `ORA-01045:user LibraryUser lacks CREATESESSION privilege;logon denied` would be generated.

To fix the situation, you need to grant the newly created user this privilege:

```
GRANT CREATE SESSION
TO LibraryUser
WITH ADMIN OPTION;
```

Now you can connect to the database using `LibraryUser/letmein` credentials, and, because of the `WITH ADMIN OPTION`, grant this privilege to other users; some RDBMSs, notably, Oracle, treat this option as more generic WITH GRANT OPTION one.

There are two more system privileges in Oracle that deserve mentioning here: `SYSDBA` and `SYSOPER. These` privileges act like roles in that they include a number of other system privileges. When connecting to the Oracle database, you can specify to connect `ASSYSDBA` or `ASSYSOPER`, assuming that these privileges had been granted to the user. `SYSDBA` is one of the highest privileges that can be granted.

IBM DB2 is somewhat similar in this aspect to Oracle; it has system privileges, and some of the privileges are associated with authority levels (see more on this later in this chapter). The hierarchy of the privileges places SYSADM authority (System Administrator) at the top, and the next level includes DBADM (Database Administrator) and SYSCTRL (System Resource Administrator), followed by SYSMAINT (System Maintenance Administrator); at the end of the hierarchy are database users. To `GRANT` the `DBADM` authority, a user must have `SYSADM` authority. Both `SYSADM` and `DBADM` can grant the other privileges to users or groups.

IBM DB2 9.7 provides additional ways to protect data, even from a user with SYSADM authority. It is called label-based access control (LBAC). It can be used to protect entire rows, columns, or both. Oracle provides similar feature called Oracle Label Security.

The Microsoft SQL Server 2008 does not have system privileges (at least, not in the sense that Oracle or IBM have them). The privileges are granted to a user (or role) for specific SQL statements. Once the privilege is granted, users can execute the statement to perform operations that they define. The SQL Server 2008 has defined a number of *securables* (database server resources such as login, database, role, user, schema, and so on) that can be granted to *principals* (user, group, role, and application role). The principals are defined on the Windows operating-system level (domain login, local login), SQL Server level (SQL Server login), and database level (database user/role and application role). Table 10-5 lists some of the permissions that can be GRANTed to the principals.

TABLE 10-5: Selected Microsoft SQL Server 2008 Permissions

PERMISSION	APPLICABLE SECURABLES
SELECT	Synonyms, tables, views, columns, table-valued functions
UPDATE	Synonyms, tables, views, columns
INSERT	Synonyms, tables, views, columns
DELETE	Synonyms, tables, views, columns
EXECUTE	Procedures, functions (scalar and aggregate), synonyms
RECEIVE	Service broker queues
VIEW DEFINITION	Synonyms, tables, views, table-valued functions, scalar and aggregate functions, procedures
CREATE	Procedures, functions (scalar and aggregate), synonyms, service broker queues, database
ALTER	Procedures, functions (scalar and aggregate), synonyms, service broker queues

The system permissions are tied to a database (MS SQL Server also uses this concept; the closest Oracle equivalent is *schema*) and are hierarchical. For example, to `GRANT` the privilege to execute a `CREATEDATABASE` statement, you must be in the context of the SQL Server *master* database, as this statement produces results affecting the whole instance of SQL Server 2008.

The security account refers to the SQL Server user, SQL Server role, Windows user, or Windows group. There is some granularity to the security accounts defined by the SQL Server. Privileges granted to a user (either on the SQL Server or Windows) affect this user only; privileges granted to a role or Windows NT group affect all members of this role or group.

Granting the `CREATEDATABASE` statement to a user/role while being in context of the LIBRARY database produces an error, as follows:

```
USE library
GRANT CREATE DATABASE
TO PUBLIC;

CREATE DATABASE permission can only be granted in the master database.
```

Changing the context to the *master* database resolves the issue. Privileges to the objects within the database are granted in a similar manner, either to a role or a user:

```
USE library
GRANT CREATE TABLE
TO PUBLIC;
```

These privileges can be revoked — either system-level or object-level — from a database user, role, or group with the REVOKE statement. Roles, which are named entities with granted sets of privileges, are revoked in a similar way:

```
REVOKE CREATE TABLE
FROM USER PUBLIC;
```

SQL Standard also specifies two clauses: `RESTRICT` and `CASCADE`. With the first option, the statement succeeds only if there is no abandoned privilege in the database. Such a situation might occur when the user, for example, already granted this privilege to some other user. When you are determined to revoke the privilege no matter what, and propagate this change across all the users who have received this privilege from the user, the `CASCADE` clause must be specified. These clauses are optional in all RDBMS implementations which support it, but in the SQL Standard at least one is required. As usual, each of the RDBMSs has its own ideas for implementing this statement.

The effects of `REVOKE` are immediate: If the privilege is revoked from `PUBLIC`, each user loses that privilege if it were granted through `PUBLIC`; privileges granted to the user directly or through a role remain unaffected in this case. The rules for revoking system privileges are complex. For example, if a privilege (or role) is revoked from a role, it is revoked from that role only; if the role granted the privilege (or role) to another user (or role), the user would continue to exercise the privilege (or role).

Keep in mind that revoking the privilege from a user has no effect on any object the user had already created. When privileges are revoked, all objects created with these privileges up to the moment will remain in the database.

Managing Security with Roles

`ROLE` is an abstract concept introduced in the RDBMSs to facilitate user management tasks by grouping users' privileges according to some criteria, usually a job function. If, for example, your accounting staff of 100 people need privileges for the dozens of objects they access daily (in addition to some system-level privileges), you have two choices: go through each and every user and individually grant him or her all the privileges required, or create a group (role), such as `ACCOUNTANTS`, grant all the privileges to the role, and grant this role to all the users in the group. Revoking the privileges poses the same choices. It seems fairly obvious which choice is better.

Some RDBMSs provide role-creating capabilities in addition to having a number of predefined system roles that can be granted to a user. Oracle 10g/11g and Microsoft SQL Server 2008 have this feature, while DB2 employs only fixed, predefined roles (authorities).

Oracle roles are collections of privileges that can be granted to (or revoked from) a user or another role, thus providing a hierarchy of privileges. A role must be enabled (with a `SETROLE` statement or by the database administrator) before it can pass on all the privileges granted to it.

Oracle 10g/11g has a number of predefined roles through which privileges are granted to users. You cannot add new privileges to a predefined role or revoke any from the role.

A package in Oracle RDBMS is a collection of precompiled routines (usually written in PL/SQL) that resides in the RDBMS itself. A user can access database functionality through procedures and functions defined in the package. By grouping these functional pieces into a package, you could establish security policy governing usage of this package on a group level, as opposed to assigning privileges on a one by one basis.

Here is an example of a role created for the LIBRARY database with a set of default options in virtually any RDBMS:

```
CREATE ROLE libUsers;
```

Now you can grant privileges to this role (refer to the `GRANT` statement discussion earlier in this chapter for more information) and later grant the privileges to everyone who needs them by assigning those people to the libUsers role.

You can enable or disable `ROLE` for the duration of the current database session using the `SETROLE` statement. There might be a limit to the number of concurrent roles that can be set by the database administrator.

A custom role can be altered or dropped by using the `ALTERROLE` or `DROPROLE` statements, respectively:

```
DROP ROLE libUsers;
```

Up until version 9.5, IBM DB2 did not support user-defined roles, relying instead on the system's predefined authorities (fixed roles) that a user can be a member of, and relies on `GROUP`, which behaves almost the same as roles that are employed in other RDBMSs. This is still supported in 9.7, but additional support for roles was added, and is consistent, by and large, with Oracle's implementation.

Some privileges for the database objects are not relevant for all discussed RDBMSs. For example, the `PACKAGE` object can be found in the DB2 or Oracle database, but it is nonexistent in MS SQL Server, PostgreSQL, or MySQL. Adding to the confusion, the concept of a package has a different meaning for Oracle and IBM.

Operating System Security Integration

It is important to remember that the OS was there before the first computer database was invented, and no RDBMS can operate without some kind of OS. Each OS comes with its own security mechanisms. All the RDBMSs discussed in this book, to some extent, provide security integration with the

OS they are running on. Essentially, it boils down to using OS accounts and privileges to access the database instead of relying on the RDBMS.

Microsoft SQL Server 2008, for example, has tight OS-integrated security, which allows users with a valid Windows account to be authenticated based on their Windows NT/2000/XP credentials. Instead of supplying a separate user ID and password, a user set up with Windows authentication could access SQL Server 2008 automatically as soon as he logs on to the machine that runs the RDBMS.

Other RDBMSs extend this functionality to multiple operating systems, and the details of implementation and usage are just as different as the systems.

RDBMSs running on some operating systems (notably, Windows 9x) do not have OS security integration, as the OS itself does not provide facilities for this.

Using Views for Security

One of the mechanisms that can be used to implement security is SQL views. Using views, it is possible to restrict data accessible to a user, the type of operations the user can perform through the views, or both.

Consider the following DDL SQL statement, which is generic enough to be acceptable by all RDBMS implementations:

```
CREATE VIEW vw_SingleTable
AS
  SELECT
     bk_publisher AS Publisher
    ,bk_title AS Title
    ,bk_pub_year AS Year_of_Publication
FROM  books
```

This view selects only three fields from the `BOOKS` table, which has a total of 11 fields. This is called *vertical restriction* because it restricts access to the subset of columns (fields). The other fields might contain confidential information that you do not want the viewer to see. If you grant `SELECT` privilege on the view only to some role (for example, the `ROLE` "friends"), everyone who belongs to that role could see customers' names and statuses, while the rest of the information that the table contains remains inaccessible to them.

You can also use *horizontal restriction* by specifying a subset of rows. For example, you may want to grant access to the historical data, something that was entered into the table a year ago or earlier, and prevent access to data added after that date. Using the example from the LIBRARY database, suppose that you would like a quick and simple access to the books with prices below certain level, say, 20 dollars. For the latter example, the SQL syntax for all RDBMSs would be as follows:

```
CREATE VIEW vw_cheap_books
AS
SELECT *
FROM   books
WHERE  bk_price < 20
```

Selecting from the following view will bring up only the books whose price is under 20.

Of course, both horizontal and vertical selection can be combined into a single view.

Additional restrictions that can be implemented in views include `WHERE` clauses and `JOIN` conditions. They are useful when more than one table is involved in a view. For example, you can restrict your view to show only authors whose books sell for less than 20 dollars.

```
SELECT DISTINCT bk.bk_title, ba.au_last_name
FROM books bk
JOIN
    books_authors ba
        ON bk.bk_id= ba.bk_id
JOIN
 authors au
  ON   ba.au_id = au.au_id
WHERE
  Bk.bk_price < 20
```

Views are used not only for `SELECT` but also for `UPDATE`, `INSERT`, and `DELETE` statements. Some of these operations are governed by the inherent properties of a view object, and some can be specified when the view object is created. For example, you cannot update or insert views that were created using aggregate functions — attempting to do so will generate an error. This is an inherent behavior. On the other hand, for an updateable view, you can create a constraint that can accept or reject data modifications based on some criteria.

TRY IT OUT Restricting Data Access with SQL Views

Let's build a view that would restrict users to see only books added up to the current year. We will use Microsoft SQL Server 2008 for this example. Please refer to `www.wrox.com` or `www.agilitator.com` for your RDBMS-specific examples:

1. Open Microsoft SQL Server Query Analyzer.
2. In the SQL Query pane, type **USE [library]** as your very first statement.
3. Enter the following code:

```
CREATE VIEW vwLastYearBooks AS
SELECT * FROM books where EXTRACT(PublishingDate, YEAR) < EXTRACT (GetDate(), YEAR)
GO
```

4. Now you need to create a user who has only privileges to SELECT from this view and nothing else; the user will be automatically assigned to the PUBLIC role:

```
CREATE LOGIN LibraryGuest
    WITH PASSWORD = 'comein";
USE library;
CREATE USER LibraryGuest FOR LOGIN LibraryGuest;
GO;
```

Alternatively, you can use the already existing login GUEST.

5. Grant the new user privileges to access your server and run SELECT statements for the view vwLastYearBooks:

```
GRANT SELECT ON library.vwLastYearBooks TO LibraryGuest;
REVOKE SELECT, INSERT, DELETE ON books FROM LibraryGuest;
GO;
```

6. Disconnect from the RDBMS and reconnect using the new credentials: user ID and password.
7. Run the following:

```
SELECT * FROM vwLastYearBooks
```

8. Try running SELECT on the BOOKS table.

How It Works

The user-created LibraryGuest was granted SELECT privileges on the view vwLastYearBooks and had its privileges revoked for selecting data from the BOOKS table. Even though the view displays data from that table, the table itself is inaccessible to the LibraryGuest.

Using Constraints for Security

Constraints often are used to maintain integrity — be it referential integrity, data integrity (also called *entity* integrity), or domain integrity.

Domain integrity constraints, such as the `CHECK` constraint, validate data for correct format and content. For example, in the LIBRARY database, the `CHK_ISBN` constraint that follows validates that ISBN number entered into the database is of specific length:

```
ALTER TABLE books
ADD CONSTRAINT chk_ISBN
CHECK (LEN(bk_isbn) = 10 OR LEN(bk_isbn) = 14)
```

Now any attempt, legitimate or otherwise, to enter invalid data outside the specified range would generate an error; your data are protected against inconsistency. Validating data before they are committed to the database table is a very efficient security practice.

Another mechanism for enforcing domain integrity is the `DEFAULT` value. When specified, this value guarantees that if any data were omitted from the query, a default value will be used instead of blank space or `NULL`.

It is open for discussion whether `DEFAULT` represents a security breach or a security enforcement mechanism. On the one hand, it prevents data inconsistency, which is a good thing; on the other, it requires less precision on the data entry end by preventing omission/sloppiness errors and less effort for a malicious intruder to insert data.

Entity integrity, which essentially refers to a row of data, is maintained with indices and constraints such as the `PRIMARYKEY` constraint or the `UNIQUE` constraint. It effectively prevents users from entering duplicate values. For example, putting these constraints on the Social Security number (SSN) column would prevent miscreants from collecting benefits more than once using the same SSN and different names.

Referential integrity maintains healthy relationships between the tables for which it is declared. It is an RDBMS version of the "No Child Left Behind" policy. It mandates that there cannot be a record in the child table if a corresponding record in the parent table is missing, and that a record in the parent table cannot be deleted as long as it has a corresponding record in the child table.

Constraints by themselves cater to a very narrow segment of database security and should be considered supplemental to the more robust mechanisms provided by the overall RDBMS security.

One of the ways to implement additional security can be stored procedures and triggers (discussed in Chapter 4). The former can help to restrict access to the database objects and implement input validation; and the latter is a variation of a stored procedure that would execute automatically upon INSERT, UPDATE, or DELETE operation performed on the table, either validating data or accumulating the audit trail.

SQL Injection

SQL injection is a technique that exploits vulnerability in the database application that uses dynamically built statements (refer to Chapter 3 for more on dynamic SQL). The idea behind the technique is to change the underlying statement, either by supplying broader selection criteria in the WHERE clause or appending additional SQL commands to the end of the statement. For example, if the client application checks for a specific user_ID using statement (admittedly lame), the expectation is that if no row is returned, authentication failed:

```
SELECT * FROM users WHERE user_id = '" + <user_ID> + "'"
```

Now imagine that the malicious attacker enters `'somebody' OR 'a'='a'` into the user_ID field. This would translate into the following statement:

```
SELECT 1 FROM Users WHERE user_ID = 'somebody' OR 'a' = 'a'
```

Because there is no user ID "somebody," the authentication would fail, but the second part, 'a' = 'a' evaluates to TRUE and a row is returned, therefore authenticating the user.

In the preceding example, the attacker also can force the server to execute an unanticipated statement by typing in the <user_ID> ;<another SQL statement>. For instance:

```
SELECT 1 FROM Users WHERE user_ID = 'somebody' ; DELETE FROM books;
```

If executed, the preceding statement would delete all records from the BOOKS table (this would require some knowledge of the database structure or a clever guess on the attacker's part).

The SQL injection attack can be defended against on many levels. The first line of defense is to assign the most restrictive permissions' set required. In the examples, that would prevent deletion of the records because the user would not have DELETE permission on the CUSTOMER table, though it still would be useless against the first scenario. To make sure that the RDBMS executes only intended statements, one can implement check logic on the application layer or resort to stored procedures use (with additional checks implemented inside the stored procedure body); additionally, RDBMSs can do a quick parsing to detect any unanticipated Boolean expressions.

Data Encryption

Encryption is a way to convert information from a directly usable format into a format that cannot be used without being decrypted. The encrypted data normally can be decrypted using the same process (algorithm) that was used to encrypt it. Encryption is *not* a part of SQL Standard, so each RDBMS provides different encryption-related services, usually as a set of built-in functions.

The data inside the RDBMS are stored as plain text (ASCII, Unicode) or binary (`BLOBS`, `IMAGE`, and similar data types). To prevent this data from being viewed by unauthorized users (who happen to be granted access to the table that contains it) or to send a data extract over an unsecured network, the data can be encrypted. The data also can be encrypted via some client software before it is entered into the database or it can be done inside the RDBMS by using its own facilities.

A lot can be learned from the SQL code used to create database objects, and in most databases it is normally stored in open text to be retrieved by querying special INFORMATION_SCHEMA view (discussed later in this chapter). To prevent this, some RDBMSs allow encrypting source code for the objects (tables, views, and stored procedures).

Encryption provides an additional level of security when, in order to view data in human-readable format (whether text or pictures, audio files, or executable files), a user would need a password and decrypting facilities, either on the RDBMS or inside his or her client software.

TRY IT OUT Encrypting and Decrypting Data with IBM DB2 Built-in Functions

IBM DB2 LUW provides ENRYPT and DECRYPT_CHAR built-in functions for data encryption:

1. Open the IBM DB2 command editor or use the command-line utility to connect to the LIBRARY database.
2. Execute the following SQL query:

```
SELECT ENCRYPT(bk_title, 'PASSWORD') AS encrypted
FROM   books
```

The results are encrypted book titles:

```
ENCRYPTED
---------------------------------------------------
x'00E61AFFE404A6D596757C7CC7AC70467884E127B6A50726'
. . .
x'00DC24FFE404A0D5F736C8A4156922A6709DD5D609EBE762'
```

To decrypt the seemingly senseless previous string of characters, you can use the `DECRYPT_CHAR` function (because we are using character data) with exactly the same password ('PASSWORD'). This will restore the data into their original form.

How It Works

The built-in ENCRYPT function accepts two parameters: character data retrieved from the table and the password with which it encrypts the characters. The result is human-unreadable gibberish that can be again converted into book titles using the DECRYPT_CHAR functions with the same password.

There are literally hundreds of data encryption algorithms, both custom and public. To devise and implement an encryption algorithm requires familiarity with programming principles, in addition to advanced math. Here are some popular algorithms in use today: DES (designed by IBM in 1970 and adopted by NIST in 1976 for unclassified data), RC5 (from RSA Data Security), CMEA (developed by the Telecommunication Industry Association to encrypt digital cellular phone data), FEAL (developed by Nippon Telephone & Telegraph), TEA, MD5, Tiger, and CAST, to name just a few.

For quite some time now Oracle had the DBMS_OBFUSCATION_TOOLKIT package to encrypt data. Beginning with version 10g, it introduced a new DBMS_CRYPTO package which somewhat alleviated the deficiencies of its predecessor. The ultimate answer came in the form of Oracle's Transparent Data Encryption feature, which is based on public/master encryption keys created with Oracle Wallet Manager. Please refer to the vendor's documentation for more information.

The data sent between an RDBMS and a client application can also be encrypted using Secure Sockets Layer (SSL) or Secure Shell (SSH) encryption over a Transmission Control Protocol/Internet Protocol (TCP/IP) communication protocol (usually the case for most networks and Internet connections). Inside the RDBMS are cryptographic functions implemented to provide an industrial-strength encryption that should be used whenever data security is required.

Database Auditing

Auditing provides the ability to trace the information flow inside a database, including connection attempts; data updates; deletes, inserts, and selects; execute functionality, and such. It is useful both for postmortem scenarios and for on-going monitoring to detect unauthorized activity.

Auditing has nothing to do with SQL Standard and is strictly RDBMS-dependent — in capabilities, implementation details, and so on.

Security Standards

While not related directly to SQL, *security standards* define the infrastructure within which SQL is employed, so these standards are therefore of interest to SQL users. Usually, RDBMS software complies with these standards to a certain degree, either voluntarily or under pressure from the government agencies that mandate requirements for the software's acceptance.

The first nationwide attempt to standardize security procedures for computer systems was undertaken in 1985 by the U.S. National Computer Security Center (NCSC). To be considered for a government contract, the RDBMSs had to achieve a certain level of security for their products through proctored testing. Dozens of RDBMSs went through years (the process has taken three years, on average) of testing procedures just to be able to sell their products to government agencies. Vendors such as Sun, Oracle, and Novell received their certifications (either C1 or B2) in early 1990s, following a directive that all computer systems storing sensitive information must be C2-certified.

A number of regulatory compliance acts have been enabled, such as Sarabanes-Oxley and BASEL II for financial records, HIPAA for medical information, PCI for credit card information, and so on.

INFORMATION_SCHEMA and SQL System Catalogs

To keep track of all objects, their relationships, and so on, the RDBMSs use the same technique they are advocating: a set of relational tables and views. The SQL Standards committee introduced the concept of INFORMATION_SCHEMA views that, with some modifications, were implemented across all RDBMSs. This schema provides read-only access to information about every database object.

In SQL Standard, a `CATALOG` is a collection of schemas that contains, among other things, `INFORMATION_SCHEMA`. It comprises the tables and views that provide all the information about all the other objects and records defined in the database: schemas, tables, privileges, and so on. The latest standard also includes structure and integrity constraints information, as well as security and authorization specifications for the SQL data. The main idea is to provide both users and the RDBMSs with a consistent, standardized way of accessing metadata (the data about data: table definitions, user-defined types, and so on) as well as some system information. By definition, the `INFORMATION_SCHEMA` tables and views cannot be updated directly, although some RDBMSs allow this (for example, IBM DB2).

SQL Standard lists more than 60 different views that can be used to get information about database objects and their usage, and RDBMSs have implemented most of them, plus some of their own. The SQL Standard–compliant INFORMATION_SCHEMA views were implemented in Microsoft SQL Server (version 7.0 or later), PostgreSQL (version 7.4 or later), and MySQL (version 5.0 or later). IBM DB2 has kept its SYSCAT schema that serves as an equivalent, and Oracle uses data dictionary views.

Microsoft Access does not provide metadata information as a view to be queried through SQL, but allows it to be accessed programmatically through Visual Basic for Applications (VBA). OpenOffice BASE, which is a front end for an RDBMS, relies on the underlying database to provide the information passing SQL requests to the RDBMS engine (embedded HSQLDB supports a subset of INFORMATION_SCHEMA).

At the very least, you can count on the views (or their reincarnations) listed in Table 10-6 to be present for you to query.

TABLE 10-6: Selected Standard INFORMATION_SCHEMA Views

INFORMATION_SCHEMA VIEW	IMPLEMENTED IN RDBMS	DESCRIPTION
`COLUMNS`	Microsoft SQL Server PostgreSQL MySQL IBM DB2 (SYSCAT.COLUMNS) Oracle (*_TAB_COLUMNS view)	Describes columns accessible to the current user/role for every table in the database, one row per column.

continues

TABLE 10-6 *(continued)*

INFORMATION_SCHEMA VIEW	IMPLEMENTED IN RDBMS	DESCRIPTION
ROUTINES	Microsoft SQL Server PostgreSQL MySQL IBM DB2 (SYSCAT.PROCEDURES) Oracle (*_PROCEDURES view)	Describes the SQL-invoked routines in this catalog that are accessible to a given user/role.
SEQUENCES	Microsoft SQL Server PostgreSQL MySQL IBM DB2 (SYSCAT.SEQUENCES) Oracle (*_SEQUENCES view)	Describes the external sequence generators defined in this catalog that are accessible to a given user/role.
TABLES	Microsoft SQL Server PostgreSQL MySQL IBM DB2 (SYSCAT.TABLES) Oracle (*_TABLES view)	Describes every table accessible to the user/role, one row per table/view.
VIEWS	Microsoft SQL Server PostgreSQL MySQL IBM DB2 (SYSCAT.VIEWS) Oracle (*_VIEWS view)	Describes every view accessible to the user/role, one row per view.

It is important to remember that INFORMATION_SCHEMA views provide standardized access to the database metadata and usage information. The information is present in every database discussed in this book and can be obtained through some other RDBMS-specific channels.

TRY IT OUT Querying INFORMATION_SCHEMA

The basics of querying INFORMATION_SCHEMA are essentially the same across all RDBMSs that support it, but there are some peculiarities that are database-specific. For instance, the following query has the identical syntax across Microsoft SQL Server 2008, MySQL 5.1, and PostgreSQL 9.0, yet the results it produces might be slightly different. The following step-by-step instructions assume that your RDBMS service is up and running.

1. Open Microsoft SQL Server 2008 SQL Server Management Studio.
2. Connect to your instance by supplying all necessary information and clicking the Connect button.

3. Click the New Query button in the upper-left corner of the SQL Server Management studio console.

4. Type in the following code:

```
USE library
SELECT * FROM INFORMATION_SCHEMA.TABLES
```

5. Observe the results, as shown in Figure 10-1.

Results | Messages

	TABLE_CATALOG	TABLE_SCHEMA	TABLE_NAME	TABLE_TYPE
1	library	dbo	authors	BASE TABLE
2	library	dbo	search_books	BASE TABLE
3	library	dbo	books_authors	BASE TABLE
4	library	dbo	location	BASE TABLE
5	library	dbo	vwPublisherTitleYear	VIEW
6	library	dbo	vwBookPublisherYear	VIEW
7	library	dbo	vwBooksFilter	VIEW
8	library	dbo	sysdiagrams	BASE TABLE

FIGURE 10-1

How It Works

The first statement sets up context for the LIBRARY database. The Microsoft SQL Server INFORMATION_SCHEMA view TABLES collects information on every custom table created in the current database. These views provide uniform standard access to the information about objects in the database and should be used instead of any other proprietary mechanism supported by the RDBMS.

Oracle Data Dictionary

Oracle uses the term *data dictionary* for its system catalogs. Each Oracle database has its own set of system tables and views that store information about physical and logical database structures. The data dictionary objects are read-only, meaning that no database user ever manually modifies them. However, the Oracle RDBMS automatically updates data in these objects in response to specific actions. For example, when a user creates a new object (table, view, or stored procedure), adds a column or a constraint to a table, and so forth, the appropriate data dictionary tables are updated behind the scenes at once, and the corresponding changes are visible through the system views (discussed later in this chapter). The Oracle's predefined user SYS owns all base tables and user-accessible views of the data dictionary.

There are literally hundreds of different views and tables that provide information about Oracle's database objects and their usage (rumor has it that there are 3,763 views and 956 tables in Oracle 11g Release 2), but most of them are only of interest to database administrators and are beyond the scope of this book.

The Oracle data dictionary views consist of static and dynamic views. The term *static* denotes that the information in this group of views changes only when a change is made to the data dictionary (a column is added to a table, a new database user is created, and so on). The dynamic views are constantly updated while a database is in use; their contents relate primarily to performance and are used to monitor the health of the database.

The dynamic data dictionary views can be distinguished by the prefix `V_$`, *and the public synonyms for these views start with* `V$`.

The static views can be divided into three groups. The views in each group are prefixed `USER_`, `ALL_`, or `DBA_`, as shown in Table 10-7.

TABLE 10-7: Oracle's Static View Prefixes

PREFIX	SCOPE
USER	User's view (objects in the user's schema)
ALL	Expanded user's view (all objects that the user can access)
DBA	Database administrator's view (all objects in all users' schemas)

The set of columns is almost identical across views; USER_TABLES, ALL_TABLES, and DBA_TABLES have the same columns, except USER_TABLES does not have the column OWNER (which is unnecessary because that view has information only about tables that belong to the user who queries the view).

The select privilege for USER_ and ALL_ views (as well as for selected V$ views) is granted to PUBLIC by default; DBA_ views are visible to privileged users only.

Oracle also has the DBMS_METADATA package that provides interfaces for extracting complete definitions of database objects. The definitions can be expressed either as XML or as SQL DDL.

Unlike the SQL Standard INFORMATION_SCHEMA, which prescribes only a handful of views, Oracle's data dictionary contains more than 1,000 objects, with dozens of columns in each. To help users find their way around, Oracle provides a subset of this metainformation through a few objects that contain the information about the system objects. The two main views are DICTIONARY, which contains a description of the data dictionary tables and views, and DICT_COLUMNS, which describes these objects' columns.

*You can use the SQL*Plus* DESCRIBE *command to obtain minimal information about the data dictionary views and tables, as well as any other database objects to which you have access.*

IBM DB2 LUW System Catalogs

IBM DB2 maintains two sets of database information views: one in the SYSCAT schema and a subset in the SYSSTAT schema (used by IBM SQL Optimizer to improve query performance). All these views are created whenever the CREATEDATABASE command is run; the views comprising the catalog cannot be explicitly dropped, altered, or updated (except for some columns in the SYSSTAT views). The SYSIBM schema has added yet another set of information views that more closely match the views of SQL Standard, bridging the gap with the INFORMATION_SCHEMA standards.

The `SELECT` privilege to views is granted to `PUBLIC` by default. IBM explicitly states that columns in the views might be changed from release to release, and recommends querying these tables using the `SELECT*FROMSYSCAT.<view>` syntax.

The following query retrieves information about the table `CUSTOMER` created in the LIBRARY database:

```
db2 => SELECT TABSCHEMA,
              CREATE_TIME
FROM          SYSIBM.TABLES
WHERE         TABNAME = 'books'

TABSCHEMA           CREATE_TIME
------------------- --------------------------
LIBRARY             2010-09-13-16.37.50.89400
```

For the sake of compatibility with the DB2 Universal Database for OS/390, IBM maintains the `SYSDUMMY1` *catalog table in the* `SYSCAT` *schema. This table consists of one row and one column (*`IBMREQ`*) of the* `CHAR(1)` *data type.*

The `DESCRIBETABLE<table_name>` command can be used to obtain information about the internal structure of the `INFORMATION_SCHEMA` objects in DB2. For example:

```
db2 =>  describe table syscat.views
Column          Type          Type name  Length  Scale  Nulls
name            schema
--------------- ------------- ---------  ------- ------ --
VIEWSCHEMA      SYSIBM        VARCHAR        128      0 No
VIEWNAME        SYSIBM        VARCHAR        128      0 No
. . .
QUALIFIER       SYSIBM        VARCHAR        128      0 No
FUNC_PATH       SYSIBM        VARCHAR        254      0 No
TEXT            SYSIBM        CLOB       2097152      0 No

  12 record(s) selected.
```

Microsoft SQL Server 2008 System Catalog

Microsoft SQL Server 2008 provides two ways of obtaining system information: through `INFORMATION_SCHEMA` views or through system stored procedures and functions. The use of the former is encouraged, and the procedures/functions (a Sybase legacy) are de-emphasized to the point of deprecation. Any supported functionality in this area is for backward compatibility only.

One of the ways to obtain system information about Microsoft SQL Server 2008 is direct querying of the system tables, tables, and views that contain information about the current database, such as `sysobjects`, `sysindexes`, `sysusers`, *and so on. Those stored in the MASTER database contain information about the RDBMS itself. While it is possible for a user with sufficient privileges to query these views and tables, Microsoft strongly discourages such a practice, stating that the system tables are for the exclusive use of the SQL Server, and that the names and structures might change in future releases. (And they certainly have: Each version of SQL Server brings new tables, drops old tables, and changes names.) Our advice is to resist the temptation of using this "back door" and instead use legitimate interfaces to obtain information: INFORMATION_SCHEMA, system stored procedures, and functions, in that order.*

Microsoft SQL Server System Stored Procedures and Functions

There are many categories of system stored procedures supplied with Microsoft SQL Server 2008, depending on the purpose and tasks performed. Only catalog procedures are discussed at some length in this chapter.

Microsoft SQL Server 2008 lists dozens of stored procedures that provide information about the system. You can use these procedures directly from the command-line interface of SQLCMD, from SQL Query Analyzer, or from a client application accessing the SQL Server through any of the programming interfaces provided. Initially, the purpose of these procedures was to implement ODBC data dictionary functions to isolate ODBC applications from possible changes to the SQL Server system tables' structure.

The use of system stored procedures is unique to Microsoft SQL Server and Sybase Adaptive Server because they both have their origins in a joint project initiated by Microsoft, Sybase, and Ashton-Tate in 1988. INFORMATION_SCHEMA views were introduced, starting with version 7.0 of SQL Server.

Getting Help

One of the most useful procedures for obtaining information about any database object is the `sp_help<>` group of stored procedures listed in Table 10-8.

TABLE 10-8: Microsoft SQL Server Help Stored Procedures

STORED PROCEDURE	DESCRIPTION
`sp_help`	Returns information about database objects in the current database.
`sp_helpuser`	Returns information about database users, database roles, and so on.

STORED PROCEDURE	DESCRIPTION
`sp_helptrigger(<tabname>)`	Returns information about triggers defined on the specified table for the current database.
`sp_helpserver`	Returns information about remote and/or replication servers.
`sp_helprotect`	Returns information about user permissions in the current database.
`sp_helpindex`	Returns information about the indices on a table or view.

`SP_HELP` is probably the most universal of the lot. If used without any arguments, it will return information about every single database object (table, view, stored procedure, index, or default) listed in the `sysobjects` table of the current database; being passed a specific object as an argument will return information about this object.

Microsoft SQL Server 2008 also provides a number of functions and system stored procedures that return information about the RDBMS server and contained objects. A comprehensive set of system functions can be found in Microsoft's online documentation.

SUMMARY

All communications with RDBMSs happen within the context of a session. When a session between a client program and RDBMS is established, it possesses certain default properties that determine its behavior. Some of these properties can be modified for the duration of the session, and the database administrator can make these modifications persistent. The enterprise level RDBMS provide transactional support ability to execute SQL statements as a batch, a single logical unit of work. SQL Standard stipulates that a SQL statement always runs as a transaction. RDBMS implementations may treat it differently: some start an implicit transaction by default, and some do not, requiring explicit statements to begin a transaction. Transactions must satisfy certain criteria (the so-called ACID test) to comply with these standards, but these details are usually taken care of by the RDBMS.

Transactions accessing shared resources must implement some concurrency control. One of a transaction's properties is its isolation level established for the transaction. The isolation level regulates what this transaction may access, and what data it is allowed to access and modify.

Some RDBMSs implement intricate locking systems to address the concurrency issue, though locks are not part of SQL Standard. The locks might be of different types. They can be specified within the SQL statement or they can be specified as properties for the session. A deadlock situation may occur in a high-volume transaction processing systems or improperly designed systems. Deadlocks are usually resolved automatically by the RDBMS or may be resolved manually by database administrators.

SQL by itself provides only limited security mechanisms. RDBMSs needed more robust security, which has been implemented in a variety of nonstandard ways by the RDBMS vendors.

There are several different macro layers of security: authentication, authorization, and audit. There are also different techniques used to protect data on the most basic levels.

All RDBMSs consider the notion of a user as some entity that connects to a database and performs actions. Further, all RDBMSs discussed in this book implement *roles*, which manage sets of privileges. Roles can be system-defined (fixed) or user-defined.

Additional security can be implemented through various mechanisms supplied by the database: constraints, views, stored procedures, and triggers. The lowest level of defense is vested in the data via encryption, which renders data unreadable by humans.

There are national and international security standards, which are recommended (but not required); some database vendors choose to get certified, while some do not. A number of laws were enacted to deal with security issues. The latest versions of the RDBMSs discussed in the book have implemented many features to help the users with regulatory compliance.

`INFORMATION_SCHEMA` was endorsed by the ISO/ANSI body long after the real RDBMS implementations moved into the market. As a result, some of the vendors implemented their own versions of the metadata repository in a form of system tables.

The information from these tables can be gathered in a variety of ways, usually through views provided by the RDBMS for just this purpose (the idea behind the `INFORMATION_SCHEMA`), or through some RDBMS–supplied stored procedures or functions to that effect.

Most RDBMSs explicitly discourage users from accessing the system tables directly because their structure might change without any notice, and the information contained in the table is not guaranteed to mean what you think it should. In short, system tables are for the use of the system, and views are for the users. The times of having to make your best guess via direct querying of the underlying system tables are over.

11

Working with Unstructured and Semistructured Data

Unstructured data is a misleading term, but we are going to use it for the lack of a better one. With the exception of absolute chaos, all data should be considered to have a certain degree of organization. Consider a paperback novel: It has a table of contents; text is organized into chapters with paragraphs; and sentences have commas, hyphens, and periods. The information is usually arranged in a logical progression; you can read it cover to cover, select chapters, look at the pictures, and so on. Yet in context of relational databases in general, and this book in particular, the novel would be an example of unstructured information because it is extremely difficult to apply information technology to this type of data. The term *unstructured*, therefore, defines degrees of suitability of data for computer processing.

We are surrounded by a multitude of unstructured data — for example, books, magazines, conversations, pictures, movies, text messages, newspapers, TV shows, and music. Most of it passes by and disappears into oblivion — or at least it used to before cheap storage came into existence, along with the hardware powerful enough to handle data in a timely manner and the software to manage it. In order for the data to be managed under an RDBMS, it has to be digitized first; once pictures and texts are stored as long sequences of ones and zeroes, the data can be further categorized into character data and binary data. The former deals with anything that is constituted of characters (words); the latter could be anything — a music file, a video, a picture, PDF or Word documents (prior to Microsoft Office 2007), or even compressed archived text files.

SQL AND XML

eXtensible Markup Language (XML) falls right in the middle between the rigor of the structured data and perceived chaos of unstructured data. On one hand, as you will see, it has a well-defined structure and rules; on the other hand, it mixes in a "free-text" approach.

It is a popular language of information exchange and is well on its way to becoming the *de facto* standard for web services, as well as more traditional software applications.

In recent years, there was a shift by users from proprietary document formats to those that are open and not controlled by any commercial entity. The vendors took notice: Starting with Microsoft Office 2007, the Office Open XML file format (OpenXML or OOXML) has become the default Microsoft Office file format as well as the international ECMA-376 standard. Several countries, most notably in Europe, have also announced adoption of the Open Office XML on national level. The hugely popular open source OpenOffice.org implemented its own, somewhat different, XML-based format called Open Document Format (ODF, governed by the OASIS consortium) for its file (though, beginning with version 3.0 it is also interoperable with OOXML), as did many other software vendors around the world. While particulars of the implementations might be different, they are all based on XML principles.

The versatility of XML comes from its venerable predecessor: Standard Generalized Markup Language (SGML). The original SGML was conceived as a means for representing text documents in electronic form. One of its prominent properties was the ability to mark up fragments of text with special tags for various purposes. The current XML standard, in version 1.0, is maintained by the World Wide Web Consortium (W3C), which is the main international organization for World Wide Web standards.

XML still uses tags extensively (more extensively, in fact, than SGML), but it uses them to establish structure instead of marking up text between two tags. Furthermore, XML does not confine itself to any particular predefined set of tags, as SGML does; any string, within certain syntactic confines, may serve as a tag. In XML, a tag must have a matching end tag; otherwise, a piece of XML is said to be "not well-formed" and cannot be parsed by an XML parser.

There are several reasons why XML is relevant to relational databases in general and SQL in particular.

One is the ubiquity of the format as means of information exchange. XML documents contain both data that could to be extracted and added to the RDBMS in order to be processed and the metadata describing it.

Another reason is that an XML document can be considered a database unto itself. The XML documents are said to be self-describing, meaning that they contain both data and metadata (information about the data, which explains the affinity to databases).

Viewed from this perspective, XML elements and attributes would roughly correspond to tables and fields in a relational database, and the document structure describes relationships — not unlike those found in an RDBMS (though there are distinctive differences as well). As of early 2007, Microsoft Office files or Open Office files are stored in XML format; one can easily see how a MS Excel spreadsheet could be a database.

Despite the apparent advantages — self-contained, self-described, and a universally understood format — there is no rush to convert RDBMSs into XML native databases as yet. On the most basic level, an XML database decoupled from its relational host is but a text file; in a sense, an XML database is a reincarnation of a hierarchical database implemented in a sequential access data file, with all the advantages and limitations of such an approach. This raises a number of issues for concurrency, performance, integrity, and security — all the problems that have been addressed over the years by RDBMSs. Nowadays, RDBMS databases routinely exceed a terabyte in size; I have yet to see an XML database approaching several gigabytes, and still cranking out a half-decent performance. The RDBMSs and XML are complementary technologies; used together they allow for a synergy to be achieved in processing structured and semistructured data.

A BRIEF INTRODUCTION TO XML

A well-formed XML document has a tree structure, or *forest structure*, for more complex composite documents. At the branches (or *nodes*, which is the technical term) of the tree are usually *elements* (although there also can be attributes, comments, and such), and there must be a single root element. An element is anything enclosed between a tag and the corresponding end tag, including the tags themselves:

```
<tagExample>Element example</tagExample>
```

As the preceding example demonstrates, a tag is enclosed in a pair of angle brackets (or between the "less than" and "greater than" signs), and an end tag is identical to its corresponding tag, except that the opening angle bracket is immediately followed by the forward slash (/):

```
<emptyElementTag></emptyElementTag>
```

This example shows that an element may contain nothing between the tags. That's fine, too. There is even a shorthand expression for this:

```
<emptyElementTag/>
```

Okay, these examples are fine, as far as they go, but they don't really go very far. Much more interesting are elements that do contain things, and not just little bits of text, either. Before we consider what elements may contain, we should mention the element *attributes*. An element may have one or more attributes attached to it:

```
<element attribute1="attr1Value" attribute2="attr2Value">contents</element>
```

Attributes are defined within the element tag, as key-value pairs, with the value part placed in the quotation marks. They are separated only by whitespace.

What is the difference between the contents of an element and its attributes? Conceptually, it is clear: We have little difficulty distinguishing between the content of a book and characteristics such as who wrote it, how much it cost, or whether it is worth the price. In the practice of XML, however, it is sometimes a matter of style or convenience, whether to define a piece of information as an attribute of an element or as part of its content, an element's content may be more complex than we have so far considered. In addition, unlike a child element, an attribute must be unique within the parent element.

In fact, an element may contain other elements, as well as text, and that's where the *structure* comes in:

```
<book>
<title>Introduction to Database Management</title>
<authors>
<author>Mark L. Gillenson</author>
```

```
<author>PaulrajPonniah</author>
<author>Alex Kriegel</author>
<author>Boris Trukhnov</author>
<author>Allen G. Taylor </author>
<author>Davin Powell</author></authors>
<publisher>Wiley Publishing, Inc.</publisher>
<price>$39.99</price>
</book>
```

In the preceding example, the element "book" contains several elements, including "authors," which contains further elements (that have identical tags, but different values).

Formatted XML

To make it easier to grasp the structure visually, it is customary to print XML with line breaks and indents; usually, however, the true XML, in a case like the preceding section, is all in one line to avoid inserting a bunch of whitespace and line breaks into elements:

```
<book><title>Introduction to Database Management</title><authors>
<author>MarkL.Gillenson</author><author>PaulrajPonniah</author>
<author>AlexKriegel</author><author>Boris Trukhnov</author>
<author>Allen G. Taylor</author><author>DavinPowell</author>
</authors><publisher>Wiley Publishing,Inc.</publisher><price>$39.99</price></book>
```

This looks very much like the result of a query on a couple of database tables that participate in a one-to-many relationship: there's a record from the `Book` table, with the columns `name`, `publisher`, `price`, and a couple of corresponding records from the `Authors` table.

The structure of XML is *hierarchical*, and in many cases just like the structure of a relational database. An XML document is a tree: for example, in the preceding fragment, `<book>` is the parent node; `<name>`, `<publisher>`, `<price>`, and `<authors>` are the children of `<book>`; and the `<authors>` node has four `<author>` children.

Because there are six authors, we cannot model them as attributes, at least not without bending some rules; attributes must have unique names within an element.

DTD and Schema

An XML parser worth its salt accepts only well-formed XML documents. The well-formed XML document is one that obeys certain rules, such as having exactly one root element, having a matching end tag for every tag, having all attribute values quoted, and so on.

However, the purpose of XML is to define structure, and a well-formed XML document may still have a cock-eyed structure by mistake:

```
<book>
<name>Discovering SQL</name>
```

```
<authors>
<book>Gone with the wind </book>
<author>Alex Kriegel</author>
</authors><publisher>Wiley Publishing, Inc.</publisher>
<price>$39.99</price>
</book>
```

The parser will not notice the erroneous placement of a `<book>` element as a child of the `<authors>` element because it is nicely closed with the appropriate end tag and does not violate any syntactic rules.

To guard against such mishaps, a validator must be instructed as to what is considered structurally legitimate. Two ways to define the structure of an XML document are to use a Document Type Definition (DTD) or an XML Schema Definition (XSD).

Document Type Definition (DTD)

The DTD is an older convention. It is a special language to define the structure of an XML document:

```
<!DOCTYPE book [
<!ELEMENT book (title,authors,publisher,price)>
<!ELEMENT name (#PCDATA)>
<!ELEMENT authors (author+)>
<!ELEMENT author (#PCDATA)>
<!ELEMENT publisher (#PCDATA)>
<!ELEMENT price (#PCDATA)>
<!ELEMENT author (#PCDATA)>
]>
```

XML Schema Definition (XSD)

The XSD is a more recent development. It is more attractive because it uses XML rather than another language; it is also more powerful and allows the definition of data types for values and other useful validating information:

```
<?xml version="1.0"?>
<xs:schema xmlns:xs="http://www.w3.org/2001/XMLSchema"
targetNamespace="http://www.wiley.com/DiscoveringSQL"
xmlns:sql="http://www.wiley.com/DiscoveringSQL" elementFormDefault="qualified">
<xsd:include schemaLocation="Book.xsd"/>
<xs:element name="book">
<xs:complexType>
<xs:all>
<xs:element name="name" type="xs:string"/>
<xs:element name="authors" type="sql:authorInfo"/>
<xs:element name="publisher" type="xs:string"/>
<xs:element name="price" type="xs:integer"/>
</xs:all>
</xs:complexType>
</xs:element>
<xs:complexType name="authorInfo">
<xs:sequence>
<xs:element ref="sql:Book" name="author" type="xs:string"
```

```
minOccurs="0" maxOccurs="unbounded"/</xs:sequence>
</xs:complexType>
</xs:schema>
```

XML schemas are replacing DTD as a means of enforcing XML structure compliance.

XSD is also more flexible. In previous examples, both `<xs:all>` and DTD specify that child elements must appear only once, but XSD does not restrict the order in which they appear.

Namespaces

The keen reader will have noticed that the preceding example of XSD has a lot of colons in the element tags. What's all that about?

The tags in the example are namespace-prefixed. If you are familiar with Java or a .NET language, you are no stranger to the concept of namespace. In Java, the equivalent notion is the package, and .NET even uses the same *namespace* term.

A namespace is the scope within which a tag uniquely exists. You may have two friends by the name of Peter. You will distinguish them with the help of their last names: `<Jones:Peter>` or `<Mackenzie:Peter>`. Two students with the same name may exist in a school. The principal will refer to `<Grade3:MarySmith>` or `<Grade5:MarySmith>`.

In XML, namespaces become important when independent pieces of XML are united in the same document. The original pieces may have the same tag, which, of course, will have a different identity in each piece; and that will create an ambiguity, when the pieces are brought together. The ambiguity will be resolved by declaring the tags from one piece as belonging to one namespace, and the other tags as belonging to a different namespace.

Okay, so let's say we are bringing together two pieces of XML that already have the namespace defined: In one of them, the namespace is "MyNamespace," and in the other, um . . ."MyNamespace." Now what do we do?

To avoid this sort of supercollision, tags in XML do not use the actual namespace, but instead use a namespace prefix. In the two pieces that have just puzzled us, "MyNamespace" is not the name; it's an alias.

The namespace *alias*, or prefix, must be resolved. It is defined within an element tag, and the definition is valid for the element and all its child elements. For the definition of a namespace, the special attribute, `xmlns`, is used:

```
<MyNamespace:bookxmlns:MyNamespace="http://www.wiley.com/DiscoveringSQL">
<MyNamespace:name>Discovering SQL</MyNamespace:name>
<MyNamespace:authors>
<MyNamespace:author>Alex Kriegel</MyNamespace:author>
</MyNamespace:authors>
```

```
<MyNamespace:publisher>Wiley Publishing, Inc.</MyNamespace:publisher>
<MyNamespace:price>$39.99</MyNamespace:price>
</MyNamespace:book>
```

Two important points must be made here:

- The URL that is used in the definition of a namespace is not addressed by the parser. In fact, it does not have to be a valid URL — it is just the means of defining a namespace.
- Unlike a "real" URL, the string that defines a namespace is case-sensitive. The following strings all define different namespaces:
    - `www.wiley.com/DiscoveringSQL`
    - `www.wiley.com/DiscoveringSql`
    - `www.Wiley.com/Discovering SQL`

      Even the following strings define different namespaces because of the special characters present:
    - `www.wiley.com/Discovering%20SQL`
    - `www.wiley.com/~DiscoveringSQL`

The namespace prefix does not have to be used within an element. Instead, the *default* namespace can be defined like this:

```
<book xmlns ="http://www.wiley.com/DiscoveringSQL">
<name>Discovering SQL</name>
<authors>
<author>Alex Kriegel</author>
</authors>
<publisher>Wiley Publishing, Inc.</publisher>
<price>$39.99</price>
</book>
```

In the preceding example, note the absence of a colon and an alias after `xmlns`, and the absence of the namespace prefix in the element tags.

A single element may contain more than one namespace:

```
<book xmlns =http://www.wiley.com/DiscoveringSQL
xmlns:auth=http://www.wiley.com/authors>
<name>Discovering SQL</name>
<auth:authors>
<auth:author>Alex Kriegel</auth:author>
</auth:authors>
<publisher>Wiley Publishing, Inc.</publisher>
<price>$39.99</price>
</book>
```

Here, we have two namespaces: the default one and a second one, called `auth`.

XML as a DataSource

XML contains both data, and the metadata (information about how the data are formatted). This makes it very handy as a standard way to store and share information. There are several models to use when extracting information from an XML document. Currently, one of the most popular is the Document Object Model (DOM).

Accessing XML Documents in an Application

A programmer has two primary ways of interacting with an XML document: DOM and SAX:

- Simple API for XML (SAX) is essentially an XML parser: It reads an XML document and parses as it goes. As the parsing progresses, events are raised (for example, "start element," "end attribute," and so on) and it is up to the developer to handle the events. Generally, as an event is being processed, at least some of the XML text has not been seen yet.
- DOM represents a well-formed XML document as a tree of nodes. By the time you have a DOM document, all the XML text has been processed and is available.

XML Path Language: XPath

Any node in a DOM document has a path to that node, just as any file in your file system has a unique path to it from the root. A path to an XML node is constructed in yet another language: XPath. It may look like this:

```
/book/author[@name='Alex Kriegel']
```

In this example, we are looking for the *author* node that is a child of the *book* node (that in turn is a child of the root) and that has the attribute name with the value of `Alex Kriegel`. Much like files with the same name may exist in different folders, so the preceding path may return several elements: in fact, all the books, ever written or co-authored by a chap named Alex Kriegel.

In a DOM tree, not only are elements represented as nodes but also as attributes and other things (content values, comments) as well. Each node is addressable by an XPath expression.

XML Query Language: XQuery

An XML document may be queried on its own. The query language for XML is called XQuery and is based on XPath. XQuery is to XML what SQL is to databases. XPath 2.0 was developed concurrently with XQuery and that compatibility with the syntax and semantics of XPath 1.0 was a primary goal. There will be a number of examples of XQuery later in the chapter.

Encoding XML

There are a number of characters that have special meaning in XML, such as `<` or `/`. If these characters have to be incorporated in an XML document as text, they have to be "escaped," or *encoded* (the parser must be instructed to ignore their special meaning and treat them as regular characters). There are two ways to accomplish this (as described in the following sections).

Working with Entities

In some cases, there are very few special characters to deal with. They may be replaced with character references or defined as entities, and then replaced with entity references. (An *entity reference* is the short name of the entity, preceded by `&` and followed by `;`.) Table 11-1 lists some predefined entities.

TABLE 11-1: XML Predefined Entities

ABBREVIATION	FULL NAME	SYMBOL
Amp	Ampersand	&
Apos	Apostrophe	'
Gt	Right angle bracket	>
Lt	Left angle bracket	<
Quot	Quotation mark	"

If some text in an XML document is required to have these special characters, the entity references may be used, instead:

```
x&gt; 10 &amp;&amp; x &lt; 15
```

That translates into the following:

```
x> 10 && x < 15
```

A *character reference* is similar to an entity reference, except that instead of a name, the character code is used, either in the decimal or hexadecimal representation. For example:

```
x&#62; 10 &#38;&#38; x &#60; 15
```

XML Character Data: CDATA

Sometimes these special characters exist in the text in great profusion; for example, in the case where a quotation of XML needs to be incorporated in an XML document.

For such an occasion, XML defines the `CDATA` section. A `CDATA` section is opened with this:

```
<![CDATA[
and ends with a
]]>
```

Characters in between are considered regular characters, with no special meaning to the parser. As an example, imagine that the page you are reading is XML-encoded (perhaps for transmission as a web page). Every example of XML would be enclosed in a `CDATA` section, like this:

```
<![CDATA[
<book>
<name>Discovering SQL</name>
```

```
<authors>
<author>Alex Kriegel</author>
</authors>
<publisher>Wiley Publishing, Inc.</publisher>
<price>$39.99</price>
</book>]]>
```

Presenting XML Documents

In the early days of the Internet, the information that was passed around included both *what to say* and *how to say it.* The language of the information transfer, HyperText Markup Language (HTML), also derived from SGML, was an adaptation of a language that was especially designed to describe *how to* present text. So the text was passed around any which way and decorated with some special words (tags) to indicate how it should look when displayed.

Eventually, there was a separation of the *what* from the *how.* Enter Cascading Style Sheets (CSS). It is yet another language with the purpose of describing, how to present the various components of an HTML document (the font, the background color, and so on).

With XML came *structured* (and semistructured) text. Structure added more power to styling: Styling instructions could now be more fine-grained.

XSL and XSLT

eXtensible Stylesheet Language (XSL) is a styling language that transforms an XML document into visual format (for example, HTML); it uses XML itself to describe how various parts of an XML document should be presented. The XSL language uses XPath, mentioned earlier in this chapter, to identify specific items of an XML document to be rendered. eXtensible Stylesheet Language Transformations (XSLT) is yet another XML-based language that describes a *transformation* of a source XML document into another XML document or XHTML.

XSL is also frequently called XSL FO (FO stands for "Formatting Objects") as opposed to XSLT (where T stands for "Transformations").

You'll see the SQL/XML functions output and XSLT working in tandem in the "Try It Out" section of this chapter.

XML and RDBMSs

There are reasons why XML is relevant to relational databases in general and to SQL in particular. As a means of information exchange, XML documents contain data that need to be extracted and added to the RDBMS in order to be processed. Also, an XML document can be considered a database unto itself. An XML document contains both data and metadata that describe data structure; this corresponds to one of the basic definitions of a database: data and storage. Viewed from this perspective, XML elements and attributes roughly correspond to tables and fields in a relational database, and document structure describes relationships — not unlike those found in

RDBMSs (though there are distinctive differences as well). As of early 2007, Microsoft Office files or Open Office files are stored in XML format; one can easily see how an MS Excel spreadsheet can be a database.

Yet despite the apparent advantages — self-contained, self-described, universally understood format — there is no rush to convert RDBMSs into XML native databases. On the most basic level, an XML database decoupled from its relational host is but a text file; in a sense, an XML database is a reincarnation of hierarchical database implemented in a sequential access data file, with all the advantages and limitations of it. This raises a number of issues for concurrency, performance, integrity, and security — all the problems that have been addressed over the years by RDBMSs. Nowadays, RDBMS databases routinely exceed a terabyte in size; I have yet to see an XML database approaching several gigabytes, and still cranking out a half-decent performance.

There are two ways to process XML in relational databases: one is to implement native SQL/XML standards, and the other (to provide support for XPath and XQuery) is a generalized technology for interpreting, retrieving, and modifying XML data. Some of the RDBMSs covered in this book allow for intermixing these — allowing, for instance, XQuery expressions to be invoked directly from within SQL. Some provide packages, and others implement only rudimentary support, treating XML essentially as a big string.

The SQL/XML standards were first addressed in SQL:2003; a revised and expanded standard was published in 2006 and then again in 2008; the next revision of the SQL/XML (along with other parts of the standard) is on target to be published in 2011.

XPath and XQuery are standards developed and maintained by W3C and are not SQL- or RDBMS-specific. XQuery supports various expressions for processing XML data, for updating existing XML objects such as elements and attributes, and can be used for constructing new XML objects from within SQL. The XPath language provides the ability to navigate around the XML document tree and compute values for the nodes.

The subset of the language includes XSLT, which can be used to transform XML documents into different presentational formats (for example, HTML) to be displayed in a browser).

As service-oriented architecture (SOA) becomes the architecture of choice for enterprise-level development that uses the XML format for communication between services, and XML becomes the foundation for document formats in many popular software tools (Microsoft Word OOXML, Open Office ODF, Adobe FrameMaker — to mention a few), the importance of the seamless integration of XML into tried, tested, and true traditional data storage (the RDBMS) becomes obvious.

Storing XML, which is character data, using internal data types such as `CHAR`, `VARCHAR`, or even `CLOB`/`BLOB` proved to be very inefficient as it required extracting and parsing the entire document just to search, access, or modify a single node. The next approach tried was to disassemble (shred) XML documents and map them onto a set of relational tables. This was more efficient, but it still incurred significant overhead and did not address the rapidly growing complexity of XML standards, which now can contain recursive structures and other constructs that cannot be easily mapped onto a relational model. In addition, a shredded XML document ceases to be a document and loses its fidelity (which might be important for auditing purposes) and becomes difficult to change and manipulate.

There was a clearly defined need for native XML support from both the RDBMS vendors and the SQL Standard committee. The new SQL/XML standard provides the mechanism for incorporating XML into a relational paradigm and introducing XQuery statements into the SQL domain. The vendors have provided some proprietary SQL/XML implementations of their own, along with full (or partial) support for standard SQL/XML syntax.

SQL Standard introduced an XML-related specification within ISO/IEC 9075-14:2003, which was then superseded by ISO/IEC 9075-14:2006. According to the International Standards Organization (ISO) documentation, it defines ways of importing and storing XML data in an SQL database, manipulating it within the database, and publishing both XML and conventional SQL data in XML form. In addition, it provides facilities that permit applications to integrate into their SQL code the use of XQuery, the XML Query Language published by the W3C, to access ordinary SQL data and XML documents concurrently. Table 11-2 lists the SQL/XML publishing functions.

TABLE 11-2: SQL/XML Standard Functions

SQL/XML FUNCTION	DESCRIPTION
`Xmlelement`	Creates a named XML element (node).
`Xmlattributes`	Creates XML attributes.
`Xmlroot`	Specifies the root node of an XML document.
`Xmlcomment`	Creates a comment for an XML document.
`Xmlpi`	Creates an XML processing instruction.
`Xmlparse`	Parses a character string and returns the parsed XML value.
`Xmlforest`	Creates a forest of XML values using the values in the columns of a table.
`Xmlconcat`	Concatenates individual XML values into a single value.
`xmlagg()`	Aggregates rows, containing an XML value, into a forest of XML values.

The following SQL/XML query creates an XML document from the RDBMS table `BOOKS` (aliased as b):

```
SELECT
xmlelement(name "book",
xmlelement(name "bk_id",b.bk_id),
xmlelement(name "title",b.bk_title))
FROM books b
```

The resulting XML document would have the following structure (assuming that the database you are executing in the previous statement supports SQL/XML — see later in this chapter):

```
<book>
<bk_id>1</bk_id>
```

```
<title>DiscoveringSQL</title>
</book>
```

Using the XMLFOREST function, the preceding query could be more concise, while producing the identical result:

```
SELECT
xmlelement(name "book",
xmlforest(
b.bk_id as ID,
b.bk_title as Title
)
)
FROM books b
```

The syntax for these basic queries is identical for IBM DB 9.7, Oracle 11g, and PostgreSQL 9.0, but is *not* supported by Microsoft SQL Server 2008, which opted for its own implementation.

While implementing the same standard, RDBMS vendors have chosen different venues, so there is no single approach that guarantees portability of the queries between different RDBMSs. The topic of XML in the world of relational databases is vast and clearly deserves a book of its own (for example, *Querying XML: XQuery, XPath, and SQL/XML in Context*, by Jim Melton and Stephen Buxton). Here we are going to provide only the basic principles and strongly encourage you to refer to vendors' documentation for in-depth information.

*There are a number of new developments in the area. One of these is SPARQL, a new query language and data access protocol for the Semantic Web (a runner up contender for Web 2.0). The specification is under development by the RDF Data Access Working Group (DAWG — no, I am not kidding!) It is defined in terms of the W3C's RDF data model and will work for any data source that can be mapped into RDF. While it is not a released standard (although it did become an official W3C recommendation in January 2008), it deserves attention from anyone looking into the next generation of web infrastructure. It follows — to a certain extent — the familiar SQL syntax (*SELECT *statement), and the results can be returned as an XML document.*

Implementation Details

Meanwhile, vendors and developers were left to their own devices, and a number of barely compatible implementations of the XML support found their ways into the RDBMSs covered in this book. The desktop databases, such as OpenOffice.org BASE and Microsoft Office Access, require XML documents to be shredded into set of relational tables and provide built-in support for importing and exporting data from and to XML, though it relates to programmatic support such as Microsoft ADO data access library (MS Access VBA) or OpenOffice.org Basic's support for the SAX parser.

The modern full-fledged RDBMS servers provide native support for XML through XML data types and XML-specific features in their respective SQL dialects. Table 11-3 lists XML-related enhancements introduced into the RDBMSs up to date at glance:

TABLE 11-3: Support for XML Across RDBMSs

RDBMS	XML SUPPORT	NOTES
IBM DB2 9.7	XML Data Type	Full support for the built-in XML data type. For instance: *CREATE TABLE library (books XML);*
	XMLAGG XMLATTRIBUTES XMLCOMMENT XMLCONCAT XMLDOCUMENT XMLELEMENT XMLFOREST XMLGROUP XMLNAMESPACES XMLPI XMLROW XMLTEXT XSLTRANSFORM	Full support for SQL/XML standard.
Oracle 11g	XML Data Type	Full support for built-in XML data type. An entire table can be created as sole storage of XML data type: *CREATE TABLE library OF XMLTYPE;* Or a column in a table can be declared: *CREATE TABLE library (books XMLTYPE);*
	XSU utility	An advanced XML SQL utility specifically built for Java. Oracle Database allows for Java-written code to be both stored and executed within an Oracle database.
	XMLELEMENT XMLATTRIBUTES XMLCONCAT XMLAGG XMLCOLATTVAL XMLFOREST XMLTRANSFORM	Partial support for SQL/XML standard.

RDBMS	XML SUPPORT	NOTES
	DBMS_ XMLGEN Package	This Oracle DBMS package creates an XML document based on an entire query.
	SYS_XMLGEN	This function creates an XML document for each record as retrieved by a query to an Oracle database.
		Full support for both XPath and XQuery.
Microsoft SQL Server 2008	XML Data Type	Full support for built-in XML data type.
	XPath/XQuery Support	Full support for both XPath and XQuery.
PostgreSQL 9.0	XML Data Type	Native support for XML data type: *CREATE TABLE library (books xml);*
	XMLCOMMENT XMLCONCAT XMLELEMENT XMLFOREST XMLPI XMLPARSE XMLROOT XMLSERIALIZE XMLAGG IS DOCUMENT IS NOT DOCUMENT	Full support for SQL/XML standard.
	XPath Support	Full support for both XPath; limited support for XQuery.
MySQL 5.5	XML Data Type	No built-in XML data type. NB: With MySQL client command line utility one can use switch –X (or --xml) to be able to format output of a SQL query as XML.
	ExtractValue UpdateXML	No support for SQL/XML standard.
	XPath support	Only a subset of XPath is supported.

The three big RDBMSs vendors — Oracle, IBM, and Microsoft — have implemented full support for XML in their respective products. The open source PostgreSQL has arguably the richest features set for SQL/XML, while MySQL's support is rudimentary at best.

Neither Microsoft Access nor OpenOffice.org BASE provide built in data types or SQL-specific support for XML; by virtue of having built-in programming environment (VBA and Basic, respectively) you have DOM to manipulate XML documents.

Oracle 11g XML DB

Oracle responded to the XML invasion by developing Oracle XML DB, which first debuted with its flagship database version 9i R1 (there were also some basic XML handling capabilities in Oracle 8i). It was further enhanced in subsequent releases and versions. The latest version, Oracle 11g, provides robust XML capabilities, following the hybrid platform paradigm, which incorporates both relational and native XML data management.

Oracle supports the full range of XML Standard, including support for namespaces, XML Schema, SQL/XML, XQuery, XSLT, and DOM. An XML document can be stored in its native format, or shredded into a set of relational tables, using mid-tier libraries and built-in PL/SQL packages. The storage options for the XML documents include the following:

- *Text-based storage* — Ensures absolute fidelity of the document, which might be required to satisfy regulatory requirements.
- *Object-based storage* — Enables node-level data manipulation; used commonly with static XML schemas, and provides near-relational performance in data exchange configurations.
- *Binary XML storage* — Used for very dynamic documents in which XML structure changes frequently.

It is important to realize that any application utilizing XML storage remains agnostic of any particular storage mechanism (files, RDBMS) or underlying operating system.

Oracle 11g fully supports SQL/XML, but XQuery-based processing offers greater flexibility and speed.

Here is the basic syntax to load data into the XML data type column as a character string:

```
UPDATE books
SET bk_notes= XMLType
(' '<books>
<book>
<title>SQL Bible</title>
<attributes>
<authors>
<author>Alex Kriegel</author>
<author>Boris Trukhnov</author>
```

```
</authors>
<isbn>0-7645-2584-0</isbn>
<publisher>Wiley</publisher>
<published>2003-01-01</published>
<bought>2003-01-02</bought>
<price>49.99</price>
<note>First Edition</note>
</attributes>
</book>
</books>')
WHERE bk_id=1;
```

In addition, an XML document can be loaded from a file or even an HTTP stream; please see Oracle documentation for a detailed discussion of the topic.

If required, the document can be bound to a schema (refer to the discussion earlier in the chapter). The most common usage of an XML schema is as a mechanism for validating that instance documents conform to a given XML schema. It can be used as a constraint when creating tables or columns of `XMLType`, as well as for defining how the contents of an `XMLType` instance should be stored.

Once data are loaded, they can be queried, modified, or deleted. The syntax for these operations is rather straightforward. The following example uses the `getCLOBVal` method of the `XMLType` (see Table 11-4 for the full list of XMLType methods):

```
SELECT b.bk_notes.getCLOBVal()
FROM books b
WHERE bk_id=1;
```

The output is an XML string. The `XMLType` data can be queried using SQL/XML standard functions `XMLExists`, `XMLQuery`, `XMLTable`, and `XMLCast`; as well as Oracle's proprietary implementation of SQL/XML standard `existsNode`, `extract`, and `extractValue`.

TABLE 11-4: Selected Oracle 11g XMLType Methods

XMLTYPE METHOD	DESCRIPTION
CREATEXML	Static function for creating and returning an `XMLType` instance.
EXISTSNODE	Takes an `XMLType` instance and an `XPath` and returns 1 or 0, indicating whether applying the `XPath` returns a non-empty set of nodes.
EXTRACT	Takes an `XMLType` instance and an `XPath`, applies the `XPath` expression, and returns the results as an `XMLType`.
GETBLOBVAL	Returns the value of the `XMLType` instance as a `BLOB`.

continues

TABLE 11-4 *(continued)*

XMLTYPE METHOD	DESCRIPTION
GETCLOBVAL	Returns the value of the XMLType instance as a CLOB.
GETNAMESPACE	Returns the namespace for the top-level element in a schema-based document.
GETNUMBERVAL	Returns the value of the XMLType instance as a NUMBER. This is only valid if the input XMLType instance contains a simple text node and is convertible to a number.
GETROOTELEMENT	Returns the root element of the input instance. Returns NULL if the instance is a fragment.
GETSTRINGVAL	Returns the value of the XMLType instance as a string.
ISFRAGMENT	Checks whether the input XMLType instance is a fragment or not. A fragment is an XML instance, which has more than one root element.
TOOBJECT	Converts the XMLType instance to an object type.
TRANSFORM	Takes an XMLType instance and an associated stylesheet (which is also an XMLType instance), applies the stylesheet, and returns the result as XML.
XMLTYPE	Constructs an instance of the XMLType data type. The constructor can take in the XML as a CLOB or VARCHAR2, or take in an object type.

The XMLEXISTS SQL function is used to verify the existence of a particular element, attribute, or value. For example, to determine whether the XML document stored in the BK_NOTES column contains information for the book with title "SQL Bible", the following query can be used:

```
SELECT bk_notes
  FROM books
  WHERE XMLExists('/book [title="SQL Bible"]')=1
                PASSING bk_notes);
```

The EXISTSNODE and EXTRACTVALUE SQL functions are proprietary to Oracle. The first one checks whether the given XPath expression targets at least one XML element node or text node, and the second one returns a scalar SQL value corresponding to the result of the XPath evaluation for the XMLType instance. While not standard features, they come in handy when there is a need to traverse the XML document and select only records that have a particular node present:

```
SELECT
extractValue(bk_notes, '/books/book/title')        Title
,extractValue(bk_notes, '/books/book/publisher)    Publisher
CASE
WHEN existsNode(bk_notes, '/books/book/isbn') = 1
THEN extractValue(bk_notes, '/books/book/isbn')     ISBN
ELSE 'no ISBN supplied
       END "grade",
```

```
FROM books
ORDER BY extractValue(bk_notes,'/name') DESC;
```

The EXTRACT SQL function extracts the element or a set of elements from the document identified by the XPath expression:

```
SELECT extract(bk_notes, '/books/book/isbn') "ISBN"
FROM books
WHERE existsNode(bk_notes, '/books/book[title="SQL Bible") = 1;
```

The XMLCAST SQL function casts its first argument to the scalar SQL data type specified by its second argument. The first argument is an SQL expression that is evaluated. Data types NUMBER, VARCHAR2, or any of the date and time data types can be used as the second argument. The following query returns only values for the BK_NOTES column XMLType, where the <title> child element has the value "SQL Bible":

```
SELECT XMLCast(
XMLQuery('/books/book[title/' PASSING bk_notes
RETURNING CONTENT)
AS VARCHAR2(1000)) "TITLE"
FROM books
WHERE XMLExists('/books/book[title="Discovering SQL"]'
                  PASSING bk_notes);
```

The EXTRACTVALUE SQL function returns values extracted from an XML document stored in the XMLType column:

```
SELECT extractValue(bk_notes, '/books/book/title') "Title"
FROM books
WHERE XMLExists('/books/book/title' PASSING bk_notes);
```

Updates for non–schema-based XML documents stored as CLOB values (unstructured storage) always update the entire XML document (replace the entire document). Updates for the documents that are stored as binary XML can be made on more granular levels — the elements and attributes themselves. Several SQL functions can be used to update XML data incrementally — to replace, insert, or delete XML data without replacing the entire surrounding XML document:

- updateXML: Replaces an XML element. The following query returns an XML document with the element <grade> replaced with a different value. Of course, underlying data are not affected by the operation. Only returned XML was modified:

```
  SELECT updateXML(bk_notes,
'books/book', '<isbn>0-7645-2584-9</isbn>') AS XML
  FROM booksb;
```

- insertChildXML: Inserts an XML element or attribute elements as children of a given element node:

```
UPDATE books
SET bk_notes =
```

```
insertChildXML(bk_notes,
/books/book,
                        'bought',
XMLType('<at>
<store>Powell's Books</store>
<gift>Yes</gift>
</at>'))
WHERE bk_id=1;
```

- `insertXMLbefore`: Inserts XML elements of any kind immediately before a given element (other than an attribute node):

```
UPDATE books
  SET bk_notes =
insertXMLbefore(
bk_notes,
'/books/book', XMLType('<genre type="technical"><description>Relational
databases</description>
</genre>')
WHERE bk_id=1;
```

- `appendChildXML`: Adds XML elements of any kind as the last child element of a given element node. The following query inserts a new node `<genre>`, together with attributes as a child node for `<book>`:

```
UPDATE books
  SET bk_notes =
appendChildXML(bk_notes,
'/books/book',
XMLType('<genre type="technical">RDBMS</genre>'))
WHERE bk_id=1;
```

- `deleteXML`: Deletes XML nodes of any kind. For example, the following query deletes the `<grade>` node for the `book ID = 1`:

```
UPDATE books
  SET bk_notes =
deleteXML(bk_notes,  '/'/books/book/genre')
WHERE bk_id=1;
```

As with "regular" data type columns, Oracle allows for indexing XML tables and columns. The syntax is part of the standard `CREATE INDEX` statement. XML indices can speed up queries against an XML data type, although its proper use requires an understanding of XML in particular and indexing in general. All index-related operations, such as `ALTER` and `DROP`, are also fully applicable to the XML indexes. For more information on this, please refer to Chapter 2.

This chapter presents the very basics of XML support implemented in Oracle 11g; please refer to vendor documentation for comprehensive in-depth coverage.

Database native web services let you expose PL/SQL stored procedures, functions, and packages as web services and also include a web service that supports the execution of dynamic SQL queries and XQuery expressions (the database HTTP server, provided as part of Oracle XML DB Repository). Because XML is the lingua franca of web services, a native XML data type provides unique opportunities for designing SOA systems.

SOA is not a new concept. It is yet another incarnation of distributed computing where a system is assembled from components running on separate hardware (such as DCOM and CORBA). Many people confuse SOA with interconnected web services. While there is a certain amount of overlap, they are not the same thing. One of the metaphors we've found especially useful when communicating the essence of SOA to the uninitiated is the two mail delivery systems: courier and post office.

If you need to deliver a package from point A to point B, a courier service could be one option. It is fast, it is secure and reliable. You can even trace the way the parcel will be delivered to the recipient. All you need to know is the exact location (address) of the point B. Oh, and you need to pay the courier.

The second option could be USPS – the United States Postal Services. It is a lot cheaper than private courier. It is reasonably fast, reasonably secure and reliable. It also could forward your mail should your intended recipient have moved without notifying you beforehand.

This is, in a nutshell, the difference between stand-alone web services and SOA. The latter is all about economies of scale, creating infrastructure with built-in fault tolerance (in case your courier company runs out of couriers just when you need to send a package) and the ability to orchestrate the deliveries according to some business rules. The former is brittle, non-scalable and has a very low fault tolerance barrier. It is also orders of magnitude more expensive in the long run (admittedly, SOA requires bigger up-front costs).

IBM DB 9.7 pureXML

XML capabilities within IBM DB2 9.7 database are implemented as a pureXML add-on. DB2 also supports an XML data type natively (as opposed to text or shredded into a set of relational data tables) and is fully integrated into the DB2 infrastructure. It provides support for XQuery, SQL/XML, or a combination of both; XML validation is supported through an XML Schema repository that stores schemas and DTD. A set of SQL/XML functions was added to extend SQL support for the XML data type. The basic queries utilizing SQL/XML are endorsed by the SQL Standard committee.

IBM provides a number of extract, transform, and load (ETL) utilities (`db2Import`*,* `db2Export`*, and* `db2Load`*) that support XML data types, as well as an application programming interface (API) for data bulk operations.*

The `INSERT` syntax for the XML data type in the IBM DB2 9.7 database is rather straightforward; it does not need any special modifiers for a character string to be recognized as XML. The only requirement is that the XML string must be well formed:

```
INSERT INTO books (bk_notes) VALUES (
'<books>
<book>
<attributes>
<title>SQL Bible</title>
<author>Alex   Kriegel</author>
<author>Boris Trukhnov</author>
<isbn>0-7645-2584-0</isbn>
<publisher>Wiley</publisher>
<published>2003-01-01</published>
<bought>2003-01-02</bought>
<price>49.99</price>
<note>First Edition</note>
</attributes>
</book></books>')
```

The entire XML document in the row can be updated (replaced with a new one) with the standard UPDATE syntax:

```
UPDATE books SET bk_notes = ('
'<books>
<book>
<attributes>
<title>SQL Bible</title>
<author>Alex   Kriegel</author>
<author>Boris Trukhnov</author>
<isbn></isbn>
<publisher>Wiley</publisher><published></published>
<bought></bought>
<price></price>
<note></note></attributes></book></books>'')
WHERE bk_id = 1;
```

Updating an XML column can be tricky as there are many options to consider: updating with hard-coded values, updating with parameterized values, updating values with schema validation, and updating the very structure of the XML document stored in the column. Here we discuss only the most common usage scenarios; please refer to IBM documentation for a more in-depth discussion.

It is a good practice to validate XML documents by using a schema. IBM DB2 9.7 provides a facility (built into every SQL syntax) for registering the XSD schema, which then can be used when manipulating XML documents.

To update information permanently in the particular node of the column, the following query comes in handy:

```
UPDATE product
SET bk_notes = xmlquery( 'transform copy $new_doc := $bk_notes
modify do replace value of $new_doc/books/book/title with "SQL Bible"
return  $new_doc')
WHERE bk_id=1;
```

As you can see, the basic element is an `XMLQUERY` function that allows you to embed the XQuery expression. The transformation starts with the optional keyword TRANSFORM followed by `COPY`, `MODIFY`, and `RETURN`. The operations that follow `MODIFY` are `replace`, `delete`, and `insert`. Some elements of this syntax (for example, the aforementioned `TRANSFORM` keyword) are in conformance with the XQuery developing standard (Update Facility), which stands to be finalized in 2008, whereas other syntax in this query might not follow it.

Another option is to perform the update/transformation on-the-fly while selecting the data in the query (the original value in the column remains intact):

```
SELECT xmlquery('transform
copy $new_doc:= $bk_notes
modify do replace value of $new_doc/books/book/title with "SQL Bible"
return $new_doc')
FROM books
WHERE bk_id=1;
```

Often, especially in stored procedures and application-specific operations, there is a need for parameterized values to be passed to update contents of the XML column:

```
UPDATE books
SET bk_notes = xmlquery( 'transform
copy $new_doc:= $bk_notes
modify do replace value of $new_doc/books/book/title with $val
return  $new_doc' passing cast(? AS VARCHAR(100)) AS "val")
WHERE bk_id=1;
```

It is always a good idea to validate whether the data being updated is compliant with the rules established in the schema associated with this particular document.

Deleting the entire XML document is no different from deleting a value of any other data type, but deleting attributes within the document is another story. The following query deletes the attribute `TYPE` from the document:

```
UPDATE books
SET bk_notes = xmlquery( 'transform
copy $new_doc := $bk_notes
modify do delete $new_doc $new_doc/books/book@cover
```

```
return  $new_doc')
WHERE bk_id = 1;
```

To rename an element node (or an attribute) within the document (in the example that follows: `pgrade` for `prod_grade`), the following syntax comes in handy:

```
UPDATE books
SET bk_notes = xmlquery( 'transform
copy $new_doc := $bk_notes
modify do rename $new_doc $new_doc/books/book/title as "SQL Bible"
return  $new_doc')
WHERE bk_id=1;
```

Manipulating XML data types extends to the capability to add/remove elements of the document. The same syntax works when replacing the entire node structure with a new one:

```
UPDATE books
SET bk_notes = xmlquery('
copy $new_doc := $bk_notes
modify do replace $new_doc $new_doc/books/book/title
with<title>SQL Bible</title>
return  $new_doc')
WHERE bk_id=1;
```

Adding a new node structure requires precise positioning within the document. You can insert an element `INTO` another element, or you can add an element `AS FIRST|LAST INTO` another element, making the new element the first or the last child of the existing element, respectively.

It is possible to perform multiple operations with a single XQuery expression by supplying multiple DO actions within MODIFY, using parentheses to group them together.

You can specify before and after insertions to position a new element within the hierarchy. For example, the following code inserts the new node <book>, explicitly defining the node <books> as its parent node:

```
UPDATE  books
SET bk_notes = xmlquery('copy $new_doc := $bk_notes
modify
do insert <cover>paperback</product>
into $new_doc/books/book/
return  $new_doc' )
WHEREbk_id=2;
```

It is important to remember when dealing with the XML data type that it requires a well-formed document; otherwise, IBM DB2 would throw a barrage of errors, which would hopefully enable you to pinpoint the source.

Special care must be taken while modifying repeating nodes (this would require FLWOR (pronounced "flower") XQuery syntax; FLWOR is the most general expression syntax in XQuery. FLWOR stands for For, Let, Where, Order by, and Return.) These keywords enable you to organize loops and conditional execution within XQuery.

XSLT can be used to transform an XML document (see the discussion earlier in the chapter and in the "Try It Out" section). Because XSLT is expressed in XML, it can also be stored in the database in an XML type column.

XML columns in DB2 9.7 can be indexed for improved performance. While similar to a standard index created on any other native data type, XML columns require a somewhat different approach. Unlike the index on any other data type, an XML column can be indexed on partial data contained in the XML document.

To specify which parts of an XML column should be indexed, a form of XPath is used, along with an indication of which data type is to be used for the index. Only single XML columns can be indexed; there is no support for composite indexes. At the same time, multiple different indexes can be created for a single XML column.

Covering the entire XML-related features of IBM DB 9.7 would require a book of its own; this chapter, by necessity, is confined to the most basic features related directly to SQL Standard. Please see IBM's documentation for more information.

Microsoft SQL Server

When archeologists excavated the more ancient layers of Microsoft SQL Server, they found some indications of early usage of XML, around the year 2000. The initial approach, introduced in Microsoft SQL Server 2000, was to map XML data onto a set of relational tables. There were several new keywords introduced to Microsoft's dialect of SQL to facilitate storage and retrieval of XML documents in this version: `FOR XML`, `AUTO`, `EXPLICIT`, `RAW`, `XMLDATA`, `ELEMENTS`, `ROWSET`, and `OPENXML`, along with numerous stored procedures for manipulating XML documents.

SQL Server 2000

SQL Server 2000 had two keywords defined for dealing with XML: `FOR XML` and `OPENXML`, which are still supported by the latest SQL Server 2008 release, and in all probability will remain there. In some cases, these facilities might be more convenient than SQL Server 2008 approach, and therefore it pays to learn more about them.

`FOR XML` was used in a `SELECT` statement to instruct SQL Server to deliver the results of a query in XML format:

```
SELECT bk_title as "Title", bk_price as "Price"
FROM books
FOR XML RAW
<row Title="SQL Bible" Price="49.9900" />
<row Title="SQL Bible" Price="49.9900" />
```

```
<row Title="SQL Server 2000 Weekend Crash Course" Price="29.9900" />
<row Title="SQL Functions" Price="39.9900" />
<row Title="Introduction to Database Management"           Price="29.9900" />

SELECT bk_title as "Title", bk_price as "Price"
FROM books
FOR XML RAW

<book Title="SQL Bible" Price="49.9900" />
<book Title="SQL Bible" Price="49.9900" /><book Title="SQL Server 2000 Weekend Crash
Course"Price="29.9900" /><book Title="SQL Functions" Price="39.9900"
/><book Title="Introduction
to Database Management"Price="29.9900" />
```

The modes `RAW`, `AUTO`, `EXPLICIT`, and `PATH` determine the format of the resulting XML document (note that there is no notion of storing an XML document besides external files or character strings). The `RAW` mode makes every row as a single element with the table columns defined as attributes; this holds true regardless of the number of tables joined in the query. The `AUTO` mode formats documents according to a hierarchical structure of the parent/child tables referred to in the query; results for a single table are virtually identical to that produced with `RAW` mode.

The `EXPLICIT` mode transforms the rowset that results from the query execution into an XML document. In order for `EXPLICIT` mode to produce the XML document, the rowset must have a specific format. The `PATH` mode, together with the nested `FOR XML` query capability, provide the flexibility of the `EXPLICIT` mode in a simpler manner, but it does require the data set to adhere to strict specifications. The first column must be named `TAG`, and can contain only non-negative integers; the second column must be named `PARENT`, and can be either `NULL` or a non-negative integer; and any other column after that must be formatted as `TAGNAME!TAGID!ATTRIBUTENAME[!..]` with `TAGID` as a positive integer.

Consider the following query and its output:

```
SELECT 1    AS Tag,
NULL AS Parent,
bk_title AS  [element!1!Title],
bk_price AS [element!1!Price]
FROM books FOR XML EXPLICIT

<rowTitle="SQL Bible" Price="49.9900" />
<rowTitle="SQL Bible" Price="49.9900" />
<rowTitle="SQL Server 2000 Weekend Crash Course" Price="29.9900" />
<rowTitle="SQL Functions" Price="39.9900" />
<rowTitle="Introduction to Database Management" Price="29.9900" />
```

`OPENXML` serves the opposite function: It creates a rowset from an XML document that exists in the file system or assigned to a variable. When an XML document is generated on-the-fly, the function is used with built-in stored procedures `sp_xml_preparedocument` and `sp_xml_remove document`. The former creates an actual document that can be loaded using the `OPENXML` function, and the latter removes the document that is no longer needed. There are numerous limitations on the use of these procedures; please refer to the vendor's documentation for more information.

Support for this approach was preserved (presumably for backward compatibility) and extended in SQL Server 2005 and 2008, in addition to completely new native XML support. It seems a safer bet to go with the more-standards-compliant XPath/XQuery features.

Support for XML is integrated into all the components in SQL Server 2008 and includes the following:

- Support for the `xml` data type
- The ability to use an XQuery expressions against XML data stored in columns and variables of the `xml` type
- Enhancements to `OPENROWSET` to allow bulk loading of XML data
- Enhancements to the `FOR XML` clause and the `OPENXML` function

SQL Server 2005 introduced the native XML data type, later enhanced in SQL Server 2008. This new data type allows for storage and manipulation of XML documents and fragments; it also implements a set of methods based on XQuery Standard. SQL Server 2005 and later allows for typed and untyped XML usage. As a rule of thumb, untyped XML should be used if there is no schema for the XML data or if schema validation is undesirable for some reason (for example, XML data contains unsupported components). Typed XML allows for full utilization of schema validation, storage, and query optimization based on the data type. Typed XML can contain XML content when used in columns, parameters, and variables.

The XML data can be entered into an XML data type column, either from a file (`BULK` import/export capabilities) or from a character string within a standard SQL query. For example, this query inserts an identical string into the VARCHAR and XML columns:

```
INSERT books(mylib_id, books, books_xml)
VALUES (2
,'<books><book><attributes><title>SQL Bible</title>
<author>Alex Kriegel</author><author>Boris Trukhnov</author>
<isbn>0-7645-2584-</isbn><publisher>Wiley</publisher>
<published>2003-01-01</published><bought>2003--02</bought><price>49.99</price>
<note>First Edition</note>
</attributes></book></books>'
,'<books><book><title>SQL Bible</title><attributes>
<author>Alex Kriegel</author><author>Boris Trukhnov</author>
<isbn>0-7645-2584-0 </isbn><publisher>Wiley</publisher>
<published>2003-01-01</published><bought>2003-01-02/bought><price>49.99</price>
<note>First Edition</note>
</attributes></book></books>')
```

While the syntax is identical, further manipulations of the respective fields would not be.

The XML document might (and usually should be) validated with the XML schema, which is created in the current database with the new `CREATE XML SCHEMA COLLECTION` *statement. Once the schema is created, the XML data type can be tied to this particular schema. This is a fairly advanced feature for a beginner's book; you may want to refer to other Wiley titles (such as SQL Bible, for example).*

XML Data Manipulation Language (DML)

Microsoft SQL Server 2008 provides XML DML as a means to manipulate XML documents contained in the XML data type fields. The XML DML adds the following case-sensitive keywords to XQuery: `insert`, `delete`, and `replace value of`; they work together with the `modify()` method implemented in the XML data type itself (see Table 11-5 for a full list of XML data type methods).

TABLE 11-5: Microsoft SQL Server 2008 XML Data Type Methods

XML DATA TYPE METHOD	DESCRIPTION
`Query`	Specifies an XQuery against an instance of the `xml` data type. The result is of `xml` type. The method returns an instance of untyped XML.
`value`	Performs an XQuery against the XML and returns a value of SQL type. This method returns a scalar value.
`Exist`	Returns a bit that represents one of the following conditions: `1`, representing True, if the XQuery expression in a query returns a nonempty result (at least one XML node); `0`, representing False, if it returns an empty result, and `NULL` if the `xml` data type instance against which the query was executed contains `NULL`.
`Modify`	Modifies the contents of an XML document. Use this method to modify the content of an `xml` type variable or column. This method takes an XML DML statement to insert, update, or delete nodes from XML data. The `modify()` method of the `xml` data type can only be used in the `SET` clause of an `UPDATE` statement.
`Nodes`	The method is useful when you want to shred an `xml` data type instance into relational data. It allows you to identify nodes that will be mapped into a new row.

The syntax for inserting a data/node into an existing XML document stored in an XML data type column is straightforward:

```
INSERT
XQuery Expression|XML Instance
(
{as first | as last} into | after | before
XQuery Expression|XML Instance
   )
```

For example, to insert a new element — say, a book cover attribute — into an XML document inserted in this chapter, the following query can be used:

```
UPDATE books
SET bk_notes.modify('insert <cover>1000</cover> as first
into(/books/book/attributes)[1]')
WHERE mylib_id=2;
```

This creates a new element `<cover>soft</cover>` and places it as the first child of the `<attributes>` parent element.

The specification at the end of the XQuery expression `[1]` *ensures a single target element — the first one, even though multiple elements might be present in the document.*

Replacing values within an XML document is also very transparent and also done within the `modify()` method of the XML data type. For example, to replace a value of the `<name>` element, the following statement can be used:

```
UPDATE books
SET bk_notes.modify(
'replace
value of (//books/book/title/text())[1]
with  "SQL Bible 2nd Edition"')
WHERE mylib_id=1;
```

The insertion/replacement/deletion can be based upon certain conditions specified within an XQuery expression using the `IF` *expression.*

All modifications — insertions, updates, and deletions — are performed in similar fashion: using the MODIFY method of the XML data type and XQuery expression. To select information from an XML document, the `query()` method of the XML data type instance is used. For instance, the following query extracts just `<title>` information:

```
SELECT bk_notes.query('/books/book/title')
FROM books
WHERE mylib_id=2;
```

To extract a single value from either an attribute or an element, you use the `value()` method. The following query extracts the value of the first `<width>` element, and casts it as an integer:

```
SELECT bk_notes.value
('(/books/book/attributes/price)[1]', 'float' )
FROM books
WHERE mylib_id=2;
```

Casts to an XML data type; a common language runtime (CLR) user-defined type; or the `image`, `text`, `ntext`, or `sql_variant` data types are not allowed, but you can use any other built-in SQL or even user-defined data type.

To utilize values contained within the XML document, SQL Server 2008 provides the `exist()` method with its XML data type. For example, the following query returns all bk_d(s) for books that have an `"SQL Bible"` value in the `<title>` element contained within the `BK_NOTES` document:

```
SELECT bk_id
FROM books
WHERE bk_notes.exist
('//books/book[title="SQL Bible"]')=1
```

XML data type columns within Microsoft SQL Server 2008 can be indexed to increase performance. The indexes fall into two broad categories: primary index and secondary index.

It is possible to create a full-text index on XML columns that indexes the content of the XML values, but ignores the XML markup. The primary XML index indexes all elements, values, and paths within the XML instances in an XML data type column. One can query the `sys.xml_indexesINFORMATION_SCHEMA` *view to retrieve XML index information.*

Dropping and modifying the XML indexes is no different from any other type of index supported by Microsoft SQL Server 2008.

The presented information and the examples cover only the basics of the XML implementation in SQL Server 2008. Please refer to Microsoft's documentation for an exhaustive discussion on the subject.

PostgreSQL 9.0

The open source PostgreSQL database provides arguably the most support for XML storage and manipulation. For starters, it adheres to SQL:2006 standards providing SQL/XML facilities and XQuery support, as well as native XML data types. (Please refer to Table 11-3 for list of all XML functions supported by the RDBMSs.)

PostgreSQL supports SQL/XML functions, and uses XPath expressions to navigate XML documents. There are no built-in validations for either DTD or XSD type instructions.

XML documents can be created on-the-fly from the relational data stored in the database or by using inline data inside an SQL query using SQL/XML functions. Here's one of many ways to create an XML document out of a relational table:

```
SELECT XMLElement(name book
XMLConcat(
XMLElement(name author, bk_author),
XMLElement(name title, bk_title)
)
)
FROM books WHERE bk_id = 1;

<book>
<author>Alex Kriegel</author>
<author>Boris Trukhnov</author>
```

```
<title>SQL Bible</title>
</book>
```

PostgreSQL does not currently support XQuery, but the XPath specification is implemented. Here is an example of extracting just titles out of an XML document stored in an XML column:

```
SELECT Xpath('/books/book/title/text()', bk_XML) as Titles
FROM books;

Titles
-----------
{SQL Bible}
{Discovering SQL}
```

One of the neat features supported by PostgreSQL is the ability to emit programming code with XML processing instructions with a bit of help from the XMLPI function. For example, the following code produces PHP script as an output:

```
SELECT xmlpi(name php, 'echo "Discovering SQL";');
xmlpi
-----------------------------
<?php echo " Discovering SQL ";?>
```

PostgreSQL also has facilities to map a set of relational tables to an XML document with functions TABLE_TO_XML, QUERY_TO_XML, and CURSOR_TO_XML. Use of these functions simplifies extraction of the data in XML format, though you have to be very careful fine-tuning the input parameters. For instance, the following query transforms the table BOOKS into an XML string:

```
 SELECT table_to_xml('books', TRUE, TRUE, '');

<booksxmlns:xsi="http://www.w3.org/2001/XMLSchema-instance"><title>Discovering
SQL</title>
<author>Alex Kriegel</author>
<isbn>123456789</isbn></books>
```

MySQL 5.5

The open source MySQL database (now Oracle's trophy following the acquisition of Sun Microsystems) provides somewhat limited support for XML.

First, there is no XML data type, so MySQL recommends use of string data types such as VARCHAR and TEXT. As such, it is no different from inserting large character string into a field using standard SQL statement.

Second, instead of the SQL/XML functions specified in the standard and implemented by other RDBMSs, there are only two: ExtractValue and UpdateXML. Both functions accept the XPath expression as a parameter. Here are a few examples of how XML can be used in MySQL 5.5 relational database:

```
SELECT EXTRACTVALUE(bk_notes,'/books/book/attributes/title')
FROM books
WHERE bk_id = 1;
```

Updating XML document is also straightforward:

```
SELECTUpdateXML(bk_notes,'/books/book/attributes/isbn','978-0-470-22906-4')
FROM books
WHERE bk_id = 1;
```

The functions are being used as part of a SELECT query, not as a stand-alone instruction, and can be combined in a single query.

XML for RDBMS: Best Practices

While it might be tempting to plunge into the wonderful opportunities offered by XML data type flexibility and power, there are certain ramifications to be considered. And its coexistence within RDBMSs, and by extension SQL, is but a strategic alliance, and not a marriage made in heaven.

While there might be situations justifying a different approach, it is recommended to limit the use of XML for performance reasons and reducing the complexity of your SQL statements; just because you can do it does not meant you should. Here are some simple rules of thumb to adhere to when considering using XML in your database:

- Keep your XML documents read-only whenever you decide to store them in the database. UPDATE(ing), INSERT(ing) and DELETE(ing) operations on XML documents stored in RDBMS could be rather expensive.
- Keep your XML documents small, as in kilobytes small.
- When producing XML documents from your relational database tables, keep it simple and use built-in facilities (such as SQL/XML functions).

TRY IT OUT Producing and Presenting XML Output as a Web Page

In this activity, you will combine all the elements presented in the chapter to produce visual output of the data in XML format. Start by defining an XSL stylesheet to assist with the transformation of bare bones XML data into something more colorful. Save the following code in a file with the .xsl extension: DiscoveringSQL.xsl:

1. Download the document titled DiscoveringSQL.Ch11.zip.
2. Unzip the file into a folder on your local computer. Among the files you will see DiscoveringSQL .xsl. You may view contents of the file in any compatible text editor, such as Notepad, or you can open it in your browser. The content should display the following structure:

```
<?xml version="1.0"?>
<xsl:stylesheet version="1.0" xmlns:xsl="http://www.w3.org/1999/XSL/Transform">
<xsl:template match="/">
<html>
<body>
<h2>Books</h2>
<table border="0">
<trbgcolor="tan">
<th align="left">Title</th>
```

```
<th align="left">Author</th>
<th align="left">ISBN</th>
<th align="left">Price</th>
</tr>
<xsl:for-each select="books/book/attributes">
<tr>
<td><xsl:value-of select="title"/></td>
<td><xsl:value-of select="author"/></td>
<td><xsl:value-of select="isbn"/></td>
<td><xsl:value-of select="price"/></td>
</tr>
</xsl:for-each>
</table>
</body>
</html>
</xsl:template>
```

3. Now, let's extract some data to work with. Assuming that you have data entered into your BK_NOTES column of XML data type, use your favorite RDBMS syntax to extract the XML string from there (refer to the preceding paragraphs). Any statements that produce valid XML will work: using SELECT from the books.bk_notes XML column, producing XML from a set of relational tables, or aggregating the document on-the-fly. The following is an example of an output that you are after:

```
<books>
<book>
<attributes>
<title>Discovering SQL</title>
<author>Alex Kriegel</author>
<isbn>0-0000-0000-0</isbn>
<publisher>Wiley</publisher>
<published>0000-00-00</published>
<bought>0000-00-00</bought>
<price>00.00</price>
<note>First Edition</note>
</attributes>
</book>
</books>
```

4. In order to be transformed with XSL, the XML document must include references to the .xsl file. Add the following two lines at the very top of the preceding XML document and save it as a file with extension .xml (for example, DiscoveringSQL.xml) into the same directory where you put your .xsl file:

```
<?xml version="1.0"?>
<?xml-stylesheet type="text/xsl" href="DiscoveringSQL.xsl"?>
```

5. Open your favorite browser and type the URL to your .xml file into the navigation bar.

Normally, the operations to extract the XML documents from the RDBMS and publish them to the Internet would be automated with some programming language, including built-in procedural extensions such as Oracle's PL/SQL or Microsoft SQL Server Transact-SQL (and they can be streamed directly to the client browser without the intermediate step of saving them to a file system). An example of such code will be posted for download at the book site.

How It Works

A browser attempts to load an XML document and at the second line encounters instructions referring to a stylesheet to be applied to the document's structure. If not for this instruction, all it would display is the code you see in Step 3 of this exercise.

But linking the Discovering.xsl stylesheet on the second line instructs the browser to transform the XML document into an HTML document — the one that the browser knows how to display. It formats it into a table with four fields and a header of tan color, and populates with data as a result of placing elements found with this instruction into the respective columns:

```
<xsl:for-each select="books/book/attributes">
```

If you are familiar with HTML, you may come up with a different way of presenting XML data as HTML with an XSL transformation:

All Bits Considered

Not all data surrounding us is text-based, or most of it is not. The information comes to us in visual, audible, tactile forms, and the first relational databases were poorly equipped to handle this (and some still are). Nontextual data pose considerable challenges for adoption into the SQL world: How do you compare pictures or sounds, for instance? Short of implementing image recognition, your best bet is comparing files. What if I changed the file format from .png to .jpeg; would it still be considered the same picture? Now, while impressive advances have been made, the RDBMSs are still best equipped to handle textual information and can handle "unconventional" data on case-by-case basis. Just remember that whether text, image, or MP3 sound files are used, for computers they are all long sequences of bits — ones and zeroes.

What Would Google Do?

It is an easy guess that search engine giants such as Google or Microsoft Bing use some kind of database to index all the things that appear in the searches: web, images, videos, maps, news, books, and so on. And while the exact details are considered top secret by their respective companies, some information became public. For instance Google's main revenue engine, AdWords, initially was run on a massively parallelized and customized MySQL open source database (and for all we know, it might still be using that database).

But how do you handle data that does not belong to you? After all, most of the information that shows up in your search window is not owned by Google, Yahoo, or Microsoft; some of it is copyrighted, and most of it is stored halfway across the world. The answer is *indexing*.

It is not necessary to own the data as long as you know where to find it. The search engine crawlers are busy day and night indexing web content and aggregating the information in some database, relational or otherwise.

Nonrelational databases will be discussed in the next chapter.

So, what can you store? Suppose that you've decided to upgrade your personal library application (and the database that backs it up) to pull data from Amazon.com instead of entering it yourself. The reasonably robust and fast Internet connection makes it feasible to rely on remote services being there when needed.

This process, SOA (mentioned previously in the chapter), although fascinating, is not part of this book. For an example on how you can use Amazon.com web services with the library database we've been using throughout this book, go to the Resources/Books section on `http://agilitator.com`.

You might decide to store a URL in your database. The obvious choices are a VARCHAR, although some RDBMSs might have to introduce a specific data type to handle this. (For example, INET type in PostgreSQL holds IP addresses and subnet in a single field, Oracle's UriType data type is designed to point to data both inside and outside the database, and MS Access provides the HYPERLINK data type.) In its more generic form, by using the VARCHAR data type, the BOOKS table would add an additional field, BK_IMAGE_URL, to store the URL pointing to the image of the book (*SQL Bible*, 2nd Edition) on Amazon.com:

```
ALTER TABLE books
ADD COLUMN bk_image_url VARCHAR(1000);

UPDATE books SET bk_image_url=  'http://ecx.images-amazon.com/images/I/51N0-
kIK9BL._BO2,204,203,200_PIsitb-sticker-arrow-click,TopRight,35,-76_AA300_SH20_OU01_
.jpg'WHERE bk_id = 1
```

Alternatively, you might decide to store all the noncharacter data on your local computer (just in case the Internet goes down). In this case, the field would be populated with a link to the file location on your hard drive (or network if you share data on your intranet; you could download the picture file from Amazon.com at the URL provided in the previous example. Just make sure you save the picture as "cover.jpg."):

```
UPDATE books
SET bk_image_url = 'C:\DiscoverSQL\images\cover.jpg'
WHERE bk_id = 1
```

The code sample demonstrating how this hyperlink data are being used — in both Java and C# — can be downloaded from the Resources/Books section on books support site at `www.wrox.com`.

Storing binary and other unstructured data outside the database frees you from the limitations imposed by database storage (though these limits might be generous in the more recent versions of the database). Table 11-6 lists binary types supported in RBDMSs.

TABLE 11-6: Binary Data Types Support in RDBMSs

RDBMS	DATA TYPE	LIMITATIONS
Oracle 11g	BLOB	Up to 128 terabytes (TB).
	CLOB	Up to 128 terabytes (TB).
	NCLOB	Up to 128 terabytes (TB).
	BFILE	Essentially a pointer to unstructured binary data stored in files outside database. By definition, they are read-only and their size is limited only by limits of the underlying operating system.
	LONG LONG RAW	Provided for backward compatibility only. Numerous restrictions: A table can only contain one LONG column; such columns cannot appear in certain parts of the SQL statement (for example, SELECT with GROUP BY clause); LONG RAW columns cannot be indexed, and so on.
IBM DB2 9.7	GRAPHIC (length)	Stores fixed length graphic string of up to 127 characters.
	VARGRAPHIC (length)	Stores varying length graphic string of up to 16,336 characters.
	LONG VARGRAPHIC	Provided for backward compatibility only. Stores varying length graphic string of up to 16,350 characters.
	DBCLOB/NCLOB	A DBCLOB (double-byte character large object) value can be up to 1 073 741 823 double-byte characters long.
	CLOB	Up to 2 gigabytes minus 1 byte (2 147 483 647 bytes) long.
	BLOB	Up to 2 gigabytes minus 1 byte (2 147 483 647 bytes) long. Character strings of the FOR BIT DATA subtype may be used.

RDBMS	DATA TYPE	LIMITATIONS
Microsoft SQL Server 2008	VARBINARY (nlMAX)	The *n* can vary from 1 up to 8,000 bytes; when MAX is used, the field can store up to 2,147,483,647 bytes (2 GB).
	BINARY (n)	The *n* can vary from 1 up to 8,000 bytes.
	MAGE	Provided for backward compatibility only. Variable-length binary data storing up to 2,147,483,647 bytes.
	SQL_VARIANT	A catch-all data type, although some restrictions do apply; for instance, it cannot store an IMAGE data type.
PostgreSQL	BYTEA	Up to 1,073,741,824 bytes (1 GB).
MySQL	BLOB	Up to 65,535 bytes (65 KB).
	MEDIUMBLOB	Up to 16,777,215 bytes (16 MB).
	LONGBLOB	Up to 4,294,967,295 bytes (4 GB).
	BINARY	Up to 30 bytes.
	VARBINARY	Up to 65,535 bytes (65 KB).
Microsoft Access 2010	OLE Object aka "Long binary data" aka LONGBINARY	Up to 1,073,741,824 bytes (1 GB).
	BINARY VARBINARY	Provided for compatibility with SQL Server; subject to SQL Server 2008 data type limitations.
OpenOffice.org BASE	BINARY	Up to 2,147,483,647 bytes (2 GB).
	IMAGE (LONGVARBINARY)	Up to 2,147,483,647 bytes (2 GB).

Microsoft went out of its way to make its desktop database user-friendly; as a result, most of the data types listed in the table will not show up in the data type selector in design view. If you are a brave heart who uses SQL to create database objects, feel free to use the listed data types in your queries!

Getting Binary Data In and Out of the RDBMS Table

Binary data was never meant for humans ever to be seen, much less understood. The "natural" number system we are dealing with on a day-by-day basis is decimal (base 10), and the most plausible reason for adopting it is that 10 is the number of fingers we have on both hands. There have been other systems used in the past: Babylonians developed a sexagesimal system (base 60), ancient Mayans used a vigesimal (base 20) number system, and the more familiar duodecimal system (base 12) is still being used on some occasions (a dozen eggs, anyone?).

For a variety of reasons, electronic computers were made to understand the binary system (base 2). At the most basic level, you deal with sequences of ones and zeroes, which on a higher level can be represented with hexadecimal values (base 16 counted system). To get a taste of what it would be like to use either of these, just fire up the Calc(ulator) application on your Windows machine and observe that the number 2010 in the decimal system becomes 11111011010 in binary and 7DA in the hexadecimal number system (toggle the values with the Dec and Bin radio buttons). This is an idea of what you would see if you manage to open any binary file — a picture, an application, or an mp3 sound file in your favorite text editor.

How do you get a binary file into a binary data type column? The answer is this: It depends on the particular RDBMS implementation, and — no, there is no standard.

If you have relatively short binary data in character form, say hexadecimal 7DA, the syntax would be rather familiar. In Oracle 11g, the following statement would insert the binary value '7DA' into a BLOB data type column, performing implicit conversion:

```
INSERT INTO books VALUES (2,'SQL Bible','978-0-470-22906-4',
'Wiley',GETDATE(),49.99,GetDate(),'Second edition', '7DA')
```

The same statement for Microsoft SQL Server would be slightly different (note the hexadecimal marker at the beginning of the binary value):

```
INSERT INTO books VALUES (2,'SQL Bible','978-0-470-22906-4',
'Wiley',GETDATE(),49.99,GetDate(),'Second edition', 0x7DA)
```

IBM DB2 requires explicit conversion from characters representing binary data into an actual BLOB data type:

```
INSERT INTO books VALUES (2,'SQL Bible','978-0-470-22906-
4','Wiley',GETDATE(),49.99,GetDate(),'Second edition', BLOB(x'7DA'))
```

The MySQL Format would also differ, albeit in a single character:

```
INSERT INTO books VALUES (2,'SQL Bible','978-0-470-22906-
4','Wiley',GETDATE(),49.99,GetDate(),'Second edition', x7DA)
```

Now, it would be all hunky dory if you could enter all these binary bytes in character form; but hexadecimal 7DA in the preceding examples is only 2 bytes long. Imagine entering all 2,147,483,647 bytes of your vacation picture. By hand. Ouch.

There are ways to make the process less painful. For a programmer, for instance, loading binary file into the database using programming language and an RDBMS-specific API (such as JDBC or ODBC) is nothing out of the ordinary. (Java and C# examples of how to write/read binary data into/from a database will be available for download at the book's support site.)

Microsoft SQL Server 2008 provides the handy OPENROWSET SQL function that allows for loading a file from the file system and inserting/updating a binary column:

```
UPDATE books2
SET bk_cover_image =
(SELECT * FROM
OPENROWSET(BULK N'C:\DiscoverSQL\images\cover.jpg',
SINGLE_BLOB)as img)
WHERE bk_id = 1
```

The rest of the world decided to extend functionality for loading binary data outside of the SQL proper domain by supplying utilities — either external or built in to the database engine. Oracle 11g provides a DBMS_LOB package to accomplish the task in PL/SQL, and IBM DB2 UDB 9.7 has the IMPORT and LOAD utilities.

Neither PostgreSQL nor MySQL provide built-in mechanisms for direct referencing of the system files in an SQL query. They rely on external programmatic solutions instead.

Reading the binary data out in a standard SQL statement is rather useless because the returned byte stream needs to be processed by an application that "knows" how to interpret it into a picture, PDF file, or MS Word document. Therefore, a SELECT statement executed on a binary field will return a long string of hexadecimal characters. The JPEG image inserted into the database will be displayed in your SQL client window as 0xFFD8FFE000104A46494600010100, and continue until all 33,636 bytes are displayed (for a file of 33 KB, that is).

Some RDBMSs' implemented features integrate SQL data types with files residing on the system's hard drive, on the network, or even streamed over the Internet, allowing them to be treated just as regular binary data fields. Such examples include Microsoft SQL Server's FILESTREAM storage and Oracle's BFILE data type. These are fairly advanced features and are beyond the scope of this book.

Best Practices for Binary Data

The decision about where to store binary data is not an easy one, and multiple factors need to be considered. Storing binary data inside the RDBMS makes the system more self-contained — no worry that the resource your database stores link to will suddenly disappear, change, or be replaced with malware with exactly the same name. The data stored inside the database is managed by the database — this means security, backup, and recovery, to mention just a few.

There are quite a few advantages of storing binary data outside the database. One — overcoming the data type storage limitation — was already mentioned, but there are more. It is easier to put character data into or get character data out of a database than to put in or get out binary data. Storing binary data in the file system makes it easier for the applications to use the data. The data files can be spread across the network, thus reducing load on the database server. This also affects performance of your application and might simplify design.

Ultimately, the choice will depend on the particulars of the business use scenario — how data will be accessed, used, and manipulated; tradeoffs among security, design complexity, and performance.

W3C is developing standards on how to describe the media content of binary data in XML, bridging both formats together.

SQL and Text Documents

The ability to store 2 GB of text into a data field is a neat thing to do. But how do you find what you're looking for inside that CLOB or TEXT data field? RDBMS developers came up with ingenious solutions to enhance SQL syntax and provide search functions.

Microsoft SQL Server 2008 has FREETEXT and CONTAINS functions that enable including large text fields into search criteria. In order to be able to execute a query, though, a full-text catalog must be created, and the fields must first be full-text indexed. There is a difference between the SQL operator LIKE, which works on patterned search, and FREETEXT, which does not require patterns.

Here is an example of how you can search the NOTES field in the BOOKS table in Microsoft SQL Server 2008:

```
USE [library];
GO
CREATE FULLTEXT CATALOG ctFT AS DEFAULT;
GO
CREATE FULLTEXT INDEX ON books(bk_notes) KEY INDEX PK_book;
GO
SELECT * FROM books WHERE FREETEXT(bk_notes, 'second' );
GO
```

The FREETEXT function in the preceding example could have been replaced with the CONTAINS function and still yield the same result. Nevertheless, there are subtle differences in the usage, and many more clauses in the syntax than would be appropriate to cover in a beginner's book. The vendor's documentation is your friend.

Oracle offers similar functionality with the CONTEXT indices and the CONTAINS function (of course, a full text index has to be created first):

```
INDEX ix_full_txt ON books(bk_notes) INDEXTYPE IS CTXSYS.CONTEXT;
EXEC DBMS_STATS.GATHER_TABLE_STATS(USER, books, cascade=>TRUE);

SELECT * FROM books WHERE CONTAINS(bk_notes, 'second', 1) > 0;
```

The full-text search setup is somewhat more convoluted in IBM DB2 9.7, but the query uses similar syntax and the CONTAINS function. Read all about the DB2 *db2ts* utility (or send me a note) before attempting to execute this query:

```
SELECT * FROM books WHERE CONTAINS(bk_notes,'second')= 1
```

PostgreSQL implementation revolves around the tsvector and tsquery functions, along with database configuration parameters. While being very powerful to assist in fuzzy searches, this is an advanced feature to be used with the full understanding of benefits and drawbacks.

MySQL requires a relatively simple process: First you need to create a full text index; then a query can be executed:

```
ALTER TABLE books ADD FULLTEXT(bk_notes);
SELECT * FROM books WHERE MATCH(notes) AGAINST ('second')
```

Neither Microsoft Access nor OpenOffice.org BASE have implemented full-text search facilities (though this functionality can be helped with clever programming in VBA and Basic, respectively).

SUMMARY

All five RDBMSs offer at least some support for XML data types and related operations. The enterprise class RDBMS such as IBM DB2, Oracle and Microsoft SQL Server have implemented most of the features defined in SQL:2006 standard. The desktop databases such as Microsoft Access and OpenOffice.org BASE do not support XML as part of their SQL implementation, but enable manipulating the XML documents using built-in languages: VBA and Basic, respectively.

Details of implementation differ between various RDBMSs.

XML documents inside RDBMSs can be stored in various formats, including an unstructured character string, shredding into a set of relational tables, and a native XML data type.

Storing, retrieving, and manipulating XML information involves understanding XQuery, XPath, and SQL/XML concepts because manipulation can be performed on very fine-grained levels — those of XML elements and attributes.

Columns of the XML data type can be indexed in a similar fashion as other built-in data type columns.

Even by itself, XML is a vast topic, and there are many sources of information about it, including the aforementioned `www.w3.org`, which is the "horse's mouth" because it is the source of the original specification (it is not always easily intelligible, however). Other sources include vendor documentation, various blogs and pages, and, of course, books.

The full-text search in the text fields is made possible with creating special indices and utilizing SQL functions implemented by many RDBMS vendors.

The binary data are supported by all RDBMSs — either through specific binary data types or via linking to external storage. There are a number of limitations to be considered when manipulating binary data in SQL queries.

12

Not by SQL Alone

SQL is the language of relational databases, and databases, relational or otherwise, are all about data. As you have seen, data come in every imaginable shape and size, and need to be structured to some degree in order to be queried with SQL. After all, it is *Structured* Query Language. With ever-faster processing speed and ever-cheaper storage, the need for preprocessing the data (conforming it to some data model in order to be queried) diminishes, and in some cases goes away. So does the need for SQL.

The latest buzz in the community is the NoSQL database. As with every latest and greatest idea, you might have heard about it before. It is a dumping ground for the data. The reinvention of the idea given up for dead in the late 1970s was made possible by the unique combination of the cheap storage, fast CPU(s), and ubiquitous high-speed infrastructure to glue it all together.

There are new usages for SQL, as data are being increasingly distributed across the globe, and data consumers adapt to ever less preprocessed data with new computing paradigms.

THE FUTURE IS CLOUDY

Not so long ago, the data that were not already on your computer or on the one to which your computer was connected were distributed by sending media via mail (no, that would be regular mail). First there were floppy discs with storage density maxing out at 720KB (yes, kilobytes); then came double density, 3.5-inch floppies encased in hard plastic with a whopping 1.4MB of storage, which were replaced by CD and DVD in a few short years.

About the same time, Bulletin Board Systems (BBSs) came into existence. Among other things, they allowed for downloading data (software, games, pictures) via dial-up connections. Then the Internet took off with the release of the first Netscape browser, which opened the small universe of academia and technically savvy hobbyists to the entire world, and the data locked into the puddles of individual machines joined together to form the ocean of information sloshing around the globe 24/7.

The data moved ever further from the individual computers. First, data were put on the servers to which client computers could have direct access through dedicated cable connections; then the dedicated connections were replaced by those provided as part of Internet infrastructure. Finally, the servers disappeared into virtual reality. You don't have to buy hardware anymore to have a dedicated server machine, not even an operating system. Now you can easily procure a virtual server at a fraction of the cost that, for all intents and purposes, behaves like the real thing. From there, it was only a matter of time before hosting of these virtual servers could be bought from a service provider on an as-needed basis. The cloud was born.

In many architectural diagrams, the Internet is represented as a fluffy cloud, with connectors going from desktops, laptops, and server machines into this unknown void where the "magic happens." This is the next database frontier, in which the on-the-premises servers go after the CFO finds out how much she can save by not owning the infrastructure. The cloud infrastructure still runs on some hardware somewhere, but it becomes inconsequential to your goals. As far as you are concerned, you are buying storage and processing power. As the saying goes, "If you only need milk, why buy a cow?"

A *cloud* can be defined by the following characteristics:

- **Self-service on demand** — Both storage and processing capacity can be procured at a moment's notice, and your application can be designed to do it automatically to meet increasing demand.
- **Pay-as-you-go pricing model** — You pay only for the resources used at the time when you use it.
- **Capacity on demand** — Your resources are virtually (pun intended) unlimited; you have all the computing power and storage in the world when you need it, and it grows and shrinks as you need it.
- **Broadband access** — Your cloud resources are not plugged into the Internet infrastructure; they *are* the Internet infrastructure.

The clouds come in all shapes and sizes: private, public, and everything in between. As you can imagine, the security concerns are a major considerations with the cloud.

The most prominent providers of the public cloud services are Amazon Web Services (AWS), with its SimpleDB platform; Windows Azure, with Azure SQL Server; IBM DB2 Cloud, as well as Google and Oracle, each providing services based upon their respective sets of technologies. The private clouds can be ether set up (and administered) by the organizations large enough to have such needs and capabilities, or outsourced to the cloud providers who would set up your very own private cloud — for a price.

Some cloud platforms, both proprietary and open source, are not tied to specific RDBMS vendors. While the specific services might differ, they all allow for on-demand procurement of a server running an operating system (Linux, Solaris, Microsoft Windows) on which you can then install your database software. The remote administration capabilities complete the cycle.

The data follow the storage, which is increasingly moving into the cloud, and it is only logical that the data management facilities go along. The shift is under way, from centralized data management to massively parallel distributed management, and most of it happens in the cloud.

Several models of the data in the cloud came into existence: one is a simple extension of the RDBMS servers, each running in a virtualized environment, and working in parallel processing the data. This is a part of the high-performance clustering capabilities of such RDBMSs as Oracle Real Application Clusters (RAC), MySQL Cluster, and DB2 Integrated Cluster Environment. You are still using SQL, but your query might be distributed across several databases/CPU for processing, and the results might be combined prior to being returned to you. Normally, you would not have to modify your SQL code to take advantage of parallel processing, though some RDBMSs allow specifying hints to force parallel execution.

Setting up and administering clusters requires expert knowledge of the RDBMSs and related technologies, and are far beyond the scope of this book.

The relational databases are holding the ground remarkably well, and many of these implementations have RDBMSs behind them, yet nonrelational databases are no longer a thing of the past as new technologies make the shortcomings of a nonrelational data model (such as the key/value pair) less of an impediment. The nonrelational data model dispatched the relational concept altogether and is using the data model discarded decades ago but resurrected by cheap computing power and storage.

As with database terms and definitions, clustering has different meanings for different RDBMSs. In the context of Microsoft SQL Server, clustering *refers to* failover cluster, *wherein one SQL Server (called* node of the cluster*) automatically takes over tasks and responsibilities of a SQL Server that failed for some reason, providing uninterrupted data processing. For Oracle or DB2, a cluster represents a number of database servers working on tasks in parallel.*

Key/Value Pair

The key/value pair (KVP) is a basic fundamental concept in organizing the data storage. As the name implies, it organizes data into a table with at least two columns, a key, to find the value by and the value to be found. The result is an open-ended structure, not molded into any particular model, such as entity-relationship.

This is a concept found in configuration files or lookup tables. The limitations are obvious, and as far as the enterprise data are concerned, this model was discarded in favor of relational databases back in the 1960s. Yet it made a comeback with advent of NoSQL databases. The term *NoSQL* was first used back in 1998, only to be reinvented in 2009. Some remarked that the NoSQL term is misleading because it is not about "not using SQL," but about ditching the relational model altogether.

We will take a closer look into particular NoSQL implementations such as Amazon SimpleDB, MongoDB, and Google BigTable.

A database based upon KVP is fundamentally different from relational databases we're dealing with in this book. Table 12-1 highlights the differences.

TABLE 12-1: Differences Between RDBMS and KVP

RELATIONAL DATABASE	KVP DATA STORE
An RDBMS database is highly structured: schemas, tables, rows; all data in the table belong to the same logical schema.	Based on the "domain" concept that is little more than a data bucket to store KVP tables; data can be organized into different logical schemas on demand.
Well-defined data model based upon characteristics of the data, not the application that will be using this data.	No data model, just a bunch of data buckets; the data can be shuffled around to meet the application's needs.
Relationships are declarative, and are usually enforced.	No relationships are defined, either between domains or within a domain.
Attributes can be of many different types.	Heavy use of character strings; in some cases, all data are character strings.
Data are organized to model a specific entity, and its structure is fixed.	Data item (value) is defined by the key, and can have different attributes attached to it dynamically.

KVP databases are item-oriented, with all data pertaining to the item bundled together. An item within a domain can be thought of as a record that contains only two columns: key and value. Table 12-2 shows a possible KVP representation of a BOOKS table.

TABLE 12-2: The BOOKS Table Organized into a KVP Domain

KEY	VALUE
1	Title: Discovering SQL ISBN: 978-1118002674 Price: 34.99 Author: Alex Kriegel
2	Title: SQL Bible ISBN: 978-0470229064 Price: 39.99 Author: Alex Kriegel, Boris M. Trukhnov
3	Title: Mindswap ISBN: 978-0765315601 Price: 16.29 Author: Robert Sheckley

A *domain* roughly corresponds to the concept of a table in RDBMS terms, but it can contain any kind of data deemed necessary for a specific application. For example, books can be mixed with authors. This leads to duplication of the data, and is only feasible because of the inexpensive storage availability. At the same time, this redundancy improves performance and scalability because no JOIN syntax is required to assemble records; it is all already there. The downside is reduced data integrity; duplicated data can quickly get out of sync.

The data access in RDBMSs requires SQL, a well-defined standardized language. Access to data in a KVP data store is exclusively through the application programming interface (API) method calls that, by definition, are proprietary and change from implementation to implementation. Some implementations provide SQL-like syntax for search filtering criteria using a basic set of (in)equality operators (for example: <, >, =, >=, =< and !=).

The API calls are almost exclusively based upon web services protocols, such as SOAP and REST, which run on top of the Internet HTTP protocol. By comparison, RDBMSs require native code provided by database drivers such as Java Database Connectivity (JDBC) or Open Database Connectivity (ODBC).

The KVP data store is a natural fit with the cloud architecture (because of built-in web protocols support) and the object-oriented programming paradigm because objects can be easily serialized and reconstituted on demand.

If you are not familiar with object oriented programming (OOP), *think of an actual object, such as a book. It has properties, such as the title, ISBN number, price, or even content. It also can have methods, such as Open() or Annotate(), which can be used to perform operations on this object programmatically. See more on OOP later in the chapter.*

All this can be represented in code and manipulated as a single, self-contained unit. This unit can be saved as a unit of data (serialized, *in programming parlance) creating a snapshot, an instance of a book with a specific ISBN, price, and so on, which further can be associated with a key value to be retrieved by. See more information later in the chapter.*

The KVP data stores have a number of drawbacks that limit their applicability. The most obvious is a complete absence of the integrity constraints, all of them: data integrity, entity integrity, domain integrity, and so on. Since all logic is vested in the application that manipulates the data, there is no mechanism guaranteeing that a proper value will be stored in the KVP data store domain. Because of the data redundancy, the synchronization might become a problem. There are no standards governing KVP data store implementations. Each will have its own proprietary API(s) and limitations. Furthermore, because of inherently multitenanted nature of the cloud, the KVP data store vendors impose additional limitations. For example, Amazon SimpleDB does not allow queries that run longer than five seconds; with Google AppEngineDatastore, a query cannot retrieve more than 1,000 items at a time.

These drawbacks must be carefully weighed against the benefits when considering an application with a KVP back-end data store.

What in the World Is Hadoop?

Finding and processing data in the distributed environment requires a different approach. The data can be anywhere; there might be duplicate sets of data; data can be stored on servers, virtual or otherwise, running different operating systems. Still, they have to be found, processed, and presented back to the client as a single data set. Now, there is a hard way to get the data, create an extraction process for each data type, bring it over into a staging environment for cleansing and conforming, do merging and aggregation — dozens of custom operations for a single query! Then, there is the Google way. In case you've wondered how Google manages to serve relevant information with intelligent search and lightning speed, all we can say is that we have no idea. The technology and concepts behind the Google's search engine are closely guarded secrets; yet some pieces do come out, such as MapReduce.

MapReduce is a software framework patented by Google that targets distributed computing on large data sets on clusters of computers. It has inspired numerous follow ups, such as Hadoop, an open source Java framework for processing and querying data on the server clusters.

The idea behind MapReduce is that instead of coding custom extract, transform, and load (ETL) processes, we have a standardized approach to finding and retrieving data based upon some search criteria, regardless of where and how these data are stored, as long as they have been indexed through KVPs. The mechanics of the data retrieval is complex, as you have to craft procedural code to take advantage of the framework and its distributed capabilities.

All of this has very little to do with SQL, and even less with relational databases. MapReduce was never designed to be used as a database (Google has its distinctly separate distributed database, the BigTable, which we will discuss later in the chapter), and it certainly lacks the functionality and robustness afforded by RDBMSs. Yet, when comes to single-pass simple data search, it leaves relational databases far behind.

Not everybody is convinced that MapReduce is the greatest thing since sliced bread. Some point out uncanny similarities to earlier technologies (such as Oracle's PL/SQL Table Functions), and some question the very approach itself. Nevertheless, the concept is powering most of the data searches on the Internet, both at Google and at many vendors running open source Hadoop implementations (such as Amazon, Yahoo, eBay, Facebook, and Twitter, among others).

Google's BigTable, Base, and Fusion Tables

The BigTable is a proprietary Google database system built on top of Google's file system, first introduced back in 2004. Just like with Amazon SimpleDB, it is delivered as a service to the users of the Google's AppEngine cloud platform. Google is using the BigTable data storage for its own applications, such as Google Earth and Google Finance.

The logical storage is organized as a "sparse distributed multi-dimensional sorted map," according to the authors, and if you feel a little bit lost at trying to decipher what that means, you are not alone. Translated into layman's language, it actually means a table with rows and columns, in which each cell is stamped with a date/time version. The dimensional component means that there might be multiple versions of the same cell (not unlike Oracle's nested tables feature). This creates a three-dimensional structure, as opposed to a flat rows/columns table found in RDBMSs. The tables in turn are divided into segments vertically by column groups, called *tablets*, spread across multiple virtual machines, which allows for load balancing: the queries can be redirected, or tablets can be moved to another machine, or even split further to meet increased workload.

By virtue of supporting MapReduce technology (along with a few other proprietary technologies, such as Chubby service), and coupled with (also proprietary) Google API/WebServices and compression technology, this structure allows for extremely fast data retrieval through SQL-like language dubbed GQL (Google Query Language).

GQL provides access to the App Engine data store query engine's features using a familiar syntax, and Google provides support for the applications using its AppEngine service, as long as the applications are coded in Python programming language.

The learning curve is quite steep, considering the sheer number of concepts one has to master to make use of the service. Unless you are willing to climb this ladder, consider BigTable as a "big black box where data can be found."

Google Base is an online database provided by Google that would store any type of data, from text to images to documents. It is a web service that likely uses BigTable as back-end storage. Its main use for outsiders is a craigslist-like functionality, with extended services for merchants.

The data can be added through so called *data feed* (a structured text file that has required attributes such as id, title, link to data, or price), or through Google Base data API (for advanced users, this requires programming skills to construct Atom RSS feed).

Google Fusion Tables is an experimental feature most recently (September 2010) posted on the Google Labs website; it might or might not have a future. The data are uploaded from either spreadsheets or comma-separated values text files. The data then can be used to visualize the data as a map or a chart, and then published in the Internet.

Open source alternatives for the BigTable are Apache Cassandra and Hypertable (among the others). The Cassandra was initially developed by the Facebook team, and later became a top-level project in the Apache Foundation. It operates on modified versions of KVPs, with keys being mapped to multiple values that are grouped in so called column families. The values in the column family for the key are all stored together which makes Cassandra a hybrid between columnar DBMS and the traditional row-based.

The Hypertable's inspiration came from the BigTable idea. The Hypertable open source database runs on top of a distributed file system, such as Hadoop. A Chinese language search engine, Baidu, became one of the major project's sponsors in 2009.

Amazon SimpleDB

Amazon SimpleDB is a distributed KVP database provided as part of the Amazon AWS cloud platform. It is a subscription service with different pricing tiers, starting with free and offering different pricing based on actual usage.

It is a highly scalable, virtually zero-administration, high availability KVP data store, written in the Erlang programming language. It provides web services interface to create and manipulate multiple data sets, to query the data and get the results back.

The data are transferred to SimpleDB and organized using proprietary Web Services API. Amazon provides a Software Development Kit (SDK) for all major technologies out there, including Java, .Net, PHP, and Python, to name just a few. You would have to sign up with the Amazon SimpleDB service to be able to create domains and save/manipulate data in the Amazon AWS cloud; the code would be in Java, C#, or whatever technology you've decided to use. Here is the basic example of creating a domain (an equivalent of an RDBMS table) in Java:

```
// the credentials assigned by Amazon when the account is open
    String AWSAccessKey = <Amazon access key ID>;
    String AWSSecretKey = <Amazon secret key>

//establish connection to the AWS cloud
   AmazonSimpleDB sdbService = new AmazonSimpleDBClient(accessKeyId
                                                       , secretAccessKey);

// create a new domain "BOOKS"
    String domain = "BOOKS";
    sdbService.createDomain(new CreateDomainRequest(domain);

//create new item (book)
List<ReplaceableItem> book = new ArrayList<ReplaceableItem>();

book.add(new ReplaceableItem().withName("book_1").withAttributes(
   new ReplaceableAttribute().withName("title").withValue("Discovering SQL"),
   new ReplaceableAttribute().withName("ISBN").withValue("978-1118002674")));

//store the item into the domain BOOKS
    sdbService.batchPutAttributes(new BatchPutAttributesRequest(domain, book));
```

To query for a book within the BOOKS domain, you use a SQL like syntax, and then scroll through the collection of the items retrieved:

```
// create query
String qry = "select * from 'BOOKS' where ISBN = '978-1118002674'";

//create request
SelectRequest selectRequest = new SelectRequest(qry);

//dsplay results in console
    for (Item item : sdbService.select(selectRequest).getItems()) {
         System.out.println("title: " + item.getName());
    }
```

This is rather similar to what you might have found in a regular RDBMS database, as the Amazon SDK abstracts the complexity. Yet make no mistake, Amazon SimpleDB is a nonrelational data store, meaning that none of the concepts you've learned so far would apply. Instead of entities locked in primary/foreign key relationships, you need to learn to think in terms of item collections organized into domains. The items are but tables containing key/value pairs, and they can be spread across multiple domains. Table 12-3 lists current limitations applied to the SimpleDB.

TABLE 12-3: Limitations of Amazon SimpleDB Usage

ATTRIBUTE	UPPER LIMIT
Domains	100 active domains
Domain size	10GB
Number of attributes per domain	1,000,000,000
Number of attributes per item	256
Attribute size	1KB
Number of Items returned by a single query	2,500
Time a query is allowed to run	5 seconds
Number of comparison predicates in a query	20
Number of predicated per expression in a query	20

The primary business of Amazon AWS is "infrastructure as a service" that, among other things, provides the capability to stand up instances of virtual machines running the operating system of your choice: Windows, Linux, Solaris, FreeBSD, and so on. Once the server is up and running, you can install a compatible RDBMS there and have your very own cloud database. Microsoft SQL Azure (see later in the chapter) implements a similar idea, only SQL Server is already installed. Instead of creating its own infrastructure, Oracle decided, at least for the time being, to offer its 11g database through Amazon Web Services Elastic Compute Cloud (EC2).

MongoDB

According to the front page at `www.mongodb.org`, the MongoDB database is a scalable, high-performance, open source database implemented in C++ programming language. It is available for download and runs on Windows, Linux, OS X, and Solaris operating systems, both 32- and 64 bits. It is one of the best known independent NoSQL data stores in existence, but you have to get it up and running yourself.

It provides indexing of the data, executable code, such as JavaScript, to be stored as part of the document, and it provides out-of-the-box support for MapReduce to take advantage of parallelization.

At the heart of the MongoDB implementation is a document (an *item*, in more generic terms) that roughly corresponds to a row in the RDBMS world. The documents are organized into *collections* (that are called *domains* elsewhere) that are the approximate equivalent of a table. The collections, in turn, are grouped into databases. A single instance of MongoDB can host several independent databases.

All is glued together with a JavaScript shell. Here is an example of how an INSERT might look in a Library database implemented in MongoDB, having PUBLISHED_DATE, ISBN, and TITLE defined as keys. The first step would be to create a document that we call BOOK:

```
> book = {
      "title" : "Discovering SQL"
     ,"ISBN" : "978-1118002674 "
     ,"publish_date" : new Date()}
```

Which translates into something like this:

```
{
     "title" : "Discovering SQL ",
     "ISBN" : "978-1118002674"
     "publish_date " : "Sun Dec 18 2010 10:23:21 GMT-0800 (PST)"
}
```

Now we can insert this object into the BOOKS collection in the Library database by using the INSERT method of the collection, at the shell prompt:

```
> library.books.insert(book)
```

To find the book we would use a different method such as FIND():

```
> library.books.find()
```

Here's the result we're getting back:

```
{
     "_id" : ObjectId("6a27d8bk2425g7j893f28b4h")
     "title" : "Discovering SQL ",
     "ISBN" : "978-1118002674"
     "publish_date " : "Sun Dec 18 2010 10:23:21 GMT-0800 (PST)"
}
```

Since our collection contained but a single document, this is all we got back because the FIND() method returns all documents in the database. We use a different method or specify some search conditions passed as parameters into the method. The other methods for data manipulation include READ(), UPDATE(), and DELETE().

The organization features quite a few high-profile customs using MongoDB in production, such as Intuit, SourceForge, SugarCRM, and *The New York Times*.

Microsoft SQL Azure

SQL Azure is part of the Microsoft Azure cloud strategy. It provides SQL Server as a service hosted in the cloud. From the RDBMS perspective, nothing changes; you are still accessing SQL

Server 2008 relational database using the very same access mechanisms and language (Transact-SQL) to store and manipulate the data.

In addition to all the usual benefits (and drawbacks) you get once your servers and your software are virtualized and managed somewhere you cannot quite put your finger on, you get built-in scalability and availability features. There are limitations, to be sure; one is a hard limit on storage size: 50GB per database and therefore limited scalability (though no limit on how many databases you might have). Other limitations include a built-in lack for distributed transactions support, the need for custom data partition logic, and so on.

With the right subscription level, your administration efforts will be off-loaded to Microsoft, your storage growth will be accommodated automatically, your data will be partitioned for performance and backed-up automatically, your fail-over clusters will be set up, and more. At least, this is the promise. Being relatively new to the game (a year or so), it still remains to be seen how Microsoft will deliver.

In addition to the SQL Azure, which is SQL Server(s) running up in the cloud, Microsoft offers Azure Table Storage which is essentially a key/value pair (KVP) data store along the BigTable lines: non-relation, non-SQL, using RESTful API to manipulate data. It provides scalability out of the box for up to 100TB and is blazingly fast; otherwise. it shares all limitations of the KVP database: no transactional support, no ACID (Atomicity, Consistency, Isolation and Durability, see Chapter 10 for more information) compliance, limit of up to 1,000 items per query, and so on. Since the pricing model is per operation, these charges might add up for high volume systems.

SQL AND BUSINESS INTELLIGENCE

Every deployed RDBMS can be arbitrarily divided into two broad categories: online transaction processing (OLTP) databases and online analytical processing (OLAP) databases. Some deployed systems may represent a mix of both.

An OLTP system is designed to support transactions; for example, order processing, inventory tracking, recording employee data, and so on, in very granular detail. Such systems are designed to process large volumes of concurrent transactions as quickly as possible. In short, the main purpose of such a system is to accumulate structured information.

An OLAP system works with aggregates and is designed to make sense out of the accumulated data, allowing for analyzing data at various levels of abstraction. These systems are used to discover trends and analyze critical factors, perform statistical analysis, and so on. While important, speed is not the main feature of such systems, as OLAP queries typically process large amounts of data. Normally, OLAP databases extract information from several specialized databases called data marts.

The foundation of the OLAP is a data warehouse. Unlike OLTP databases, the data warehouses are not normalized (at least not to the same degree as OLTP databases). The data model of the data warehouse is different from the OLTP database, and there are at least two major flavors deployed: dimensional and relational. The former is advocated by Dr. Ralph Kimball and operates within the concept of a specialized data marts comprising a larger data warehouse; the data are organized into fact tables and dimensions. The latter, pioneered by Bill Inmon, turns the concept upside down; data warehouses feed data to data marts, and the data are organized into a set of relational tables usually normalized to third normal form (3NF).

The dimensional data warehouse deploys star and snowflake data models; the latter being extensions of the former. In both models, the base table is called a fact table; it contains core information about some business entity, say, sales figures. Surrounding this table (and related to it through a primary/foreign key relationship) are dimension tables, which contain relevant contextual information (time, geography, products). The dimensions are selected arbitrarily, based upon some business needs, ideas, and available information. The star schema stops here, while the snowflake schema allows for more complex design where dimension tables can in turn also serve as fact tables.

Usually, data are gathered from various data sources (including nonstructured sources, such as text files or spreadsheets). Before it can be loaded, a data warehouse must be validated and cleansed. This is where the extract, transform, and load (ETL) process comes in. Once in the warehouse, the data are ready for being shaped into multidimensional cubes using visual tools (like Cognos, Brio, MS Analysis Services, and so on) or manually created using the MDX extension of the SQL (yet another dialect of SQL specifically created to address complexities of the OLAP "slicing and dicing").

OLAP Rules

The term *OLAP* was introduced in 1993 by Dr. E. F. Codd, who also was the first to propose the relational data model about 20 years earlier. At the heart of an OLAP database lies a *cube*, a multidimensional aggregate of information. With its various flavors (determined by the actual data storage type), *relational OLAP* (*ROLAP*), *multidimensional OLAP* (*MOLAP*), and *hybrid OLAP* (*HOLAP*), it is taking data analysis from a manual, tedious combination of art and science into a computer-aided, exact science. (OLAP does not remove the need to program for data analysis, yet it is a major improvement over just about any other way of analyzing large amounts of data.) Dr. Codd established 12 OLAP rules to follow, and most OLAP products conform to them in one way or another:

- **Multidimensional conceptual view** — OLAP operates with cubes of data that represent multidimensional constructs of data. Even though the name implies 3-D data, the number of possible dimensions is practically unlimited.
- **Transparency** — OLAP systems should be part of an open system that supports heterogeneous data sources.
- **Accessibility** — The OLAP should present the user with a single logical schema of the data.
- **Consistent reporting performance** — Performance should not degrade as the number of dimensions in the model increases.
- **Client/server architecture** — The architecture should be based on open, modular systems.
- **Generic dimensionality** — Not limited to 3-D and not biased toward any particular dimension. A function applied to one dimension should also be applicable to another.

- **Dynamic sparse-matrix handling** — Related both to the idea of nulls in relational databases and to the notion of compressing large files, a sparse matrix is one in which not every cell contains data. OLAP systems should accommodate varying storage and data-handling options.
- **Multiuser support** — OLAP systems should support more than one user at a time.
- **Unrestricted cross-dimensional operations** — Similar to the rule of generic dimensionality, all dimensions are created equal, and operations across data dimensions should not restrict relationships between cells.
- **Intuitive data manipulation** — Ideally, users shouldn't have to use menus or perform complex multiple-step operations when an intuitive drag-and-drop action will do.
- **Flexible reporting** — Save a tree. Users should be able to print just what they need, and any changes to the underlying financial model should be automatically reflected in reports.
- **Unlimited dimensional and aggregation levels** — The OLAP cube can be built with unlimited dimensions, and aggregation of the contained data also does not have practical limits.

Most OLAP tools, either integrated or stand-alone, generally conform to these rules. There are many more rules defined by theorists, as well as *de facto* rules established by the heavyweight database market players. Please refer to OLAP-specific literature and the vendor's documentation for more information.

What is OLAP used for? Decision support, sales analysis, marketing, data consolidation, the list goes on. Once data are accumulated, OLAP steps in to make actual sense out of it by providing an ability to traverse data along predefined dimensions (Time? Region? Customer's age?). OLAP provides multidimensional representation of data contained in OLTP data warehouses through the cube structure, which allows for creating views of data according to different sets of criteria, and manipulating them using sophisticated analytic functions.

ROLAP, MOLAP, and HOLAP

All these acronyms refer to the way data for the cube, the primary operational unit for the OLAP queries, is stored. The functionality, methods, and principles of OLAP remain identical across all three major RDBMSs:

- MOLAP refers to the situation when relational data for a cube, along with aggregation data, are stored in the cube itself. It provides for the fastest response, and is most appropriate for frequent use (like on-demand OLAP, without the need for real-time data).
- ROLAP refers to the situation when relational data for a cube, along with aggregation data, are stored in the relational database. This provides for real-time querying, though responses might be slower than MOLAP as all the data need to be assembled from scratch.
- HOLAP refers to the situation when relational data for a cube are stored in a relational database, while the aggregation data are stored in the cube itself. It was designed to get the best of both worlds. It is somewhat faster than ROLAP, and the cube structure is much smaller than in the MOLAP case.

The independent vendors' market shrank dramatically in the last decade: Oracle acquired Hyperion, IBM swallowed Cognos, and SAP got both Business Objects and Sybase. Microsoft continues developing it own business intelligence platforms: SQL Server Analysis Services (SSAS) and SQL Server Integration Services (SSIS).

Oracle 11g

Oracle also has incorporated business intelligence capability directly into Oracle 11g Database by providing embedded OLAP Server with its Enterprise Edition of RDBMS. It allows OLAP cubes to be compiled directly to be executed directly against the OLTP database without transferring it into a specialized OLAP-specific database. This approach has its pluses and minuses. One plus would be that the need for a time-consuming and expensive data transfer (and transformation) process is eliminated. On the minus side is the fact that ad hoc cubes still have to be compiled first, and running an OLAP query against your production database may slow down your operation with a resource-intensive process.

Oracle 11g Database lays the foundation for the Oracle OLAP, providing data storage and management capabilities, analytic functions, security, and so on; whereas the OLAP services themselves support multidimensional calculations, forecast functions, models, and the like. A number of wizards are provided to guide users through the maze of choices.

The Oracle cube can be queried directly using SQL and some OLAP-related functions that were added to it. Because cubes already include aggregation on many levels, there is no need for the GROUP BY clause, and any joins required to access this data are already highly optimized. To use the dimensional nature of the cube, applications would utilize the Java OLAP application programming interface (API). Oracle's Discoverer Plus OLAP is an example of such a dimensionally aware business intelligence tool that utilizes OLAP API(s). In addition, Oracle provides a set of Java OLAP APIs to allow users to program additional rich functionality, which enables building cross-platform solutions using Java applications, applets, Java Server Pages, and so on. It can be installed separately, on middle tier hardware, or integrated with an RDBMS.

IBM DB2

Previous versions of IBM DB2 UDB provided OLAP capabilities through DB2 OLAP Server and OLAP Server Analyzer. Both are add-ons developed in collaboration with Hyperion (and its Essbase product) for Windows and UNIX customers, and a similar product for iSeries customers in collaboration with SPSS. Then, IBM withdrew from marketing and supporting the DB2 OLAP Server (and OEM versions of the products from Hyperion and SPSS that subsequently were acquired by Oracle), and introduced DB2 Data Warehouse Edition (DB2 DWE). Later, it had acquired Cognos to be the core of its business intelligence (BI) strategy.

IBM supports only ROLAP and MOLAP functionality. IBM DB2 UDB also features OLAP Miner, branded by IBM as an "opportunity-discovery" component of the IBM OLAP Server. It applies data mining algorithms to the OLAP cubes to pinpoint the "surprise" areas and present them to an analyst for further investigation.

It appears that our ideas about databases are influenced by our storage capabilities. We still think in two dimensions, not far ahead of the original sheet of paper upon which the first table was drawn. Since every idea of computer persistent storage is ultimately based on strings of ones and zeroes arranged on a flat surface, so is our visualization of the data. No matter how you look at it, the access to a particular piece of data are by coordinates (x,y), which pretty much defines our thinking. Once we move to multidimensional storage (for example, holographic), the data table can become a sphere, for instance, where data are accessed by spherical coordinates, by a position vector. This paradigm shift, in turn, might require a different language to access and manipulate such a structure.

Microsoft SQL Server

Microsoft provides OLAP capabilities through SSAS, bundled with SQL Server, and has introduced two distinct dialects of SQL specifically designed to address the needs of BI based upon SQL Server SSAS.

Multidimensional Expressions (MDX)

The Multidimensional Expressions (MDX) language is used to manipulate the base unit of any OLAP analysis: the cube. The language is similar to SQL in many respects, and enables the manipulation of data stored in OLAP cubes. Microsoft also provides external access interfaces like OLE DB, ActiveX Data Objects (ADO) ADO/ADO.NET and ASQL-DMO (Data Analysis Management Objects) for accessing OLAP functionality within SQL Server 2000–2008.

In addition to its predefined functions, MDX permits the creation of custom functions for use in the OLAP cubes. While having somewhat similar syntax to SQL, MDX is not an SQL extension; it is a different language, designed specifically for OLAP. Though it is not an open standard (being introduced by Microsoft), it is one of the most popular OLAP tools, and enjoys solid support from OLAP vendors such as IBM, SAP, SAS, Brio Technology, and Microstrategy.

Data Mining Extensions (DMX)

The Data Mining Extensions (DMX) query language, which was introduced for data mining in Microsoft SQL Server, is used to create and work with data mining models. In the broadest sense, data mining is a process of discovering patterns in the data, "unknown unknowns," so to speak. It usually involves very large sets of data to be sifted through, and requires sophisticated algorithms and advanced math techniques to be deployed.

Unlike MDX, it is SQL Server only, and to date hasn't gathered much support from other vendors. The leaders in data mining, SAS and SPSS (recently acquired by IBM), prefer to stick to their own technologies, though there is a shift toward cooperation and standardization with advent of new technologies such as Predictive Modeling Markup Language (PMML) to represent learned knowledge in XML format.

XML for Analysis (XMLA)

XMLA, which stands for XML for Analysis, represents yet another industry standard for data access in BI systems. It is specifically attuned to the distributed cloud-based data, and incorporates web technology standards such as XML, SOAP, and HTTP protocols. The standard is maintained by the XMLA Council, with Microsoft, Hyperion (by extension, Oracle), and SAS as founding members.

As a language, it has only two methods executed over SOAP protocol: EXECUTE and DISCOVER. Both use MDX as their embedded query language to access data and use SOAP messages to shuffle data back and forth between multidimensional OLAP data sources.

There is a robust open source OLAP market represented by products such as Pentaho Mondrian OLAP and Jedox PALO projects.

ELEMENTARY, MY DEAR WATSON!

A new era of was officially introduced on February 14, 2011 with an IBM Watson computer taking on a "uniquely human" activity — playing Jeopardy games. The machine was named after IBM founder Thomas J. Watson (should anyone wonder why it was not named after Sherlock Holmes), and it represents a next giant step towards something that was dubbed "artificial intelligence" in 1956, and was almost exclusively in the domain of science fiction ever since.

For a long time it has been understood that simply to possess information does not equal ability to answer questions, let alone provide intelligent answers. A search engine, even the most advanced one, relies on keywords to search for information; it is up to humans to come up with clever strings of keywords, and it is ultimately a human task to decide whether the information returned constitutes an answer to the question. Watson takes it a step further. It has to figure out the question, deduce the context, and come up with the statistically most-probable answer. This is very different from the Deep Blue computer which beat chess grandmaster Garry Kasparov in 1997. The chess game can be reduced to a set of well defined mathematical problems in *combinatorics*, a very large set to be sure, but ultimately susceptible to the number-crunching power of the computer — no ambiguity, no contextual variations. The IBM Watson had to deal with the uncertainty of human language; it had to interpret metaphors; it had to understand the nuances of human language.

The tables had turned again. Instead of humans learning the machine's language to query for answers, it was the machine that learned to understand questions posed with all the ambiguity of the human language. With clever programming algorithms, the computer was able to "understand" natural language query, and come up with a correct answer — most of the time, that is.

Does Watson use SQL to come up with the answer? The details of implementation are a closely guarded secret, at least for now. Given the limitations imposed by the Jeopardy rules, the narrowly focused purpose and relatively modest computing power (around 2,000 CPU "connected in a very special way," according to Dr. Christopher Welty, a member of the IBM artificial intelligence group; that is a far cry from the 750,000 cores of the IBM Mira super computer being built for DOE's Argonne National Library), it most probably did *not* use a relational database to store data. Rather, it most likely relied on proprietary data structures and algorithms to search and retrieve the information. Eventually, these advances will make it into the mainstream database technology, and the way we transform data into information into knowledge will change, again. The future is near.

COLUMN-ORIENTED DBMS

As the name implies, the column-oriented database stores data in columns as opposed to standard row/ fields orientation. This turns the relational model upside down, as it flies in the face of the normalization rules. The concept can be illustrated with AUTHORS table in our Library database (see Table 12-4).

TABLE 12-4: Columnar Representation of AUTHORS Table

AU_ID	AU_FIRST_NAME	AU_LAST_NAME
1, 2, 3, 4, 5, 6	Alexander, Boris, Mark, Paulraj, Allen, Gavin	Kriegel, Trukhnov, Gillenson, Ponniah, Taylor, Powell

One advantage comes from the fact that the data are not stored as a text in these columns, but is compressed into binary uniform data type (yes, a columnar database operates with but a single data type per column, as opposed to rows, which usually contain different data types); this allows for using advanced indexing techniques (bitmap indices, for example). Another advantage comes from the fact that the database optimizes physical storage, so all data can be read in one pass, without multiple calls to the storage (such as the hard drive).

Unlike NoSQL options, such as SinpleDB or BigTable, the columnar databases actually do use SQL and sometimes even integrate with relational databases (for example, Infobright columnar database runs with MySQL, and Sybase IQ runs on top of Sybase ASE).

Most benefits are realized in data warehousing applications, which deal with aggregate data computed over a number of data items. At the same time, it slows down insert/update/delete operations, making it a really poor choice for an OLTP database.

There are few commercial implementations and just a handful of open source implementations. Adoption is rather slow, though. Sybase IQ is at the forefront of enterprise-level, columnar database computing, and even it claims just over 3,000 world-wide installations (compare this with hundreds of thousands of servers running Oracle, DB2, and Microsoft SQL Server). Another leader in columnar databases is Vertica (its founders include Dr. Michael Stonebraker of Ingres/PostgreSQL fame).

There are quite a few open source columnar databases usually built upon RDBMSs, such as MySQL or PostgreSQL, with complementary layers of storage and optimization to take advantage of the columnar data storage paradigm. The examples include InfiniDB and Infobright (both integrated with MySQL), while Greenplum and Aster have chosen PostgreSQL for their columnar extensions.

OBJECT DATABASES

The object-oriented (OO) approach, an interesting academic topic in the 1980s, became mainstream in the early 1990s and the de facto standard for most of software development efforts thereafter (the *object-oriented* term is explained later in this chapter).

Nearly every modern programming language is (or claims to be) object-oriented; however, even though the OO approach proved to be successful in computer programming (in terms of increased development speed, increased robustness, and code maintainability), it hadn't caught on in the database market so far. The objects have structures of their own, and RDBMSs prefer to work with data shredded into bits and pieces of a normalized schema.

Translating objects back and forth between an application and set of relational tables makes performance less than optimal. An obvious solution would be a system that allows direct storage of the objects and the ability to manage them in a fashion similar to data in relational tables. Although there are some purely object-oriented databases, their market share is rather insignificant. Many major RDBMSs vendors, including Oracle, DB2, Microsoft SQL Server, and PostgreSQL, provide some kind of objects for use with traditional RDBMSs: the *object-oriented RDBMS (OORDBMS)* approach. Even though the object-oriented paradigm is not directly related to the contents of this book, we will briefly introduce it in the database context in this chapter.

In the RDBMS world, OO refers to the ability of the database to store and retrieve instances (explained in the following paragraph) of objects in much the same way as XML documents are stored and retrieved, either by parsing into text and reconstituting on demand or by saving the entire object as-is, be it a Java or .NET object. In addition, some databases sponsor object data types, which introduce OOP principles into their procedural SQL programming.

Object-Oriented Programming (OOP) Paradigm

In object-oriented programming (OOP), everything is an object that can be defined as a distinct programming structure capable of containing data and having some relevant methods. Usually, objects are representations of real-life entities, reduced in their complexity to a few well-defined features and tasks they should be able to perform. A person, a tree, a book — all can be represented as objects; the same goes for some abstract objects such as bank account or data access object. Consider an object that models, say, a bank account. It might have the attributes "balance" and "account ID," and the methods "withdraw" and "deposit," all representing some functionality that is expected of an object of this type. The main principles of object orientation are encapsulation, inheritance, polymorphism, and identity, all of which will be discussed in the next paragraphs.

Objects and Classes

Each object has its own attributes and methods. For example, for the object CAR you can have such attributes as engine size, engine type, wheel size, interior color, exterior color, shift type, and so on. The methods may include "drive," "turn(left|right)," and so on.

The objects are defined through the programming concept of classes. An *object* is an instance of a *class*. The common analogy here is the blueprint of a house and the actual house built based on that blueprint. You can instantiate many objects of the same class in the very same way as many houses can be built from the same blueprint, being different only in their attributes, color, or location, for example.

The three main concepts of OOP are encapsulation, inheritance, and polymorphism, as discussed in the following sections.

Encapsulation

The main idea of *encapsulation* is to hide implementation details and make them accessible only by explicitly defined methods that reduce the impact of changes made to the internals of the objects and enforce security. The nonprogrammer's world analogy would be any programmable electronic device you may have at home, such as a VCR or a microwave oven. You normally can manipulate them only through buttons devised for this purpose, though it might be possible to open the cover and use your best judgment to control its operations through manipulating electronic components.

Security is usually enforced by using public, private, and protected methods. Public *methods are available for all users of the class,* private methods *limit the internal code access, and* protected methods *are accessible to objects instantiated from classes inherited from the parent class.*

Inheritance

Another important concept of OOP is inheritance. *Inheritance* is a mechanism that allows the programmer to create a new class based on (or inherited from) the old (existing) class. The new class, called (unsurprisingly) the child class, has all the attributes (properties) and methods of the old class (parent). Some of them can be ignored or modified, while some new characteristics can be added. For example, subclasses Chevrolet, Ford, Honda, Toyota, and Nissan can be derived from class CAR. This allows for reuse of the code this class contains and makes the development process more rigorous.

Polymorphism

Polymorphism means that a given method can be applied to different objects. For example, the same method can perform logically consistent actions when it gets a different number of arguments or arguments of different data types. For example, a hypothetical function ADD can add numbers, concatenate strings, and increment a date by the given number of days, depending on the internal implementation. For the programmer, that means that as long as he or she calls the method with correct arguments, he or she does not have to worry about details of implementation and expect correct results.

The term object *might cause some confusion when used within common relational database terminology. From the very beginning, in RDBMS language, a database object means a table, a view, an index, and so on. An* object *within your program is different from a* database object.

The closest the RDBMSs came to OO are user-defined types (UDTs), which allow you to create complex types out of those defined in the RDBMS. Imagine defining the data type BOOK that would have all the properties such as title and price, and then creating a table with a column of this data type. While such constructs are useful in transforming computer-oriented design into human-oriented design, there are penalties to be paid: numerous limitations on how this custom data type can be used, decreased performance, and incompatibilities with SQL Standard and other RDBMSs.

Among the RDBMSs discussed in this book, currently only Oracle, DB2, Microsoft SQL Server, and PostgreSQL offer full support for UDTs.

Compensating for the lack of OOP features, SQL Server 2008 can use .NET languages to create database-stored procedures. In addition, the ability to invoke legacy provides the ability to invoke and use ActiveX/OLE objects from within Transact-SQL code through system-stored procedures. Both Oracle and IBM DB2 allow for use of Java programming language in a similar fashion. PostgreSQL has a unique ability to use virtually any programming language to create stored procedures by registering it with the RDBMS.

With the advent of OOP came the idea of object storage. Relational databases, in spite of all the modernization, new data types, and functionality, remain by and large text-based; that is, they parse, store, and search textual data. While various new media formats such as video, sound, PowerPoint presentations, and Microsoft Word structured storage were accommodated by the inclusion of the new data types, essentially it remains the same text-based approach, although somewhat expanded.

As OO languages (C++, Java, C#, Visual Basic.NET, Delphi, Smalltalk, Eiffel) become increasingly popular, it began to makes sense to store information in objects as they are defined by the classes implemented in these languages. Imagine a Java class BOOK, which has its properties (attributes) and methods defined. When an application creates an instance of this class to add a new book, it populates its properties and then saves the instance into a database. In RDBMS context, this would mean extracting pieces of data and populating a number of tables. For an OO database, it would mean serializing the object as it is — as a binary, byte-code, or text description version — and still being able to track this object by, say, BK_ID, without the need to assemble all relevant data from the tables. This is what OODBMSs and OORDBMSs are all about.

While pure OO databases try to implement their own "pure OO" method of storing information, OORDBMSs rely on relational technology to establish a hierarchy of the objects. Because of a rather tight coupling of the OO database with the programming language, the application written for one database might be impossible to use with some other products. There are several initiatives to establish a standard for OODBMS, which so far have resulted in the ODMG 3.0 standard, in addition to a number of proprietary ways to do things.

While still a novelty, OODBMS are making it into the mainstream of the academic and corporate worlds, fueled mainly by adoption of OO technologies such as Java, Enterprise Java Beans (EJB), and Smalltalk.

One of the commercial successes of OO databases is InterSystems Cache multiplatform DBMS, which supports both SQL and object interfaces to the data (through proprietary Cache ObjectScript), allowing for a mix-and-match approach. It has especially strong following in the U.S. healthcare system, being adopted as the DBMS of choice by many hospitals, and Electronic Health Records (EHR) management systems providers.

There are also open source DBMSs, such as the db4o embeddable database (with a corresponding commercial version from Versant) supporting Java and .Net, and the Zope Object Database, which supports objects for the Python programming language.

The main advantage of the OODBMSs over OORDBMSs comes from eliminating the mapping of the objects from the application (client) to the RDBMS structure, something we will talk about in the next section. In the current environment, in which data are still coming as text or numbers, RDBMSs are much faster than comparable OODBMSs/OORDBMSs. At the same time, there are situations when the object approach might prove to be superior to the "old" relational model. While it seems that ORDBMS databases have made the biggest progress in the recent years, the jury is still out.

The SQL Standard ISO/IEC 9075 defines extensions of database language SQL to support embedding of SQL statements into programs written in the Java programming language, commonly known as SQLJ. An object created with SQLJ has both advantages and disadvantages when compared with more traditional applications. The main advantage is that SQLJ is strongly typed; that is, if the class compiled, there would be no unexpected errors because all embedded SQL statements were checked against the database. The second advantage is that SQLJ programs are more concise than corresponding JDBC programs because SQLJ operates on a higher abstraction level. Disadvantages include an additional step in compilation (all SQLJ programs must run through a preprocessor first), and the lack of support from many popular frameworks (such as Hibernate).

Because of standardization, SQLJ is uniquely suited for exposing the relational nature of a database through the OO front end (for example, object-relational mapping). In addition, many databases support invocating external modules as part of the RDBMS-defined data types. SQLJ seems like a natural candidate for these tasks.

OBJECT-RELATIONAL MAPPING FRAMEWORKS

Object-relational mapping (ORM) is a way to bridge two inherently different world views. The OOP languages model their world in terms of objects, properties, and methods, while relational databases use entities and relationships, and normalized data models are best suited to store and retrieve scalar values (numbers, character strings). To have an OO client software talking to a relational database means constant translation between the two; at some point, it became obvious that this translation process could be automated, and ORM was born.

There is no shortage of different frameworks created for every technology supporting OO out there, Java, .Net, Deplhi, Groovy, Perl, and Python, to name a few. Currently, the most popular by the number of users in the Java community is the Hibernate 3.0 ORM, with Microsoft developers using NHibernate, LINQ to SQL, and the nascent Microsoft Entity Framework, in no particular order.

Hibernate/NHibernate

Hibernate is an ORM specifically designed and implemented for the Java programming language. It is released as free open source software under the LGP license. The project was started back in 2001 out of frustration with the complexity of EJB, then the hottest environment for constructing enterprise applications. The current implementation, in version 3, is certified for the +Java Persistence API standard. Although being free and open source, it does have an owner, JBossInc, itself owned by Red Hat, which retains all intellectual property rights.

Its purpose is to map Java classes to a set of relational tables and provide two-way communications between the objects and the database. Once configured, it will automatically generate SQL calls and marshal data between the application and the database, freeing the developer to concentrate on implementing applications logic, not on persistence layer plumbing.

NHibernate is a direct port from the Java-based predecessor Hibernate. It is also free, open source software released under the LGPL licensing scheme. The latest version as of the time of writing is NHibernate 3.0, released on December 4, 2010; it supports Microsoft .Net framework up to version 3.5.

Microsoft LINQ and Entity Framework

LINQ is a .Net library extending .Net Framework family of languages. It purports to be a unified framework providing query, set, and transform operation abstraction layer to a variety of data sources, including RDBMSs. The latter is called LINQ to SQL. The basic relational entities, such as tables, are defined as classes in the .Net code, and the query is constructed in an SQL-like syntax with the underlying LINQ libraries handling all complexities of the database communications, including establishing connections, submitting queries, and fetching back the result sets. The classes can be linked together in relationships, modeling the underlying RDBMS data model, or creating one dynamically.

Touted as the "first step in much larger vision of an entity-aware data platform," Entity Framework was introduced as evolution of ORM. The latest version as of the time of writing is 4.0, released in April 2010. Microsoft provides tools such as Visual Studio Entity Designer to facilitate creating of the data maps between .Net objects and entities in the RDBMS. It uses a variant of SQL, aptly named Entity SQL, to manipulate the data in the .Net classes inside the application. In order to work, an RDBMS-specific provider is needed. As of today, with the exception of HSQLDB, such providers were created for all databases discussed in the book.

SUMMARY

New developments such as cloud computing, XML, OLAP, NoSQL, and OO technologies continue to change the ways we are collecting, storing, and consuming information; the very nature of the information keeps changing and often involves new media and new formats. The very fundamentals such as rows and columns might go the way of the dodo, being replaced with new paradigms.

Cloud computing represents the next step in distributed storage and computing. The main characteristics of it are self-service on demand, resource pooling, capacity on demand, and a pay-as-you go approach. Infrastructure as a Service (IaaS) encompassed paradigms of Software as a Service (SaaS) and Platform as a Service (PaaS); storage and computing capacity on demand were made possible by advances in virtualization technology and ubiquitous connectivity. A variety of different frameworks, ranging from proprietary to open source made cloud computing a reality. Cloud computing allows RDBMSs to be installed, configured, and administered on virtual environments, created and destroyed on demand. Combined with plummeting storage prices and ubiquitous connectivity, it also enabled the NoSQL phenomenon, a reincarnation of the key/value data organization that harkens back to the prerelational era.

XML emerged as the de facto information exchange standard. Not surprisingly, relational databases responded by incorporating XML into their cores. The approaches taken by each of the RDBMS vendors might be different (XML documents might be mapped and parsed in familiar text-based records, or stored as complete documents), but the details of these implementations have become increasingly irrelevant to the vast majority of developers and users.

OLAP became the standard for BI. With the enormous amount of data, accumulated since the dawn of civilization (structured or otherwise), it was only a matter of time before someone would take data comprehension to the next level, which is to discover statistical trends. While not part of the RDBMS technology, BI does not make much sense without some kind of a database (relational in our case). The main processing unit of this information is a multidimensional cube, which can be manipulated using either some general-purpose language (such as Java) or some proprietary language (such as Microsoft MDX and DMX). Some vendors bundle BI tools with their RDBMSs, and some BI tools are stand-alone tools built by third-party companies.

The OO approach became the de facto application programming standard, and as such made a compelling case for OO databases. As we model the surrounding world in terms of objects, we need a place to store these objects. An RDBMS maps the objects to words; an OODBMS will accept them as they are. You may compare it with a book, in which images are created by your brain from mere words. A movie stores and communicates visual objects directly to your senses, bypassing the verbalization step.

OODBMSs may well be the wave of the future, which is notoriously unpredictable. As of today, many companies have implemented OO databases, designed to store and retrieve objects created within some particular language (Java, C++, Smalltalk, C# (.NET)). Eventually, new standards will emerge and performance gaps, if any, will be eliminated, making RDBMSs outdated. For now, RDBMSs remain the pillars of the business community, though they do pay lip service to the objects, incorporating them as data types but warning against the inefficiency of using them.

Installing the Library Database

The instructions in this appendix assume that all scripts are located in a single directory `C:\discovery`. Table A-1 lists all the scripts available for download from the book's site `www.wrox.com` and `www.agilitator.com`. The .sql script file contains all Data Definition Language (DDL) creation code, including one for creating a database. The `.dat` file contains data to populate tables.

The examples are given for the most ubiquitous operating system, Microsoft Windows, but would run with cosmetic modifications on any other operating system for which a particular RDBMS installation is available. The SQL scripts will run identically in each environment regardless of the underlying operating system.

Before you can use any of the scripts, you must make sure that your RDBMS is up and running. For simplicity's sake, the SQL syntax for creating a database does not use any of the options that normally accompany such an important act as that of database creation. Everything is left to default, which is not *a recipe for a production database.*

With the exception of PostgreSQL script, all other scripts contain database creation code. The PostgreSQL has a separate script for this purpose because it cannot run the CREATE DATABASE statement as part of a multi-command string. Additionally, there are two versions of the Oracle DDL script: one for SQL*Plus and one for new Oracle's web interface. Each script was specifically crafted to take into account respective RDBMS requirements such as data types, date formatting and so on. Please make sure that you are using the appropriate script for each RDBMS.

Step-by-step instructions for each of the most commonly used interfaces are given in the following sections.

TABLE A-1: Sample Library Database SQL Script Files

RDBMS	SQL SCRIPT FILE
Oracle	DiscoveringSQL.Oracle.Library.sql DiscoveringSQL.Oracle.Library.4.Web.sql DiscoveringSQL.Oracle.dat
IBM DB2	DiscoveringSQL.DB2.UDB.Library.sql DiscoveringSQL.DB2.UDB.dat
Microsoft SQL Server	DiscoveringSQL.MSSQLServer.Library.sql DiscoveringSQL.MSSQLServer.dat
PostgreSQL	DiscoveringSQL.PostgreSQL.CreateDB.sql DiscoveringSQL.PostgreSQL.Library.sql DiscoveringSQL.PostgreSQL.dat
MySQL	DiscoveringSQL.MySQL.Library.sql DiscoveringSQL.MySQL.dat
Microsoft Access	DiscoveringSQL.Access.Library.sql DiscoveringSQL.Access.dat
OpenOffice.org HSQLDB	DiscoveringSQL.OpenOffice.HSQLDB.Library.txt DiscoveringSQL.OpenOffice.Data.txt

ORACLE 10G XE

We are using Oracle 10g in this book because this is the latest Oracle Express edition freely available at the time of this writing; the latest commercial release is Oracle 11g. There is no difference in functionality within the scope of this book, and the installation process described here will be identical between these versions.

Installing Library Sample Database with SQL*Plus

1. Launch Oracle's SQL*Plus utility; Figure A-1 shows the Windows XP menu location.

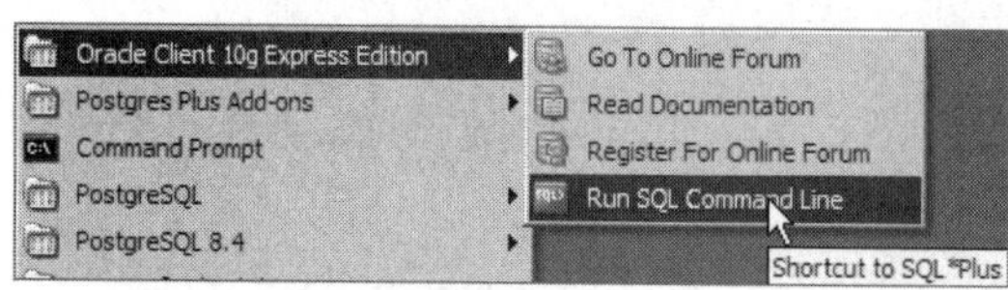

FIGURE A-1

2. At the SQL prompt, type the following statement: `@C:\discovery\DiscoveringSQL.Oracle.Library.sql`. As shown in Figure A-2, @ instructs SQL*Plus to load and execute scripts contained in the file.

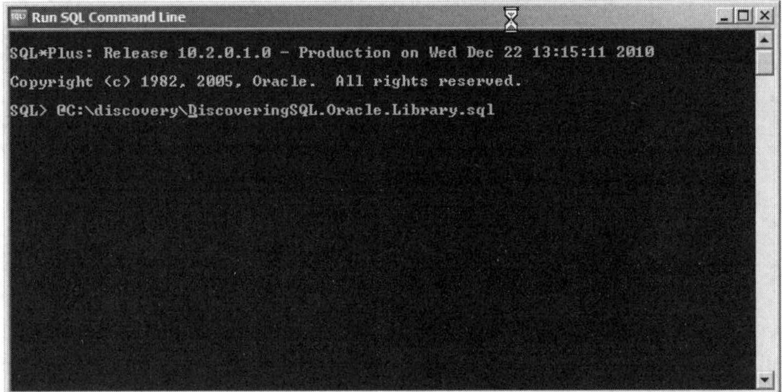

FIGURE A-2

3. Figure A-3 shows successful execution of the DDL script and the syntax to load yet another script to populate tables with data.

FIGURE A-3

4. Load data into the newly created tables by executing the `DiscoveringSQL.Oracle.dat` file that contains the INSERT statement. The results are shown in Figure A-4. You can verify that your new Library database tables indeed contain data by executing SELECT statements against them (BOOKS, AUTHORS, and so on; see the database model in Chapter 2 of the book).

FIGURE A-4

*In case SQL*Plus prints out any error message, you can try to troubleshoot the issue by looking on the Oracle website for the specific error produced or send an e-mail to* discovery@agilitator.com *(make sure to include as many details as possible).*

Installing with Oracle Web Interface

The web interface provided with Oracle Express installation provides a very nice graphical user interface (GUI). It runs in the browser. The link on Programs/All Programs opens the site in a default browser. The examples in this appendix use Mozilla Firefox 3.6.13.

1. Launch the application GUI in the default browser and connect to the database as a SYSTEM user using the password you've created during the installation process (see Appendix B for details), as shown in Figure A-5.

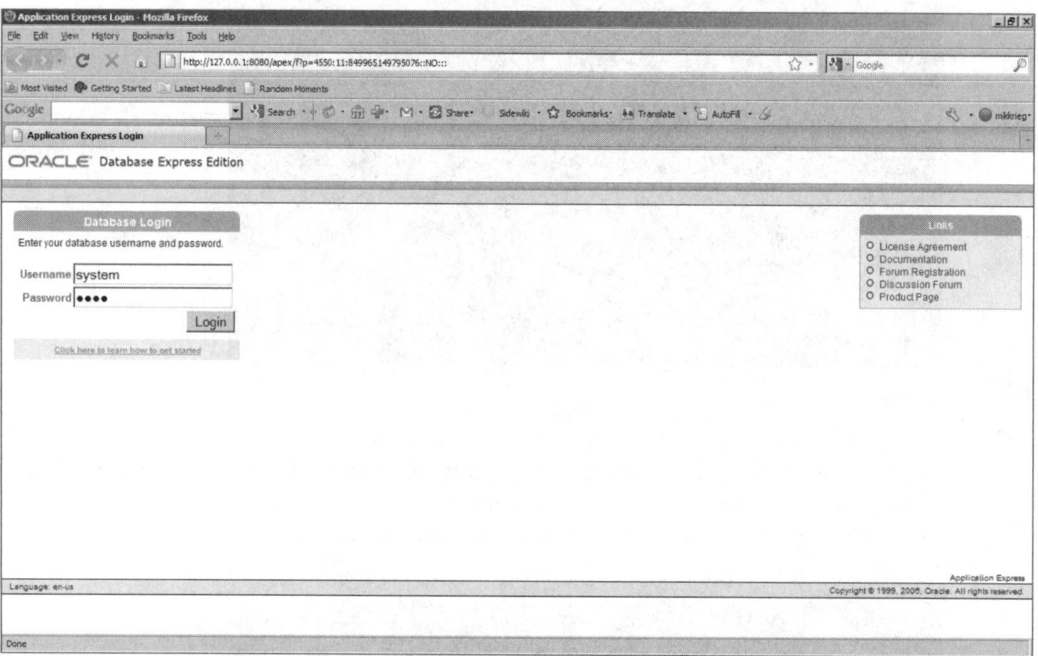

FIGURE A-5

2. From the main menu, click the Administration icon and then click Create User task within the administration panel. This will take you to the screen displayed in Figure A-6. Make sure that the newly created user will have sufficient privileges to create and query database objects. Alternatively, you can grant all these privileges (and more) by assigning the DBA role to the user (see Chapter 10 of the book on more information about Oracle privileges).

Create Database User [Cancel] [Create]

* Username: library
* Password: ••••••••
* Confirm Password: ••••••••
Expire Password ☐
Account Status: Unlocked
Default Tablespace: USERS
Temporary Tablespace: TEMP

User Privileges

Roles:
☑ CONNECT ☑ RESOURCE ☐ DBA

Direct Grant System Privileges:

☐ CREATE DATABASE LINK	☑ CREATE MATERIALIZED VIEW	☑ CREATE PROCEDURE
☑ CREATE PUBLIC SYNONYM	☐ CREATE ROLE	☑ CREATE SEQUENCE
☑ CREATE SYNONYM	☑ CREATE TABLE	☑ CREATE TRIGGER
☑ CREATE TYPE	☑ CREATE VIEW	

Check All Uncheck All

FIGURE A-6

3. Log out of the system by clicking the Log Out link in the right topmost corner of the screen, and log back with the credentials of the just created user. This time, instead of the Administration icon, click the SQL icon, as shown in Figure A-7.

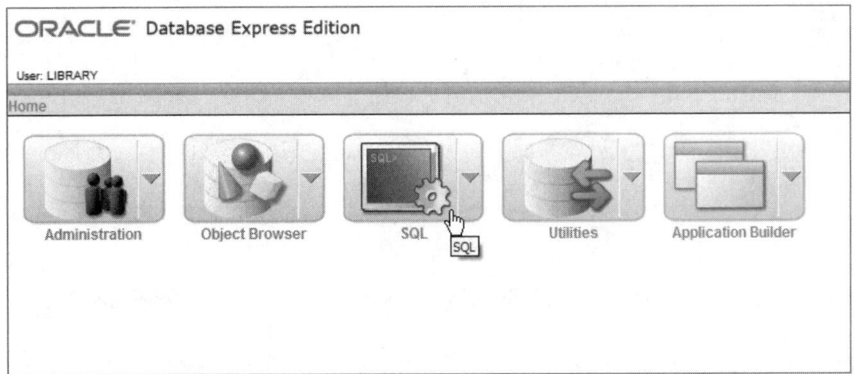

FIGURE A-7

4. Upload the script `DiscoveringSQL.Oracle.Library.4.Web.sql` to the Oracle administration site using the upload button. This script is slightly different from the one you would have used with SQL*Plus; it does not create a user.

   You can upload more than one script at a time, as shown in Figure A-8. (While this seems like a wonderful idea, in our experience there are some bugs not yet worked out; working with only one script at a time tends to be more reliable.)

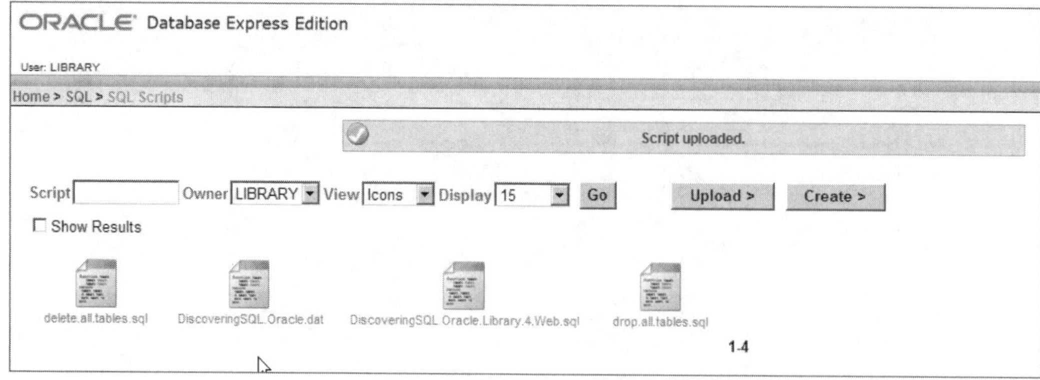

FIGURE A-8

5. Click the script's icon to load it in the editor, as shown in Figure A-9, and click Run.

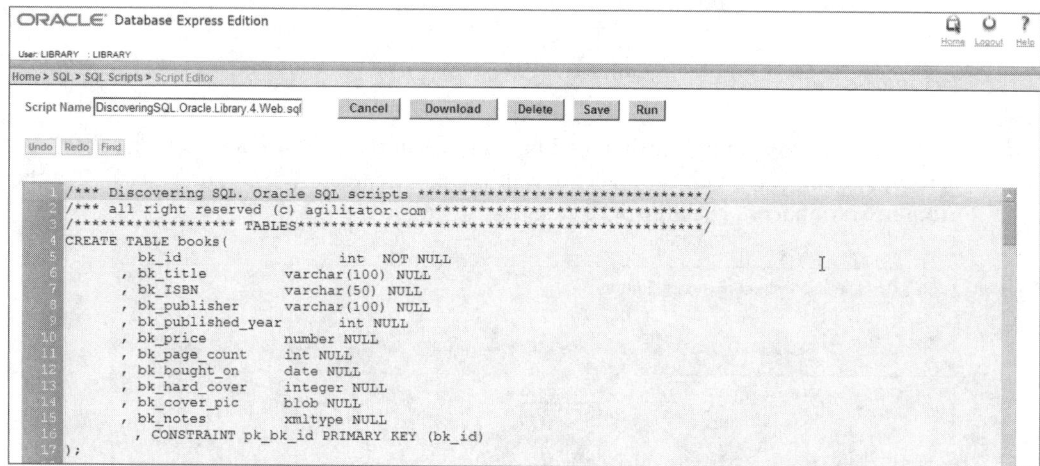

FIGURE A-9

6. Confirm your command on the following screen (Figure A-10) by clicking Run again.

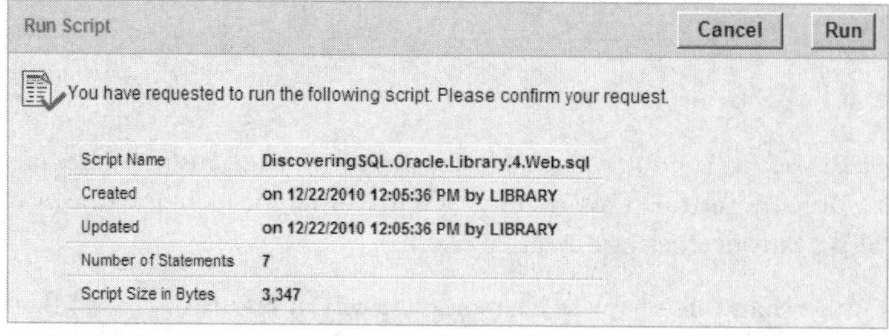

FIGURE A-10

7. You can check the results of the submitted script by clicking the View Results icon, as shown in Figure A-11.

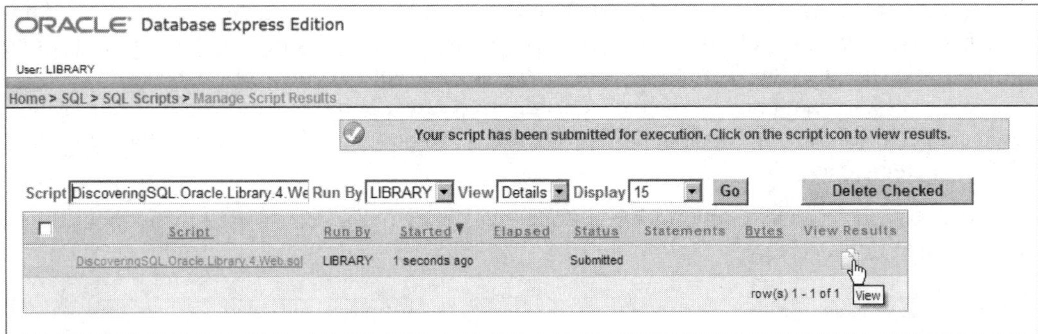

FIGURE A-11

The results of the script that created the Library database objects are displayed in Figure A-12.

Script: **create_tables** Status: **Complete**

View: ○ Detail ◉ Summary Display 15 Go Edit Script

Number	Elapsed	Statement	Feedback	Rows
1	0.03	CREATE TABLE books(bk_id int NOT NULL	Table created.	0
2	0.02	CREATE TABLE authors (au_id int NOT NULL , au_first_n	Table created.	0
3	0.01	CREATE TABLE searchTags(tag_id int NOT NULL ,	Table created.	0
4	0.02	CREATE TABLE books_authors(ba_id int NOT NULL , bk_id	Table created.	0
5	0.03	CREATE TABLE location (loc_id int NOT NULL , fk_bk_	Table created.	0
6	0.03	CREATE TABLE search_books(bt_id int NOT NULL , bk_id	Table created.	0
7	0.03	CREATE VIEW vwPublisherTitleYear AS SELECT authors.a	View created.	0
8	0.00	CREATE VIEW vwBookPublisherYear AS SELECT bk_title ,	View created.	0
9	0.00	CREATE VIEW vwBooksFilter AS SELECT bk_title , bk_l	View created.	0
10	0.08	ALTER TABLE books_authors ADD CONSTRAINT FK_bk_au_au FOREI	Table altered.	0
11	0.00	ALTER TABLE books_authors ADD CONSTRAINT FK_bk_au_books FO	Table altered.	0
12	0.01	ALTER TABLE location ADD CONSTRAINT FK_location_books FO	Table altered.	0
13	0.00	ALTER TABLE search_books ADD CONSTRAINT FK_search_bk_searc	Table altered.	0
14	0.00	ALTER TABLE search_books ADD CONSTRAINT FK_search_bk_bk	Table altered.	0

row(s) 1 - 14 of 14

Statements Processed	14
Successful	14
With Errors	0

FIGURE A-12

Oracle's web interface offers another possibility to execute scripts through the SQL Command interface, as shown on Figure A-13.

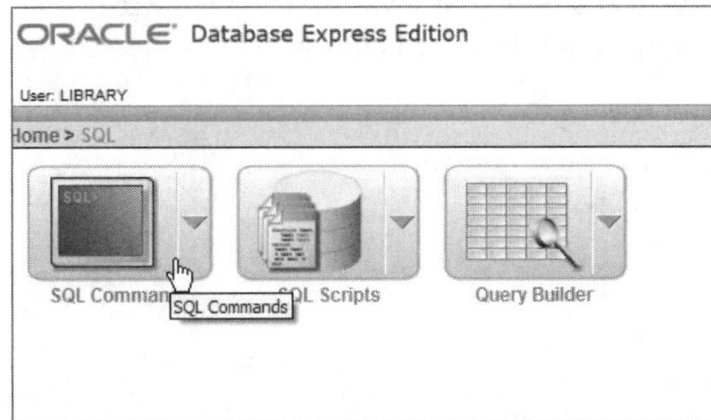

FIGURE A-13

The SQL Command (see Figure A-14) allows you to run ad hoc SQL statements against the database. The main drawback of using it for creating Library objects is its built-in limitation: It can only run one statement at a time. If you copy and paste, say, the entire contents of `DiscoveringSQL.Oracle.*` files, it would return an error. In order to create all objects, you would have to run it one statement per database object (view, table, constraint). To populate the tables, you have to run one INSERT statement at a time.

Nevertheless, this interface comes in handy for the majority of the scripts used throughout the book to illustrate SQL concepts.

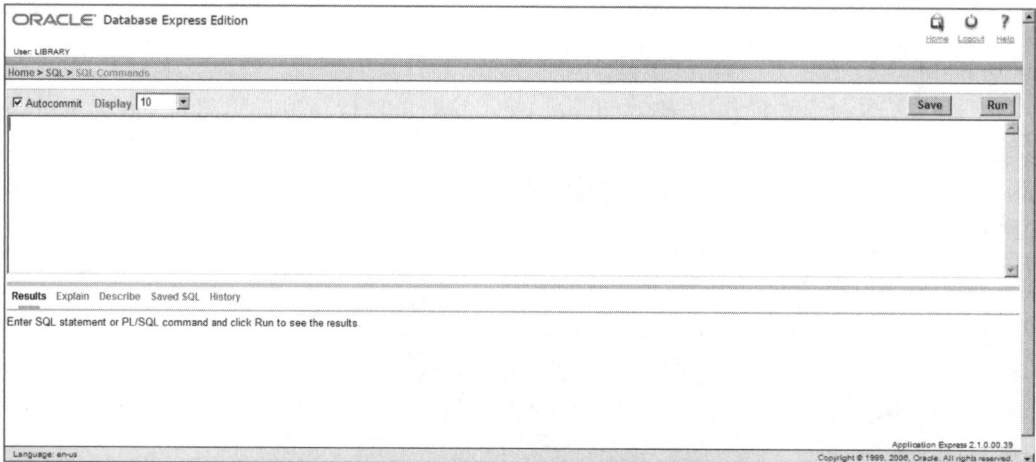

FIGURE A-14

IBM DB2 9.7 EXPRESS-C

IBM DB2 provides three different utilities to access its database server: the interactive *command line processor (CLP)*, the commanA-line *db2* utility, and the graphical user application *Command Editor*. Here we will discuss the latter two.

IBM Command Editor

1. Once the database server is up and running, launch the application from the `IBM DB2` ➪ `Command Line Tools` ➪ `Command Editor` menu option. It takes some time for the application to start up. Figure A-15 shows the Command Editor GUI console with some SQL code already loaded.

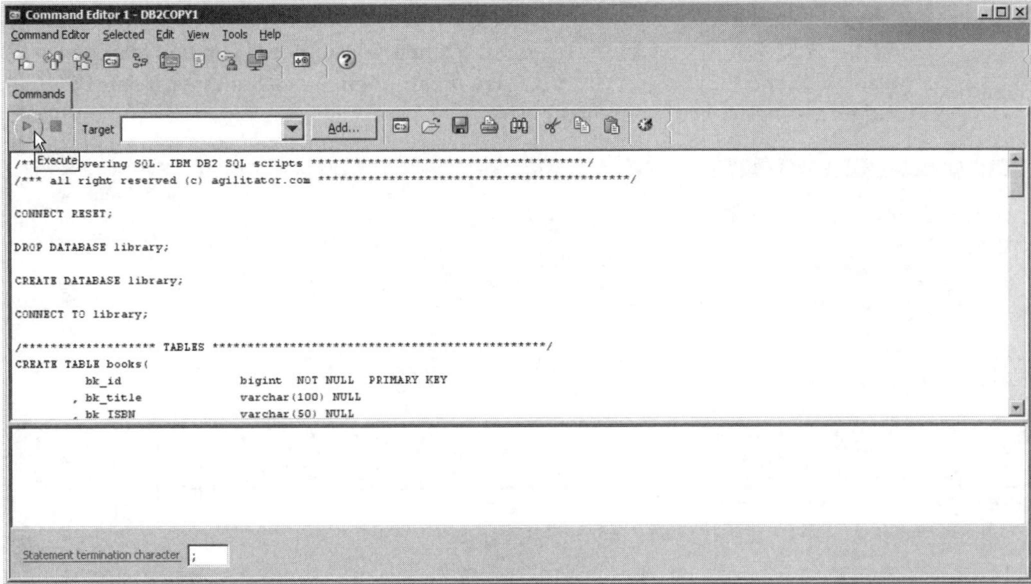

FIGURE A-15

2. Open the `DiscoveringSQL.DB2.UDB.Library.sql` file by clicking the Open Folder icon on the toolbar and navigating to the file's location. Once the file is loaded into the pane, click the Execute button (a green triangle icon on the toolbar). Figure A-16 shows the results of the execution: The Library database and all database objects are created. The process might take up to several minutes, depending upon your computer's characteristics.

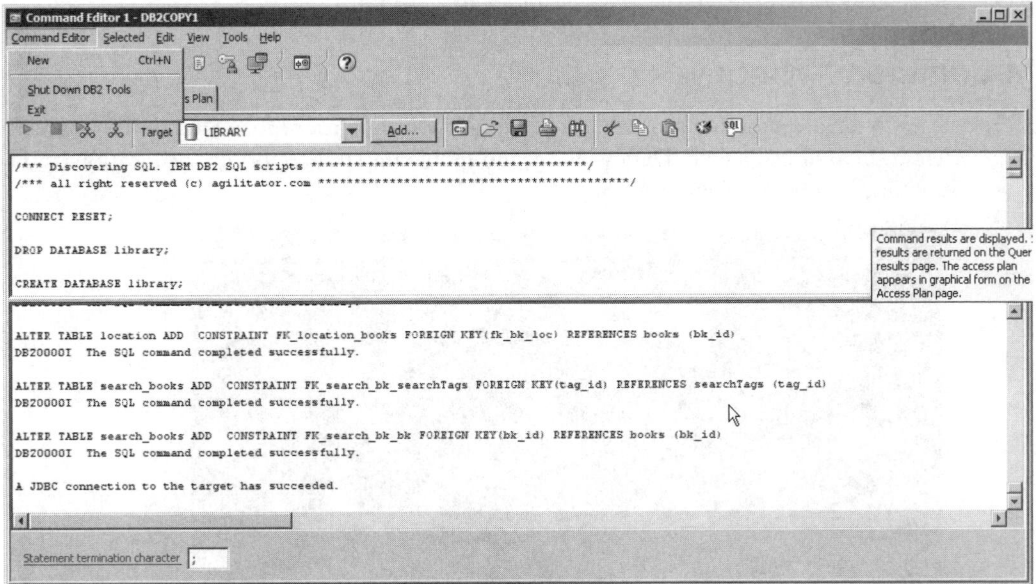

FIGURE A-16

3. Once the Library database and its objects are created, connect to the Library database by clicking the Add button and selecting Library from a pop-up list. Then you can load the code contained in `DiscoveringSQL.DB2.UDB.dat` file to populate its tables with data. The process and its results are shown in Figure A-17.

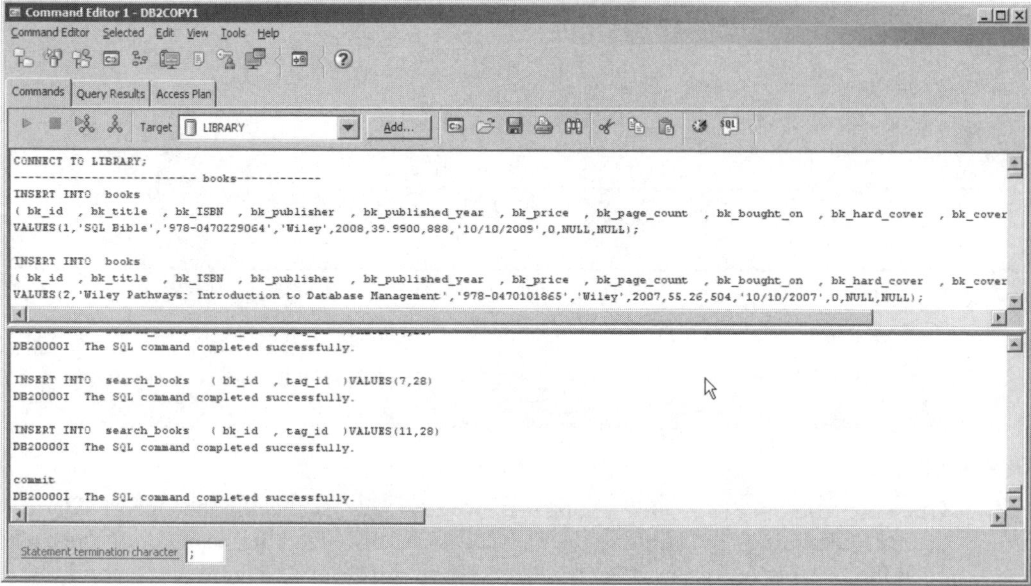

FIGURE A-17

4. You can use the very same window to query your database with query examples from the book. The results will show up on the Query Results tab.

IBM Command Window

1. The Command Window accessible from the same menu group: IBM DB2 ➪ Command Line Tools. It will open an MS DOS window and set the initial directory to the location of IBM utilities, as shown in Figure A-18.

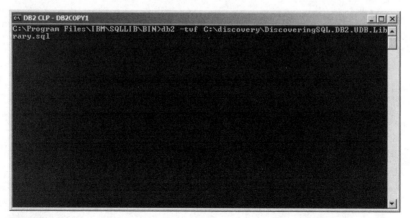

FIGURE A-18

2. Figure A-18 also shows the commanA-line syntax to run the SQL script to create the Library database. The utility db2 accepts the file `DiscoveringSQL.DB2.UDB.Library.sql` from the directory `C:\discovery`. The switch (tvf) gives the DB2 special processing instructions, such as specifying commanA-line terminators an echoing command to the output window. Once the database and the database object are created, you may run `DiscoveringSQL.DB2.UDB.dat` file in the very same fashion. The results of the data population script executed against the Library database are shown in Figure A-19.

```
DB2 CLP - DB2COPY1
DB20000I  The SQL command completed successfully.

INSERT INTO  search_books   ( bk_id   , tag_id   )VALUES(7,26)
DB20000I  The SQL command completed successfully.

INSERT INTO  search_books   ( bk_id   , tag_id   )VALUES(7,27)
DB20000I  The SQL command completed successfully.

INSERT INTO  search_books   ( bk_id   , tag_id   )VALUES(11,27)
DB20000I  The SQL command completed successfully.

INSERT INTO  search_books   ( bk_id   , tag_id   )VALUES(5,28)
DB20000I  The SQL command completed successfully.

INSERT INTO  search_books   ( bk_id   , tag_id   )VALUES(7,28)
DB20000I  The SQL command completed successfully.

INSERT INTO  search_books   ( bk_id   , tag_id   )VALUES(11,28)
DB20000I  The SQL command completed successfully.

commit
DB20000I  The SQL command completed successfully.

C:\Program Files\IBM\SQLLIB\BIN>
```

FIGURE A-19

The third member of the command-line tools group is the interactive CLP utility. It allows you to execute SQL statements one by one, including SELECT statements.

MICROSOFT SQL SERVER 2008 EXPRESS

There is no lack of tools to access the Microsoft SQL Server, from the built-in graphical console SQL Server Management Studio, to the commanA-line interface SQLCMD, to thirA-party utilities such as Quest SQL Server Management Tools and open source SQuirreL introduced in Appendix D.

SQL Server Management Studio Express

The Management Studio is an integral part of SQL Server and is available as an adA-on for the Express editions. It is the primary tool for administering the SQL Server installation, and we are going to use but a small piece of it: the Query Analyzer.

1. Start up the SQL Server Management Studio from Programs ➪ Microsoft SQL Server 2008 ➪ SQL Server Management Studio, and log onto your SQL Server installation, as shown in Figure A-20.

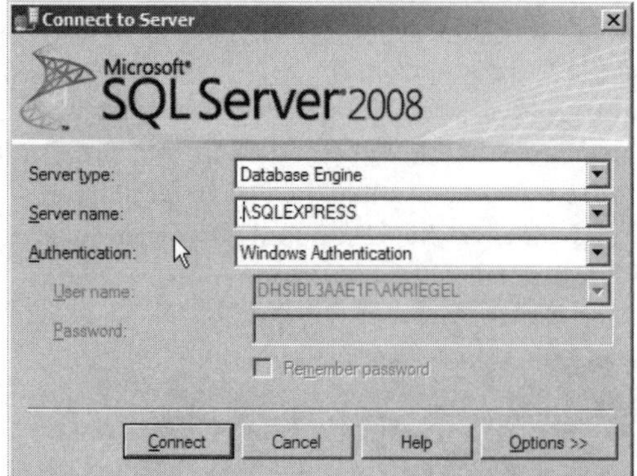

FIGURE A-20

2. Once the Management Studio consoler is up, click the New Query button at the top-left corner of the console, as shown in Figure A-21.

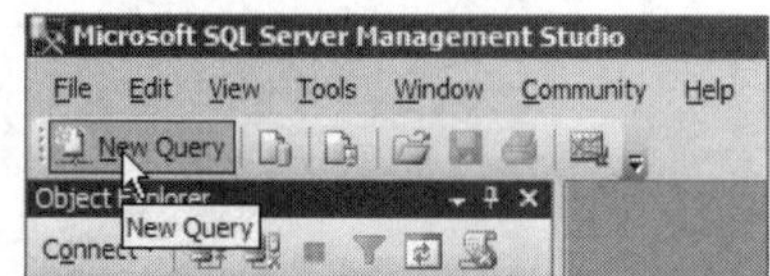

FIGURE A-21

3. Load the file `DiscoveringSQL.MSSQLServer.Library.sql` into the new query window by clicking the Open File icon on the Studio Management toolbar or by opening the file in a text editor and copying its contents into the query pane. The loaded (and already executed) script for creating a new database and all database objects is shown in Figure A-22. Click the Execute button on the query toolbar.

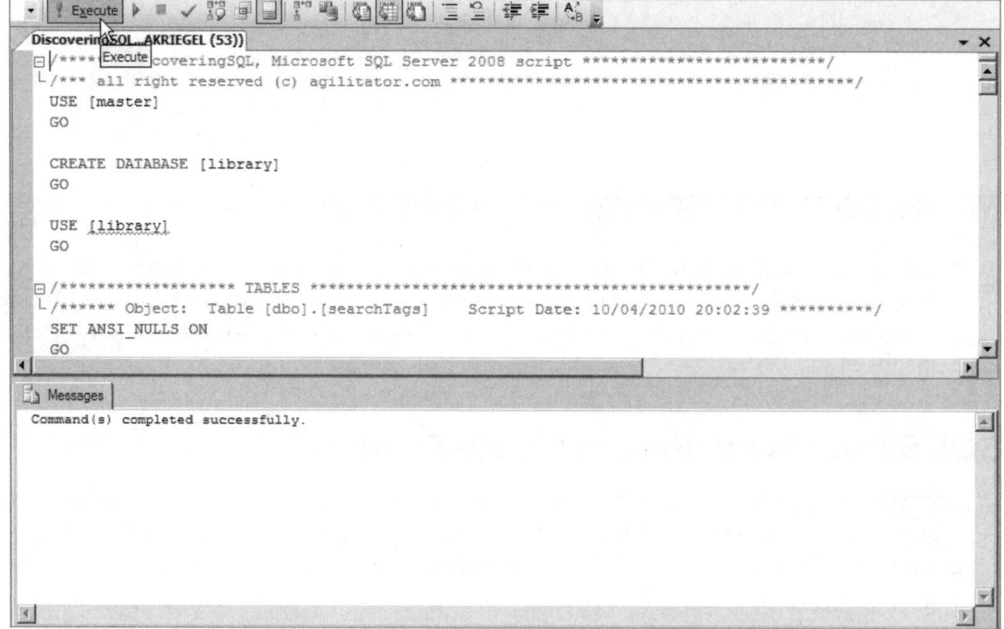

FIGURE A-22

4. Once the database and all the database objects have been created, you can load the data into the tables by executing INSERT statements from the script file `DiscoveringSQL.MSSQLServer.dat`. Load the file in the same fashion, as described in Step 3, and click the Execute button, as shown in Figure A-23.

```
DiscoveringSQL.MSSQLServer....
USE [library]
GO
-------------------------- books------------
INSERT INTO [books]
([bk_id],[bk_title],[bk_ISBN],[bk_publisher],[bk_published_year],[bk_price],[bk_page_count],[bk_bou
VALUES(1,'SQL Bible','978-0470229064','Wiley',2008,39.9900,888,'Oct 10 2009 12:00:00:00',0,NULL,NUL

INSERT INTO [books]
([bk_id],[bk_title],[bk_ISBN],[bk_publisher],[bk_published_year],[bk_price],[bk_page_count],[bk_bou
VALUES(2,'Wiley Pathways: Introduction to Database Management','978-0470101865','Wiley',2007,55.26,

INSERT INTO [books]
([bk_id],[bk_title],[bk_ISBN],[bk_publisher],[bk_published_year],[bk_price],[bk_page_count],[bk_bou
VALUES(3,'Microsoft SQL Server 2000 Weekend Crash Course','978-0764548406','Wiley',2001,29.99,408,'

Messages

(1 row(s) affected)

(1 row(s) affected)

(1 row(s) affected)

(1 row(s) affected)

(1 row(s) affected)

(1 row(s) affected)
```

FIGURE A-23

The Messages pane in the query window will display the execution acknowledgment steps, as shown in Figures A-22 and A-23. This is also a place for errors to be displayed. If you got any errors during the installation process described in this appendix, you may e-mail them for troubleshooting to discovery@agilitator.com.

As mentioned before, Microsoft SQL server also supports command-line interface to its database: the SQLCMD utility. It is a powerful tool for automating many administrative and development tasks. Nevertheless, its arcane syntax might be intimidating for someone without much experience with the command line, and since Microsoft always put emphasis on visual interfaces there is little reason for using it instead of Management Studio Query for the purposes of this book.

POSTGRESQL 9.0

PostgreSQL ships with a rather slick pgAdmin management console that facilitates most of the administrative tasks conducted both through the visual point-anA-click interface and the SQL queries window. There is also a commanA-line SQL Shell interface that until recently was the only native interface to the PostgreSQL RDBMS.

Installing with pgAdmin III

1. Launch pgAdmin from `Programs` ➪ `PostgreSQL 9.0` ➪ `pgAdmin III`. The initial screen is shown in Figure A-24.

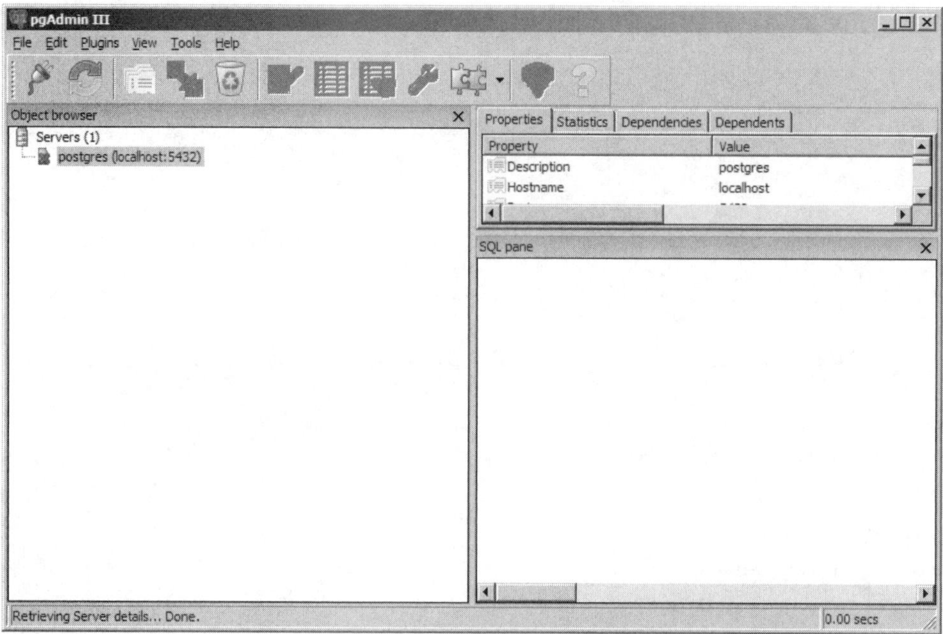

FIGURE A-24

2. Connect to the *postgres* server by selecting the server node and selecting the Connect menu option from the right-click pop-up menu, as shown in Figure A-25.

3. In the next step, bring up the SQL query console by clicking the SQL icon on the pgAdmin toolbar, as shown in Figure A-26.

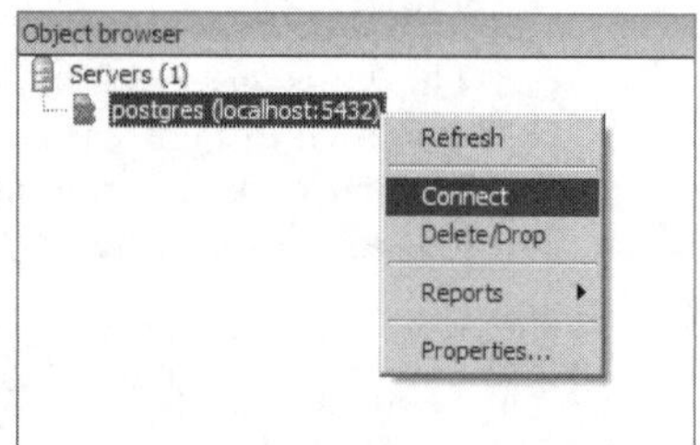

FIGURE A-25

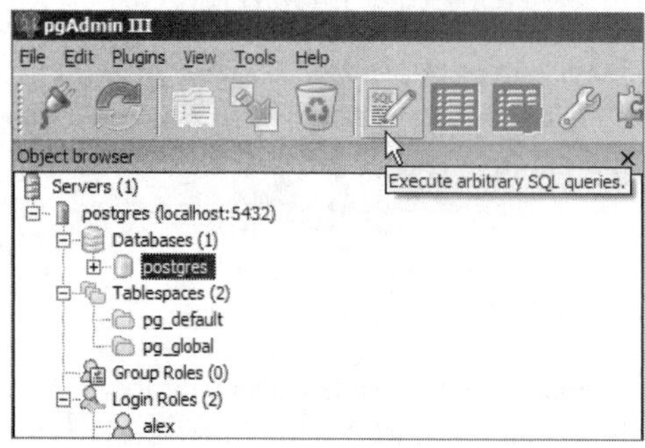

FIGURE A-26

4. Load the CREATE DATABASE script by clicking the Open File icon on the toolbar and navigating to the `DiscoveringSQL.PostgreSQL.CreateDB.sql` file, or simply type the statement shown in Figure A-27. Click the Execute button (a green triangle icon). As you can see in the Output pane on the same screen, it took 8,687 milliseconds to create a database with all the default options.

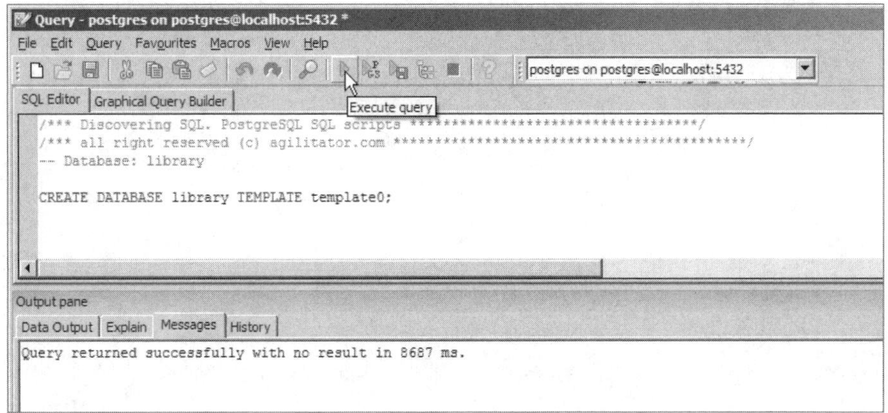

FIGURE A-27

The SQL syntax in the Figure A-27 query pane has an additional TEMPLATE specification (as opposed to a simple CREATE DATABASE statement). This is to avoid a potential error message resulting from some PostgreSQL idiosyncrasies related to the way it handles default connections. Without this qualification you may experience an error complaining about "source database 'template1' being accessed by other users."

5. After the Library database is created, you need to switch to it to run the rest of the DDL statements and complete the installation. From the drop-down box on the toolbar (displaying the connection to the *postgres* database), select <New Connection>, and from the pop-up window shown in Figure A-28 select Library database on *localhost:5432*.

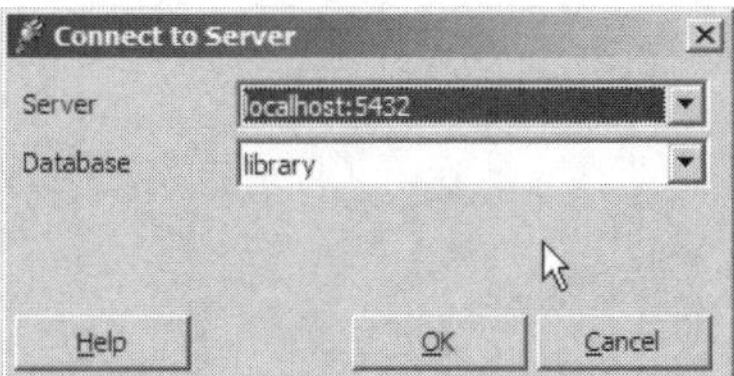

FIGURE A-28

6. Load the DDL script contained in the `DiscoveringSQL.PostgreSQL.Library.sql` file in the same fashion as described in Step 4 of this tutorial and click the Execute button. The results are presented on Figure A-29.

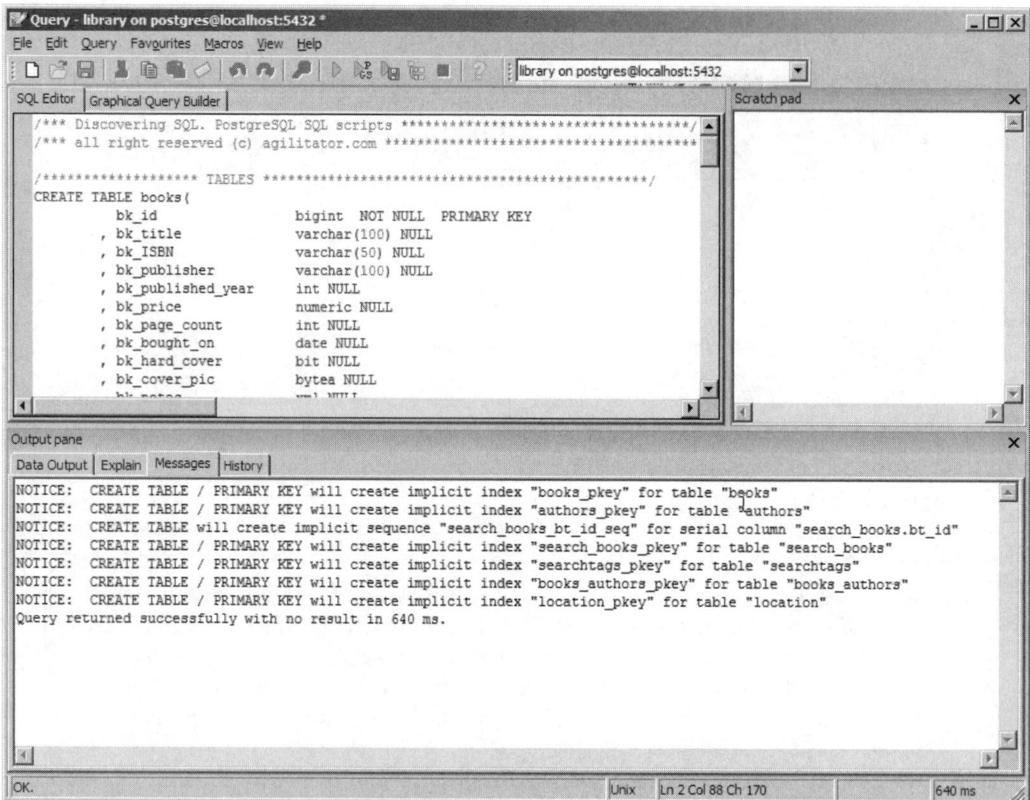

FIGURE A-29

7. Load the `DiscoveringSQL.PostgreSQL.dat` file into the query window and execute the scripts. Even though the output window would read "1 rows affected," as shown in Figure A-30, all data will be entered into the database table, and you can run SELECT statements to verify this.

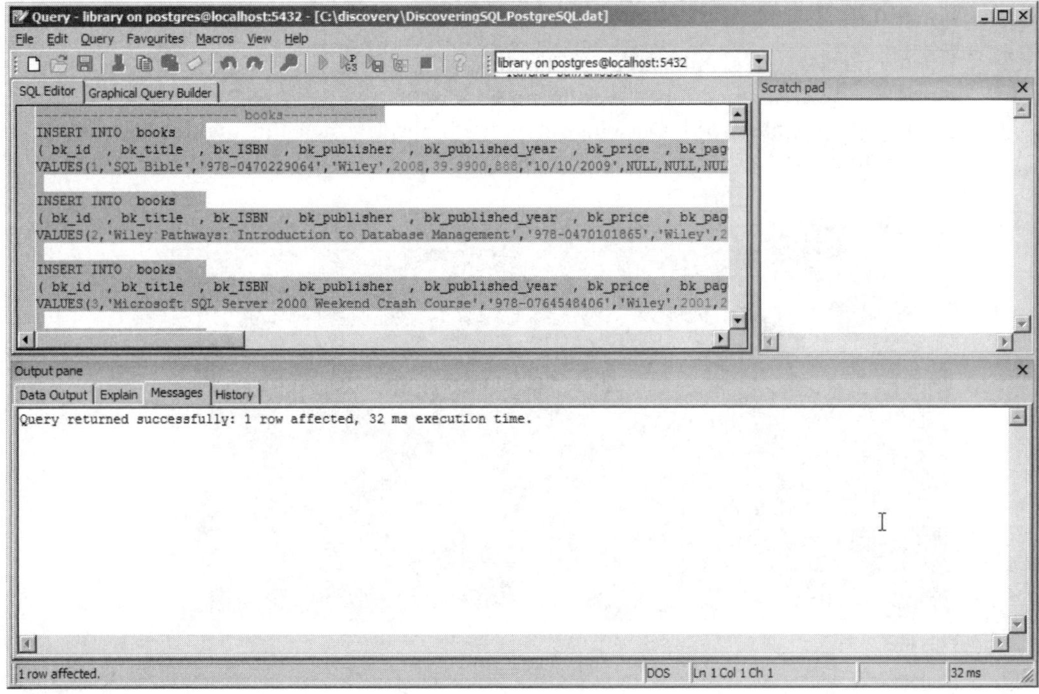

FIGURE A-30

MYSQL 5.1

The MySQL Command Line client is the only utility installed with the MySQL community edition installation, even though dozens of GUI interfaces exist to fill in the void, from commercial to free and open source, in virtually every programming language out there. This variety attests to the popularity of this open source relational database. Here we are going to use the built-in Command Line Client (of course, you can always use SQuirreL Universal SQL Client's GUI to do visual installation; check the resources available at the book's support site, `www.wrox.com`, and `www.agilitator.com`).

MySQL GUI tools, long-time staples of the MySQL community, are being discontinued, and the new MySQL Workbench is currently available for download as free Community Edition (CE). This is yet another application to be installed and configured, and I've decided to leave it out for now. Check the book's support website at both `www.wrox.com` *and* `www.agilitator.com` *for updated tutorials, or go to tool's website:* `http://wb.mysql.com/`.

Installing with the MySQL CommanA-Line Utility

1. Launch the MySQL Command Line Client from the `Programs` ➪ `MySQL` ➪ `MySQL Server 5.1` ➪ `MySQL` Command Line Client menu option. It will log on as `root` and will prompt you to enter the password. Once logged in, it will display the banner with basic instructions on how to use it, as shown in Figure A-31.

```
MySQL Command Line Client
Enter password: ****
Welcome to the MySQL monitor.  Commands end with ; or \g.
Your MySQL connection id is 13
Server version: 5.1.53-community MySQL Community Server (GPL)

Copyright (c) 2000, 2010, Oracle and/or its affiliates. All rights reserved.
This software comes with ABSOLUTELY NO WARRANTY. This is free software,
and you are welcome to modify and redistribute it under the GPL v2 license

Type 'help;' or '\h' for help. Type '\c' to clear the current input statement.

mysql>
```

FIGURE A-31

2. Execute the database creation script by typing in the following command at the prompt, as shown in Figure A-32: `source C:\discovery\DiscoveringSQL.MySQL.Library.sql` (this assumes that you have downloaded all relevant scripts into `C:\discovery` directory; if this is not the case, please specify the full path to the location on your computer).

```
MySQL Command Line Client
Enter password: ****
Welcome to the MySQL monitor.  Commands end with ; or \g.
Your MySQL connection id is 13
Server version: 5.1.53-community MySQL Community Server (GPL)

Copyright (c) 2000, 2010, Oracle and/or its affiliates. All rights reserved.
This software comes with ABSOLUTELY NO WARRANTY. This is free software,
and you are welcome to modify and redistribute it under the GPL v2 license

Type 'help;' or '\h' for help. Type '\c' to clear the current input statement.

mysql> source C:\discovery\DiscoveringSQL.MySQL.Library.sql
Query OK, 9 rows affected (0.39 sec)

Query OK, 1 row affected (0.06 sec)

Database changed
Query OK, 0 rows affected (0.05 sec)

Query OK, 0 rows affected (0.02 sec)

Query OK, 0 rows affected (0.02 sec)

Query OK, 0 rows affected (0.01 sec)
```

FIGURE A-32

The alternative execution syntax is to type `.\` *(dot-backslash) instead of* `source`. *For some of the most commonly used commands, please see Appendix C or the vendor's documentation.*

3. After the database and all database objects are created in Step 2, you can load the data by executing the `DiscoveringSQL.MySQL.dat` script following the very same syntax rules described in Step 2: `source C:\discovery\DiscoveringSQL.MySQL.dat`. The results are presented in Figure A-33.

```
MySQL Command Line Client
Query OK, 1 row affected (0.01 sec)
Query OK, 1 row affected (0.02 sec)
Query OK, 1 row affected (0.01 sec)
Query OK, 1 row affected (0.02 sec)
Query OK, 1 row affected (0.02 sec)
Query OK, 1 row affected (0.01 sec)
Query OK, 1 row affected (0.02 sec)
Query OK, 1 row affected (0.02 sec)
Query OK, 1 row affected (0.01 sec)
Query OK, 1 row affected (0.02 sec)
Query OK, 1 row affected (0.01 sec)
Query OK, 1 row affected (0.02 sec)
mysql>
```

FIGURE A-33

MICROSOFT ACCESS 2007/2010

The easiest way to get the Microsoft Access version of the sample Library database is to get a ready database file for your version — Access 2000, Access 2003 (.mdb files), Access 2007, or Access 2010 (.accdb files) — from the book's accompanying websites at `www.wrox.com` or `www.agilitator.com`.

Alternatively, you can run Microsoft Access–specific SQL scripts available for download from the same sites. Unfortunately, Microsoft Access, even in its latest version, operates on the concept of named query, which means that you cannot run more than a single statement from the query window. For those brave souls, the steps would be as follows:

1. Create a blank Library database file.
2. From the Create tab, click the Query Design icon on the toolbar.
3. Dismiss the Show Table pop-up window by clicking the Close button.
4. Click the SQL View button in the upper–top-right corner of the application window.
5. Open `DiscoveringSQL.Access.Library.sql` file in a text editor and copy each DDL statement for creating file, one by one, pressing the Run ("!") button every time. Make sure that only one DDL statement is present in the query window at a time.
6. Repeat the same for `DiscoveringSQL.Access.dat` file, one INSERT at the time (and there are about 150 INSERT statements in this script file...!).

True to its all-in-one nature, Microsoft Access provides an opportunity to write a Visual Basic for Applications (VBA) script to load the SQL script files and both create database objects and populate the tables. Programming MS Access is outside the scope of this book, but there are many helpful sites available.

OPENOFFICE BASE 3.2

There are several ways to install the Library sample database with the OpenOffice BASE desktop RDBMS. The easiest one is to download the fully populated database file *library.odp* from the book's support sites at `www.wrox.com` or `www.agilitator.com`.

Alternatively, you may want to run scripts to create the database structure and populate it with data. Here is a step-by-step procedure to install the Library database through SQL scripts. Keep in mind that the purpose of OpenOffice is to hide as much complexity as possible from the users, so it is not as tuned to manipulating raw SQL as full-fledged RDBMSs such as Oracle or Microsoft SQL Server. Please refer to Appendix C for an overview of the OpenOffice.org SQL facilities.

1. Launch the OpenOffice BASE application from the menu and select the Create New Database option, as shown in Figure A-34, and click Next.

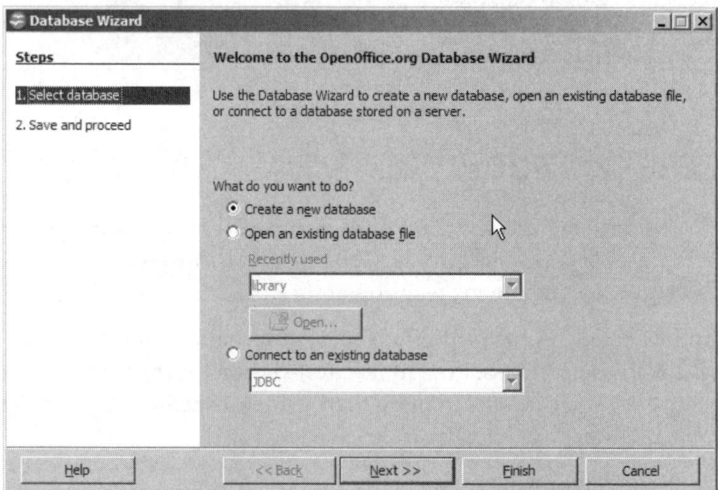

FIGURE A-34

2. On the next screen (see Figure A-35), select the registration option (registering it allows other components of OpenOffice to access it if needed; it is *not* a registration with the outside of your computer), and make sure that the Open Database for Editing checkbox is checked. Click the Finish button.

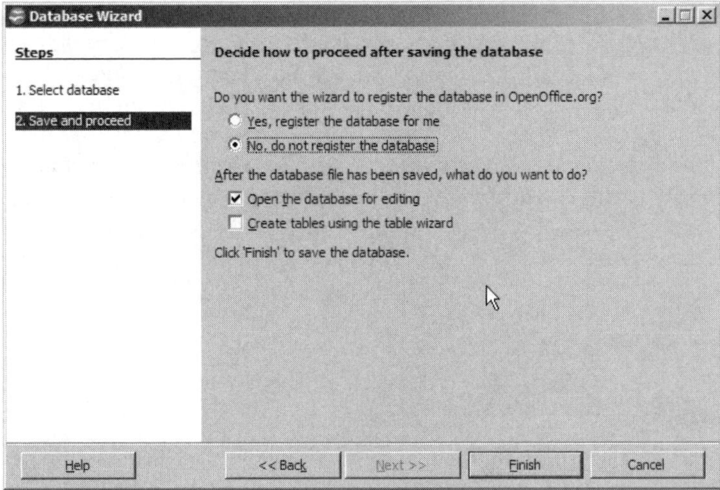

FIGURE A-35

3. When prompted, save the database file into the directory of your choice or accept the default location. It is saved with the default .ODF file extension.

4. When the main window of the empty Library database is opened, from the Tools menu on the toolbar click the SQL option to access the Execute SQL Statement window shown in Figure A-36.

5. Open the file `DiscoveringSQL.OpenOffice.HSQLDB.Library.txt` in a text editor of your choice (Notepad, TextPad, and so on), and copy its content into the Command to Execute pane, as shown in Figure A-36.

6. Click the Execute button and verify the status in the lower pane of the window.

7. Open the data file `DiscoveringSQL.OpenOffice.Data.txt` and copy its contents to the Command to Execute pane, replacing previous DDL statements, as shown in Figure A-37.

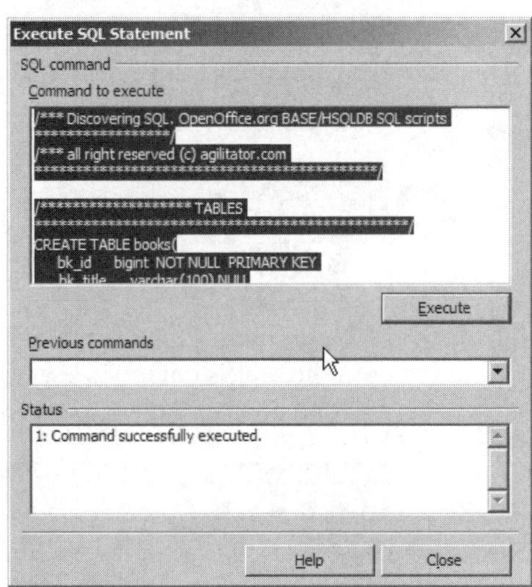

FIGURE A-36

You may purge all data from the tables at any time by running an additional script provided in the `delete.all.tables.txt` *file and then repopulate the tables by repeating Step 7. The script will not drop the tables, only empty them. To DROP a table, you need to execute the DROP TABLE command from the Execute SQL Statement window, or from the right-click menu of a particular table. Referential integrity constraints would enforce in which order tables might be dropped.*

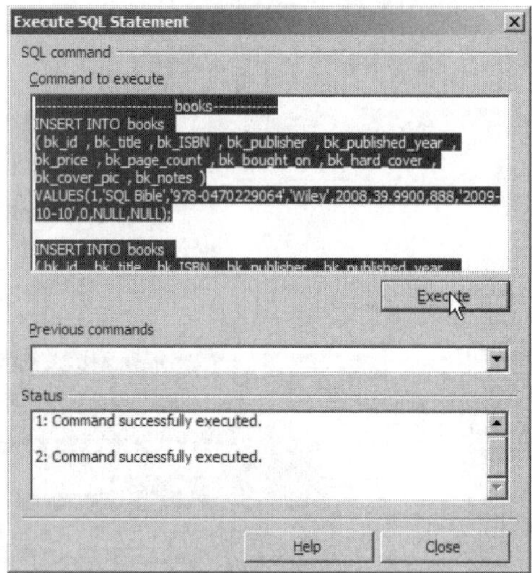

FIGURE A-37

8. Make sure to refresh the tables list using the Refresh Tables menu option (Figure A-38). To open the table's data for viewing/editing you may double-click a table in the Tables pane or select an appropriate option from the right-click pop-up menu for a given table.

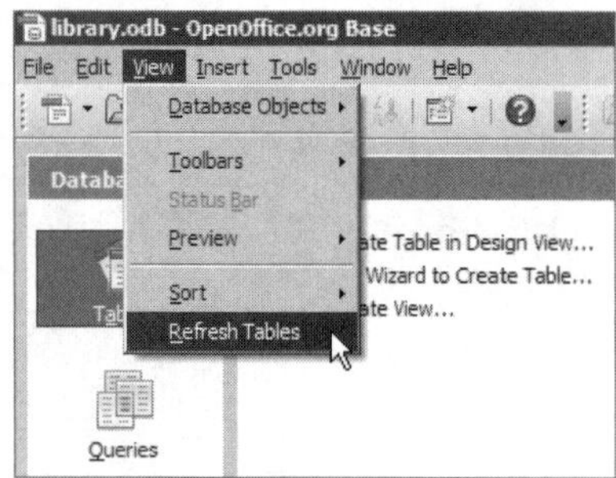

FIGURE A-38

Installing RDBMSs Software

In the days of yore, you would start the installation by popping a disk into your computer. With the price of bandwidth falling, you can now download the software off the Internet. Still, be prepared for a sizeable download (to the tune of 100+ megabytes).

Over the years, the installation procedures have improved dramatically, and, assuming that you go with most of the default options, the installation should be a snap. At the same time, there are a few things you need to know. The full version of the Appendix, available for download at `www.wrox.com`, describes the setup of RDBMS servers on a Windows 7 machine. Even if your environment is different, this might help you to select options as you proceed with the installation. For the full text of this Appendix as well as step-by-step PowerPoint/Open Office Impress slides describing the installation process, please visit `www.wrox.com` or `www.agilitator.com`.

Accessing RDBMSs

The full Appendix C available for download from the accompanying website at `www.wrox.com` has details on how to launch and use built-in utilities to access the RDBMS of your choice, and execute SQL commands.

ORACLE

Oracle 10g provides various utilities for communicating with its RDBMS, such as SQL*Plus, SQL Developer, Oracle Enterprise Manager, and Application Express. The new tool in the box is a rather sleek web interface, a scaled-down version of Oracle's Application Express that allows communications with an Oracle database through a web browser. The full Appendix details the use of SQL*Plus Command-Line Tool and Oracle Application Express Web Interface.

IBM DB2

IBM DB2 installs two database access tools grouped under Command Line Tools (plus a shortcut to the Microsoft MS-DOS command-line utility), in addition to those used for configuring and administering DB2 databases. The full Appendix outlines the use of IBM DB2 Command-Line Processor (CLP) and DB2 Command Editor, a Java-based GUI utility used to generate, execute, and edit SQL statements, work with output, and more.

MICROSOFT SQL SERVER 2008

There are two "native" client tools supplied with Microsoft SQL Server 2008 Express: the SQLCMD command-line utility, and Management Studio Express — the GUI administration console. The use of the SQL Server Management Studio for purposes of installing the Library sample database is described in Appendix A. Appendix C will touch briefly on the SQLCMD interface.

MYSQL

The MySQL Command Line client described in Appendix C is the utility installed with the MySQL community edition installation. It has been the default interface to MySQL RDBMS since the beginning. There are several GUI tools available, the latest being MySQL Workbench, available for download from the MySQL site `http://wb.mysql.com/`.

POSTGRESQL

PostgreSQL provides two built-in mechanisms: the pgAdmin III graphical user interface tool, and the original *psql* command-line tool. The use of pgAdmin is described in detail in Appendix A for purposes of installing and populating the Library sample database.

MICROSOFT ACCESS 2007/2010

Microsoft Access is a desktop one-stop solution combining RDBMS capabilities with reporting and built-in programming environments to create database solutions. It can act as a pass-through client connecting to other RDBMSs, such as Microsoft SQL Server or Oracle, or use its own RDBMS to store and retrieve relational data via SQL. The basics of the SQL Design feature are briefly described in Appendix A.

OPEN OFFICE BASE WITH HSQLDB

Just like Microsoft Access, the Open Office BASE offers a "pass-through" interface to connect to other RDBMSs, but it also includes an SQL engine of its own based upon open source Hyper Structured Query Language Database (HSQLDB) embedded with the application. There are a number of graphical tools for building database objects and reports, as well as the ability to execute arbitrary SQL statements. The latter capability is described in Appendix A of this book in conjunction with installing the Library sample database.

Accessing RDBMSs with the SQuirreL Universal SQL Client

Besides the native RDBMS utilities discussed in Appendix C, which are, by definition, specific to those databases, there are universal clients that, at least in theory, can connect to any RDBMS. There are numerous commercial tools, free tools, as well as open source tools that span both categories. The open source, free SQuirreL Universal SQL Client represents the best of both worlds.

In its current version, 3.2.0, it is a robust versatile application with many advanced features suited both for a casual SQL user and a heavy-duty SQL/RDBMS developer. The latest version features SQL syntax highlighting (with vendor-specific extensions recognition), code completion ("intellisense" in the Microsoft lingo), which provides a list of the contextual hints based upon the SQL code you're typing into the pane. The advanced features include the ability to browse database objects, create visual ERD diagrams representing relationships among the tables, localize environment in several languages (including French, German, and Spanish), and more. The full version of this Appendix, available for download at `www.wrox.com`, explains in detail how to install and configure the tool to connect to the RDBMSs covered in this book.

INDEX

Symbols and Numbers

A

D

E

F

L

M

N

O

P

Q

R

S

T

U

V

W

X